Reinventing the Economy

The Third Way

ALSO BY DAVID SIMMONS

Economic Power (Third Avenue Press, 1976)
Ideals and Dogma (Third Avenue Press, 1981)
Open Conspiracy (Mulberry Books, in press)

Reinventing the Economy

The Third Way

David Simmons

JON CARPENTER

Jon Carpenter Publishing
The Spendlove Centre, Charlbury, Oxfordshire OX7 3PQ

First published 1996

ISBN 1 897766 17 3

Printed and bound in England by J.W. Arrowsmith Ltd., Bristol

Contents

Preface

With the deterioration of Britain's economy and society becoming more and more visible with each passing year, there has been much discussion of methods for handling the economy. The constraints of inflation and imports are seen as insurmountable, while the Conservatives constantly present themselves as doing the best possible thing given the chaos of world recession, inflation, and the problems they inherited from Labour.

Some Tory politicians still believe that the methods of Thatcherism must be allowed to continue, so that the Smith Square Soviet's Fifty Year Plan can be fulfilled. Others recognise the existence of failure, and argue that new approaches are needed; but usually they have no coherent policy platform to suggest. Even the Tories' own internal opposition seems to accept that inflation has to be conquered before the economy can be set to rights.

Labour has deftly stepped into this policy vacuum, arguing perceptively that bold new somethings must be done, and new marketing strategies undertaken. Confusing electoral success with policy correctness, Labour has taken large chunks of Thatcherism on board. The policy clichés of a strong pound and high interest rates have been revered as truth eternal. Not that this is surprising for a party that has always been more concerned with the ideological purity of policy than with the end results.

Part of the reason for Labour's policy limpness is that its old-style socialist policies are seen as discredited. Some, such as those on trade unions and nationalisation, were out of favour even before the Thatcher revolution of 1979. Others were gradually marginalised by the policies and propaganda of each passing Tory administration. Labour was seen as dominated by extremists, and anti-business — what little thought it paid to business involved either corporate giantism or state ownership.

But for all the failings one might attribute to Labour, the Thatcherites were even worse. Under a series of Chancellors who raised incompetence to new heights, the economy was plunged to new depths. Mrs Thatcher said it would take more than one term to turn the economy round; she and her successors have now had more than three terms. And we have had the worst recession since the 1930s, with the lowest growth rates this century. Poverty has reached unheard of levels, while homelessness and crime can be portrayed without exaggeration as threats to society.

It is argued that Britain's economic deterioration has been due to world events, while the growth of inequality has either not existed, or been a result of the economic problems. The evidence suggests that both are a direct, even deliberate result of Tory policies.

It might be argued that the term 'Thatcherism' is no longer meaningful, with the

Lady from Dulwich's fall from grace. However, all the evidence is that Majorism is simply Thatcherism with fewer road cones. It is not a different set of policies; merely a different style of presentation.

However, it is not my intention to disprove Thatcherism, although that is a useful task. But many Tories already admit the failure of past policies; Nigel Lawson admits to mistakes, while John Major refers to a 'golden age that never was'. The purpose of this book is merely to sweep up the dead leaves of last year's ideology so as to create room for next year's growth.

As a result, some of the faults of Thatcherism have been covered very briefly, or not at all. For example, the trickle-down effect, the merits of the service sector versus manufacturing industry, the unspoken policy of shadowing the Deutschmark, and the encouragement of inward Japanese investment have not been mentioned at all. While the Laffer Curve, joining the ERM, and the social and personal effects of unemployment have all been given little more than a modest mention. There simply is not the space for a full analysis of all the many weaknesses of New Right economics. Nor is this the place for it. To disprove all the many faults and flaws of the Tories' ideology would take several books.

Similarly, this is not the place to analyse all the various policies of the New Right. Some, such as education and health, seem more worthy of mention, while others, such as the Conservatives' industrial policy, if that is not a contradiction, are relevant to the present thesis. However, this is not the place to examine health, housing, state ownership, public transport, or the attack on the welfare state. Also, it is not the place to consider the morality of the Falklands conflict. Nor is it the place to examine the Conservatives' political and personal morality. The vision of this book is to look to the future, rather than bemoan the past.

Any open-minded observer will agree that recent Conservative policies have effectively disproved themselves. The appalling recession which began in 1990 survived longer than the credibility of the forecasts of its end. By the beginning of 1993 it qualified for the label 'slump' and earned its creators all the respect they deserved. However, many other writers have followed the critical path, with excellent, detailed analyses, some of which have been cited in the present book. Particularly worth mentioning are the books by Lord Kaldor, and by Ian Gilmour.

My objective here is simply to point out some of the flaws, and argue that there is, despite Mrs Thatcher's claim to the contrary, an alternative. It was a pointless thing to say, although in the era of good soundbites, 'There is no alternative' had a strong ring to it, the steel tone of conviction. But as a scientific analysis of policy choices, it was three hampers short of a picnic. It had all the truth of a three pound note.

On the other hand, because the failings of the Conservatives are all too obvious, there is a temptation to see everything they have done as bad, or wrong. There has not been, although some might suggest otherwise, a total abnegation of democracy. Nor has every aspect of economic and industrial policy been completely in error. It might be more accurate to regard them as utterly misguided; but totally convinced of the correctness of their own directions.

In the past, too many attempts at policy creation have looked at issues in isolation, or at symptoms rather than causes, or at the creation of quangos to 'deal with' the problem. Worst of all, politicians on both sides of the House have started from the belief that certain methods and instruments were more valid than others, to the complete disregard of actual effects. On the rare occasions when we have looked at the ideas of other countries, we have usually turned to America, despite the fact that the United States is notably unsuccessful in many ways.

Any successful attempt at policy construction should look at society as a whole. It should look at the causes, rather than symptoms. And it should look at countries which are successful right across the social spectrum, rather than simply allowing a small minority to be wealthy. We should look for nations which score on all the personal indicators, not merely those which have large Gross National Products. The United States is undeniably a rich and powerful nation, as well as being one that Britain often looks to, to copy. For some reason, American fashion, trends and ideas are seen as the ones to follow. Yet it is also a country of great poverty, racism, and crime; whole cities have become near war zones, and teenage street gangs carry more guns than some European armies. We should not copy their economic policies, simply because they make good films.

There is much that is good in the United States, but it is not the ideal example to follow. It would be far better to copy selectively, to look at the more egalitarian nations. Those that come immediately to mind include Denmark, Norway and Holland. One might say these countries are not perfect, but then, is perfection a necessary requirement? Or do we simply want somewhere that is better? A goal should be something that is an improvement, not something that is unattainable. And most importantly, we should look for examples that work, policies that actually do what they claim, and that have some sort of rationale to justify their operation.

It may seem to a few readers that some ideas are repeated at various places within this book. I hope that this only occurs where it is intended, because each actor in the social drama plays many parts. It appears first as cause, then as effect. In some cases, it walks on wearing a mask, and no one knows its true part. Perhaps one of the roles this book will play is to get us a little closer to some of the real motives behind the socio-economic stage.

There may also be repetition because some arguments or social trends reinforce policy solutions that have already been stated. And in some cases, moral and practical arguments reinforce one another. With such items, both supports have to be given, because the truth is not some theoretician's fevered imagining, but built-in to the fabric of reality.

I have attempted to follow a logical sequence in writing this book, so each chapter relates to the previous one. Chapter 1 looks at the development of economic ideas, from the post-war consensus to the rise of the New Right and Thatcherism. It also considers how successful these two trends of thought were, as practical policies. Then Chapter 2 examines who benefits from Conservative policies; is it government for all, or are some groups more favoured than others? The evidence seems to indicate the latter view.

Chapter 3 considers the impact of Tory economic and industrial policy, again to see who gains. Once more, some groups seem to be more blessed than others, specifically, the rich and big businesses. Chapter 4 looks at the nature of democracy, and compares the Conservatives' actions with the three possible definitions of democracy. It is a comparison which does not flatter. Then Chapter 5 makes the argument that every theory must have a methodology, a way of operating, in order to make the claim that it is scientific. But the New Right have no discernible methodology to support their theories.

Chapter 6 begins the process of putting working economic ideas together, to create a complete economic structure. This is based on Keynesian demand management, the idea that the government should intervene in the economy when there is insufficient demand. The following chapter looks at the importance of competition, often praised in the abstract by the Tories, but rarely created in reality.

Chapter 8 argues that there must be decentralisation of all possible aspects of the economy — in the political system, in government, and so on. This is necessary for true democracy to exist in practice. Chapter 9 then makes the case for a broader approach to policy. Too many politicians talk about the economy as if only a limited range of factors affect it. The case is made for including social, cultural, and environmental factors — among others — within our calculus.

Chapter 10 looks at ways in which society can be improved — do we take the broad brush, or seek to better ourselves as individuals? It concludes that any method which yields visible improvements can and must be tried. The next chapter looks at some possible methods. These range from local political action, to changes in the business or personal sphere. There is also a need for people to reappraise their values, and Chapter 12 looks at the impact of society's existing values, and the need for a more caring approach to the world. The last chapter is a conclusion, and draws together all the preceding arguments.

In writing this book I have drawn heavily on the ideas and evidence created by other writers. It would not have been possible for me to re-create the research they carried out, so there is a considerable debt to the work of others. In addition, I have had help and advice from informed and perceptive friends. Their comments have greatly improved this book, as it steadily progressed from being a collection of ideas to being a coherent thesis. However, the final choice and the final word has been mine, so I bear any responsibility for errors.

I would like to thank Nigel Perkins, Masato Oka, Janet Alty, Brian McGonagle and Yogi Patel for their careful reading of various drafts. I would also like to thank Katharine J. Fairclough for her help with research. For a book of this scope, there is so much information that needs to be examined — or at least considered — that the task is overwhelming. Katharine has considerably lightened that load. Finally, I would like to thank Angela Barst, not just for her perceptive comments, but also for her constant support. A project of this magnitude is not undertaken lightly, but her help made it very much easier.

1

The darkling plain

FROM 1942 UNTIL around 1971, there was in the major economies of the west a general agreement, a consensus on political and economic issues that was shared by academics, politicians, business leaders, and the average voter. In Britain this was called the Keynesian social-democratic consensus. It was never shared by the far left, or the far right, but it was sufficiently widely accepted by all the major parties for it to represent a single view of government policy.

The main beliefs were — Keynesian demand management, a welfare state, and a mixed economy. The war radicalism of the second world war affected society in a similar way to that in which the 1914-18 war had led to a desire to create a 'home fit for heroes'. And in 1945 the massive unemployment of the 1930s was seen as unacceptable. The Keynesian prescription of demand management to control unemployment made heavy government spending politically acceptable, and provided an economically valid justification for budget deficits. This negated the argument that politicians had made in the 1920s, that it was not possible to spend more money than one had. The Keynesian argument was that *the government should spend in order to create demand*, and that temporary budget deficits were not a problem. The increased demand would create jobs, thus creating extra taxpayers.

The welfare state had an element of both social justice, and the provision of certain benefits for society. Its transfer payments created demand in times of slump, and the schools and hospitals provided educated, healthy workers. As regards state ownership, it had for some years been Labour Party policy to nationalise certain sectors of the economy. Nationalised industry was seen as both more efficient and more equitable.

Kavanagh and Morris point out that the Keynesian consensus was supported by two separate groups, the 'administrative rationalists ... who were interested in efficient, cost-effective schemes' and 'the social democratic intellectuals ... whose research and writing made the case for a more equal society'. (Kavanagh and Morris, *Consensus Politics*, p76.)

In other words, there were those who supported the Keynesian system because it was the most rational, and those who approved of it on moral grounds. The rationalist approach included such arguments as that it was cheaper to finance demand management policies than to pay dole to the unemployed. An expansion of the economy not only eliminates the need to pay dole money; it also creates a new group of taxpayers, adds demand to the economy, and therefore encourages production and thus further employment. The moral stance points out that we should look after the well-being of society's members.

The era of the Keynesian consensus was one of low and stable prices, growing economies, increasing affluence and expanding world trade supported by a strong US dollar. The world had only just recovered from a major world war that had destroyed lives, homes, factories and infrastructure, yet within six years the major nations were on the brink of the longest period of sustained economic expansion that has ever been. With the help of Marshall Aid, Germany was lifted out of its war-ravaged chaos, to become a major economy. Britain moved from post-war rationing to the frivolity of the Festival of Britain in 1951. And the United States entered what seemed like a time of limitless wealth.

But the commodity price boom of the 1970s, and the oil price shock of 1973 and 1974, lifted the world out of the cheap post-war market. As commodity prices rose, the terms of trade turned against the industrial nations, and the Bretton Woods system of currency stabilisation was in danger of collapse. In essence, it did collapse in 1971, when President Nixon announced that the US would no longer buy gold at the agreed rate of $35 per ounce. This was the equivalent of devaluing the dollar, while at the same time ending the Bretton Woods system.

The social-democratic consensus came to an end, partly because of the rise in world commodity prices, plus the oil shocks; perhaps we simply couldn't afford the high living, high spending policies of the 60s. Perhaps the consensus was only possible because of the conditions of the time. Money, raw materials and labour were cheap, and business treated all of them as if supplies were infinite. As the American economy faltered, and prices rose, so an era came to an end. That at least is one common explanation. The conclusion that is usually drawn is that the Keynesian consensus was only able to survive at that time, and economic conditions were no longer suitable for it. New policies were needed — or so it was said — and the right was full of ideas as to what these were.

But it is necessary to ask whether or not Keynesian policies had actually failed. Keynesians themselves did their influence no good when they stated, probably correctly, that the economy had a built-in propensity towards inflation. Big business and powerful trade unions had grown up over the years, as they pointed out. The big corporations were able to control prices, while the unions were able to control the price of their product — wages. The companies would then pass the added costs on to the final consumer, where such rises would be experienced as inflation.

Thus, say the Keynesians, we have an economy where inflation is almost inevitable. In fact, there is little we can do about it, within the framework of conventional economics. Which is a pity, given that inflation has now become a key policy issue. However, there is a *political* solution. That is, the government can initiate a prices and incomes policy of some sort.

This sounds like an acceptable approach, but it has two major flaws. First, the prices and incomes policy has never been properly integrated into the body of theoretical economics; that is, it may work, but it has no academic status. It doesn't fit into the traditional price-determination framework, it doesn't fit in with the free market, and it lacks a coherent logical or analytical underpinning.

Even worse, it is an approach that doesn't seem to work. It has been tried a number of times, under the auspices of the Prices and Incomes Board (NBPI), then via the Phase 1, 2 and 3 of the Heath government, and lastly via the 1974-79 Labour government's Social Contract. All of these failed to control their chosen targets, for various reasons and in varying ways. This is despite the fact that the NBPI, for example, had the help of the Monopolies and Mergers Commission in dealing with abuses of monopoly power. But it had the disadvantage that 'it could handle only a relative few of the many thousands of price and wage changes taking place each year'. (*The Labour Government's Economic Record*, W. Beckerman, ed. p305.) For most students of politics, control of prices or incomes is very much an unsettled argument.

The Social Contract was a compromise measure that bought trade union support with the offer of price subsidies, higher pensions, and the promise of better standards of living: in exchange, the TUC promised restraint in pay claims. It ended in disaster. It was not merely a failure; it was a failure which showed both parties in a bad light. The unions seemed untrustworthy for not upholding their agreement, while Labour appeared naive to have accepted union commitments. Worst of all, it led to the strike-prone period of 1978-79 when public and private sector workers from a variety of industries caused enough chaos for the media to label it 'the Winter of Discontent'.

The net result was quite enough to discredit prices and incomes policies for all time. It was certainly enough to discredit the unions, the Labour party, and any idea of collaboration between the two. Nationalisation and the welfare state were also becoming discredited, and inflation was beginning to be seen as a greater problem than unemployment. Thus, the structures proposed by the left were seen as failing, while the left's chosen policy instruments were not able to deal with the problems of the day.

The move to the right was perhaps inevitable, and was signalled by the election of Mrs Thatcher in 1979 and of Ronald Reagan in 1980. Both of these supported what has become known as the New Right, a system of economics based on individual choice and the minimal state. The emphasis on the individual was combined with a rejection of collectivism, even to the extent of denying the existence of society, as Mrs Thatcher once did.

The New Right argued for low taxes and low welfare payments, to create incentives. This would encourage people to work harder, rather than live off the state, as they would supposedly earn more money from work than they had previously. Also, with lower benefits, unemployment would be a less attractive option. Workers, in this highly ideological view of society, were motivated only by money, but they were also lazy. State welfare payments had to be kept low to persuade people to take jobs. Strangely, the New Right often seemed to co-exist with low wages for the workers, while high wages were the preserve of management. Only the bosses were motivated by incentives, it seems.

However, the argument for low taxes fitted neatly with the concept of the minimal state, according to which the government was not entitled to spend citizens' money for them, that it should not be in the role of making choices that individuals could best make for themselves. Also, the government was not qualified to take commercial decisions, and the economy would operate more efficiently if business was left to company management. For both reasons, the state should avoid taking an active role in the economy.

The New Right's style of economics is known as *supply side*, as opposed to the Keynesian *demand management*. It is concerned with the efficient provision of goods and services rather than with any attempt to create demand. It is the economic corollary of the role of the individual, with personal choice being the central facet of the market. Only in the free market, it was argued, could individuals make the choices that they wanted. As part of this, the New Right argue for privatisation and deregulation. This involves removing publicly provided services from public ownership or control, and introducing an element of private ownership or market forces. These are supposed to allow business to function freely, and subject nationalised industry to the forces of competition. By implication, those industries will then be more efficient, and more responsive to the consumer's demands.

In fact, in many cases the government was privatising monopolies, so there could be no competition. It is worth comparing this with the approach to nationalisation taken by the Swedish government until the 1980s. The state owned a small percentage of some industries, sometimes in the form of owning one or two small companies. This ensured that there would always be competition in those industries. State ownership also acted as a defence against predatory multinationals. It guaranteed that some part of the economy would be locally owned. And given the multinationals' liking for transfer pricing, and their awareness of the profits that can be made in host markets, perhaps there is another reason why big business objects to state ownership.

It is also worth mentioning that companies were allegedly privatised for the good of the taxpayer. Yet if that was true, then each company sold should have been sold for the highest price, and with the lowest rate of commission. Not only were commissions to City merchant banks said to be more than generous, but also, many of the shares were sold at a significant discount. This was to encourage the average saver to invest in shares, so one might say it was the taxpayer, wearing a different hat. When these sales become really distasteful is when the government gives the offending business away, and throws in a generous dowry as well. For example, when a division of the Property Services Agency was 'sold off,' the 'buyer,' W.S. Atkins, received £11.5 million. (*Private Eye*, July 30, 1993.)

It was also argued that governments should not be engaged in commercial activity, as this was the role of business. To mix the roles would be unhealthy, and less efficient. The state had no right to spend the taxpayer's money on whatever the politicians of the day felt was appropriate. It was not the state's money, and they had no idea of what people wanted. Worst of all, said the New Right, there was a danger of politicians deciding for themselves what people should have. This was unspeakable arrogance, said the upwardly mobile ideologues. Government would serve the taxpayer best by spending the least.

The free market, with individuals making their own choices, buying what they wanted, was regarded as the most efficient way of allocating goods. It sounds reasonable, but it ignores the fact that special equipment, known as money, is needed to buy goods, and this 'money' is very unequally distributed. Also, in a sense there is no market; there are merely a number of related markets, where some products may compete, but others are not even relevant. For example, Hawaiian beach clothes are not a competitive product in the UK clothing market. Also, some suppliers may be so slightly known that they would not truly be in the market by any economist's definition.

But given all the arguments for the market, any interference with it was seen as unhealthy, as it could lead to inefficiency, and small groups of people gaining excessive power. This is a problem for the New Right if the group involved is a union, but for big business to wield power is acceptable. In some cases the New Right sought to control this market imbalance by weakening the powers of trade unions; in others it sought privatisation and deregulation. The unions, it was said, interfered with the free determination of wages, while state ownership lifted companies out of the market, removing the need to worry about profits, costs, and efficiency. Similarly, the host of official regulation that had grown up in many industries was seen simply as a way of preventing ordinary business people from getting on with their jobs.

Just as one of the arguments underlying nationalisation was that the state could run businesses more efficiently, more rationally than greedy capitalists, so privatisation depends on the advantages of the market. To the New Right, the market is seen as an objective allocator of goods, pure and unbiased.

Writers such as Hayek object strongly to small groups of people — for example, elected governments — imposing their ideology on the population. If, however, small unelected groups — such as business executives — choose to run an entire industry in a way of their own choice, regardless of its impact on others, that is merely the free market in action.

Supply siders have claimed that their new economic regime has been successful. In Britain productivity was said to have risen dramatically since 1981, proof of the increased efficiency of British industry. However, a close look at what has actually happened shows that productivity — measured in terms of output per person — has not changed when we consider the *whole* economy. It is only industry that has improved and only slightly. And it has done so only by closing down vast swathes of Britain's industrial heartland.

Yes, it seems that productivity from 1979 on rose in comparison to 1973-79, with output per head rising by 4.2 per cent in 1979-88 against a 0.7 per cent rise over the period 1973-79. But 4.2 is only slightly impressive when compared with the 3.8 per cent growth over the period 1964-73. Also, there is evidence that much of the improvement in productivity occurred as a result of the 1981 recession, with factories closing down all over Britain. Naturally, companies closed down their oldest factories, the least efficient ones. So with these shut down, the average productivity rose. Rather than a re-birth of manufacturing industry, we have a change in the composition of the average.

In fact, there is only the most fragmentary evidence of any increase in efficiency. In many cases, alleged productivity gains are merely lower costs, as a result of lower wages, which are a short-term gain for each employer, but represent a long-term restriction on the use of new technology, as well as a long-term constraint on demand in the economy.

One of the primary skills of the New Right politicians has been that of presentation. They have portrayed their policies as being successful, but the reality is at best open to doubt. The Conservative Party, which claims to be the party of low inflation, has been faced with rates of inflation higher than that existing when they took office. It has been almost traditional in Britain for politicians to blame the previous government for economic problems. But when one's own party has been in office for more than a decade, that excuse no longer seems valid.

Despite the loss of this all-purpose excuse, the Thatcherite regime has managed to present itself as successful, and the range of policies available to it as limited. They have since moved on to condemning those who 'talk down' the economy. Apparently, a badly phrased speech could have more impact on the economy than wiping out the manufacturing sector. The converse was that ministers need do nothing to get the economy out of a recession, apart from making rousing speeches. It was a perfect symbol of the minimal state; industrial policy extends no further than speech making.

There are many comparisons between the Great Depression in the US in the 1930s, and Britain's recession in the 1990s. One of the most striking similarities is the total inability of the powers that be to see either the real cause of the slump, or a workable cure. President Hoover's failure to understand the causes of a slump led to what may have been, literally, one of the more entertaining ways of dealing with recession.

> Hoover sent a telegram to a comedy team saying the country needed some jokes to wash away the Depression and would they think of some. He told Christopher Morley a poem might do it — 'something simple enough for a child to spout in school on Fridays'. And he said to Rudy Vallee, 'If you can sing a song that would make people forget their troubles and the Depression, I'll give you a medal'. (James David Barber, *The Presidential Character*, 1992, p20.)

For many people nowadays, such a simplistic belief is almost unbelievable, to imagine that one could 'wash away the Depression' with a few jokes. But Hoover, like Mrs Thatcher and her successors, was totally incapable of seeing that the policies were not working. And it is strikingly similar to John Major's belief that the economy can be 'talked up' or down. This glib confidence masked a simple inability to understand what the real economy was.

Another striking similarity between depression America and slump Britain is the pattern of false boom and inevitable collapse. In the United States in the 1920s, easy money seemed to be available if one speculated in Florida land. As a result, land prices inflated to unrealistic levels. Millions borrowed to cash in on the easy riches, and the stock market boomed. In Britain, the borrowing was fuelled by deregulation, and encouraged by banks looking for easy profits. Once a false boom had been created, the collapse was inevitable.

Under the New Right, both Britain and the United States acquired massive trade deficits. And both countries have introduced heavy cuts in income tax. This had led to a United States federal budget deficit of $294 billion predicted for 1991, while in Britain the tax cuts have been financed by the sale of state-owned assets. Despite that, the overall burden of taxation in the UK has risen from 34 per cent to 36 per cent of GDP. But because the cuts were aimed at income tax, there has been an increase in inequality. The rich have benefited most from the cuts in income tax, while the rise in indirect taxes has hit the poor disproportionately. One key difference between Britain and the United States in the effect of the tax cuts is that the US maintained government spending — and so created a massive budget deficit — while Britain cut spending, thus avoiding a budget deficit but creating a recession.

Other features of New Right thinking include the belief that government should not limit the actions of business, so that unwanted rules should be removed; that is, deregulation. It is said that these rules impose unnecessary costs on industry, adding to the consumer's final bill. However, complete deregulation could lead to companies cutting costs on safety and wages, and reducing the quality of their products. Also, as the regulations are removed, consumer faith in their purchases could fall, so fewer purchases are made. This could harm the economy. For example, how many holidaymakers would want to take the Mystery Tour, knowing that it might be no more than a five-minute ride to the council tip. Each consumer purchase is a small mystery, and anything that increases the consumer's uncertainty adds to their reluctance to buy.

In the United States deregulation as a major component of policy was introduced by Reagan, although the principle of deregulation was established slightly earlier. There had been a gradual move away from the idea that industry had to be controlled, towards the belief that too much control was economically harmful. There was also a tendency, especially in America, for regulatory agencies to be 'captured' by the industries they were supposed to be responsible for. For example, ex-managers of oil companies would go to work in the Department of Energy, and media executives would work for the Federal Communications Commission. This was understandable as the regulatory agencies needed some level of expertise to know what was or was not possible in their chosen industry. It is equally natural that these hired experts would sympathise with all the needs and problems of their previous employers. The eventual result was a regulatory agency that spent much of its time protecting that which it should be disciplining.

However, New Right pundits presented regulation as a cost imposed on the economy; the unspoken implication being that it carried no benefits. But experience suggests that regulation carried both costs and gains, and that the removal of those rules actually imposed a considerable burden on the economy.

One of the most expensive items of Reagan's legislation was passed in 1982, and allowed Savings and Loans (S & Ls) — the American equivalent of UK building societies — to invest their funds in any place of their choosing. They did so, placing some money in junk bonds, and some in bribes and luxury goods, in high living for the S & Ls' directors, and in dubious land speculation. Because of this, the assets of the S & Ls — also known as thrifts — no longer covered the deposits of their customers. As a result, literally thousands of S & Ls have gone bankrupt, leaving the federal government with a bill for financial support that started at $100 bn. The federal government was responsible for savers' funds, and so had to guarantee their investments. The bail-out bill later rose to $500 bn, and is now estimated to be heading for $1,000 bn.

According to one American writer, the cost of deregulating the S & Ls 'will very probably exceed, in real terms, all the aid given to Europe under the Marshall Plan, plus the subsequent bailouts of Lockheed, Chrysler, Penn Central, and New York City combined'. (David P. Calleo, *The Bankrupting of America*, Avon Books, 1992, p135.) A new Marshall aid plan had been suggested by many experts as essential for the unstable economies of eastern Europe and the one-time Soviet bloc. New Right ideas, and deregulation, have united to make this necessary aid to development an impossibility.

It has been suggested that the S & Ls had a unique problem of borrowing 'short' and lending 'long'. That is, they borrow short-term from ordinary savers, and lend long-term on house purchases. This, say the New Right apologists, leads to unavoidable instability: therefore, their collapse is not the result of deregulation. It is a superficially convincing argument — if one ignores the fact that many financial institutions borrow short and lend long. To take one British example, building societies do this, yet they seem to have relatively few problems with instability. No, the collapse of the S & Ls, the most expensive American blunder this century, was a direct result of deregulation.

Fortunately, the federal government recognised the lessons to be learnt. Not only did it set up a regulatory body, specifically to monitor the S & Ls, but the intended deregulation of banks was very carefully thought out, to prevent a recurrence of the thrift bail-out.

Deregulation has brought its own special problems for Britain. It has been said that making macroeconomic policy is like driving a car when the windscreen has been painted over, and all you have is the rear view mirror. We cannot know the future, so we make policy based on the past. To do this, our economic data must be absolutely accurate. Increasingly, this is not the case. One problem is the changing structure of the economy, moving from industry to services.

> *The second blight has been deregulation, which has blocked off sources of data. The scrapping of foreign exchange controls, for example, makes it harder to monitor inflows and outflows, so balance-of-payments figures have become murkier. It may be no coincidence that America and Britain, two of the speediest deregulators, have the loudest complaints about numbers.* (*The Economist*, July 28, 1990. Italics in the original.)

All economic laws have some truth for their own time. Say's Law was created in a time of scarcity, while Keynes created his ideas at a time of great unemployment. Deregulation would certainly be a good idea for a tightly regulated economy like Japan's. And perhaps the New Right had some truth for an age of rising inflation, and over-powerful trade unions. Certainly, the world has been less stable economically since 1971 than it was previously. It may be that the so-called global economy is too complex, and that very specialist financial systems will have to be evolved to allow us to cope with the many changes that occur.

Part of this complexity is due to the growing competition from the Newly Industrialised Countries (NICs), many of whom are in south east Asia. Once they were under-developed nations, now they threaten to create unemployment in the developed nations of the west, as they expand into ever-new product lines. For the time being, they compete partly with the help of low wages, but partly through high levels of capital investment. Aiming for the global market, in carefully targeted product lines, the tiger economies of Asia have aimed a well-placed karate kick at the flabby gut of western capitalism. It is the trickle down effect in glorious technicolor.

Perhaps the New Right is partly correct about the laziness of the working class. There is a tendency for state benefits to create what the New Right calls a dependency syndrome, where people find it temptingly attractive to remain unemployed, rather than find an uninteresting, low-paid job. And the trade unions have at times misused their powers. They have rigged votes, intimidated members, and regarded the strike as the automatic response to any provocation.

But the New Right's view is somewhat jaundiced, seeing the world through chrome yellow spectacles. All unemployed people are seen as scroungers, who have to be forced back to work, union members are portrayed as strikers, the sole cause of the nation's economic problems, people who must limit their excessive pay claims. Yet no attention is paid to the reasons behind this behaviour, or to the excessive pay or exorbitant pay rises of the company executives. No consideration is given to the fact that many top executives are making no positive contribution whatsoever to their company's success, judging by the company's performance. Nor is there any awareness of the fact that workers' motivation does not come solely out of the pay packet. As the sociologist Maslow pointed out, all human beings have a hierarchy of needs, beginning with food and shelter, and extending through to the need to create. The New Right pays no heed to these subtler forms of motivation.

The New Right sees the economy as being influenced by a very limited range of variables. Only certain types of workers cause inflation if their wages are too high. All problems can be solved by paying more — or less — money to the people involved. And economists do not need to concern themselves with such details as actual production, the dirty, practical aspects of economics. The New Right belief in the minimal state leads to a total separation of state and industry. The problem is that commerce needs many of the things that are best provided by government, such as education, training, and infrastructure. And the Tories show no interest in design, investment, R & D, or in the success of government intervention, as demonstrated by Japan. Because of its historic indifference to such factors, British industry does not provide these features by its own initiative. Therefore, if the government does not support provision, then it will be, truly, minimal.

Thatcher and her acolytes took this to extremes with their lack of any industrial policy, and the use of monetarism to control inflation. And in terms of policy, it did not seem to matter that Mrs Thatcher was replaced as Prime Minister by John Major. The name changed, and the personal style was different, but the policies carried on. They both leave the success or failure of industry entirely up to industry itself. This sounds reasonable on the surface, but there are many things that are needed by the world of commerce that it fails to provide for itself, such as training and infrastructure. With monetarism, Friedman argues that failure to control the money supply will result in too much money chasing too few goods. So the monetarist solution is to control the amount of money. It is because the New Right is so dominated by the theoretical dimension of the supply side ethos that it totally fails to grasp the practicalities of increasing supply.

Not only does the government need to take an active role in encouraging the production of goods, it also needs to manage the economy so that people can buy the goods. Again, the Tories have seen one side of the picture; they see a need to reduce interference in the supply side, but they cannot see the need to assist in manufacturing. They are aware of the concept of supply, but they cannot see that it needs to co-exist with demand. Even in the event of a catastrophic collapse in demand, top Tories still talk as if confident speeches will end the recession.

The belief in a minimal state also leads Tories to argue that the state should sell off the companies that it owns, through privatisation. However, some people have argued that privatisation is just a short-term way of funding necessary spending. There is also the fact that many state-owned businesses were providing essential services, and to privatise them could reduce the quality of the services. After all, the state's job is not to save money for the hypothetical taxpayer, but to look after the interests of all members of society. Of course, Mrs Thatcher denied the existence of society, but that was empty rhetoric. We are all individuals operating within a complex socio-economic system that we refer to as society. The label that we apply to the system cannot deny the reality of our interdependence.

For example, in its desperation to privatise British Rail (BR), the government has effectively jettisoned the BritRail pass, which is mainly used by tourists from abroad. The pass is worth more than £30 million a year, and takes tourists away from the densely-crowded capital to the less popular resorts. (*The Observer,* June 20, 1993.) To a sensible government, the pass has a tourist revenue-generating value far in excess of its immediate sales value. But the private sector will have no interest in the pass's benefit to the nation; the nature of the market is to look only at one's own costs and income.

In addition, the changes to BR's operations to allow for privatisation itself is likely to cost £500 million, according to transport consultants Steer Davies Gleave (*Modern Railways,* July 1993). On top of that, there will be the cost of the financial aspect of the privatisation. Then there will be the costs incurred by breaking BR up into separate profit centres. Lew Adams of ASLEF told of a case of a high speed train being sent from London to Derby to refuel. It could not refuel any nearer, because the nearest sites were part of different profit centres (*Railwatch,* December 1992. All in all, it would seem that the costs of privatisation will outweigh any likely savings. Indeed, no one has yet given any evidence that there will be savings. There may well be cost reductions to be made, but the cost of finding out where BR is inefficient may exceed the savings.

BR is typical of the whole privatisation programme. An organisation of moderate efficiency, no better and no worse than most in private ownership, is being disrupted for the sake of alleged savings, while the social gains to the nation are simply lost.

The same argument of interdependence could be made about government spending cuts. The savings are simply not relevant if the average person is worse off afterwards. Quite clearly, the withdrawal of a provision impoverishes those who received the service, as well as the people who actually delivered it. Such a loss places a heavy burden of proof on the cost-cutting government. To argue a benefit to the taxpayer does not make the case, as that is merely one aspect of our identity. If a small tax cut necessitates a drastic reduction in state provision, the 'single-role' gain of the taxpayer is wiped out by the overall loss to the person.

The New Right is a simplistic ideology, seeing all aspects of the economy as being determined by purely financial factors. This alone is a serious distortion, because people are motivated by many other factors. Why people choose to work, or work hard, or perhaps remain unemployed may be a purely personal matter for each individual, not something to be labelled unthinkingly by some arrogant Westminster power-seeker, or the inhabitant of a Chicago university ivory tower. People work because it is the norm, for an identity, to provide for their family, to acquire status, and so on. They may also choose to work at their particular job because it allows them to make a contribution to society, to help others, and gain a sense of personal value.

The sociologist can point to Maslow's hierarchy of needs, from basic survival needs, to the need for self-expression. Of course, a basic income covers all the essential needs for life, but — assuming an income in excess of the basic — what does the person spend the rest of their money on? And why do they choose to do a particular job, maybe one which earns less than the maximum they could earn?

All this is a mystery to the New Right ideologues, because they simply do not understand the power of human motivation. In overlooking this force, they are making their theory less accurate. But as well as being shallow, it is also a selfish ideology. It overtly justifies the corporate executive's high pay as a natural facet of the economy; it represents an incentive. It is not greed, it is a stimulant to make that person give of their enormous value to society, their irreplaceable skills. Of course, the ordinary worker does not have such value, and must be grateful for the incredible benefits bestowed on the working class by the unique company bosses.

And this means that it is a divisive approach as well. The treatment government policy gives to the worker or the trade union is completely different from that applied to the company director or to a professional association. We are truly in a world of 'them' and 'us'. The workers must restrain their pay claims, and are blamed for inflation and unemployment if they do not. The bosses are under no pressure whatsoever to limit their wages. They have often justified their increases with the claim that their pay is profit-related, yet they have been known to receive pay rises when their companies are performing badly. This is a perfect breeding ground for the class antagonism that has been a major source of so many of Britain's economic problems. If the next Labour government reverses even a fraction of the Thatcher regime's union law, we may see a floodburst of pent-up hostility towards management that will colour industrial relations for years to come.

This divisiveness is both economically and socially damaging. It turns the economy into a battleground, where one of Thatcherism's achievements has been to bring industrial peace by weakening one side. It also creates attitudes within the populace that impinge on all aspects of society. The state, in the guise of the Conservative government, is saying to everyone, get ahead on your own effort, and if you do, fine; if you don't, tough. We are not interested in fairness, we are only interested in power for ourselves, and wealth for our colleagues. But if the state disregards fairness, it is not too surprising if the ordinary citizen thinks it is unimportant. This is not to say that the Conservative government openly espouses such views, but rather, that its underlying message and its actions suggest these to be its true beliefs. It is significant that the phrase 'hidden agenda' crept into the language during the Thatcher regime.

If a reduction in the number of strikes was one of the Tories' achievements, low inflation was another. Yet this was obtained at the cost of 2.9 m unemployed, with a real rate that could have been as high as 4.1m. It is a small victory, realised at great sacrifice, yet it could only have been maintained with the continuing revenue from North Sea oil. In other words, for fourteen years oil money has been poured into state benefits, so that insecure workers can be forced to take lower pay rises.

Judging by the results in the economies of Britain and America, the New Right demonstrates perfectly the triumph of presentation over content. We have two countries where production by domestic companies is declining rapidly, where the quality of education is collapsing and the degree of inequality is rising. The consensus has broken down, and the fabric of society is threatened by that breakdown. The basic social groups of traditional society are breaking up into the New Right, the hard right, the old Tory right, and perhaps even a Victorian right, with on the other side, the traditional left, the hard left, and perhaps even a new left. Then we can add on all the new, environmentally based groups — the greens, and green sympathisers, on the margin electorally, but very influential in terms of policy.

This enormous diversity of views could mean that a stable two-party system based on the old working class-Labour Party *vs* upper/middle class Tory Party lines is no longer possible. Some of the groups that see themselves as allied to one or other of the main parties would be so unacceptable to the mainstream of that party that no agreement on policy could ever be reached. This could create exactly the sort of instability that is often cited as a reason for not having proportional representation. But perhaps, given this new-found diversity, PR is the only way of creating a government that would be acceptable to a majority of the population.

Keynesian policies were flawed because of their over-emphasis on demand, while supply side economics focused too heavily on production. Yet the latter was doubly cursed, because not only did it, like Keynesianism, ignore one half of the economy, but it was not even effective at promoting the half it did concern itself with.

Some alternative economic system is needed, one with the welfare gains of the Keynesian Social-Democratic consensus, and with the productive efficiency that the New Right has sought to create. This alternative system must be practical, visibly workable, with some evidence that it will function in the way claimed. That is, there should be empirical evidence that it is workable. Ideally it should not be rooted in nineteenth-century theory, as Marxism was. This limits its validity for twentieth-century society and modern economies. When I first started working on this new consensus, it seemed that it needed to be a path halfway between Keynesian ideas and Marxism, which I then (1980) chose to call the Third Way.

The new way must also be coherent, covering the major aspects of the economy, not just isolated fractions. It is easy for ideologues to deal with some small aspect of the economy, such as the money supply, and develop complex arguments that somehow allow one to link that with every facet of economic life. Thus, they say, control the money supply and you control inflation, unemployment, interest rates and the general state of the economy. But the evidence for this has been limited. To treat the economy, and therefore the whole of society, in this simplistic manner is dangerous.

The new alternative should also use policies that reinforce one another, rather than conflict with one another. This has been a problem with much of Thatcherite policy, and has tended to make a difficult situation even more problematic. For example, using interest rates to control the economy, and supposedly reduce inflation, has had the side effect of raising inflation yet again, as interest rates have pushed up the cost of buying a house. It is a policy that clashes even with itself. Similarly, cuts in government spending have the effect of creating unemployment — and this adds to the state's budget, because of the cost of benefits. So the attempt to control prices has simply destroyed itself, while the spending cuts re-appear as new costs elsewhere.

In other cases, the policies might create related problems, so the policy is, in a literal sense, effective. But the side issues throw doubt on the value of that effectiveness. For example, cuts in spending on education might result in teachers having larger classes, and thus being less able to cover the curriculum properly. As a result, students leave school or college alienated, or not properly qualified. Money has been saved, but social friction might increase, and industry would have greater difficulty finding skilled workers. Thus, the overall value of the cuts is open to question.

The mere possibility of such a conflict means that policies should be costed and analysed before anyone attempts to put them into practice. This does not mean setting up a committee on every tax increase or budget proposal. In most cases, there is already evidence as to which actions are beneficial or not — it is just a matter of getting governments to listen to the evidence. But if the Prime Minister and the Cabinet feel that they already know the answers, then the facts can be ignored. And all the indications are that high interest rates, low taxes, deregulation, supply side economics, and all the rest of the Thatcherite paraphernalia are just washed-up reactionary tat.

The main function of high interest rates is supposed to be the control of credit. But if interest rates are high, then it is more profitable for banks and other financial institutions to lend money, so they actively encourage lending. Thus, the volume of lending may actually go up because of high interest rates. If this happens then the policy will have been totally ineffective. Worse, it will have been exacerbating the very problem that it was intended to control. Yet this is an inevitable result with a policy that contains internal contradictions, and the mere possibility of such a conflict should raise doubts as to the policy's efficacy. The problem is that many of the policies we associate with Thatcherism have these in-built clashes.

However, it is worth noting who benefits from high interest rates — banks, the City generally, and those with hefty savings, or a low mortgage. All of these, plus big business, are the natural constituents of a Tory government. New Right policies implicitly say, here are the people we are looking after, the rest are a tool to be manipulated for the sake of our economy.

Given that most people are harmed by high interest rates, a more sensible approach with this particular problem might be to combine high interest rates with credit controls, and agreed credit ceilings for the big financial institutions. So the consumer would find borrowing slightly less attractive, because of the cost, but also less accessible because of the credit controls. But this fails to state the degree to which policies could reinforce one another. A more apposite example could be if one sought to create and protect competition through a strict anti-merger policy, combined with a corporate break-up policy, encouragement for new small businesses, an education system that encouraged people to see themselves equally as being employers or employees (rather than only as employees), plus a level of equality that allowed them to save enough money for the start-up.

This is not to say that there can be a policy with no conflicts, no inconsistencies. If a policy is put into practice, it must live in the real world, with all the complexities that implies. And there is no reason to assume that any theory can be put into practice without it having some side effects other than its main aims. To say, 'here is my theory, let's put it into practice,' is to take on enormous responsibility. Clearly, there are people who are willing to do this from a very simplistic base, but ideally they should incorporate all aspects of society into their theory.

One of the problems is that as an electorate, we are willing to allow a small group of people to take over the whole country. We collectively surrender all responsibility, so that our leaders, the so-called experts, can run things. Britain, as a nation, respects its leaders and looks up to them. Perhaps this is because Britain is a hierarchical, class-ridden society. We tug the forelock and mark the ballot paper in one smooth movement. But it is certainly not because our leaders have outstanding qualities of knowledge and expertise. And perhaps the leaders are not even looking after us.

As well as avoiding any inconsistencies, we should avoid having a system with too many compensatory mechanisms. Society has a broad range of faults, and any social scientist creating a theoretical utopia will typically design a range of quangos or state organisations to deal with these faults. These bodies will then punish, ban, or tax the forbidden behaviour so that society will more closely follow the accepted path.

This approach is understandable, but has two problems. First, it leads to the creation of a blueprint that is covered with an untidy scrawl of quangos, as government bodies proliferate to deal with every conceivable form of mischief. Secondly, it is an expensive way of dealing with the task, employing a horde of bureaucrats to correct and monitor wrongdoers' behaviour, as a permanent component of the state's apparatus.

It would be far more effective if one could create a social structure which had built-in mechanisms to minimise or prevent the faults which concerned us. This might seem over-optimistic, but if we compare Britain with the Scandinavian countries, say Sweden or Denmark, we can see mechanisms which operate in roughly that way. For example, in Britain we have a cumbersome and not very effective set of anti-merger rules; political bias often creeps into the application of these rules, and competition is not very well protected by them. In Sweden or Denmark, competition is protected by the ease with which people can start up their own company, something which is partly due to the low level of inequality, and partly because of the culture. This vague term covers many things, from the high level of education, giving people the skills they need to be able to choose their own career, to the fact that Scandinavian society values individual choice.

Perhaps one cannot simply change a nation's culture, although there is no doubt that Japanese society was transformed during the Meiji era, and later under General Macarthur during the American occupation. Radical social engineering is possible, although it does reek of the misuse of power. Yet smaller changes are more acceptable, such as the move away from teaching children to be factory fodder, towards education as a source of personal growth. Similarly, progressive taxation might be used as a way of improving the quality of life for the working classes. Yet such small differences, which Popper might regard as piecemeal change, may add up to a radical transformation of a nation's culture.

Also, the new approach must be flexible, and able to cope with changing economic circumstances. That is, it should not impose any policy as absolute, regardless of situation. Policies should be pragmatic, aimed at alleviating situations rather than presented as universal cures. It is possible to deal with the problems of the here and now, because that is something we can see. It is not utopian to suggest a solution, although that is what Marxists would claim. It is simply a matter of seeing all the problems, and determining which combination of solutions would best deal with the existing combination of problems.

However, one of the most powerful influences on government action is the underlying values of the policy framework being used. Many politicians would deny that they have an ideology, arguing that what they do is simply the application of common sense. But large areas of policy-making are determined by value judgements, which throws into question the real worth of the policies. This is doubly true, given the gross ineffectiveness of policy, and the uneven distribution of gains.

The whole philosophy of deregulation, privatisation and spending cuts all revolve around the idea of getting the taxpayer better value for money. But cuts in government spending, or in the funding for privatised or deregulated services, do not mean a better quality of service. So the taxpayer as a person is not getting better value for money. Nor is the average person better off materially under New Right economics.

This makes some writers wonder who the policies are intended to work for. Is there a hidden agenda, and what are the *real* values behind the ideology? The next chapter examines the values behind the New Right.

2

This blessed plot

AFTER 13 YEARS of Tory misrule, a surprise election result pitched us into a rollercoaster, heading towards a total of 18 years of Tory government. Not only was this result deeply unattractive to many voters, it also led to the worrying prospect of a nation in which a large proportion of the electorate have not experienced any type of government apart from the Conservatives. Yet although many see the Thatcher experiment as a ghastly failure, clearly there is still sufficient support in the country for the Tories to get re-elected. One might say that only 43 per cent of voters wanted the Conservatives; but only 35 per cent wanted Labour. So calls for proportional representation (PR) are not a full answer. It is not just the electoral system that brought the Tories back, but the voters. The key issue here is, why did the voters not want Labour, despite the economic chaos wrought by the Conservatives?

It might be said that with the ousting of Mrs Thatcher as party leader, the Conservative government was no longer following the precepts of Thatcherism, that we returned to mainstream Conservatism. In fact, the only observable difference resulting from the change in party leader was the new PM's attitude to the European Community, now the European Union (EU). Whereas Mrs Thatcher was bluntly hostile, John Major saw Europe as an opportunity, although it might be worth asking for whom the EU is an opportunity. However, the government's policy programme is still referred to by some as Thatcherism (see *The Economist*, February 9, 1992), and since it still seems a valid description, it will be used here as well.

The similarities in policy include the desire for low taxes, low levels of government spending, the minimal state, no government intervention in industry, supply side economics and the use of market forces. There is a continued refusal to manage the economy, while the government's only economic policy instrument is interest rates — just as Lord Kaldor said in June 1979. (*The Economic Consequences of Mrs Thatcher*, p17.)

One difference is in the apparent personalities of the two Prime Ministers. Whereas Mrs Thatcher seemed like a shrieking harridan, imposing her policies, John Major is too meek and mild to be seen as malicious. As a result, while Mrs Thatcher was seen as strong in the face of 'temporary' difficulties, Major is seen merely as incompetent. He is too anodyne to hate, and so generates less emotional opposition.

A large part of post-1979 Tory policy has been, and still is, ideologically motivated. That is, it has been carried out, not for observable economic reasons, or for some demonstrable social benefit, but because of ideology, a particular view of the world. Although the system is sometimes referred to as *liberal* economics, one could argue that the Conservatives have hijacked liberalism from its true meaning. The English philosopher, John Locke, portrayed liberalism as an implicit contract between rulers and ruled. Part of that unspoken agreement can be seen in the American Declaration of Independence, which says that all people have 'certain inalienable Rights, that among these are Life, Liberty, and the pursuit of Happiness'.

Thus, the explicit values of liberalism relate to the freedom and well-being of the individual. The Tories have corrupted the concern for the individual into attacks on collectivism. Often, the main aim of policy has been to destroy or weaken one group or another within society. That is, there was neither rational analysis, nor a valid moral stance; simply the removal of political enemies.

The miners were the subject of a deliberate and carefully planned attack, with the primary purpose of demonstrating that the government was the more powerful of the two. Teachers have been blamed as the sole cause of any and every failure in the education system — whereas the record number of GCSE passes in 1992 was seen as a triumph for the government, when concerns were expressed about falling standards and lack of uniformity, it was the teachers who were responsible. New requirements were imposed on local authorities, while some policies were forbidden. Thus, councils were obliged to allow tenants to buy their council houses, but the revenue from the sales could not be used to build more houses.

This was changed by the Chancellor's Autumn Statement in 1992. This allowed councils to spend more of their capital receipts (revenue from the sale of council houses) on building new houses. But as the sale of council houses was likely to fall, due to greater caution, the effect of the recession, fear of high interest rates and so on, it was not a great gain for local authorities. Also, as the government cut councils' borrowing limits, it is likely that the overall impact of the changes will be to make them worse off. However, councils still had a legal obligation to house the homeless, even though they were not allowed to build houses.

The result of the constraints has been rising homelessness, as local authority provision has been drastically reduced, and increased costs for councils because hostel and bed and breakfast provision has been necessary to replace the lost housing. But, unsurprisingly, short-term housing is far more expensive than council-owned housing. Thus, the result of government intervention has been a reduced service, and increased costs. It has been said that John Major is a very nice man. But his policies are just as vicious in their effects as anything that Mrs Thatcher introduced. To say that Thatcherism has faded away is to misunderstand the effects of current policy.

It might be said that Thatcherism was not an ideology, but an assortment of unrelated and sometimes conflicting ideas from a variety of sources — the Adam Smith Institute, the Centre for Policy Studies, the Institute of Economic Affairs, and so on. Yet there are several consistent themes running throughout the body of Thatcherism. There is the belief that everything can be solved by the market, the corollaries of this belief being the minimal state and the primacy of the individual. Then there is a parallel if conflicting theme, that governments must, if necessary, intervene to ensure that markets do operate — as through privatisation, deregulation, opening up state organisations to market forces, or reducing the power of the unions. In encouraging opt-outs from the state health or education systems, the government is ensuring that market forces do apply, so that in future, schools and hospitals will provide what 'customers' want. The conflict in logic occurs when the state intervenes to impose quality standards; if ministers really believed in the market, they could leave quality to arise naturally as a result of customer pressure.

Another conflict involves the belief in the individual, freedom of choice, and the minimal state. These values imply a state which is weak, decentralised, and plays only a small role in running society. Yet what we actually have is a powerful, highly centralised government apparatus, imposing its beliefs over a wide range of areas, from local government housing policy and the structure of the education system to the content of education and the ownership of the media.

Most of the conflicts have been within the *practice* of New Right ideas, rather than the *theory,* although there does seem to be some uncertainty over the control of inflation. The Thatcherites started with a clear assurance that the control of the money supply would automatically reduce inflation. This belief has been discreetly dropped, but there is still a policy link between money and inflation in the unswerving adherence to high interest rates. Yet at the same time, ministers insist on promoting the view that high wages somehow cause inflation as well. To control this, 1.5% pay limits for the public sector were introduced in 1992. This is similar to the view held by the Labour government of 1974-79, although it does clash with the Conservative government's monetarist ideology.

The problem with such conflicts occurs if a policy sets up counter-posing forces operating in different, even totally opposing ways. The effectiveness of the original policy may be reduced, and may even be rendered worthless. This is especially likely to happen with a government that can only see one side of issues, viewing a complex landscape with monoculars. For example, from 1988 onwards, Tory chancellors sought to control inflation, and the money supply, using high interest rates. But in doing so, they forced building societies to put up interest rates as well, thus adding to rising prices.

Also, the deregulation of the 1980s led to a credit boom, as banks and building societies competed with one another for customers. Demand rose to unsustainable levels, further fuelling inflation. The high interest rates made lending much more attractive to banks and other financial institutions, so they actively encouraged customers to take out loans. Thus, the high interest rate policy, aimed at controlling the money supply, actually led to an *increase* in the money supply. Yet it should have been no surprise to any intelligent chancellor that putting up the price of money should make the banks want to 'sell' more.

A more serious example came with the government's attempt to cut spending. As public sector expenditure was reduced, or held steady in the face of rising costs, workers were made redundant. This reduced the state's tax revenue while increasing its costs. Thus, while public sector spending was being held down, welfare costs were rising. As a result, what was happening was not a reduction in spending, but a redistribution of government funds. There was no benefit for the economy or the taxpayer, although there would be a loss of demand with each job lost.

Many of the policies comprising Thatcherism can be traced back to Milton Friedman or the New Right — a belief in monetarism and the free market, a limited role for government, and supply side (or neoclassical) economics. This last is also known in the United States as Reaganomics, or voodoo economics, after the president who first brought it to public attention, and the scientific proof which underlay the theories. Many of those theories originate in the US, where they failed to work, with the result that they were imported into Britain. It is as if the total lack of effectiveness of the policies was counteracted by the fact that they had been applied in the United States, so must be copied.

Although monetarism has no logical connection with supply side economics, it is notable that many New Right thinkers tend to support an entire package, from control of the money supply to cuts in welfare spending. Because of this, some writers refer to the theory as 'political monetarism' (see K. A. Chrystal, *Controversies in Macroeconomics*, p129). Even where there is no logical or empirical link, the values are such that supporters see the ideology as a consistent whole. Yet the only apparent common factor between all these disparate policies is the end result: the New Right's entire programme seems to work to the disadvantage of the average worker.

It is also worth noting that much of the New Right's programme is very much a theoretical construction, untainted by such concepts as proof or practicality. For example, the Laffer Curve is a key concept underlying the belief that lower rates of taxation could generate greater tax revenues. However, no-one knows where any given country might be on the Laffer Curve, so there is no possibility of knowing what the effect of changes in the rate of tax would be. Despite this, faith in the principle was sufficient for Reagan to slash tax rates in 1981, thus paving the way for the federal budget deficits of the 1980s.

Most of the New Right's ideas fit together to create a coherent whole, so that the rare ideas which do not fit in are jarring. However, consistency is not a necessary requirement for an ideology. It is in essence a view of the world, an explanation of how the world operates, and is more comparable to a religious faith. It is an emotional rather than a rational system. Thus, presenting it as if it were consistent is more important than whether or not it actually is consistent.

To examine the values underlying this economic belief system, it is worth looking at how New Right policies are meant to work. The essence of supply side economics is that if resources are used more efficiently, production and growth will be higher (see John A. Tatom, in *The Supply Side Solution,* Bruce Bartlett and Timothy P. Roth (eds.)). The measures deemed necessary for greater efficiency include government policy, tax law, and controls on trade union power (see Bartlett and Roth, p33).

Thus, if taxes are reduced, while both unions and market barriers are weakened, and government policy is directed towards freeing rather than controlling market forces, we will all supposedly be better off. In other words, if we allow the production system to operate freely, the market will take care of everything else. The market will allocate resources, goods and income, and levels of income will be determined by the effort of each individual.

The post-1979 Tory governments have duly introduced trade union legislation, reduced both the basic and the top rates of income tax, and opened various sectors of the state to the rigours of the market. They have sought to control both the money supply and state spending, while reducing the role of the state in the economy.

The result of all this should have been a boom in growth, output and productivity. The evidence suggests minimal growth, low output, and a disputed increase in productivity. It might also be said that we do not need more growth or greater output, which may well be true. But if we just take what is argued by the New Right, we see that its claims have not been borne out. As a separate issue we can consider the value of the New Right's goals; the argument here is merely that the Thatcherites did not deliver what they promised.

However, some still claim that Thatcherism was a success. It transformed British political and industrial attitudes. It made people aware of the need to be efficient and cost-effective, although some Tories regard the destruction of socialism as its main achievement.

> That London — and Britain — is not like Liverpool today and that the Labour Party dare no longer own up to its socialist soul is the most graphic and dramatic encapsulation of what was achieved in Margaret Thatcher's time. (Norman Tebbit, *Unfinished Business*, p23.)

Of course, people will see events through the mists of their own beliefs, especially if they personally have gained from them. But there is no doubt that attitudes towards state ownership and management have changed, and often for the good. The pre-1979 approach to nationalisation took as its norm a failure to question the need for state ownership or the policies applied. At the extreme it included Tony Benn's desire to nationalise twenty-one major sectors of the economy, from chemicals to banking and insurance. There was a belief that 'capitalist' ownership was bad, but if the government owned everything, that would be good.

This dogmatic view of nationalisation, combined with a total inability to see the need for proper management, meant that Labour Party policies were in need of a thorough review. But politicians never listen to what ordinary people are saying about society, so it took the loss of an election to make Labour carry out even a perfunctory re-evaluation. Yet even after the election defeat of 1979, the far left managed to retain control of Labour's policy-making apparatus, so that the 1983 manifesto was simply a re-phrasing of Bennism. The politics of collectivism were still being offered as the road to good government, even though most people seem to reject the collectivist, state-run approach.

And popular opinion on some subjects has changed. Nationalisation is seen by many as having been discredited, as are trade unions and unlimited state benefits.

The unthinking promotion of the collective has been replaced by an unthinking obsession with individualism, often in extreme forms. Mrs Thatcher set out to destroy socialism — and any high profile body which disagreed with her beliefs — and to a large measure she succeeded. But this, like the attacks on the unions, local government and teachers is more reminiscent of the 'enemy within' aspect of fascism than it is of a rational approach to managing a nation. On the other hand, many union leaders abused their power, and some local authorities carried out policies that verged on lunacy. To a certain extent these groups brought the deluge down on themselves.

We have also moved away from the employment seeking, anti-capitalist beliefs of the 1950s and 1960s. During much of the post-war period, people were brought up to regard the function of education as equipping them for a life as an employee. A good education was one which would equip you for a 'good' job. The system worked, so no-one questioned it. It was unexciting and authoritarian, and there was no impetus for change. Over the same period, the far left were promoting an aggressively anti-capitalist ideology, so that some teachers and textbooks presented business as a slightly repulsive process, to be tolerated rather than emulated. This attitude too has changed, hence the growth in the number of small businesses. 'Today despite the recent recession, the number of new small businesses is still increasing and self-employment is now some three and a quarter million against less than two million in 1979'. (Norman Tebbit, *Unfinished Business,* p30.)

Of course, it is very likely that this trend is not despite the recession, but because of it. Millions of ex-workers have sought a way of dealing with their unemployment, having seen that the government had no intention of doing anything for the macro-economy. So each person chose to do the best they could for their own personal economic situation. And although normally this increase in the number of small businesses would be a good thing, given the recession it may be that people have been going into business at the worst time possible. As a result, the long-term gain may be negative, as companies go bankrupt and workers lose their savings.

It is also claimed that the productivity of industry rose sharply during the 1980s, and this can be seen as a statistical fact. However, it is very easy to create a rise in productivity if one merely closes down the least efficient of one's producers. The average level of efficiency duly rises, but not because any of the existing firms is in any way more efficient. There is still some controversy over the origin of this rise in productivity, but there are indications that it did not represent any real improvement. For example, both capital investment and industry's expenditure on training fell throughout the Thatcher years; by 1992, manufacturing investment was lower than it had been in 1979. Given this, it is hard to see where any increase in efficiency could have come from.

According to the *World Competitiveness Report*, Britain fell three places in overall competitiveness in 1991, from tenth out of 22 countries, to 13th. France was one place behind Britain overall, but 'leads the UK in management, science, technology and qualified people — so building for long-term competitiveness,' the report says.

The report also 'ranks the availability of skilled workers in Britain 21st and says that managerial rewards encourage short-term thinking in industry to a greater extent than any of the UK's rivals'. (*The Guardian,* June 22, 1992.)

We fell from 13th to 16th in 1992, and then from there to 19th out of 22 leading industrial nations. For industrial production, Britain is last of the 22. (*The Guardian,* June 22, 1993.) Given the continuing failure of Tory policies to offer any improvement for the British economy, it is hardly worth reading future reports. Future editions will simply repeat the tale of relative decline, while our league position remains bottom.

According to a report by three Warwick University academics, even if there was a rise in productivity in the 1980s, which is doubtful, it was 'still not sufficient to close the productivity gap between the UK and its competitors'. (Paul Stoneham, Derek Bosworth, and Anne Gibbons. *Investment, Productivity and Competitiveness in UK Manufacturing Industry.*)

Britain has been doing all the wrong things for decades, with both management and government sharing the responsibility. UK management have paid very little attention to investment, R & D, or training. There has also been a great deal of short-termism in management attitudes. 'Short-termism' is being used here in the sense of a complex of attitudes in both business and government, encouraging short-term policies. Business leaders tend to seek immediate profits, while the City and government undervalue both industry and the structural supports that industry needs. For years there has been a shared culture in Britain's commercial establishment, which has played a major role in the UK's economic decline. All that has happened is that the Tories have added new types of incompetence. (See Martin J. Wiener, *English Culture And The Decline of The Industrial Spirit 1850–1980.*)

Nor is this something that the government is unaware of, although the chancellor might not wish to make it too widely known. However, in March 1993 it emerged that the Department of Trade and Industry had compiled a report on the competitiveness of UK manufacturing industry. The evidence in the report suggests that the underlying damage to Britain's economy, in terms of low investment, skills shortages and insufficient R & D, will take years, perhaps decades to put right. (*The Guardian*, March 15. 1993.)

Evidence of Britain's current weakness can be seen in the steadily deteriorating balance of payments deficits. As our industrial capacity has fallen, so has our ability to supply the UK domestic economy. In 1987, the deficit for the entire year was £1.67bn. The deficit for the first three months of 1988 was larger than that, at £1.87bn. The deficit for August 1988 was, at £1.3 bn, 'the second worst deficit ever recorded in the history of the UK'. (*The Guardian*, September 28, 1988.) The worst was the July 1988 deficit, at £2.15 bn. Britain had moved rapidly from having annual deficits in the one to two billion pound range, to having quarterly deficits of the same order, to having monthly imbalances of that order. Equally significant is the fact that in 1983 Britain suffered its first deficit on manufactured goods in history.

Part of the cause of these deficits can be found in the two major recessions suffered by Britain since the Tories took office. Thousands of companies have been destroyed by these recessions, thus reducing Britain's capacity to produce manufactured goods. So even in the event of an official economic recovery, the UK will still be unable to make enough goods to satisfy domestic demand.

It has been said that governments since 1950 have not made all that much difference to the macro-economic performance of Britain. Clearly, there are structural and cultural factors, in addition to the traditional targets of state intervention. However, although Britain has been in long-term decline since as early as 1850, the decline in output and competitiveness — as well as several other indicators — was particularly strong during the 1980s. Governments do have an impact, if only by targeting different variables. But it seems that Westminster has been singularly inept, when compared with other countries.

One would not wish to place all the blame on the Conservatives, but on the other hand, they did promise to revitalise British industry, reverse the previous decline, and boost growth. Total growth over the period of the Thatcher/Major administration up to June 1992, was 4.5 per cent, somewhat less than Japan would have achieved in a normal year. Of course, growth is not the best way to measure a nation's achievements; but it is one for which the New Right have claimed their policies to be superior.

Apart from the manner of increasing output, there is the question of whether we actually *need* to make more. Britain is surely so wealthy in terms of its total manufacturing capacity that it has no great need to produce more. What is needed is a willingness to *redistribute* the wealth that we now have. The Conservatives have not merely ignored this; their taxation and union policies have made the distribution of wealth more unequal. Poverty, inequality, homelessness, crime, infant mortality and other social ills have all increased under the Tory regime.

Thus, not only has supply side economics failed to deliver the goods — the economy has no need of more production. What is far more important is making rational use of existing resources, so that everyone is better off. For the poor, this requires a material improvement, and a re-distribution of wealth. But all of us could have a better quality of life if social conditions improved.

It is difficult to see how any rational administrator could continue with policies that are so obviously harming the nation. This is not to say that politicians are necessarily rational, but at least they present themselves as being so. They could, however, claim that short-term disruption is necessary for the long-term improvement in health. Perhaps Major's 'if it isn't hurting, it isn't working' is not an example of governing by cliché, but a colloquial expression of a well thought out policy. Perhaps the New Right is moving away from its materialist style, towards the view that suffering is not only good for the soul, but is somehow good for the economy as well. And naturally, as long as the politicians and their business-worshipping advisors are adding to their own family silver, they will assume that somehow, everyone must be doing well. It is quite likely that part of the readiness to stick to the hard path is due to the well-loved

Victorian values, the stern paternalism that in the nineteenth century virtually idealised the suffering of child workers.

Apart from supply side economics, and the controversial increase in manufacturing productivity, one of the New Right's other contributions was via monetarism, as a tool for controlling inflation. The argument is that stable prices create competitiveness, thus boosting economic growth. One New Right pundit argues that inflation reduces investment, by opening up a gap between cash returns and real (after inflation) returns. (Bartlett and Roth (eds.) p69.) This would be a problem if it were not for the fact that in both Britain and the United States, companies have been cutting back on investment anyway. Inflation has taken second place to short-termism.

However, there is the claim that 'inflation reduces real growth by worsening our net foreign trade balance, since exports cost more and imports cost relatively less'. (Bartlett and Roth (eds.) p70.) But all the evidence suggests that value for money, quality, after-sales service, design, product reliability, and a variety of other non-price factors are actually more important for international competition than price. The obsession with price and inflation while ignoring all other factors is a recipe for economic disaster.

There is no evidence to justify this emphasis on low or stable prices. We do not import more Mercedes and BMWs because they are cheaper than British cars, but because their quality and style are better. We buy Japanese products because they are known for their reliability. The customer buys a product for its characteristics, choosing the balance of features that seems most attractive. And value for money is usually far more important than mere cheapness, which is after all, only saving on price, only to spend later on repairs or replacements. Some customers, on some products, will go strictly for cheapness; but low price is not the route of the successful companies or the successful economies.

All the evidence is that non-price factors are as important, if not more so, than price alone. As a result, price competition can be less important than non-price competition. But these factors, such as reliability, style, or after-sales service, are not areas in which Britain excels.

Thus, there is no real reason for focusing entirely on inflation as the key economic evil — but even if there were, monetarism is not necessarily the best way to deal with the problem. It has been found that controlling the money supply can be enormously difficult; apart from which, the amount of money in circulation must react to the level of activity in the economy. That is, the supply of money responds to the demand for it. If there is a shortage of money in one form or another, people's spending will be constrained. If they are unable to purchase as a result of the limits, this may have an impact on sales, and hence on unemployment. That is, tight monetary policy often creates unemployment.

This link is widely recognised by economists, and even by many Conservative politicians. Indeed, when he was chancellor, Lamont had dismissed concerns about unemployment by saying that it is a price worth paying to get inflation down. This casual indifference to the suffering of more than three million people is morally offensive, regardless of the value of the policy. But the causal link raises two further questions. First, unemployment is naturally deflationary; if people are out of work, they spend less, while those still in work push less for wage increases. Given this, how do we distinguish between the deflationary impact of monetarism, and the effect of the unemployment caused by the monetarism? In other words, is the monetarism actually reducing inflation, or is it simply that anything which makes several million people jobless will control prices?

Second, can there be any moral or social justification whatsoever for a policy that reduces inflation from 12 per cent per annum to 4 per cent, while forcing an additional two million people out of work? Anyone who is at all concerned about the well-being of society, and the welfare of the individuals within it, would have to say no. For some reason this does not seem to apply to any member of the post-1979 Tory governments.

Yet, for the Conservatives, the main concern has been inflation, which some ministers have gone so far as to call an evil. They found it difficult to control the money supply, partly because successive chancellors chose not to use certain traditional methods of control, such as credit controls. As mentioned, supply responds to demand — as with every commodity. Money is not something which is normally oversupplied, except by deliberate government action. However, the complete removal of credit controls, combined with the deregulation of the financial institutions, will tend to lead to over-supply.

Once the Thatcherites had realised the difficulty of controlling the money supply, they turned to controlling the demand for money. This meant putting the price up — raising interest rates. This led to all sorts of other effects. High interest rates meant a strong pound, and this held down the price of foreign goods, so that we did not import inflation along with the products we imported. Unfortunately, a strong pound made imports cheaper and our exports became more expensive. This resulted in the series of ever-growing balance of payments deficits mentioned above.

The high interest rates, combined with the high pound, also led to an increasing number of bankruptcies, thus creating unemployment, and the worst recession for 60 years. This made Britain less able to produce the goods needed for domestic demand. The government argument is that if we control inflation — and there is no evidence that interest rates rather than unemployment were doing this — then the economy will grow, encouraged by our lower prices. This did not seem to be happening.

A strong pound had always been a macho status symbol to British chancellors. Part of this appeal may be due to the fact that a strong economy will tend to have a strong currency. Therefore, even if a chancellor has totally botched the management of the economy, he can still pretend that everything is all right, because actually, we have a high exchange rate.

But also, by holding interest rates high, Britain was able to enter the Exchange Rate Mechanism (ERM) at DM 2.95 to the pound. The ERM is yet the last in a series of superficial measures to create economic success. Starring Jacques Delors and Norman Lamont, European Currency Union is a grandiose scheme to unite the currencies of twelve nations in one. The ERM is merely the overture to this fiscal opus. Sterling joined the ERM at a fixed rate, and the theory was that this would impose discipline on the British workforce. Once in the ERM, it was said, devaluation of the currency ceases to be an option. If workers demand excessive wage increases and make their employers uncompetitive, they risk unemployment as their companies' products lose sales. In this view of course, the only thing that affects the competitiveness of British companies is the workers' wages. The theory was so flawed that it was probably the main cause of Britain's subsequent need to devalue.

The currency upheavals that culminated in the devaluation of the French franc in August 1993 merely showed the inability of a currency system to fix the exchange rate at a given level. The French finance minister wanted, as a political status symbol, a strong franc. In the real world, one needs a healthy economy to support a strong currency. For both France and Britain, the desire to determine indicators rather than actual conditions cost the exchequers dearly. For Britain, defending sterling cost at least £4 bn, while for France defending the franc cost about £11 bn.

No self-respecting member of the New Right could imagine that economic success might be affected by dirty industrial factors like investment, R & D, or the level of either the workers' or the managers' skills. But then, the New Right is by its very nature opposed to the workers; it seeks to blame the workers at every opportunity, and it is not concerned with improving their lot. The possibility that Britain's managers might be less than perfect would simply not occur to them.

Nonetheless, Britain joined the ERM at what was recognised to be an unrealistic exchange rate. The reason for this is the theory that a high exchange rate reduces inflation. Certainly, devaluation causes a one-off rise in the price of imports. But that is not the same as saying that an unrealistically high currency value will hold inflation down. However, both the macho high rate, and the ERM, fail to recognise that exchange rates are a symbol of the economy's real performance. Just as it is not possible to impose a high rate of exchange in the long term, so it is not possible to unite twelve disparate economies.

Despite this, the two-pronged attack created by high interest rates seemed like a good idea. But whereas credit controls only affected credit, high interest rates hit credit, mortgages, corporate borrowing, and investment. And each of these had a knock-on effect on the economy. With every 1 per cent rise in the mortgage rate, between five and seven billion pounds is taken out of consumer spending. And of course, increased hire purchase costs also reduce spending. And lastly, corporate demand for capital goods falls as investment is cut back due to the cost of borrowing.

The extent of government spending cuts may be disputed, but these cuts are undeniable. And this is just a part of the Tories' attack on the average person, as we shall see later.

Meanwhile, the other half of the high interest rate policy has attracted foreign investors to buy pounds, so that they can take advantage of the generous rates on

British bank accounts. All this buying pushes up the price of the pound, allowing UK consumers to buy foreign goods more cheaply. At the same time, British goods become more expensive for foreign customers, so fewer of them are sold. This adds even more to our trade imbalance. We are not producing enough; what we are are making is often uncompetitive, because of our low manufacturing productivity. High interest rates just make our goods a little bit less attractive.

As mentioned, British goods are already failing in non-price competition; the high exchange rates that occur as a result of high interest rates merely add to their lack of appeal. However, because we are falling behind on non-price factors, British industry becomes increasingly vulnerable to price competition.

If the exchange rate is artificially propped up for any length of time, as has been the case with sterling, then the likely result is a series of balance of payments deficits. If this happens, the country may be forced to use all its foreign currency reserves to pay its bills, and may even have to borrow money to support its currency, as Britain did in 1992, unsuccessfully. When the economy is really weak, and output is low, such borrowing, indeed any such support, is utterly pointless, and will not be able to hold off a devaluation. This was the case for Britain in September 1992. To blame the devaluation on speculators is merely another example of the government's refusal to be shackled by such boring constraints as factual accuracy.

It might be argued that all of this is glorious hindsight vision, seeing the obvious once it is blindingly clear. Perhaps the Tories had untried ideas that might have worked had the economic circumstances been different. However, many writers had already pointed out the flaws of monetarism and Thatcherism, in some cases even before Mrs Thatcher took office. The logical and factual weaknesses were visible from the beginning.

Lord Kaldor argued in a speech given in 1980 that the government's policy plan, the Medium Term Economic Strategy, 'contains bold assertions, logical *non sequiturs* and tautologies masquerading as empirical laws which will provide rich source material to teachers of economics... for many years to come' (*The Economic Consequences of Mrs Thatcher*, p53).

One could also mention the early predictions of Cambridge economist Wynne Godley. In 1978 Godley predicted that unless the monetarist policies of the day were dropped, and replaced with more suitable ones, unemployment would rise towards five million. (*New Society*, April 6, 1978.) Given a 1994 official figure of three million unemployed, with at least a four million total using the pre-1979 methods of counting, one has to say that Godley was not far off.

As early as June 1979, Kaldor was arguing against the use of interest rates as a sole instrument of policy. 'The only weapon at the disposal of the monetary authorities... is to keep on raising the rates of interest in the hope that there is some rate which is high enough... at which sufficient economic activity becomes unprofitable or a sufficient number of business firms go into bankruptcy, to create a level of unemployment at which the resistance of trade unions is broken...' (*The Economic Consequences of Mrs Thatcher*, p17).

Kaldor speculated as to the number of unemployed that would be necessary for the Thatcherites to be able to control inflation, suggesting it could be three, maybe five million. At that time there were one and a half million jobless, and a level of even three million would have seemed totally unacceptable. But by the method of calculation used in 1979, we may now have more than four million unemployed.

In fact, there was no evidence that New Right ideas were practical in any way. Indeed, the arguments made by Conservative writers themselves add up to a condemnation of Thatcherism. For example, Norman Tebbit suggests that centralisation is a bad thing. '...A centrally directed system is bound, sooner or later, to go awry on a large scale, whilst a market-based system will naturally correct its own errors and failings incrementally' (*Unfinished Business,* p87). Yet from the very beginning, political control from Westminster had been one of the consistent themes of the Thatcherite regimes.

While centralised political control stifled local authority freedom of action and individual initiative, in the economic arena there was no control. New Right ideology rejected any form of industrial policy or state intervention; it ignored any need for the state to maintain the nation's infrastructure; and it rejected all forms of state subsidy. This was bound to go awry, which it did, with huge balance of payments deficits, and massive borrowing to prop up the pound.

Indeed, the whole Thatcher experiment has been a disaster; but it is interesting to see how the collapse has affected different sections of society. Because strangely, although the economy has deteriorated to a degree that many people find frightening, some social groups have actually benefited. Of course, the rich have got richer, but this is not all. One of the many achievements of the Tories is to improve on the situation which Disraeli described in the nineteenth century, with Britain being split into two nations. The Tories have divided Britain into *three* groups.

The old divisions based on social class are still a useful way of categorising people's attitudes, but increasingly they are not appropriate for evaluating people's life chances. More important, social class is no longer relevant as a method for determining someone's ability to control their own life. Once, 'middle class' meant a strong likelihood that the parents could influence the outcome or quality of their child's career. Under Thatcherism, people are lucky if they can control their own lives. And this provides the basis for distinguishing between the three groups — the extent to which they control their life chances.

The first group is well known, and has been described many times before. They are still alive and well, although their exact social composition and origins have changed slightly in recent years. They are the establishment, the rich, those at the centres of power. This is a group which has the ability to control its own wages and conditions, and has access to sufficient wealth to ensure that its rewards are more than generous. The source of their power may vary, some have vast wealth, and some might only have their incomes. But all have privileged positions.

MPs and company directors are able to vote themselves massive pay rises, although both groups tend not to abuse this ability. Indeed, in 1992 MPs voted against a pay rise, as a gesture of restraint. But there have been many cases of company executives presenting themselves with pay increases that have crossed the border from generous to immoral. Very often, these have been voted through by pay committees, or a director's pay has been raised when that particular director was out of the room. But this does not imply an objective decision on company pay structures. It is more likely that the pay committee is made up of executives from other companies, all of whom vote for one another's increases, in an interlocking elite. Or if there is no committee, directors will leave the boardroom one by one, while those remaining will vote a massive rise for the absentee.

Some professionals can simply raise their fees. Their specialist knowledge and the rarity of their skills allow them a degree of self-determination that others cannot match. But the fact that some professionals are now seen as more vulnerable shows the dividing line that marks the establishment. Some groups, such as journalists or television producers, might once have been seen as being in the same social class as the business elite. The Thatcherites have clarified that. The groups who walk arm in arm with the politicians and civil servants along the corridors of power are in the establishment. Those who are potential enemies are out. Naturally, those who share golf or lunch or clubs with top politicians are able to press for their incomes to be maintained, for their privileges to be protected, for their tax perks to remain exempt. They may not wield power directly, but they have access to it, and hence are part of the establishment.

The Thatcherite view of the establishment is quite sharply defined. Many professions that were once members of the affluent elite have seen their privileges eroded. And market forces have been allowed to rule in an extraordinarily wide area. But the heavy tread of ideology can be seen in the degree to which professional privileges have been reduced. For solicitors, there has been a surgical removal of their house conveyancing monopoly. The television industry has simply been put through the grinder.

Unlike the Marxists, I am not suggesting that the power of the establishment comes only from their control of the means of production. Clearly, for some of these people their wealth and security stems from neither the ownership of business nor its control. It may do so, but it may also originate in political power, or simply in the privileged access to those with power. Thus, social contacts can be a greater source of power than trade union solidarity, or the barrel of a gun.

At the other end of the social spectrum is a group that I propose to call the underclass. Galbraith uses the term to describe a global subclass, used as menial labourers by the more affluent nations. The group I wish to look at is a purely local phenomenon, made in Britain.

Galbraith argues that the affluent middle classes have engaged in a tacit conspiracy against the lower classes. The middle classes can afford to pay for private provision of pensions, life insurance, health insurance and so on from their large incomes. They object to paying higher taxes so that these things can be provided for the poor. This collusion of selfishness is what helps to create the underclass.

This group is made up of the poor, the weak, the vulnerable. The label may seem unattractive, but then so is the situation that these people have to put up with. For our purposes, it does not matter if they are poor because of low pay or low welfare benefits. The low income is their defining characteristic, along with their inability to affect their income to any noticeable degree. These are people who must struggle to survive, with little or no savings, and small chance of affording any luxuries. Most pensioners would fall in this class — but not all; the top ten per cent of pensioners earn, from various sources, over £600 per week (*The Independent*, September 16, 1992). Most of these would be retired company directors and their relatives, struggling along on anything from £500 a week to £500,000 a year.

Those of working age fall within the underclass if they lack the skills to get a full-time job, or a well-paid one. Hence, many who would be described as traditional working class would, as a result of changes under the Tories, fall within the new group. Their skills have been either devalued, or rendered impossible to acquire. The New Right emphasis on individual incentive allows the rich and poor alike to spend three years at university. By strange chance, working class youngsters cannot afford this, or choose not to seek graduate qualifications. They leave school, and enter the world of work immediately. For them, life is a struggle to survive. They may be in debt, or perhaps are too poor to obtain credit, and they will have difficulty maintaining even a modest standard of living.

They live at the margins of society, more vulnerable to unemployment, but the last to be taken back on when the economy picks up. They lack skills, but equally important, they lack political power. This seems strange, given the number of people who must fall within this group, but because many members of the working class vote Conservative almost automatically, while those who do not are neither vocal, nor sufficient to create an electoral majority, the government does not need to court their approval. It can write off the underclass, just as society has done. However, the fact that an elected government is willing to dismiss the welfare of such a large section of the populace says a lot about Tory values. Quite simply, the dominant Tory clique in Westminster does not care about the well-being of the less fortunate.

The economic significance of the underclass is that we now have a large section of the population whose purchasing power has been drastically reduced. They are partly removed from the economy, and by reducing demand overall, employment is also reduced. What is particularly worrying is that the government is still taking actions that will lower wages for many groups. It intends to abolish those few Wages Councils that still exist, and is allowing jobs to be lost on the railways and in the mines.

One report argues that employers are using the threat of unemployment as a tool for holding down pay and conditions, and increasing working hours. 'The report accuses employers of imposing dramatically worse pay and working conditions on their staff. ... Some employers routinely dismiss staff weeks or even days before they complete two years in the job and thereby qualify for unfair dismissal protection'. (*Job Insecurity*, National Association of Citizens Advice Bureaux, cited in *The Guardian*, March 2, 1993.)

Trade unions' negotiating power has been steadily weakened by a series of anti-union laws. Some of it is well-known, such as the ban on secondary picketing, or the requirement to hold a strike ballot. Less widely known are such restrictions as the ban on picketing the head office of an employer, unless one either works there, or has no fixed place of work. Then there is the ban on picketing a factory owned by the same employer, even if the company is diverting work to that factory (*LRD Guide to the Tory Employment Bill*, LRD, 1980). Such changes in the law make the worker almost powerless, even when the strike is justified.

But many employers are going a stage further than this, and demanding de-recognition of unions within the workplace. According to Labour Research, in some cases this may be a by-product of a single-union deal, but more often it is a way of simply removing the trade unions from the industrial landscape. According to a University of Warwick study, many employers 'hoped to introduce a new climate in which unions were rendered irrelevant'. (*Industrial Relations Review and Report,* November 1992, IRS.) And de-recognition is becoming more common; four times as many cases were found in the 1988-92 survey as in the 1984-88 survey. Increasingly, the average worker has little or no protection from the predatory employer. (*The Union De-recognition Bandwagon*, LRD, 1992.)

As a result of Tory legislation, working conditions in Britain have steadily deteriorated. More and more workers are part-time, and as a result have less job protection. For example, a full-time employee is entitled to protection from unfair dismissal, and a written statement of the reasons for dismissal, after two years. A part-time worker doing between 8 and 16 hours a week must be employed for five years before they have the same entitlements.

The lack of protection and the negotiating weakness makes the part-timer a very attractive proposition to the money-conscious employer. Not only can they save on National Insurance contributions, but they can also reduce overtime payments. 'In retailing, where part-timers are used extensively to provide cover across what may now be an 80 hour shopping week, extra payments to part timers for Saturday working are rare. A 1988 survey by the National Economic Development Office found that only 15% of part timers received Saturday premia'. (*Part-Time Workers — A Negotiators' Guide*, LRD, 1992.)

Given the gains to be made, it is not surprising that the number of part-timers has increased since 1979. At the present time, a quarter of Britain's workforce, 5.5 million people, are part-time workers. The percentage is greater in some areas, especially retailing. 'The food retailers, in particular, relay heavily on part-timers with 60% of the workforce, primarily in supermarkets, now working part-time compared with just over a third 20 years ago. At J. Sainsbury, the UK's biggest food retailer, 52,000 out of 68,000 store staff are part-time'. (*Part-Time Workers — A Negotiators' Guide.*)

According to one survey, the movement towards part-time work has accelerated rapidly in recent years. In the retail trade, for example, part-timers were fairly stable from 1985 to 1989, at about 42 per cent of the full-time workforce. But from 1989 onwards, the percentage shot up rapidly, reaching 48 per cent in 1992. Women are the main beneficiaries of this, with the result that female unemployment is growing at a slower rate than male unemployment. Any economic recovery that does occur is unlikely to alter this trend, says the survey company, Income Data Services. It is more likely 'to accelerate the shift towards more female part-time workers'. (*The Guardian*, May 10, 1993.)

It is worth noting that in Belgium, Denmark, France, Germany, Greece, Italy, Luxembourg, Holland, Portugal and Spain, the part-timer has exactly the same legal rights as the full-time employee. Part-time working could so easily imply freedom and flexibility, with the worker choosing their own hours, and enjoying a reasonable standard of living. But with minimal legal protection, and almost non-existent union power, the employee is merely a reducible cost in the company's production schedule.

For many workers, the quality of their job has also declined. Market forces have brought a pressure for efficiency that totally ignores such factors as enjoyment. For example, many NHS cleaners used to get some pleasure from small jobs, helping the nurses. They felt that they were making a contribution. With the new tendered-out contracts, the job is narrowed down even as the hours expand, and all pleasure is burnt out of it. For other workers, the increased hours, the loss of tea breaks, the demands for 'performance' all take their toll. Work has returned to being pure drudgery.

Daily, the process of wage cuts and job losses continues. The government intends to abolish the few remaining Wages Councils, as well as carrying out more spending cuts, as are many private companies. Also, newly privatised companies are imposing new wages and working conditions on their employees. In most cases, the new agreements involve wage cuts, sometimes quite significant ones. And opted-out schools and colleges are gradually moving to new working agreements. In addition, many people are now on short-term contracts, part-time working, or on the new 'zero contracts'. This latter item means effectively the casualisation of the job, with no employment benefits whatsoever, and no job protection. Workers are taken on as and when needed, and when not needed, are simply dumped. There can be advantages in this for the workers, in that they can work as and when they want. But given the employer's bargaining power, the worker is likely to be marginalised by casual work, rather than freed by it.

Many workers have found their pay or working conditions hit by privatisation or deregulation, although recent developments show that companies who have used their negotiating power to reduce wages have been breaking European Community law. An EU directive says that 'staff transferring from public to private employment are entitled to keep the same pay and conditions as before'. (*The Observer*, May 9, 1993.) A quarter of a million workers have lost wages and conditions as a result of the Conservatives opening industry up to market forces. All of these are entitled to their old pay and conditions, and one hopes that the unions will ensure that workers' rights are returned to them.

The Tories' attack on the welfare state, reducing the value of pensions and unemployment pay, makes workers even more vulnerable. Society's safety net has been replaced by a brick landing pad, so that those who cannot find work — or sufficiently well-paid work — will have to manage on a bare survival income. Although Mrs Thatcher had promised to limit the burden of poll tax on the poor, the Social Security minister at that time, John Moore, made an offer to the Treasury to abandon that commitment. Even the incomes of the very lowest paid can be sacrificed to the hungry maw of the Treasury.

Those who claim off the state, especially the unemployed and single parents, are seen as scroungers, and energetically vocal campaigns are organised to ensure that these people do not defraud the state. A large part of the zeal is a flag of war, to cover the penny-pinching in a cloud of patriotism. The villains who steal £30 a week from the state are a threat to society, and tabloid hostility is an excellent way to justify scrounger hunts.

One should also compare the effort that is put into tracking down those who unrighteously claim state funds, with the effort put into ensuring that members of the upper income groups pay their full tax liability. The Tories have made the latter form of villainy far more difficult, by minimising the rate of tax. However, some tax evasion does still occur, and for those for whom emigration to northern Cyprus is too drastic, the traditional forms of dealing with the law must do. For the lower and middle income groups, this may involve rude letters marked OHMS. For the very rich it usually seems to involve making meaningless promises about public access to rights of way.

It is worth noting that all the well-spoken hysteria about the various categories of claimant is both pointless and misdirected. If the problem is that these people are costing the Treasury a fortune each year, then the best long-term solution would be to create a few jobs. Given that each unemployed person costs the state £8,000 a year, it makes economic sense to create jobs, even at a cost of £20,000 per job. If the job, or business that is set up, is even moderately permanent, then the state will profit by the action. The key fact is that each unemployed person costs the state money, in benefits of various sorts. If that person then gets a job, they are contributing to the Exchequer, rather than taking from it. It is a self-evident truth that does not even need figures for the sense of it to become apparent.

The Conservatives, however, do not take this approach. They seek to save money on welfare benefits, regardless of whether this is the best solution or not. It seems that workers will in future be more insecure, more vulnerable, and less able to negotiate a decent wage. More workers will be pushed into the underclass, and spending power in the economy will fall yet again. This in turn will reduce consumption, thus reducing the size of the economy.

The argument is that people have to accept lower wages to price themselves into jobs, thus creating the necessary jobs to eliminate the existing unemployment. In other words, people should accept low wages in order to become wealthy. The way to make Britain wealthy again is for us all to accept the lowest wage possible. The cheek of it is the only thing that is rich.

There is a problem that lower wages mean less spending power. So wages cuts generally lead to a decline in economic activity, and a greater emphasis on price competition. This can be seen in the growing number of High Street shops specialising in low quality, unbranded goods. There has also been a fall in the cash value of brand names. In the past, big name products could command a premium price; but as we move towards something like a world slump, even top names must become price competitive.

As the workers' purchasing power falls, their quality of life also declines, along with their health. Their diet is often lacking in essential minerals, and is unlikely to have the full range of vitamins. In addition, they are not likely to have a car, so cannot travel to the larger supermarkets. According to Tim Lang, of Parents for Safe Food, 'the poor are being quietly removed from the contemporary food economy'. (*Time Out*, February 17, 1993.)

Because of the steady reduction in purchasing power under the Tories, there is a danger that many employers will now have to hold wage levels down, simply to survive. And this process could become a self-propelling vicious circle. Each round of wage cuts could create a further round, as demand spirals downwards, and competition intensifies. What we may see is a steady shrinkage of the UK economy, fuelled by the continuous impoverishment of a large section of the population.

Although people often say that the recession has got to end sometime, if we accept the spiral decline hypothesis, there is the possibility of there being no end to the recession. At least, not in any reasonable time-scale. The economy might simply continue to deteriorate until it can go no further. Temporary recoveries may look reassuring, but they may be no more than a double-dip or even triple-dip slump. History will make its judgement, but at the present time, all the signs for the UK economy are at stop.

In some ways, modern Britain is similar to the Philippines — we are encouraging inward investment by foreign multinationals, and the economy is being directed towards exports. In addition, we are becoming a low wage, low skill, assembly operation economy. More worrying is the possibility that we may be heading for a Philippine-style decline, with upwardly spiralling levels of poverty, and collapsing living standards.

Given the policies followed by the UK, such a scenario is not totally impossible. Repeated cuts in government expenditure mean repeated pay cuts for public sector workers, as well as lost jobs. There is a worryingly accurate echo of the Philippines here. Although it is argued that the low-wage, foreign investment approach is the best way to create growth in the economy, if we look at the experience of the Philippines, one suspects that this method is actually very damaging.

There has been a rapid growth of poverty in the Philippines. It has risen from 60 per cent of the population in 1985, to 70 per cent in 1988, to 90 per cent in 1992, according to the IBON Information Service of the Philippines. However, it has to be admitted that the US army was their second largest single employer. Apart from the rent Washington paid for Clarke and Subic Bay, the US bases probably added nearly a billion dollars a year to the Filipino economy. (*The Observer Magazine*, November 15, 1992, p48.) The loss of those bases was undoubtedly a major factor in the growth of poverty.

The growth of poverty in Britain has been relatively modest, but then, we have only been following this particular path to economic success for a relatively short time.Every additional year of Conservativism means another significant increase in poverty. As in the Philippines, the Tories are actually promoting policies which encourage the shift towards a low wage, low skill workforce.

In a speech to an EU conference in Copenhagen, John Major warned that, 'It is not a solution to drive down wages to the levels which exist in eastern Europe'. (*The Guardian*, June 22, 1993.) But he then went on to warn of the dangers that excessive wage costs could bring. The government's wages policy will ward off such dangers. Instead we have, according to Chris Pond of the Low Pay Unit, a security guard earning £1.19 an hour for an 84 hour week. Or a beauty therapist who earns 53p an hour, working a 66 hour week. To treat workers in this way is inhuman. The economic impact will be a steadily declining economy.

It is worth noting that in the Philippines also, the private sector is given pre-eminence. 'Economic policy-making in the Philippines is guided by the idea that the private sector is the medium for economic progress and the prime mover for development'. (Rosa Linda P. Tidalgo and Emmanuel F. Esquerra, *Philippine Employment in the Seventies*, p52.) The success of the private sector in creating progress can be judged from the fact that the level of poverty has steadily increased since the 1970s.

The market, and the emphasis on private ownership, lead inevitably to growing financial and social inequality. Those with the power to negotiate, move their operations, close factories, or choose who they employ, can simply impose wage settlements on the entire workforce. Those who have no source of income, other than their own effort, or a miserly dole handout, must accept the wage offered. Here, the United States becomes a more appropriate comparison. The market uncaringly rewards success and power, and discards those who have no saleable skills. But such uneven allocations must have their impact on society.

There is no doubt that the Tories recognise both the absence of competition, and the failure of their policies. Seeing that we are worse off now, their argument is tending to shift to a hypothetical future. Thus, the claim becomes, under Conservatism, people will be better off in the future. One good example of this is the suggestion that we will be better off as a result of inheriting huge amounts from our parents. This sounds emotionally unhealthy, but given the demands of the state for payment for care of the elderly, it also sounds improbable. Family savings are disappearing into nursing home bills, so that as a direct result of government cuts, there will be no inheritance whatsoever for many families.

The social impact of the underclass is that of millions of people living in slums, cardboard boxes or on rundown estates, scraping a living, and knowing that they will never be able to do any more than scrape. For young people, condemned to a future of slums and unemployment, the best that life can offer is the occasional burst of excitement. They turn to drugs or crime or casual violence as a natural response to their environment. For some, it may be the only way of surviving, or of making a decent living. The fear that this crime brings into the lives of the comfortable middle class is insignificant compared to the tragedy that some of the underclass must suffer.

But if politicians can call muggers evil, or heap tabloid scorn on unmarried mothers, what words can we use to describe the person who knowingly creates a society which generates crime, and isolates women? What adjective is suitable for someone who is responsible for impoverishing millions, making thousands homeless, and creating massive insecurity?

This is not to say that all crime is the result of Thatcherism or poverty. There are many causes, and many changes have occurred in society since the 1950s to contribute to the rise in crime since then. Among the factors which concern us are the rise in both inequality and materialism, and the failure of both schools and parents to teach children a coherent set of moral values. (The contribution of politicians to the lack of respect for morality is considered below.) The greater inequality is clearly the result of Thatcherism, but we cannot blame the government for inaction by teachers and parents. There has also been a decline in the sense of community, and again, Tory values must be the primary factor.

One can, however, make clear links between the increased inequality and unemployment, and the higher levels of crime. In addition, the reduction of opportunity as a result of education cuts creates a sense of hopelessness and oppression. The jobless youngster has little to look forward to, because there are so few ways of attaining the few opportunities that do exist. And those still at school are aware that whatever they may achieve in terms of qualifications, their chances of getting a decent job are slim indeed.

Those people on very low incomes will suffer additional stress, beyond that of the insecure, but relatively wealthy middle classes. Those at the bottom of society's income pyramid may often feel that their very survival is under threat. The ordinary working people described by Hoggart in *Uses of Literacy*, were comfortably safe in comparison. They might have missed a meal occasionally on a bad week, but their home was assured. The new poor of post-Thatcher Britain may have to fear starvation and homelessness.

The stress that this creates can isolate both family and friends. Some may reach a point where they cannot cope with the stress, others find they can no longer be supportive to those close to them. Relationships may break up, or they may continue in name only. Like so many other factors, this actually works in the Conservatives' favour. Increasing insecurity causes people to move to the right, while stress-induced isolation prevents people from working together. Solidarity becomes no more than a concept for those struggling as lone individuals simply to survive. It could be described as the fractionation of society, as one by one supportive social groups collapse under the pressures of Thatcherism.

In addition to the immediate environmental effects, there is also the fact that the government sets the tone of society by its own behaviour. The main components are the Thatcherite ideology of 'look after yourself', and the actual behaviour of Tory ministers, which can best be described as 'get away with what you can'. To the Conservatives, there is no right or wrong; morality is merely a word. Anything that you can get away with, is completely acceptable.

The combination of governmental indifference and the Tories' emphasis on the individual must be a significant contributory factor to the rise in crime figures. On the one hand, for the lower income person, there must be a sense of being totally alone. There is no guarantee of state support in the event of financial disaster. Yet on the other hand, there is a government that overtly ignores morality, while saying that the individual must look after themselves. It is a veritable invitation to go out and help oneself.

With the government setting the moral tone in this way, naturally all other members of society will tend to follow. The underclass are more likely than most to adhere to such an attitude, although one wonders if some top business executives have not also decided to take up this pragmatic philosophy. However, it will be understandable if the poorer members of society choose to emulate the Tory philosophy. Indeed, it seems as if quite a few of them have. Crime has grown at a frightening rate under the Thatcherites, and it is very likely that Britain's new criminal class are able to justify their actions in terms of what you can get away with. Morality is dead, killed off by a government which has abused virtually every aspect of moral behaviour.

In addition, as the level of crime has grown, so has the amount of money spent on security precautions. Householders may buy burglar alarms, shops will fit security grilles, and other businesses will increase their expenditure in various ways. It is not consumption for pleasure; it is merely compensation for the ills of society. Clearly, since 1979 a growing proportion of GNP has been spent on security, and with a low growth economy, one cannot say that what growth has occurred implies a rise in standards of living. It would not be inconsistent with changed patterns of spending to say that standards of living have actually fallen. People are not acquiring consumer goods, but compensatory goods.

And by blaming the victim, the government has also reduced the scope for rational discussion of social issues. Some people have been so antagonised by ministers constantly blaming the poor, the homeless, and the welfare recipients for their own plight, that they refuse to see the underclass as responsible for anything. But once you reject responsibility, you also reject any possibility of changing the situation. This is not to say that all the socially disadvantaged are even significantly to blame for their situation; merely that some of them could do something to minimise the problems. That is, taking the current situation as the responsibility of government, the individual can still do something to ameliorate their situation. But with attitudes polarised between 'it is' or 'it isn't' the government's fault, what little can be done may often pass ignored.

The size of the underclass has increased considerably under Thatcherism. This is not to say that the Tories are solely responsible for inequality. The Labour Party has also contributed its fair share to the apathy and incompetence of post-war British economic policy. With Labour, this was due to their obsession with state ownership, the creation of harmonious relations with the unions, and industrial giantism. In addition, they promised a wealth tax, and then discreetly dropped it. With the Tories it is due to their mixture of cuts in welfare benefits, the abolition of Wages Councils, the weakening of trade unions, and the unequal impact of tax cuts. 'Curiously, every single new tax relief, tax perk or tax subsidy introduced in Britain since 1979 has benefited the rich more than the poor'. (John Rentoul, *The Rich Get Richer*, p49.)

The 1992 *PSI Report* stated that 'the poorest tenth of households shared between them a mere half of one per cent of the increase in national disposable income between 1979 and 1988. Meanwhile the richest tenth of households shared nearly half the extra money. As a result the richest tenth enjoyed a 50 per cent increase in their real incomes; the income of the poorest tenth barely changed over the period'. (Richard Berthoud and Elaine Kempson, *Credit and Debt. The PSI Report,* pp9-10.) This is inequality on a massive scale, with the Tories' responsibility made quite explicit.

Obviously, the Conservatives' first budget, which cut top tax rates from 83 per cent to 60 per cent, offered a massive gain to the rich. What is less obvious is that cuts in the basic rate of tax also give more to the rich than the poor. For example, the 1988 budget cut the basic rate of tax to 25 per cent, which suggests that all would gain equally. In fact, the saving is proportional to the size of the income, so the larger the income, the larger the tax cut in cash terms.

Over the period 1979-86, the changes in income tax and national insurance raised the contributions of those earning half the average wage by five per cent. Those earning ten times the average wage had their tax and national insurance costs reduced by 15 per cent. (*New Society*, February 6, 1987.) Overall, from tax year 1978-79 to 1986-87, the changes gave top wage earners a saving of £3.6 bn. (*The Rich Get Richer*, p48.)

An enormous shift of resources has taken place, enriching those who have, and impoverishing the less well off. From 1979 to 1986, the number of people earning less than the Supplementary Benefit level rose from 6.1 million to 11.9 million. (*The Rich Get Richer*, p35.) That is an indication of the growth of the underclass. However, given the rise of the market philosophy, and the willingness of Tory governments to apply cuts regardless of suffering, it is likely that the stress and anxiety associated with low income has utterly degraded the quality of life for those on low incomes. The loss of income is exacerbated by the loss of hope, the feeling that all outside help has been removed.

Indeed, there is much anecdotal evidence to suggest that although quality of life has deteriorated for many, and job and education prospects have virtually collapsed, the individuals themselves are often managing with great dignity. It is comparable to working class poverty of the 1930s, in terms of lifestyle, but with more of the modern conveniences. The main source of anxiety seems to be the awareness that, rightly or wrongly, the state will do nothing for them. The government will not act on a macroeconomic level, creating jobs, nor will it act on a local level, and improve welfare benefits or local authority funding. The low income individual is entirely on their own, with no-one to help them.

As mentioned above, Galbraith argues that the affluent middle classes have engaged in a tacit conspiracy against the lower classes. The middle classes can afford to pay for private pensions, life insurance, health insurance, and object to paying higher taxes so that these things can be provided for others. And this group, which Galbraith calls the contented majority, wields the most voting power. It is individualism unchained, the revolt of the white-collar, but fomented by New Right propaganda. The middle class wish to take the material blessings of the affluent society, but without paying the membership fees.

The Conservatives have taken this conspiracy a stage further. The leaders of business, and top politicians, have colluded to weaken the value of the vote. In Britain, the middle classes do not gain anything by their lack of concern for the lower orders. In Britain, we have a contented minority who have gained most of the benefits from New Right policies.

What we see in the middle of society can best be described as the precarious class. Whereas the underclass finds it a struggle to survive, the precarious class are struggling to live in comfort, to keep their past standard of living. They are affluent and unsettled, people who once were wealthy and secure, but are no longer both. Some have ceased to be wealthy, while most are no longer secure. Some, like Fleet Street printers or television technicians, are worse off in real terms. Their current real income is significantly lower than what they were previously earning. Others, such as teachers, are earning more, but their pay has slipped down the scale, relative to the average wage.

But many have made little improvement. Wage cuts have been threatened or imposed, and it has been a great effort simply to minimise the impact of cuts. For example, bus drivers have been hit by deregulation and cuts in central government spending on public transport. Train drivers have suffered from BR's cuts and the privatisation. Many industrial workers have had their negotiating position weakened by the recession and by the erosion of trade union powers.

Civil servants have been made more vulnerable by market testing, where the provision of administrative services is put out to tender. It is in essence a form of Compulsory Competitive Tendering (CCT), but for white-collar workers. The effect of market testing is to put downward wage pressure on both the civil servants, and the employees of the tendering companies.

The unions have been weakened by various items of Conservative legislation, with the result that millions of workers are less secure. Others may see changes to their jobs on the horizon. They may or may not have already had their pay or conditions reduced, but such changes are increasingly likely in the future. Perhaps they may be affected by privatisation, or by Local Management of Schools (LMS), or by new technology. But the types of change are multiplying, while the worker's ability to deal with it, and ensure that change works for his or her benefit, is diminishing.

The precarious class are those with valuable skills and qualifications, and an important contribution to make to the economy. Their reduced status is not only symbolic of the way in which the Tory government undervalues professionals and skilled workers; it is also symptomatic of Tory contempt for the economy. It also damages the economy in the immediate sense. If we use the concept of lifetime earnings, we will see that millions of workers in jobs will have reduced their consumption, simply because of government policy. The chancellor may talk about a recovery of consumer confidence; but there will be no full recovery of confidence while the present government is in office, with its existing policies.

As a result of the many changes, the typical worker feels deeply insecure. People react to insecurity by spending less. This is not merely common sense; it is an inherent part of Milton Friedman's monetarism. Friedman postulates that people spend according to their expected lifetime income, so if their expectations of future earnings change for any reason, clearly the amount of spending will alter as well. (See Robert J. Gordon (ed.), *Milton Friedman's Monetary Framework*, p11, p16. Visser, *The Quantity of Money,* p148, p242.)

The worker's fear is that future changes will eliminate either their job, their job security, or their current high pay levels. And there is good reason for such fears, given the government's constant spending cuts, deregulation, privatisation, and other alterations to the job market. The concern for the future is that many jobs we now see as secure, well-paid, even middle class, may slip down the scale into the underclass. Teachers, television technicians and bus drivers may not yet have entered the underclass, but their pay levels are severely threatened.

This too is reminiscent of the Philippines, where once-secure middle class jobs have been marginalised to the edge of poverty. But given the number of trends that weaken the workers' union power or negotiating position, declining pay levels are almost inevitable. The combination of lower pay and greater insecurity means a significant drop in personal spending, and thus, a shrinking of the economy.

This trend is a natural feature of the New Right concept of the free market, in which efficiency is elevated above all other values. The worker is subordinated to what may be called 'the economy', but is in fact the wishes of the corporation.

It is also a reversal of the traditional relationship between worker and employer. Trade unions in most western countries had established the principle that employment was a contract between the two parties, for mutual benefit, and by mutual consent. Wages, hours, and working conditions were all to be agreed by the two sides, on the understanding that both gained from the pact.

The New Right approach is that workers are merely another factor of production, to be deployed as and when needed. They are to be used in whatever way maximises efficiency, as measured by the corporation's needs. It is not just a narrow definition of efficiency; it also de-humanises the workforce. And it denies that companies have any social responsibility — a subject which we will return to in a later chapter.

The attack on the welfare state makes many of the middle classes more insecure. Changes in legislation have removed the various forms of job protection; for example, the government's abolition in 1991 of the 1972 Industrial Relations Code of Practice. Privatisation and deregulation then eroded working conditions even further, by creating new profit-oriented private sector employers, who claimed the legal right to start employment contract negotiations anew. In nearly every case, the new contract gave workers lower pay, fewer rights and less protection. As mentioned, this is illegal under EU law, but one has yet to see the cuts being reversed.

If, however, we restrict our analysis to the known impact of past policies, we can see that the reduction in current spending is not the full extent of the government's impact on people's feeling of insecurity. The combination of recession, wage cuts, and record mortgage rates, all the direct result of Tory policies, has hit both house-buyers and house prices. House prices have slumped as potential buyers have fled an expensive market, while existing purchasers are trapped in a house with a declining value, while their wages may also be falling. If they sold the house, they would lose money; they are buying what is in effect, a worthless asset. Building society figures suggest that one million housebuyers were trapped in this impossible situation. (*The Observer*, August 23, 1992.) For many it is even worse; they are trapped by falling values, but they cannot afford to continue the repayments. Housebuyers in this situation have simply handed in their house keys to their local building society, and walked away. Their life's savings have been destroyed.

In the past, people borrowed money against the (rising) value of their house, to pay for holidays or a new car. No one trapped by house price falls or wage cuts will be doing this. Some have left the housing market forever, and have no intention of ever again trying to buy their own home. All who have houses will be wary of borrowing against the value of their home. Even if they can currently afford the mortgage payments, they know only too well how high those payments can go. They know that when the Chancellor talks about interest rates, it could spell subsistence level spending for months.

With growing concern about jobs, mortgages and savings, people are increasingly insecure. And it has been observed that at times of great insecurity, voters look for somebody who can offer them certainty and safety. The actual policies become less important than the confidence and assurance offered by the politicians. And it tends to be the right-wing politicians who offer such assurance, the paternalistic promise to look after people, as long as everything is left for the state to decide. The Conservatives are the natural actors for this role, although the integrity of the performance has declined in recent years. However, it has not declined sufficiently for another party to take over the act. But there are a large number of people affected by this anxiety.

If we add up those caught by falling property values, those who have handed in their keys, and those who are wary of future interest rate rises, it may well be two million buyers. Then there are those with normal credit debts to pay off, surprised by the cost of borrowing in late 1980s, and now cautious about getting into debt again. And many people will have been hit by the share collapses of 1990 and 1992. Most shares are owned by the big financial institutions, but after years of skilful promotion by the Thatcherites, presenting each new privatisation as a wonderful opportunity, there are now eleven million individual shareholders, compared with three million in 1982. Many of these only hold shares in one company, and only have a few, so there has not been the intended shift to a share-owning society. But there has also been a backlash from the extended share ownership; by reducing the value of people's wealth, the stockmarket crashes also reduced their perceived spending power. The result of this was to reduce their spending.

When considering those who have been made worse off, we should also include the unemployed, most pensioners, the low paid, part-time workers, and those on short-term contracts. Simply counting the unemployed would give us an official figure of 3 million unemployed, with 4 million a more likely figure. Then there are the 9.4 million poor, defined as those living below the Council of Europe's 'decency threshold' (*The Poor Decade*, Low Pay Unit, 1988). Then there are nearly 12 million pensioners (OPCS figure for 1991) and 5.5 million part-time workers.

If we take these groups, we then add the 1.8 million people who are in debt, plus 1.5 million with negative equity. Even if we make allowances to discount for double counting, and the fact that ten per cent of pensioners are actually very wealthy, we still have a total in excess of twenty million people, all of whom are spending less for one reason or another. This is twenty million people who have been made measurably worse off by the Conservative government's policies. This is the other face of the loss of production caused by the government's attack on spending. And it makes a hefty contribution to the continuing recession.

There are also the billions of pounds transferred by the tax system since 1979 from the lower and middle income groups, to the rich. As well as impoverishing the losers, the transfer itself alters the balance of purchasing power in Britain. The money has been moved from groups which may spend 80 or 100 per cent of their disposable income, to a group which might spend only 20 per cent of its disposable income. The rich already have most of the things they want, therefore their additional spending from any increase in income will be minimal. Thus, with no apparent change in the quantity of money in circulation, the total spending power in the economy has been dramatically reduced. Every budget that transfers income to the rich, at the same time reduces purchasing power.

But the problems go beyond the economic. There is also the impact of continuing insecurity on the structure of family life. Parents who are worried about the safety of their job, or whether they will be able to pay the bills, may not be able to spare the emotional strength that their children need. Young people need love, support and understanding; sometimes they need discipline, encouragement and gentle pushing. Parents who find it hard enough to keep away from the bottle are not best placed to create the secure environment that allows a healthy childhood.

As parents crack up under the pressure, relationships crumble. Divorce rates soar, ex-partners wield unresolved hatreds for one another, and children get hurt in the emotional crossfire. Very often, nobody gains from the separation, and certainly few learn to handle relationships any differently. In the United States, youngsters turn to membership of street gangs, as a surrogate family, but this gives neither the emotional depth nor the educational or career support of a real family. However, the expansion of the gangs is yet another factor in the deterioration of the quality of life in the US. Other forms of emotional support, such as drink and drugs, have equally damaging aspects for both the individual and society.

Perhaps the suburban middle classes are happy to blame the vandal, the drug addict or the gang member — blaming the victim clears the conscience of the tax-efficient white-collar worker. But as the behaviour of the gang members, vandals and others affects the daily lives of the middle class, they too might see the need for change.

There is also the political impact of insecurity and marginalisation. Arndt suggests that the main source of success for the Nazi party was their realisation of the importance of job security. The Nazis eliminated basic freedoms, raised taxes and militarised Germany. Yet the people continued to support them, regarding full employment as an acceptable trade-off. (See H. W. Arndt, *The Lessons of the Nineteen-Thirties*, p169.)

There is a danger that the continued insecurity created by Lamont and Major, coupled with the failure of the Labour Party to present a credible alternative, will lead to the rise of a new third party. It has often been noted that insecurity leads to political extremism, and the average Briton is probably feeling less secure under the Thatcherites than at any other time this century. The third party may not be concerned with such fragile myths as democracy, and may seek simpler remedies for the ills of society. Scapegoating racial minorities is both easy and emotionally satisfying. The rise of racism throughout Europe could be the beginning of a long phase of fascism in Europe.

The constant struggle to survive demeans both the individual and society. The personal impact of insecurity has a lower profile than the public face of racism and extremism, and is easily overlooked. We choose to ignore the damage done to our lives, the compromises for the sake of a job, the daily struggles we endure. In a state of perpetual anxiety about work, we are less able to think about more general issues, such as the underlying causes of the economy's difficulties, or higher thoughts, of art or philosophy. Our activities increasingly relate to work, while our minds, even when free of work, are unable to rise to higher levels.

Gradually, life has changed from being a source of pleasure or a path of enlightenment, to being a process of survival. We have become worker drones for the industrial hive of Thatcherism. Humanity and personality have been sacrificed for the sake of creating an obedient, but modestly paid, workforce. The New Right's employees will march into their offices and factories, do their work without striking or complaining, and march out at shift's end. It is a vision from Fritz Lang's *Metropolis*, a future that is being pieced together all around us.

There are growing dangers from the underclass. Being on the margins of survival, many people have to turn to whatever source of income they can. Others, feeling marginalised, turn to whatever source of comfort or mental relief they can find. And all of us have seen the shining example of Tory morality, that there is no right or wrong, what counts is what you can get away with. There is no justice, there is no final authority to set the record straight, there is no good or evil. There is only expediency and survival. Against this, the minor sexual adventures of some politicians are merely chaff in the wind. The real immorality of the Conservatives lies in their total degradation of basic moral values, such as truth or compassion.

What also seems to be happening is that the political dishonesty is corrupting the functions of the state generally. In Parliament we see Norman Lamont using Treasury money to pay his legal fees, or John Gummer opposing moves to fight fraud in the European Community. (*The Observer*, July 19, 1992.) As the rot spreads, we see the director-general of the BBC, John Birt, employed as a 'freelance consultant' for the BBC. We then discover that senior civil servants at the Ministry of Defence and the Property Services Agency have been involved in a complex fraud worth at least £20 million. Finally, there have been a series of cases involving top diplomatic personnel, 'including at least two ambassadors'. (*The Observer*, July 12, 1992.) Their crimes ranged from the misuse of public funds, to smuggling heroin — and none of these misdemeanours led to a criminal prosecution.

The effect of this moral bankruptcy can also be seen in the rising toll of crime, drugs, prostitution, violence and rioting. If this continues, we will find Britain heading down the same dead-end alley as the United States, with its teenage gangs, and its top-security suburbs. The poor will do whatever they regard as necessary to survive, while the middle classes will have to manage as best they can in their downwardly-mobile armed suburbs. This is of no concern to a government whose real agenda is the welfare of big business, its managers, acolytes and executives. Thus, we do not have a democracy, we have a façade which is so skilfully presented that most voters take it for the genuine article.

Quite clearly, we do not have a genuine democracy. We have the ideology of business, a free market philosophy which allows the rich the right to do what they like, and governments that have done nothing about rising recession. The only difference between Britain and the United States is that whereas George Bush simply ignored the economic problems, Tory ministers put up a convincing show of caring about the recession, but being unable to actually cure it. Thus, the apathy, the callousness, and the wilful disregard for human welfare were there in both cases; the Tories merely gave a better performance.

If we look at post-79 policies, we see the consistent concern for the needs of business, running parallel with an actual indifference to the needs of the vulnerable. These themes can be seen quite clearly in education policy, in housing, and in industrial policy.

A key point to recognise is that ministers are economical with the truth; they tell porkies, they utter terminological inexactitudes — in short, they lie. They also cover up the truth, and employ less than objective sources to investigate the truth. One rare example of good practice was when 'the National Council for Educational Standards, the right-wing pro-grammar school group', published a report claiming that 'a combination of grammar schools and secondary moderns performed better than comprehensives in examinations'. Keith Joseph asked the Department of Education and Science to carry out a study of the value of the NCES research. The DES found the research to be seriously flawed, and its findings were in doubt. The report remained unpublished. (*The Guardian*, October 14, 1983.) The fact that Keith Joseph had the report checked indicates a greater concern for the truth than can be said of latter-day Tories. If electoral victory corrupts, repeated electoral power corrupts absolutely.

In addition, ministers encourage schools to opt out of local authority control, as a way of weakening local government. At the time of writing, there is no evidence that either parents, pupils or teachers gained from opt-outs, or that these groups have any greater amount of choice because of them. Secondly, there is the recurrent theme of cuts in government spending. Occasionally this conflicts with a stated desire to improve the quality of education, as in Kenneth Baker's call for a doubling of the proportion of young people going into further education by the year 2000. However, despite the importance of this for the economy, Baker never suggested that more money might be available for this worthy goal.

The overall effect of all the government's changes to the education system has been to emphasise the two-tier nature. In the 1960s and 70s, the growing number of universities made the old Oxbridge/redbrick divide seem less important, as students from working class backgrounds could gain respected degrees. Under Thatcherism many working class people are unable to go to university. Those at school or college are in overcrowded classrooms, with overworked teachers. And if they do go on to higher education, it may be under new scheduling arrangements, which allow more 'efficient' use of university premises, but may lead to lower quality degrees.

Thus, working class students will have the new, low cost qualifications, while the children of the elite class will have gone to Oxbridge, or a select private university. Ministers, despite their claims that large classes do not harm educational attainment, send their children to private schools. There is no increase in parental choice; parents now have the choice of a range of underfunded schools, whereas previously, they had only the local school, well-funded and well-run, and generally with a good range of books and equipment, and dedicated teachers.

In fact, the impact of the education cuts may be less than was intended, and certainly less than would be the case in a more market-oriented society. In America, the conversion of schools into profit centres has been followed by the replacement of all skilled and experienced staff by cheap, unqualified teachers. This has not happened in Britain, because of what could be called a social infrastructure. That is, over the years of the welfare state, Britain has built up a body of educated and concerned administrators who can run the institutions of society efficiently, and in the interests of all. These people want education to be managed in the interests of the population generally, rather than for the sake of the hypothetical taxpayer.

The welfare state, and the belief that one should look after the interests of others, is a longstanding part of Britain's culture. In America, where market ideas have ruled for longer, the dominant values are those of money and materialism. If New Right Toryism is allowed to run amok for too long, our caring administrators will retire, seek other jobs, or simply be overwhelmed by the task confronting them. Of course, the argument applies to all public sector services, most of which are doing an excellent job. It may not stay that way for long.

In addition, the introduction of student loans has converted further education from a right to an expensive luxury. Most middle class parents can afford to keep their children for a few years, while they get the qualifications that will be so useful for their futures. But working class students will often be unable to afford the cost, either of the loan, or the loss of earnings. This is not only inegalitarian, but also it reduces the pool of qualified, trained experts from which society has to choose. Thus, both the individual and society are made worse off.

It seems that virtually all of the changes made under Thatcherism have led to one group or another being disadvantaged. Miners, Fleet Street printers and television technicians have lost their jobs, indeed their entire industry. Many professional, white collar, or industrial workers are worse off because their unions are now weaker. Others are more insecure in their jobs, because of weaker unions, the recession, or the impact of privatisation. And millions more are unemployed. Others have lost their homes or their life savings because of government policy.

It was said that Thatcherism would bring greater choice, freedom, and concern for the individual. This is meaningless if millions of individuals are worse off as a result of the chosen policies. For example, there has been a significant decline in the quality of welfare provision; Britain faces an estimated shortage of 20,000 teachers, and up to a third of London's ambulances are out of action at any given time.

One can take specific cases, such as education, or look at the overall impact of the programme. The result is the same. The ideology, the theory, all the justifications in the world are irrelevant if the actual result is to make people poorer, with a lower quality of life. No excuses, no statistical juggling, no 'economy with the truth' can hide the reality. Thatcherism has not worked. It has totally failed to bring any benefit whatsoever for ninety per cent of the population.

It has made the middle classes insecure, and impoverished the lower income groups. It has ended the battle between government and unions by rendering the latter virtually impotent. And none of us, in our part-time, low paid jobs, gains from this victory. Even the relatively wealthy, with well-paid secure jobs, have to worry about crime and burglary committed against their electronically-defended homes.

A crucial division in society now is that between those who control the political system, and those who do not — the old middle and working classes. It is nothing to do with capital, or with ownership, but simply to do with the effective exercise of political rights. If voters use their franchise unthinkingly, their vote becomes valueless.

This group, the self-disenfranchised, can be sub-divided even further, into the overt victims of the controlling group, and the marginalised, those who see themselves as being beneficiaries of society, yet can so easily be pushed into total vulnerability. Both groups, the underclass and the precarious class, could so easily re-take the power they have yielded. It is only because of the apparent complexity of economic issues that they have given in to apathy.

Such arguments however, raise the question, who does benefit from the Conservatives' changes? The answer is clear to many people, but it is worth examining some of the facts. This will be done in the next chapter.

3

The government of the few

FOR MOST OF the twentieth century, the values of business have been, in the words of J. K. Galbraith, the conventional wisdom. Free enterprise, a balanced budget, and the importance of capitalism have been taken almost for granted, apart from the brief post-war glitter of affluence. For the rest of the time, the voice of big business was supreme, 'not only on business policy and economics but also on the role of government in society, the foundations of foreign policy, and the nature of a liberal education'. (*The Affluent Society*, p39.)

For Britain in the latter part of the twentieth century, Thatcherism is the ideology of business. This does not mean that it operates for the benefit of all companies, or even that New Right policies are good for commerce generally. And they are certainly not good for the economy. What can be said is that New Right economics are supported by both government and by business leaders. That is, it is an ideology which politicians and business people share, rather than one that necessarily operates to anyone's advantage.

It is a view which is just not open to discussion, so that its truth or validity or practicality is simply not an issue in public debate. Not only can one not say that any aspect of New Right economics has been proved correct; it is not even relevant to its acolytes. They apply it, espouse it and uphold it regardless of its validity.

But although it is the ideology of business, it is not a school of thought which functions for the good of all companies. It certainly has not benefited the 150,000 companies that have ceased to exist since 1990. And although New Right theory or supply side economics might refer to competition and market forces, in practice they both ignore such details. These are the 'come ons', the carnival huckster's ploys to attract custom, and have no inherent value.

Genuine competition by definition requires the existence of many suppliers, lots of small firms. Similarly, market forces can only operate where there is no abuse of power, indeed, no power to abuse, no monopoly, and no firm large enough to influence prices or dictate to the customer. This means that the market must be comprised of small or medium sized firms, because only when there are a multitude of suppliers does the consumer have real freedom of choice. If customers have complete choice, then suppliers have no power.

One of the less appealing aspects of the current obsession with the market is the desire to cut costs, regardless of the effects. The impact of this on pay levels was examined in the previous chapter, but one could also consider the effect on the quality of service. Many companies have cut their level of provision, as for example charging for air at petrol stations.

In a genuinely competitive market, firms will seek to offer more than their competitors, to attract customers. It is worth noting that Lloyd's insurance got started in a coffee house, owned by Edward Lloyd. Much commercial business was done in the London coffee houses of the day. That particular location became the centre for the insurance market because Mr Lloyd decided to provide paper and ink for his customers, so that they would spend more time there, drinking coffee and doing business.

Competition is ideal for consumers, indeed for society and the economy generally, as it is best in terms of providing what customers want, maintaining business efficiency, and promoting innovation. In the real market, it is not always *price* competition, as with Lloyd's coffee house, but it does involve trying to offer whatever it is the customer wants. For the New Right, it is only a theoretical ideal, trotted out in support of each new lunacy, and then put back in its box. For the actual practice of libertarian economics, competition is totally ignored, market forces are spurned, and small firms are dumped on from a great height. Any alleged concern for competition or for customers' welfare is just a collection of words sharing the same page in a speech. It is sound only, signifying nothing.

This is reflected in the Thatcheroid regimes' talk of caring for small firms — it has been a mixture of pure bull, and low-grade PR. The hidden agenda of Thatcherism has always been to look after the interests of the rich and powerful — rich individuals, and big business. The welfare of the average person, although a fundamental goal of both democracy and economics, was totally ignored by the Thatcherites.

Thus, there has been a clear gap between stated goals, and the actual results of policy. In some cases, the gap was so wide as to be near unbelievable. Norman Lamont's repeated claims that green shoots of economic spring had appeared was heading for status as a music hall joke. Perhaps his main achievement was in retaining office, even though most of the population recognised that his policies had been disastrous. However, because of the effectiveness of Tory propaganda, most people also accepted the basic tenets of New Right economics — the need to control inflation, the importance of the market, and the reduced role of the government.

This could be seen as a change in beliefs, but in fact many people had never been entirely convinced of Labour's overall policy platform, partly because Labour had not really sought to explain or justify its ideas in detail. The post-war consensus was largely a product of elite circles, and as party leaders moved further and further away from their popular roots, they ceased to be aware of any need to explain or discuss their ideas. Most people shared the values of the Labour Party, and they probably still do; but a gap opened up in the agreement on policy details. The Conservatives duly filled this gap. They explained all their policies in full detail, explaining the links between cause and effect, and arguing why they could not take action in some areas. To a certain extent, such justification was necessary, because their policies and their values conflicted with past ideas. But the constant repetition of New Right ideas also acted as a smokescreen, covering up the gap between reality and stated intentions.

Part of the Tories' hidden agenda was to eliminate the natural Labour constituencies, such as council house tenants and state employees. Such people, perhaps because they were so conscious of their dependence on the state for their well-being, expressed this realisation in their voting behaviour. The Tories sought to break this link by selling off council houses, and by privatising various sectors of central and local government. Another approach was to remove services from local authority control, making them independently managed, for example, schools, colleges and hospitals.

The other aspect of this agenda was to promote the interests of big business. It has quite explicitly not supported small firms as a group, although there has been much rhetoric along those lines. The reality has been a massive recession, in which thousands of small companies have been forced out of business. At the same time, the large corporations have been allowed to ignore the needs of competition, have received hidden subsidies, and been given preferential treatment by government policy.

And as a general rule, big business does not want small firms to be supported. For example, the Institute of Directors has actually criticised EU plans 'to stimulate Europe's small business sector' on the grounds that it could lead to corruption. (*The Guardian*, April 13, 1993.) Such an outcome is theoretically possible, given the EU's embarrassing track record for corruption. But funding can and should be controlled more sensibly. And the IoD's attitude is extremely worrying, given the small firm's recognised job creation abilities.

Coakley and Harris argue that the true beneficiaries of Thatcherism were intended to have been the City financial institutions — the bankers, analysts, and stockbrokers. They refer to 'the best efforts of successive Thatcher administrations to promote its interests at the expense of other sectors of the economy'. (See Jonathan Michie [ed.], *The Economic Legacy 1979-1992*, pp37-38, 49.) Certainly, the Tories have been extremely deferential to the economic views of the City, although whether the City has received better treatment than big business is too fine a point to be decided here. It is sufficient to say that both have been given greater attention than the population as a whole.

This is largely because the distinction between City, business leadership and the Conservative Party is of little meaning. The individuals come from similar social backgrounds, and share a common culture. They tend to regard manufacturing industry as a dirty, grubby way of life for the lower orders. Dealing with money, with paper, or simply making deals has been much more of the gentleman's way of earning a living. This is part of the reason why Thatcherism so quickly took root in the cultural desert of Britain's establishment. The City, the leading force in generating Britain's commercial attitudes, was perfectly in tune with an ideology which was both abstract, and dismissive of such things as industrial investment.

This is not to say that the City did actually gain from Thatcherism. Coakley and Harris point out that deregulation and other financial changes instigated by the

Tories weakened London's competitive position, with a resulting loss of its previous financial pre-eminence. This was not entirely the result of the Conservatives' policies in respect of the City, because financial centres gain much of their strength from the economy in which they are based; hence the growing importance of Japan's banks. It is interesting, however, that the New Right economic policies are so ineffective as to harm even the groups that the Tory government most wanted to help.

This is perhaps an inevitable result of the Tories' rigid adherence to an ideology. The belief overrides all real-world events; facts, evidence, failure, or disaster are but chaff in the face of the heel-clicking certainties of Thatcherism. And naturally, the acolytes of this faith have sought every opportunity to convert the ordinary citizen to their views.

As well as weakening local councils' role in education, ministers have used education to promote an explicitly pro-business attitude. What was presented as educational reform actually had a blatantly political agenda. There has been a constant emphasis on business, both as a yardstick for judging schools' performance, and as an input into educational content. This has been visible in qualifications such as BTEC (Business and Technical Education Council) or TVEI (Technical and Vocational Educational Initiative), both of which have a strong vocational component, and in the move to increase the vocational element of A Levels. In a similar way, a 1991 White Paper on Adult Education argued that vocational courses should be financed differently from those which were merely 'leisure interests'.

The City Technology Colleges (CTCs), proposed by Kenneth Baker in 1988, were supposed to be 'beacons of excellence'. They were also supposed to be very practical, science and technology-based, and funded by the private sector. The marriage between business and the state was intended to bring out the best in all concerned, while meeting the needs of local industry, but at no extra cost. The reality is that CTCs 'are being funded at 2½ times the rate of some neighbouring schools'. (*The Guardian*, July 13, 1991.) Despite Kenneth Clarke's protests the following year that there was no link between funding and results, the CTCs show a strong link. Ministers are not able to be honest about what is in fact business-oriented elitism. Were they to do so, there would be an implied obligation to spend equally on all pupils. But continued underfunding of ordinary schools and colleges leads to declining standards, which ministers can then blame on schools or local authorities.

Because the difference in funding is not widely referred to, nor recognised, it is possible for ministers to speak of the 'success' of the CTCs. In fact, allowing for the funding levels, CTCs are somewhat unsuccessful. But their very existence is an added plank in the government's promotion of business ideology. They can talk about business involvement in education, and emphasise the role that commerce can play in schools. And of course, they can emphasise the need for business-related content at all levels of education. Because of our heightened awareness of the career returns provided by education, we tend to accept the validity of this business-education link-up. Ultimately, all state bodies, whether funded by central government or not, may be preaching the same New Right economics, the ethos of commerce.

The use of school opt-outs not only reduces the power of local authorities, it also forces school management to be more business-minded in its approach. Thus, head teachers and principals become part of the forces promoting New Right ideals. In addition, the use of the National Curriculum allows the government to ensure that commercial values are promoted wherever possible, and that most references to socialism or the Labour Party are excluded. This would explain why the official history curriculum stops at 1945.

Having established their perceived ideology of competition, small business, and the individual, the Tories can then impose their actual agenda with relative ease. Although there has been some help for small firms, especially those just starting up, there has been no protection for small firms against predatory large companies. There has been no attempt to protect competition by tightening up the rules on the acquisition of small firms. And there has been no recognition of the impact of the recession on small businesses.

The government has also ignored the way in which high street banks and Customs and Excise have trampled all over the needs and rights of small firms. It has wiped out tens of thousands of small companies in an avoidable and destructive recession. It has closed down many of the DTI's Small Business Advice Centres, and allowed the big four banks to misuse the so-called Loan Guarantee Scheme. And although it has talked freely about competition, it has in practice been more concerned about profit for big business than about the life's work or employment of thousands of ordinary people.

It is also promoting policies and institutions that ignore or harm the interests of small firms. The EEC introduced this approach with its value added tax, which ensured that every company in the production and distribution process had to calculate the tax, and charge it to the next person/organisation in the process. Assuming identical rates for purchase tax and VAT, the final consumer pays no extra tax because of VAT, but a huge burden was placed on all the small firms who lacked the office staff to cope with this illogical tax.

And there is no rationale to VAT. It performs the same function as a purchase tax (as operated in Britain prior to the introduction of VAT in 1970), or a sales tax, as used in the United States. That is, it raises revenue for the state, by imposing a tax on consumers. But unlike purchase tax, VAT requires that everyone involved in the entire chain of manufacture and distribution work out a nominal tax rate, which they charge to customers, even where those customers are intending to reclaim the tax. The burden of the paperwork involved is both massive, and unnecessary.

The British government may have used the same principle — covert anti-small firm legislation — with BS 5750, a British Standards Institution (BSI) seal of approval for management quality. It is claimed that BS 5750 shows that a company has reached a certain level of managerial competence, but in fact, it merely shows that the company's procedures have been formalised. Inspectors simply write down exactly what is done by the company, what the manufacturing or communication procedures are, and that becomes the firm's operating manual. In other words, no upgrading of quality occurs; but the level of quality is standardised.

Despite this minimal contribution to manufacturing efficiency, many firms feel under pressure to acquire BS 5750. Most of the pressure comes from big companies, the BSI and the Department of Trade and Industry (DTI). Although Dr. Michael Sanderson, chief executive of the BSI, denies that there is any coercion, others suggest that it is a 'monster,' or an 'inherent threat'. (*Director,* December 1992.) Dr Sanderson says, 'BS 5750 guarantees that you're manufacturing consistently to the specification you claim you are manufacturing'. (*Director*, December 1992.) As another businessman quoted in the article says, it might simply show that you are guaranteeing 'consistent crap'.

In addition, 5750 can be an excellent barrier to small businesses. For a start, it is expensive. The certification organisations claim that it can be done for as little as £1,000. But Tim Leeder of Strood was quoted £3,000. If he gained accreditation through his professional association, it would cost him £2,000 plus one day a month for a year. Whether or not Tim needs to learn new management methods is uncertain, considering that his company totals himself, his wife Linda, and his two pals, Neil and Richard. (*Daily Telegraph*, December 15, 1992.)

According to management consultancy PERA International, it takes 552 days for a company with 200-500 employees to gain accreditation. Yet it still takes a company with less than ten employees a full 445 days. This is time that the owner of a very small firm can ill afford, and would almost certainly mean lost wages, sales or output. (*Director*, December 1992.)

It is also doubtful whether 5750 is actually relevant to the small business. Indeed, it is the offshoot of a quality control system created by the Ministry of Defence to monitor the performance of its big business suppliers. It is no doubt ideal for managing a large bureaucracy, for controlling the disorganised inter-departmental communications. But there may be no advantages for the small business; a management tool designed for big business is not necessarily appropriate for small companies. In addition, certification could be a very effective threat to the survival of many small firms.

If the government was genuinely concerned about manufacturing quality, rather than impose a system of uniformity such as BS 5750, it should encourage manufacturers to improve the quality of their products. In Japan, the ideas of guru W. Edwards Deming were enthusiastically adopted to the extent of creating a medal of honour named after him. The Japanese are now renowned for the excellence of their products, and their goods are highly sought-after. BS 5750 offers Quality Equals Fitness for Purpose. Along with product uniformity, the BSI offers appropriateness; not exactly a ringing declaration, but perhaps more suitable for a nation whose industry is slowly shifting down-market.

The same formal approach is taken with BTEC courses, in further education. The argument is that one cannot measure a student's understanding, as that is something which is happening within the person's head. Yet one has to measure something, to show that the process of education is working. So the BTEC teacher measures 'competences', or observable skills. If we know that a student is able to perform a given skill, then for all practical purposes, they have grasped it as fully as any government education expert would wish.

The problem is that any observable skill is more quantifiable than the understanding that most teachers would wish the students to have. And when skills or competences are highly valued, the actual gain in knowledge may be reduced. For example, 'when a girl who is using a pair of scissors to cut her nails can be described as learning how to 'put together two metal blades unpowered', then we are clearly living in a universe of discourse in which anything goes!' (Philip Cohen, from Bates, Clarke et al, *Schooling for the Dole?* p115.)

This competence-based approach has a variety of side-effects. It reduces the skill and the judgement necessary for teaching, and therefore also reduces the teachers' power. It also allows a reduction in the quality of mass education, in such a way as to allow ministers to claim that an increase has taken place. There may have been a decline in the academic content of education, but there would also be an increase in the number of qualifications given out. This allows the state to continue its two-tier education system, with the sons and daughters of the rich getting a knowledge and understanding based approach, while the masses get a basic skills-based method.

But, to return to the government's policies affecting small business. Many companies have been forced into bankruptcy by the high street banks, or by Customs and Excise. Some studies have argued that the banks treat small businesses quite fairly, and that interest rates are not significantly higher for small firms (see *The Independent*, December 15, 1992.) However, for both private and small business customers, the issue has been not the level of interest rates, but the various operating charges.

Customers have been charged up to £47 for having a cheque bounce. Banks have bounced cheques, knowing that a salary or other payment would be coming into the account within days. One customer was informed that their account had become overdrawn, and that they would be charged £1 per day for the overdraft — and that the account had actually become overdrawn two months earlier! Some customers have been invited into the bank for a discussion with the bank manager. When, a month later, they queried an unexplained charge, they were told it was a fee for their consultation with the bank manager.

Such ploys do not create good relations between bank and customer, nor do they show the banks in a good light. To claim that interest rates have not been excessive is simply an irrelevancy. The only purpose such a claim has is to draw attention away from the problem of account charges, towards an agenda where the banks knows that they can justify their actions, although it is worth mentioning the fact that the big four English banks' charges have been consistently higher than those of the Scottish banks.

Similar treatment occurs in the way that large companies deal with small firms when it comes to the time to pay the bills. Often the large companies will delay payment for months, and in some cases, indefinitely. Occasionally, the result is that the small company goes out of business, having no income from its main customers. This has the advantage for the large company that its debt effectively ceases to exist. In Europe, this would be illegal, and prompt payment is obligatory. It would be very easy to make excessive delays in payment illegal in Britain also.

In contrast to the discreet hostility to small firms, the Conservatives have always been very willing to help big business. This has covered a range of approaches. There has been deregulation, to prevent companies being inconvenienced by nasty, petty restrictions on their activities. There has been government spending, to create demand for the companies' products. There are lax merger rules, so that if a company wants to buy another company, they are allowed to do so, whatever their reason. And if, through bad luck or incompetence, the firm suffers financial disaster, the government will compensate it, from taxpayers' money.

Deregulation has covered a range of fields, but in most cases, it has been at the expense of the consumer. It has allowed water quality to be degraded, so that poison and filth has poured out of taps, with no punishment or sanction suffered by the bosses of the newly-privatised water companies. It has allowed the government to end the monopoly position of the mails and telephones, opened up the financial markets, and reduced controls on buses and coaches.

Most dangerously, there has been a heavy ideological element to the deregulation, with the costs and benefits of existing rules ignored. Nor has cost-benefit been taken into account in the abolition of rules. Even worse, some regulation has been left to the organisations themselves to monitor. For example, financial institutions, newspapers and schools are more or less free to monitor their own activity. But while newspapers make their own rules, television broadcasting is subject to two different regulatory authorities. The fact that most newspapers have been active sympathisers of the Tories is, of course, pure coincidence.

With schools, the previous inspectorate, Her Majesty's Inspector of Schools (HMI), has been privatised. Future control of schools may be carried out by private organisations, hired by the school to regulate its effectiveness. Similarly, industry may find that health and safety inspection will be privatised. Companies will employ their own health and safety consultants. Cases like this raise the possibility of a conflict of interests; the regulator is in the employ of the organisation, and may be subject to that organisation's influence.

It is unlikely that the Tories would see this as a problem in education. It assists in creating the two-tier system, where the rich will attend high status, traditional schools and colleges, starting at private prep schools, and moving on to Oxford or Cambridge. The average person will go to a state school which has minimal funding, overcrowded classrooms and harassed teachers. It will be regulated by an inspector of the school's choice, which allows the government to wash its hands of the matter; it has done its job, and can blame the falling standards on the local council or the teachers.

This is an excellent ploy to remove such tedious aspects of democracy as accountability. The government does not manage, regulate or organise schools or colleges, so it can stand back, and deny all responsibility for the results. The fact that it is the the ultimate funder of all state education can be veiled by intermediary local authorities or arm's-length state agencies.

The contracting out of local authority work has been another form of privatisation. It has been known as compulsory competitive tendering (CCT), and was estimated to release a billion pounds worth of contracts to the private sector. 'This opportunity has led to intense competition between the international giants who have largely taken over the smaller companies and compete with each other by lowering wages, hours and cleaning standards'. (*The Guardian*, January 21, 1987.) Thus, both consumers and employees are made worse off by the change, while the only gain goes to the giant corporations.

There is also a contradictory aspect to deregulation, because at the same time as the government has been eliminating legislation constraining business, it has been adding new requirements to the public sector. Local councils, schools, colleges and hospitals are all subject to rules and controls that did not exist prior to 1979. The implication is that private business is the sector that least needs regulating.

It is also counter-productive. Many sectors of business depend on public trust, and as industry is deregulated, problems of quality, honesty, reliability, and ease of replacement occur. As the customer is less able to trust the supplier, the customer becomes less willing to buy. Naturally, this problem is far more likely to affect the small business than the large corporation, with a national reputation. However, it will affect companies of all sizes, and lead to a gradual loss of confidence, and a decline in sales. This is of particular concern to new industries, who often seek to create trade associations to give themselves an image of respectability, in the absence of credible state control.

The probable motive behind deregulation is that it is being promoted by a sector that is not concerned about reputation, or about loss of customers. This happens to be true of big companies, who dominate their markets, and are often able to sell in the face of customer reluctance. Sheer size alone is enough to create a reputation in most buyers' minds, as the buyer thinks that such a large company must be honest. This is not always true, but big corporations are not averse to taking advantage of the consumer's gullibility.

For example, when General Motors (GM), owner of Vauxhall, was being accused of selling a dangerous car, the Corvair, it told all critics that no one else had complained. In 1965, when three cases concerning the Corvair were brought to court, GM blamed the accidents on the drivers. This was despite the fact that over one hundred similar cases had been brought, and that four years previously GM had introduced a factory option designed to cure exactly the problem that caused the accidents. (Ralph Nader, *Unsafe at Any Speed,* pp4, 6.)

Because of their size, and their volume sales, large corporations are assumed to be beyond reproach. Regulations do not enhance their image in the public mind, but they are a nuisance to the corporate cost-cutters. All the major American, European and Japanese car manufacturers see component costs as something to be reduced as much as possible. At times this conflicts with product quality, safety or reliability. But the car makers are primarily concerned with profit, while the governments are no longer concerned with consumer welfare. Elected politicians are more likely to find themselves dependent on corporate financing, to fund future election campaigns. If necessary, they will spend government money to ensure the survival of large corporate donors.

One example of government's willingness to spend money to benefit big business is in road building. The Department of Transport adds to the nation's stock of motorways, as a way of boosting the car industry. There is a cosy relationship between the government and all components of Britain's transport industry, which of course existed long before the Thatcherites came to power. However, the Conservatives, especially post-1979, have been much more sympathetic to the needs of road transport than previous administrations. For example, from 1974 to January 1979, the road transport lobby was pushing for maximum lorry weights to be raised from 32 tonnes to 40 tonnes. The Labour minister initiated an inquiry on the subject. The Conservatives duly won the 1979 election. 'The new Tory Transport Secretary, Norman Fowler, decided to continue with the inquiry, although he restricted its terms of reference'. (Mick Hamer, *Wheels within Wheels*, p86.)

This was perfectly in keeping with the government's 'public transport policy, which was to cut subsidies, and drive people off the buses and into private cars'. (p66.) The official line was market freedom, individual choice, and no state intervention. The reality was that while subsidies to British Rail were ideologically repellent, indirect subsidies to the road and freight industries were seen as perfectly natural.

The report on lorry weights appeared in December 1980, and in essence, accepted all the evidence given to it by the road lobby. And while the Freight Transport Association (FTA) had argued for a 40 tonne weight limit, the Society of Motor Manufacturers and Traders (SMMT) had argued for 44 tonnes — the figure which was accepted. However, after a Labour motion in the House of Commons opposing the report was supported by 11 Tory rebels, the government decided to opt for only 40 tonnes. Having got Department of Transport approval for the higher limit, the road lobby set to work to get the upper figure into the legislation. The FTA, Road Haulage Association, SMMT and the Confederation of British Industry all wrote to the national press, and sent out press releases. David Howell, Minister for Transport, said that increasing vehicle weight would reduce the number of lorries on the road. Despite this, when Howell finally decided the new limit, it was for 38 tonnes. Not that this could be seen as a victory for the environmentalists. The punishment for exceeding the legal weight was determined by the Department of Transport, and the road lobby used this as a way to avoid the limit, without needing any new laws. The Ministry simply altered the rules on prohibition and prosecution, so that 'lorries had to be 5 per cent overweight before they faced a prohibition notice, and 10 per cent overweight before they were liable to prosecution. ... So the maximum weight of lorries that can now be run on Britain's roads, without fear of any penalty, is 39.9 tonnes'. (*Wheels within Wheels*, p89.)

Thus, without any legislation being necessary, lorry weights have been increased. This keeps both lorry manufacturers happy, as well as having a predictable spin-off for oil and tyre companies, and road construction firms. But absolutely nothing about the process could be described as democratic.

Indeed, the process of decision-making over motorways shows a constant lack of consultation. Civil servants, in discussion with the road lobby, agree on the need for a motorway. It is then planned, costed, and virtually put into construction. Transport consultant Jonathan Bray describes it as 'road engineers talking to road engineers'. For the civil servants, Bray says, their career prospects depend on the success of each road plan. Only if there are serious local objections will there be even a public inquiry. However, as the case of Twyford Down, Hampshire, shows, even if there is massive local hostility to the project, it will go ahead. In that case, as in many others, civil servants have totally ignored local residents' objections. There is usually little or no democratic involvement in such decisions. It is not 'building for the nation's needs,' but building according to the wishes of the road lobby.

The everyday loaf of bread reveals the same struggle between two sides, although in this case, the two choices are white flour versus brown. It is just one of many stories about how food quality has been sacrificed to the interests of commerce. As with road versus rail the battle has been going on for many years, in this case involving a battle between nutritionists and big business. And again, under the Tories, big business has won.

As long ago as 1936, the League of Nations condemned white flour for its lack of nutritional content. The millers, however, were concerned with other things. 'First, white flour keeps longer. Second, it holds more air and water. Third, bran and germ are valuable sold as animal feed. Fourth, white flour and bread therefore give the trade more turnover. Fifth, wholegrain bread takes more skill and time to make'. (Geoffrey Cannon, *The Politics of Food*, pp237-238.) Thus, all the differences between white and brown come down to the fact that white is better business for the baker; although brown bread is better for the customer.

As in so many other areas, the Second World War was a turning point. When the nation depended on the working class to fight, it decided to look after the health and well-being of that class. Viewed cynically, it could be seen as enlightened self-interest. After the war, food manufacturers continued to press the case for white bread, arguing that as vitamins could be added in the mixing process, the white loaf could be just as healthy as a brown one. This gave us the 'fortified' loaf, which by the 1960s was Britain's standard loaf.

This 'fortification' primarily meant adding iron filings and chalk. This allows the manufacturers to advertise the product with moderate conviction as healthy, assuming that processed food is as good as food in its natural state. The evidence suggests that chemicals, whether added to food or the soil, tend to simply leach out. Thus, fertilisers end up in the nearest river, doing more harm than they ever did good, while the additives in bread simply pass through the body, doing nothing whatsoever in nutritional terms.

There was also evidence that dietary fibre was essential to health, and in 1977 the Royal College of Physicians commissioned a report on fibre. When the report appeared three years later, it recommended wholegrain bread. Meanwhile, the Council on Medical Aspects of Health (COMA) suggested that 'fortification' should no longer be compulsory. The baking industry's official lobbying organisation protested. The fortification gave white bread credibility; the fact that it was required by law meant that consumers knew the bread was fortified. The lobbying worked, and MAFF rejected the COMA recommendation.

Despite their empty rhetoric about competition, by 1987 'the British milling and baking industry is dominated by two firms... Associated British Foods and Rank Hovis McDougall. The trade maintained that white bread was what the British public wanted. Consumption of white bread dropped steadily from 41 ounces a week in 1957 to 20 ounces a week in 1984'. (*The Politics of Food*, p244.)

The decline in white bread consumption is a clear indication that consumers are not happy with the standard loaf. However, the big companies have sufficient market power to impose the product and at one time were able to charge a premium price. In a situation that approaches monopoly, the consumer has to take what is given.

The government's stance can be seen even more clearly in the battle between British Airways (BA) and rival airlines such as Virgin Atlantic. 'When, finally, British Midland was allowed to compete with BA on flights from London to Edinburgh — providing a better service including free drinks and seat allocation as well as cheaper fares — BA suddenly found it possible to reduce fares'. (Nicholas Bethell MEP, *Evening Standard*, January 12, 1993.)

Despite this, British Airways was allowed to take over the failing British Caledonian, as well as buying a 49 per cent stake in TAT, the French airline, and a stake in the Australian airline, Qantas. It was also allowed to take over Dan-Air, a move that the Civil Aviation Authority argued should have been investigated by the Monopolies and Mergers Commission. The chairman of the Commission implied that one cannot talk about competition, and then allow unquestioned takeovers, and still maintain any sort of credibility.

BA's management has occasionally claimed to want competition, and has often said that it actually faced competition in the market. Richard Branson has argued, however, that BA controls about 40 per cent of the scheduled slots at both Heathrow and Gatwick, Britain's two main airports. This severely limits the choice available to the consumer, and washes away any claims by the government or by BA that there is a healthy market.

BA is not a company that likes competition, and in 1985 was fined £8 million for forcing Freddie Laker's Laker Airlines out of business. BA was also forced to pay $65 million to Laker's creditors, some of whom had taken anti-trust action in the United States against it. The seriousness with which BA took these charges can be judged by the fact that it offered some litigants cheap fares in exchange for dropping their anti-trust cases.

It must be said that British Airways did not act alone to wipe out Laker Airlines — five other airline companies were involved, with the help of McDonnell Douglas, the DTI, and the British and US governments. The conspiracy was successful, and no serious action was taken against BA or its management. Clearly, neither of the governments involved genuinely believed in competition.

So when Virgin Atlantic set up operations, BA tried to drive it out of business. Not by being more competitive, or by offering a better service, but by simply destroying the company. It was a policy that had worked before, and the Tory government had obligingly not done anything to stop such a method working again.

A member of BA's staff said that 'there was a dirty tricks campaign, but it was standard commercial practice; like supermarkets handing out leaflets'. (*The Guardian*, January 12, 1993.) This 'standard commercial practice' included running a press disinformation campaign, planting stories in the press about Virgin's finances or safety standards, and stealing Virgin's customers. It must be pointed out, however, that BA's top management, including the fragrant Lord King, knew nothing about the campaign.

BA employees would phone up customers who had booked with Virgin, having broken into Virgin's computer network to get details of their customers. This was not too difficult, as Virgin had rented space in BABS, BA's computer booking system. The BA staff would then pretend to be Virgin staff, tell the customer that the Virgin flight was now full, and offer to book the customer on a BA flight. The customer thinks, 'how helpful Virgin are'; but the money goes to BA. Virgin was particularly vulnerable as BA staff, because of their access to BABS, also knew how full each flight was, and how much each customer had paid. Thus, BA could target its efforts in such a way as to make every Virgin flight unprofitable. If this campaign had taken even a quarter of Virgin's customers, it would have wiped out the company. Yet Virgin was the company that was trying to offer the better service, and the lower prices. And BA, the 'successful' company, would have committed criminal acts to achieve its victory.

Given the Conservative government's purported belief in competition, it should never have allowed BA to take over British Caledonian. This merger should have been referred to the Monopolies and Mergers Commission. One might also say that the takeover of TAT should have been blocked by the European Union. However, there is no evidence that the EU is concerned about competition; as with the Tories, it is one of those words that are used to give the impression of caring about the population as a whole. Politicians can justify their actions by using such phrases as 'standard of living', 'competition', or 'growth'.

The initial decision to ignore the competition aspect of BA's sale was taken for simple commercial reasons — allowing the Civil Aviation Authority (CAA) to open up the airways to more competition would reduce BA's value at privatisation. Allegedly the whole purpose of privatisation was to create more competition, a better market. To privatise a monopoly provider seems a strange way of creating competition, but the Tories' market philosophy has always been full of contradictions.

The advantages of the free market have long been accepted, not just for the economy in general, but for airlines in particular. Under the 1964-70 Labour government, Anthony Crosland set up the Edwards Committee, to investigate the industry. One of the committee's findings was that a monopoly airline might achieve economies of scale, but that any gains as a result of this would be more than eliminated because of the loss of competition. Not that Labour actively sought a free market. Indeed, Freddie Laker had to take the government to court, all the way to the Court of Appeal, just to get his transatlantic Skytrain operating.

But then, Labour have never been very keen on the market philosophy. Their approach has been control via state intervention. But given the overwhelming dominance of market forces in the Conservatives' ideology, for them to ignore the needs of competition is highly significant.

The actual indifference to market forces is cleverly disguised by the frequent use of market-related words or phrases. *Competition* is a good one, as is *deregulation,* or *level playing field.* This last can be used to imply fair competition, but in practice it is more likely to mean no action to block mergers, or no rules to protect small businesses. In fact, it can be used to justify almost any action or inaction that protects the highly uneven existing playing field.

The case of BA is just one of a range of special treatments for big business. The big firm is given grants to set up in Britain, and regulatory bodies are less likely to prosecute corporate polluters, or indeed any form of corporate misbehaviour. Mergers will be allowed, regardless of 'industrial logic', and in the few cases where the regulatory authorities seek to break up a company, the government will back down at the slightest sign of protest.

The reason for this disregard is that the Conservatives' real agenda is to allow big business the freedom to buy whatever it wants, and do what it wants. The big corporations want to be able to put prices up whenever they want, and pay their executives whatever they want. Naturally, they resent any state control of prices — although if prices do rise, they can always blame the unions. If anyone suggests that prices are too high because of the lack of competition, they will deny that, and demand the right to acquire any other company they choose. And of course, company bosses dislike any government action which might reduce their take-home pay — like taxes.

Although it is generally recognised that competition benefits the consumer, companies do not like it. Competition is hard work, it cuts profits, and therefore tends to reduce directors' pay and shareholders' dividends. The only people who gain from it are 95 per cent of the population. And most of those would either be working class, middle class, or nouveau riche, so their needs can be discounted entirely.

One should not blame the Conservatives for all increases in corporate pay, although obviously the Tories have created a culture of self-interest, of individualism. Company bosses have duly taken advantage of the legislation and the atmosphere created for them, and offered themselves generous perks and pay rises. But one of the most distasteful trends of the 1990s seems to be that of shedding large chunks of the workforce to pay for pay rises for the management.

One of the most dubious schemes was that created by London Weekend Television (LWT). 'The first stage of the plan involved reducing the value of each existing share to the company's net asset value, 83.2p. This operation cost LWT £122.5 million (most of it borrowed), but was considered money well spent because it reduced the possibility of the shares going down in value, and hence management losing out'. (*Stage Screen and Radio*, May 1993.) The next step was to invite 44 of LWT's top bosses to join the new share option scheme. Then if LWT won its franchise bid, share values would rocket from the deliberately reduced level to a market-driven peak. In fact, share prices peaked at 385p, offering the chance for enormous profits to be made. For example, a manager who put £19,159 into the scheme made a profit of £339,663.

For ordinary workers, LWT was not such a generous employer. Technicians had their 'take-home pay and working conditions even further reduced in January in order, they were told, to secure their jobs and futures. No doubt it will have a favourable impact on the share price'. (*Stage Screen and Radio*, May 1993.)

The usual justifications for top bosses' generous pay and perks are that the company must reward its most valuable employees, and that much of the pay is a direct result of the higher profits that skilful executives have generated. A study by the London Business School and the London School of Economics found that up until 1988 there was a link between pay and profits; after 1988 that link ceased to exist, and pay levels rose regardless of what happened to profits.

The people who are so ready to accuse others of the politics of envy are not averse to lining their own pockets when the tax breaks are generous. And this is regardless of the health of their company, or the well-being of the more vulnerable members of society. We can disregard euphemisms such as 'incentives'; this is greed and selfishness. This is a section of society that sees rising crime and homelessness, increasing unemployment, poverty and despair, and while watching this growing misery, simply does not care.

One cannot say that the government acted out of ignorance, or did not realise the issues involved. Even if ministers had been unaware of the impact of their market philosophy on the economy when they first entered office, after a few years the effects became obvious. With the privatisation of BA we see a government with an explicitly pro-free market ideology deliberately ignoring the needs of competition. One cannot imagine a regime more likely to understand the importance of the market, yet it ignores its own principles, so that revenue can be maximised and asset sales can create scope for greater tax cuts. Given the uneven gains offered by tax cuts, one could say that BA was sold on the cheap so that the upper income groups could pay less tax.

One of the more worrying examples of the government's failure to regulate business involved P&O Ferries; the Zeebrugge ferry disaster. It was said that an inefficient management system combined with pressure to sail on time were significant contributory factors. Although poor relations between senior masters and P&O's operations department, unclear rules and chaotic work schedules certainly did not help, even more worrying was P&O's refusal to install warning lights which could prevent the *Herald of Free Enterprise* sailing with its bow doors open. This was despite there being requests from three ship's captains, including the master of the *Herald*, for warning lights to be fitted.

It was not enough that P&O's directors were cleared of any wrong doing. 'P&O European Ferries, owner of the *Herald of Free Enterprise*, was cleared of corporate manslaughter. Sir Jeffery Sterling, the P&O chairman, received a peerage in Mrs Thatcher's resignation honours list'. (*The Guardian*, December 31, 1990.)

The Conservatives have not only created an environment in which company directors can exploit both the company and its workforce, they have actively encouraged this corporate piracy with generous tax schemes and low rates of taxation for high earners. The growing inequality that has emerged under the Tories is merely a reflection of their concerns. This is a government that works for the interest of corporate management.

There is also the worrying lack of accountability. Under the Conservatives, the whole idea of ministerial responsibility seems to have been discarded. It is now the relic of an era when failure to govern properly required an admission of guilt, and loss of office. Under the Tories, ministerial errors are seen as no more than unfortunate, with no bearing on a person's career. Ministers may take money from anonymous sources, or ruin the economy; they may sell arms to Iraq, arrange special tax rates for the Conservative Party, or ask the privatised companies to give pre-election rebates... yet still not need to resign.

An atmosphere of dishonesty has developed, probably the result of ministers' increasingly cavalier attitude to the facts. They have been economical with the truth, they have juggled with statistics, and they have treated economic forecasts as a Joycean stream of consciousness. A Westminster culture has developed, in which any statement is seen as valid, and all that counts is, can the MP get away with it?

Not only do we find that Norman Lamont had his legal bills paid by the Treasury — we find that 'six other ministers received public money, totalling just over £10,500, to help with their legal bills'. (*The Observer*, January 17, 1993.) We find that five former ministers and ten Tory MPs have found well-paid jobs in the privatised industries. And what may be more disturbing, as an indicator of the trends within British justice, is that the Crown Prosecution Service has been supplying defence lawyers with incorrect information. Equally worrying is the fact that in the case where this is known to have happened, the defendant was an Asian, and one of the witnesses against him was a white youth who had been charged (in a separate case) with an attack on the Asian defendant.

One of the worst examples of ministers not being accountable was Nicholas Ridley's refusal to discuss the Fayed brothers' takeover of the House of Fraser, owner of Harrods. A DTI report had condemned the Fayeds as having 'dishonestly misrepresented their origins, their wealth, their business interests and their resources'. Keith Hampson, a Conservative MP, said that the Fayeds had 'made a monkey out of the regulatory process'. Yet in Parliament, Ridley refused to even 'discuss the ground rules for considering the disqualification of company directors'. (*The Guardian*, March 29, 1990.)

Given a lack of accountability of this order, one might wonder, not merely about the quality of democracy in Britain, but also about the motives and attitudes of our elected representatives. The implication was that anyone could run a business in Britain, and if they had Ridley's approval, that was enough. There was no need in his eyes for MPs, or people in general, to know what he regarded as the rules necessary for holding company office. In other words, checks and balances and constitutional protection were mere trivia in Ridley's eyes; his opinion was sufficient to decide government policy.

The question of democracy will be examined in more detail in the next chapter, but for the time being, one can say that the economy is not being managed for the benefit of the population as a whole.

The examples given here are typical of post-1979 Conservative policy. As individual consumers, we find the quality of our purchases have deteriorated, while large companies are making monopoly profits at our expense. The examples were bread and air travel, but one could just as easily cite beer and CDs, water and cars. There is not the space in this book to describe all the corporate and governmental malpractice that has occurred since 1979. Not only could one write a book about it, several excellent books have been written.

At the same time as our quality of life has been declining, state spending has concentrated on those areas which give profits to big business, especially those sectors with long-established lobbying links. Roads and defence boom, while health, education and railways are allowed to run down to unsafe levels. At the same time, the government is talking about a £23 bn road programme, and planning 12-lane motorways. And at no time, regardless of the nature of the offence, are company directors held legally liable for their corporate actions.

The welfare of the citizen as consumer is of no interest to the Conservatives, whatever they say. Prices escalate while competition is ignored, and the quality of life is hardly mentioned. It is certainly not okay, but commerce rules. The New Right's alleged concern with market forces is meaningless; their real goal is the well-being of their exclusive constituency — big business and its management.

4

Agreeing to differ

IN SOME CANTONS of Switzerland it is still possible to see the direct democracy of the village square in action. People gather together, discuss what is needed, and vote on it. But as we move from village life to mass society, we have to accept representative democracy, where our elected servants act on our behalf. The concept of democracy as 'government of the people, by the people, for the people' becomes unwieldy in a nation of 50 million inhabitants. Our representatives duly take over that role, on our behalf.

As a group, with their institutional apparatus, we call these servants, 'the state'. The seventeenth-century political philosopher, Hobbes justified the existence of the state, on the basis that it protected the individual against threats from internal or external agencies. The individual yields some power to the state, which becomes the monopoly user of force. It then uses its power on our behalf.

The immediate controller of the apparatus of the state is the government, which can be seen as the temporary manager of the machinery of the state. Governments need further justification beyond that given by Hobbes to legitimate their power. At a minimum, they need consent to rule, and validate their existence. This legitimacy depends partly on the number of people who support the government, and partly on the ideology of the regime. In a democracy the consent is active, in elections, but in a communist regime the leaders may seek to legitimate their rule by appealing to an abstract 'will of the people'. That is, the communist leaders would claim to be carrying out an idealised will, what is best, in their opinion, for the people.

But true legitimacy should involve consent, although even that is a minimal claim to fame. It merely means a sufficient level of support to show that the population is not actively seeking the overthrow of its rulers. Thus, one could say that the Soviet Union had the consent of the people up until 1989. And mere numbers do not give a government validity, especially where there is a polarisation of attitudes, a narrow majority, or a close margin on specific policies. For example, the French voted for acceptance of the Maastricht Treaty by a margin of 50.95 per cent of the population for the treaty, compared to 49.05 per cent against. Such a slim margin of victory means that neither of the existing alternatives genuinely represents the will of the people.

In a basic 'one person, one vote' democracy, we assume that the government is legitimated by the election, with that election expressing the will of the people. In a system like Britain's, we then say that those who are elected have a mandate, an explicit right to enact the legislation they promised. And in a sense, numbers do not matter under the British system. Suppose that a government is elected with 51 per cent of the vote; do we then say it has a mandate? If so, can it do as it wishes? Does it need 51 per cent for a mandate? If so, do we then say that not only the post-1979 governments in Britain, but also the Clinton administration in the United States, lack legitimacy?

For John Locke, there was an implicit contract between the citizen and the state. The state was obliged to protect its subjects and their lives, maintain law and order, and defend the nation from external enemies. In this way, legitimacy depends on the government's fulfilment of this unspoken agreement. The argument is similar to that of Hobbes, who also implies an unspoken agreement. However, the government need take no action to enter this contract, nor can it deny its commitment. The duty is inherent in the state's role.

For consent to be meaningful, there must also be participation. One cannot regard a regime as legitimate if it ignores the welfare of the population or their calls for action, under the pretext of serving their best interests. No state can have sufficient knowledge to understand all of the population's needs; officials tend to be both geographically and socially remote from the masses, and have little appreciation of their day to day needs. For the government to be both effective and democratic, it must be open to some input from the people. It must at least listen to what they say they need. That input is the minimum level of participation needed for some semblance of effective government.

The process of formulating the public's opinion can be compared to a properly chaired meeting. Everyone who wishes to speak is allowed a voice, with each person's opinion carrying an equal weight. Open debate then thrashes out the facts and the implications of each competing view, with the rationality and evidence for each view open to detailed scrutiny, until the most valid arguments emerge as victors.

In a democracy such as Britain, the input to government covers a wide range — voting for candidates, public discussion of policy, and with proposals put to the voters before each election — thus giving a mandate to the victorious party. Legislation is discussed openly, in both Houses of Parliament and in the press, information is available on the policy alternatives, and weaknesses are thrashed out in parliamentary debate. There must also be accountability, so that those who object to the policies can make their complaints.

With all this apparent openness and debate, revolving around the need to provide for the public good, one might think that Britain was an ideal democracy. If we take the strict definition, perhaps it is: government is responsive to public opinion, this is tested regularly, and in cases of conflict, the majority opinion rules. However, in their detailed analysis of the failings of the British political system, Hillyard and Percy-Smith show that our nation is far from perfect.

If we examine the reality of our democracy we find that the Cabinet keeps secrets from Parliament, while occasionally, the Prime Minister and Cabinet committees make decisions from which the full Cabinet team is excluded. In some cases, new laws are created by civil servants, while in other cases, acts are passed into law without ever passing through the Commons. All of this is hidden from the public by a mixture of convention, media collusion, and the Official Secrets Act.

Hillyard and Percy-Smith compare Britain to the ideal that it is sometimes alleged to be, a liberal democracy. This type of democracy is the best possible form of representative government, where the welfare of the citizen is the highest priority. Some people say that we can define it simply as the system displayed in Britain and the United States. But liberal democracy can be defined, even though the New Right do not devote too much effort to the subject, while Roger Scruton does not mention liberal democracy in his dictionary of politics. Francis Fukuyama, creator of 'the end of history' thesis, strikes out in a totally new direction, making up his own definition.

Scruton does however, mention liberal democracy is passing, in his analysis of the writings of J. K. Galbraith. Scruton refers to 'the real differences between the communist world and the world of liberal democracy' (*Thinkers of the New Left*, p165). One presumes that he means to contrast the communist nations with those nations that are sometimes called the free world. To refer to them as the western democracies might be a loose generalisation, but to call them liberal democracies is a generalisation that, as we shall see, fails to grasp the concept.

Hillyard and Percy-Smith state that, 'According to liberal democratic theory, central government in Britain should be based on popular participation, regular 'free and fair' elections organized on the basis of 'one person, one vote, one value', informed consent to government, rational debate and discussion at all stages of the policy-making process, legitimate political authority, scrutiny and accountability'. (*The Coercive State*, p22.)

The central theme in liberal democracy is the openness of decision-making, and the accountability of the democratic process. And some writers add the proviso that in a liberal democracy, the government must be working for the welfare of all citizens, not just those who voted for it. Such a requirement is essential if the system is truly to be 'government of the people, by the people, for the people'. The process may be carried out by elected representatives, but it must be done for the benefit of the citizens. Thus, it is not merely a set of legal structures, but a way of managing society, an implied set of values. (See Finer, pp62-74.) It does not mean, however, that everyone should be involved in every step of the decision-making process. This is impractical, given the number of people involved, and is not absolutely necessary, if there is accountability and proper representation.

To a certain extent, all the characteristics specified by the writers quoted are present in the British democratic process, although one might object to the quality that exists. That is, we have consent, but it is not fully informed consent. We have public debate, but neither in the media nor in the Houses of Parliament is it fully rational and open to all possible arguments. It is clearly not open to all voices equally, with politicians endlessly repeating their views, while calmly ignoring public opinion. Nor does the debate occur at all stages of policy-making, given the existence of Cabinet committees. The legal rights, the checks and balances, also exist, but in emaciated form. We have a constitution that is largely unwritten, much of it rooted in tradition, or common law. And it is all too easy to ignore an outdated tradition, or find a precedent to overrule an aspect of common law. The effect is that our constitutional protection is minimal.

John Major limply attempted to introduce some small modicum of openness into the political process, firstly through the Citizen's Charters. However, this has primarily been the imposition of additional obligations on the state sector, but without the finance to make any meaningful change possible. One other small step was when Kenneth Clarke decided to publish the minutes of the discussions between himself as Chancellor, and the Governor of the Bank of England.

This effectively destroyed the Cabinet's 30 year rule, but did little or nothing to create real openness. All that was involved was the Bank's interest rate policy. Thus, it represented a significant change of direction, but not a noticeable step towards democracy. That would occur when ministers revealed the discussion processes involving core economic policy, such as government spending, income distribution, or welfare.

Most importantly, we lack participation and accountability. As mentioned in the previous chapter, the education system has been so re-structured that ministers can deny any responsibility for the disasters that might occur. The same arms-length device has been applied to many other sectors of government. Politicians talk glibly about their beliefs in the correct policies. Yet not only are their policies not working, but they refuse to take any responsibility for such failures. Given the arms-length agencies, they are not technically involved in the decision-making processes. And having made serious errors in both management and in constitutional propriety, they refuse to admit to making a mistake.

It is particularly distasteful as so many of the executives of these new agencies are Conservative place-men and women. They are put in to ensure that someone sympathetic to the ideology is in charge, which may imply a belief that the policy is workable. However, there comes a point when over-active patronage becomes corruption.

Thus, if we have a liberal democracy, it is only a partially effective one. According to Warren, 'Critiques of liberal constitutionalism typically involve unmasking the numerous ways in which formally equal protections and guarantees both hide and perpetuate substantive inequalities'. (Mark Warren, 'Liberal Constitutionalism as Ideology', in *Political Theory*, November 1989, p512.) We can interpret this in one of two ways; either this structure has serious flaws — or else what we have is not actually a liberal democracy. If we take the definition of liberal democracy, and consider whether or not it is an accurate description of the British or American political system, we find that it is not.

The requirement of liberal democracy that the state acts for the welfare of all its citizens becomes a cause for concern when the population is of mixed racial origin, and the government represents only one of those races. For example, in Los

Angeles, 40 per cent of the population are Hispanic, 14 per cent black, and 10 per cent Asian. There is a fear that any future mayor of Los Angeles will ignore one or other of these groups, thus causing resentment, perhaps even riots. It is not unreasonable to expect such reactions, given the Watts riots of 1965, or the way in which white policemen were found innocent of beating black motorist Rodney King, despite a video showing them beating him. In the United States, as in many other societies, justice and equity seem to be the prerogative of those in the same racial or social group as the government.

In Britain, there is cause for concern as the government represents the ruling minority, while as shown in Chapter 2, the needs of the precarious class and the underclass are largely ignored. Our MPs and civil servants are primarily white and male, so the needs of women and non-whites tend to be seen as being of less importance. The power structure has a significant class dimension; women and ethnic groups can, as individuals, become part of the ruling elite, and absorb the values of that group. However, the two largest social classes remain effectively powerless, as long as sufficient numbers of them continue to vote for the government on the basis of its confident, trustworthy manner, rather than the results of ministers' policies.

Of course, the Conservatives would say that their problems have been caused by exceptional circumstances, a world recession, the Bundesbank, and maybe even alien invaders. These are excuses that will not detain any informed commentator. Quite simply, the Tories have deliberately chosen to disregard the welfare of 90 per cent of the population. And given this, the regime they are offering is not a liberal democracy.

There is an element of truth in some of the excuses. For example, when Tory leaders point out that there is a recession in Europe as well, this is, at the time of writing, true. But the implied argument that everyone is suffering from it, therefore our recession is not our fault, is a weak one. Most importantly, the same monetarist, high interest rate policies that we associate with Thatcherism have been built into Maastricht. There has also been steady integration of European economic policy since the mid-eighties, as part of an attempt to create economic convergence. As a result, the recession that blights the EU has probably been caused by the same policies that created Britain's slump.

One could say that the Tories are carrying out policies that were on their election platform, and that therefore they have a mandate from the voters. This however, ignores the requirements of accountability and participation. Genuine democracy should not be a process which occurs at the ballot box, after which total power is handed over to the victors. People have the right to participate, as well as the right to express their dissatisfaction at any time. And of course, a truly democratic government would actually listen to the voters' objections.

There is a cautionary note in this case, as the British public are known — even notorious — for not complaining. They do not complain about poor food, bad service, or incompetent governments. It was not until the poll tax fiasco that even a moderate percentage of the population decided to voice their objections. Given this

British reluctance to make a scene, concerned politicians should actually seek out indications of public opinion. Not that this could be an excuse for the Tories. One cannot say that they merely failed to identify the public's views. They actively disregarded clear statements of popular opinion.

The Labour Party cannot shout too loud; it should have been much more open-minded at the time of the 'Labour Listens' campaign, having lost three elections in a row at that time. Yet at one meeting, 'Roy Hattersley was on the platform 'listening' to a local man tell him that Labour would never get elected until it dropped its opposition to private schooling. Instead of merely noting the man's views, he came back with a ten-minute speech on why he found the private and privileged education sector politically repugnant'. (Colin Hughes and Patrick Wintour, p100.) Hattersley had failed to listen to an electorally significant point of view, and thus had lost the opportunity to find out what people object to in Labour's policy. But in addition, he had also missed what might have been an informed discussion; he might even have learnt something!

It also appears that there has been no discussion of policy within the Labour Party. For example, Neil Kinnock presented unilateral nuclear disarmament as a subject that would not even be discussed in the Shadow Cabinet. And Bryan Gould is said to have resigned from the Shadow Cabinet because of the lack of debate. If there is no open-mindedness within Labour, it is not surprising that there is no wish to create a consensus with the voters. The Labour hierarchy from Tony Blair downwards have chosen their opinions, and are not willing to discuss them with anyone.

In the United States, Senator Bob Dole has alleged that Bill Clinton did not have a mandate, as only 43 per cent of the electorate voted for him. Given the three way split, one wonders what percentage Dole would have considered a mandate. In Britain, Roy Hattersley has argued that proportional representation (PR) would undermine the concept of the mandate. The traditional theory of first-past-the-post politics has been that voters choose the party they want, and that party then has the right to push for all the legislation that was in its manifesto. Hattersley argued that in a PR system, the majority parties would have to negotiate policy, leading to an outcome which might not reflect what the voters had wanted.

This objection ignores the fact that in a liberal democracy, the government, whatever its party composition, would be working for the benefit of all voters, regardless of whom those people had voted for. Therefore, it would not matter how many people had voted for the government; their MPs should be introducing what they believe to be the best possible policies for the whole nation. Hattersley's argument implies that each party would have a set of policies for its chosen constituency, and would ignore the supporters of opposing parties. This is not unexpected for a party so closely identified with a single type of pressure group — the trade unions — but it does not reflect a commitment to liberal democracy.

The other fear concerning the mandate is the tyranny of the majority. Supposing the government's policies served the interests of 90 per cent of the population; would that be acceptable? Or given the nature of the electoral mandate, one could imagine a 51 per cent majority imposing its wishes on the minority. And this would be just as wrong if the majority comprised 95 or 99 per cent of the population. Under a true liberal democracy this would not be a problem; the conflict would not exist because the government should seek to look after the interests of all members of the population.

Galbraith's picture of middle class electoral collusion against the less fortunate is a form of tyranny of the majority. He refers to a contented electoral majority who are quite happy to ignore social and environmental problems, and see the poor taxed unjustifiably, as long as they don't have to pay more taxes themselves.

One could see the Conservatives' concern with the welfare of the taxpayer in exactly the same light. A certain percentage of the population pay the government's revenue, and one could make the argument that they were, therefore, the government's employers. Given this relationship, these people therefore demand that for their sake, the tax burden be minimised. And to do this, government spending must also be minimised. But this argument would be weak for a number of reasons. First, the state's implicit contract is with the entire population, including those who happen, for one reason or another, to be non-taxpayers. Second, there is the fact that 'taxpayer' is merely a role that many of us play. We have other roles and other needs, and for the government to focus exclusively on one aspect of our persona is short-sighted.

Even if the majority want to minimise their tax burden, and claim the right to lobby, protest and shift their tax liability, there is still the fact that a true liberal democracy should be concerned with the welfare of all. Of course, not all countries come up to the theoretical ideal, with Britain and America not being among the more successful. The fact that a middle class conspiracy can exist proves the scale of the political failure.

The danger of the tyranny of the majority is one reason why Marxism, with its dictatorship of the proletariat, is morally and politically offensive. No country should be run by, or for, any one group. For the same reason, the Labour Party's obsession with the working class, and its close ties with trade unions, are seen as unhealthy by many voters. It can be argued that the Tories' links with big business are just as unacceptable, which is true. In a healthy society there should not be such strong links between the government and other institutions with an interest in the content of state policy. Such links give the institutions, which may be outside the realm of democratic processes, undue influence over the activities of government. The only difference is that the Tories' links with business are seen as acceptable.

Technically, the Tories have consent. They have been voted into office, under free elections, by secret ballot, and thus have been democratically elected. One might say that 57 per cent of the electorate had voted against them, but equally one could say that 65 per cent of the voters had voted against Labour. In fact, the argument is spurious in both cases; one cannot say that simply because one decides not to choose a given item, that one is opposing it. Those people who put their cross against the Labour candidate did not necessarily feel any hostility to the Tory.

Thus, on mere numbers, the Conservatives have consent. But consent by itself is no more than tolerance, lack of action against the government, which is not sufficient to legitimate the leaders. The regime may have achieved nothing more positive than apathy or alienation — and there are clear signs that large sectors of the population in many western nations feel one or both of these. In Sweden, voters apathetically accepted the rush into Maastricht, because, on a superficial interpretation, they actually wanted integration with the EU. It now seems that they felt overwhelmed by the stampede, unable to stop the inevitable. That is, until the Danes voted against Maastricht, and showed that the oncoming tidal wave was not inevitable. That was when Swedish citizens started campaigning against the treaty.

One additional requirement for liberal democracy is that there be consensus. Part of the government's job is to recognise that there are conflicting needs and opinions, and that these have to be reconciled. That is, the government must create a policy framework on which all can agree.

Also, there must be not merely tolerance, but active support for the broad sweep of the state's policy framework. At the minimum, this involves agreement between the key players in the economy, say, ministers and business, and/or trade unions. However, the post-war consensus was seen to include government, civil servants, academics, and the general public. Thus, a majority of the population gave their active approval for the post-war Keynesian style of governing. This broad support is only likely to exist if the majority of the population recognise that policy is carried out in their interests. And this will only occur if the state is performing the key feature of a liberal democracy; working for the interest of all. Thus, consensus is a natural part of liberal democracy.

This does, however, raise the question of what percentage of the population one needs for consensus. For example, if sixty per cent of the population believed in a certain group of policies, would that make theirs the consensus view? The answer is that it would have to depend on the number of alternate views, and the intensity with which they were held.

Both the French and the Danish referenda on Maastricht showed such narrow majorities that that there was no agreement. To have initiated any policy in such a situation would have been politically inept. However, if there had been a large percentage of 'don't knows', or if the minority group was not deeply convinced of its views, then there would be fewer objections in taking action. Where this division could be a problem was if the two (or more) sides were evenly balanced both in numbers, and in the intensity of their beliefs.

Thus, rather than seeking to allocate a percentage to consensus, it might be more appropriate to see it in terms of balance. If a majority believe strongly that their policy choices are the correct ones, should it ignore the mild dissent of a minority?

This brings us to the question of whether consensus is a group of policies, or a style, a method of governing. That is, is it a product or a process? The answer is that it is both; it is a process of participative democracy as well as being the agreement that is reached. It is only through discussion that society can resolve potential conflicts, and reach a set of ideas that it can agree upon. And because everyone has had the opportunity to put or defend their views, people will be much happier with the outcome. Thus, the consensual process leads to a platform of consensus policies.

As mentioned in Chapter 1, the Keynesian social-democratic consensus was based in both the rational and the moral analysis. This strengthened the Keynesian consensus, as whichever fundamental method one took, one reached the same conclusion. However, had the two approaches led to different conclusions, a participative democracy would have found a way of combining the two. In a façade democracy, such as that of the Thatcher and Major governments, the dominant ideology is simply imposed on society.

We saw above that the imposition of policies can lead to alienation. This has been associated with the Marxist use of the word, in which the worker is isolated from and distanced by the work process. But to imagine that alienation only occurs at work is a distortion of the concept. Indeed, there are many disturbing comparisons to be drawn between work and the political system suggesting that their psychological effect could be the same. For example, Marxists say that as work is not inherently satisfying, workers have to be given instrumental rewards, such as pay or status, to motivate them. This can be compared to the voter's response to tax cuts; not trusting either the politicians or the political system, the one thing that voters can believe in is the personal reward offered them in tax cuts. This would explain their role in helping the Conservatives win the 1992 British election. Tax cuts also enabled Bush to halve Clinton's lead when Bush offered them as part of his election campaign of that year. A large number of US voters were aware of Bush's inaction on the economy, but may have felt reluctant to trust anyone to end both the budget deficits and the recession. A rise in one's own take-home pay is believable, however.

Similarly, Marxists see alienation as caused by an inability to control the work process. This is comparable to voters' inability to control their political leaders, as happened in Sweden, and as has been happening constantly in Britain with the post-1979 Conservative governments.

Part of the problem is that politicians are almost completely isolated from voters. In the past, politicians sprang from among the ordinary people, and understood their lives, their attitudes, and their needs. Nowadays, politics is a career move, a line of employment like any other, but with better pay, and relatively good job security, especially in the case of the power elite of each main party. The exponents of the craft learn how to move themselves up the career ladder, which rising stars or policies to associate themselves with, and how to present themselves to the great unwashed.

Peter Jenkins paints a picture of Neil Kinnock as the consummate political animal, his skills revolving entirely around the rules and the battle strategy necessary to rise through the Labour Party. (*Mrs Thatcher's Revolution.*) We see Kinnock's delight as the Labour Party's constitution is changed in a way that improves Kinnock's chances of becoming leader (p116). Or campaigning at unions' seaside conferences, because the power of the block vote is his key to success. But we see nothing which suggests a dedicated leader of the opposition looking for a credible and workable set of economic policies.

However, this may have been an unflattering picture of Kinnock. Hughes and Wintour, in their study of Labour's post-1987 policy review, make it quite clear that Kinnock 'craved' electoral victory (p202). But they also show the compassionate person, who explicitly recognised that the real price of defeat at the ballot box is paid, not by the politicians but by the poor, the pensioners, the unskilled, the vulnerable. It is a shame, and a tragedy, that many Labour politicians failed to take account of those who paid the price.

In the United States we saw George Bush, having failed to do anything of any significance for the US economy, struggle desperately to win the 1992 election. He had not only done nothing, he was not even aware that his inaction was in any way a failing. He too was a political animal who knew the rules, the structures and the presentation. He was able to project confidence and competence, which may even be enough for some politicians to win elections. But there was no understanding of what the rest of us refer to as the real world.

Mancur Olson suggests that if nations are undisturbed, their social and economic structures generate powerful vested interests, as groups with power create organisations or lobbying procedures to press their case. Countries like Britain have been able to plod along as the vested interests proliferated, stultifying enterprise and growth. In Germany and Japan, the shake-up brought about by losing a major war destroyed or re-organised the power structures, eliminating those groups whose power had no economic value, or where the individuals retained their positions for some outdated reason. In Britain, such groups have continued to hold and accumulate power, entrenching themselves further.

This has been visible in the City, the civil service, and in such financial institutions as the Treasury and the Bank of England. Not surprisingly, when a senior figure from one of these august bodies speaks, it is usually in support of the government. These organisations have not changed significantly since the nineteenth century, and as they have grown powerful and respected, they tend to attract people who seek power and respect. After a few decades or so, the ethos of the workforce becomes the institutional ethos. Protection of entrenched privilege becomes more important than the original purpose.

For example, the Inland Revenue sought to re-assess the non-domicile status of foreign businessmen who are not technically resident in Britain, and who therefore do not pay tax. This reassessment was halted by the Treasury. By coincidence, foreign businessmen had contributed several million pounds to Tory funds. As a result of the Treasury's intervention, these wealthy non-residents will be considerably better off, by being relieved of the tedious need to pay tax. The Exchequer will however, be slightly worse off.

Certainly, big business has become much more influential under the post-1979 Conservative governments; it is a living example of Olson's hypothesis in action.

The corporate vested interests, using the well-paid lobbyists and research groups such as the Adam Smith Institute, have been extremely successful at putting their views into the ears of ministers. Olson argues that the increasing influence of outdated but powerful interests ultimately destroys the dynamism and creativity of the nation. And this is what is happening in Britain; the ruinous economic policies are gradually destroying the country.

Political parties are just another aspect of this hierarchy, with career politicians being the logical development of the process. Politics has changed from being a way to serve one's country or region, to being an attractive job in itself, regardless of any other characteristic it might have. An added attraction of the European Union is that it provides politicians from each nation with yet another career ladder to climb onto, bringing a whole new field of promotion opportunities into view. This encourages some MPs to support the EU, and to approve of the expansion of its powers, knowing that they might be able to walk the corridors of Brussels one day.

Olson points out that the more complex the laws, the greater is the need for experts to analyse and interpret those laws, whether for the benefit of governments, individuals or companies. Thus, there is a vested interest for all those involved in the growing complexity of regulation. For politicians, there is their impressive achievement in getting benefits for their constituents, despite the difficulty of dealing with complicated laws. MPs can then present themselves as being especially skilled, and therefore especially deserving of re-election. 'Interestingly, the proportion of incumbents getting re-elected has increased over time'. (*The Rise and Decline of Nations*, pp70-71.) This probably means that politicians are getting more adept at persuasion.

It is possible that one of the effects of Thatcherism is the shake-up of many of Britain's traditional institutions, of the sort described by Olson. Trade unions, the media, education and local government all needed a shake-up, and they certainly got one. We had taken them for granted, and assumed that the status quo was impregnable and everlasting. Mrs Thatcher showed us that things could be changed, and in that sense, may have left some lasting benefit for the country. Even if the impact was not as comprehensive as that which Olson suggests revitalised Germany and Japan, at least some re-thinking was necessary.

However, Mrs Thatcher chose to attack only selected institutions. She ignored the most powerful establishment bureaucracies, like the Treasury, the Bank of England, and top judges. Naturally, the entire party political system was also overlooked. Links between political parties and commerce were retained. Yet it is the City, and the old duffer culture of big business, that are responsible for keeping the policies of government and industry so firmly in the nineteenth century. An interventionist government would at least encourage the use of modern methods. But as we mentioned in Chapter 1, industry tends not to provide many of the facilities which it actually needs for survival.

Also, because of the rejection of consensus, the political system became even more adversarial, more image conscious, and more career orientated. We have moved from having two dogmas, locked in sightless combat, to having two versions of the same dogma, still in combat. And neither of these senseless gladiators seems to have any interest in the welfare of the average person.

In such a situation, alienation is inevitable. Our political servants have become our masters, but being socially isolated, they do not know what policies are needed. Even worse, they do not care. Their employment does not depend on their skill in satisfying our needs, but on their presentational skills, in persuading us that they are the best candidates for the job, that they are doing the best that can be done. Because we live in a consent democracy they can get away with it. Since the 1970s, ministers have managed to lower our expectations of them, so that we consent to their leadership, even though we are not happy with the quality of life they have generated, or the moral standards they set.

The post-1979 Thatcheroids have been seen by many as total failures in the policy sense. The economy is falling apart, sterling was devalued despite protestations that Lamont would never devalue, the balance of payments has become a major policy constraint, and the recession has turned into a slump. The Prime Minister's claims of economic health are known to be false. Perhaps this is why John Major said, in a television interview, that he and his party had failed to spell out what they were doing. The prevailing attitude of post-1979 politics has become one where politicians tell the people what is correct, rather than listening to what the people want or believe. This is not consensus; it is not even democracy.

It is not merely that Mrs Thatcher dropped the idea of consensus when she came to office; she also discarded the whole idea that government is responsive to the needs and wishes of voters. It is a reverse of the theoretical concept of democracy, that the state responds to the needs of citizens. The New Right view is that citizens must learn the truth as espoused by the state. It is not merely liberal democracy that has been rejected; by denying consensus, democracy itself has been removed.

There are many similarities in the political and economic structures of Britain and the United States, and the same sort of process has been going on in parallel in both countries. However, in the US it became visible in 1968, 'a year when the pollsters reported ever increasing difficulty in interviewing citizens, who refused to talk politics; and when a national public-opinion survey brought back the news that 43 per cent of all those polled said that, in their hearts, they preferred somebody else to the candidates offered them'. (Theodore H. White, *The Making of the President 1968*, p352.)

In Britain, voters have found it difficult to make a choice between what was, for many, two equally unattractive parties. On the one hand was the Labour Party, incompetent, untrustworthy, and constantly changing its mind about its policies. On the other hand, the Conservatives, confident, but with unattractive policies and candidates. It was a hard decision, especially in the 1992 election, and could well explain the late swing away from Labour.

Labour is stuck with an outdated ideology that many of its parliamentary members have refused to drop, or even re-appraise. It has been obvious from opinion polls that voters do not like some Labour policies, and there are clear indications that some of those policies have not been the best, or most efficient way, of dealing with issues. In addition, Labour has become very adversarial in its stance. Jim Callaghan once said that the job of the opposition party is to oppose. And in Parliament, very often, Labour has done just that. It has simply opposed any and every Tory proposal; and that is not a healthy or rational way to conduct politics.

An opinion poll found that less than half the population trust either party with running the economy. It found that 19 per cent trust none of the parties, while 25 per cent did not know. Given the incompetence that both main parties have displayed, one by governing, the other by not knowing how it would govern, the 19 per cent is surprisingly low. But the figure for don't knows is unusually high, suggesting a disoriented electorate.

It might be suggested that even if there is no liberal democracy, there is a broad consensus that is more positive than mere assent. At the very least, there is a basis of support for Britain's political institutions. That is, one might say that most people support the institutions of Parliament, the judiciary, the civil service and so on. This, however, is more comparable to Hobbes' justification for the existence of the state, than it is to approval of a given elected regime. The state, as a basic structure, may have consent; but that does not mean that the government also has.

A variety of polls taken throughout the Thatcher/Major years suggest a wide gap in opinion between Westminster and the constituents. For example, even though John Major was pushing full force for the Maastricht Treaty, two thirds of voters were against more power for the EU, according to both an ICM poll for *The Guardian* and a Harris poll for *The Observer*. (*The Guardian*, November 14, 1991. *The Observer*, November 17, 1991). On transport, more than sixty per cent of motorists want increased spending on public transport, while eighty per cent reject the Department of Transport's plans for privately funded roads (*The Guardian*, July 26, 1991).

On the issues that are most central to the Conservatives' ideology, we find 'Growing public hostility to water privatisation... that nearly half of all Tory voters fear that it will lead to a worse service for customers' (*The Guardian*, May 17, 1989). The figure for Labour voters was nearly seventy per cent. Similarly, faced with the choice between a cut in tax, or more spending on the NHS, 84 per cent of all those polled preferred more spending. (*The Guardian*, March 14, 1988.)

It might be said that this finding is disproved by voters' behaviour at the 1992 election, but decisions at the ballot box are influenced by far more than the offer of a penny off taxes. The growing hostility to the Tories' policies is matched by uncertainty concerning the recession, and doubt that Labour can deal with it any better than the Conservatives. The final decision in the polling booths is the outcome of many factors, but the worst part of it is that all the candidates seem unappealing. The choice is between two sets of careerists, both of whom have nothing to offer in terms of policy ideas, and may even deliberately ignore what the electorate wants.

It is one thing for a government to reject a consensus between the parties, saying that it does not wish to compromise, or water down its policies. That may be pragmatism, or at worst, narrow-mindedness. To reject it when it represents what a majority of the voters wish to see, and it is what is best for the country, is offensive.

This is not consensus; it is not even democracy. It is tyranny. All that governments have nowadays is the bare minimum level of consent needed for them to survive.

But in surviving, politicians create alienation, disenchantment and apathy. Eventually voting turnout will fall, and extremism will increase as a natural reaction against the bland indifference of the mainstream politicians. Values such as morality, fairness and compassion are being daily eroded by example as the elected dictators get on with the business of running the country for the good of their social equals. Reaction against New Right policies could manifest itself in political extremism of the worst kind. Lord Kaldor points out that the Weimar Republic was managed according to the same obsession with monetary control, until unemployment reached 7 million, and the architect of the disaster was removed by the president. It is a pity that Britain has no constitutional machinery for removing or impeaching ministers who are obviously incompetent.

A lack of consensus is socially divisive at least; at worst, it can lead to the Beirut syndrome, and a total collapse of the society. Harmonious multiracial societies show us that it is possible for people from a wide range of backgrounds to live together peacefully. But this can only exist where people are willing to talk freely, and accept the other person's need, and point of view. In the process of discussion, we may sometimes find that we are not as correct as we thought; we may change our minds, and accept some of the other person's ideas.

Thus, for consensus to exist, there must be open and informed discussion of the problems, the policies, and the alternatives. That is, the various groups within society, and their political leaders, must debate their chosen policies until they can agree on a mutually satisfactory compromise. The normal method in most Western nations is for the most powerful groups to put their requests to the elected leaders, and the leaders then agree a compromise. But whatever the result, it will be primarily in the interests of the two parties to the negotiation — weaker groups are invariably excluded from the process. In a consensual society, all groups would take part.

Some might argue that the interests of certain groups are inevitably opposed. For example, Marxists would say that the needs of the working class and the owners of industry are in conflict, by the nature of their role. The owners of a business seek to exploit the workers, and the workers must get as much as they can from the company's wealth. Such a conflict scenario led directly to the management/union clashes of the 1970s, with the unions' assumption that the bosses were dishonest and exploitative, and that the unions had the right to demand as high a wage increase as they could.

There is a large element of truth in the view that the interests of workers and management are in conflict, especially in reference to British industrial management. Bosses' attitudes have been short-term, selfish, and simplistic. They have not even been sufficiently informed to manage their companies properly. Indeed, much of the management/worker hostility has been a direct result of the way in which workers have been treated. They have had separate works entrances, separate canteens, and the perpetual contrast in working conditions. While executives have spent their days in quiet, carpeted offices, workers have laboured away in noisy, dirty, and unsafe factories to which even the Health and Safety Inspectorate would have objected.

But it is a massive step in logic from saying that their interests do now clash, to saying that by the nature of their roles in society their needs automatically clash. And that is the Marxist position. However, if we were to consider the possibility of management and workers discussing their needs over the boardroom table, we open up the possibility of an agreement being reached in which conflict could be severely reduced. All that is needed is for the two sides to see their mutual interdependence, instead of seeing only narrow self-interest.

For example, while management have seen the company as a source of pay, perks and fringe benefits, the workers have seen the firm simply as a source of employment, with the bosses as the enemy. In fact, neither side could have its benefits without the other. If both sides recognised their mutual interdependence, they could begin to work as partners, rather than as enemies.

This might begin with management taking less pay and smaller fringe benefits, while workers might moderate their pay claims for the here and now, in consideration of the benefits that come in the future from investment and greater efficiency. Discussions between bosses and unions could revolve around areas of mutual interest like investment, planning, new markets for products, innovation and so on. Such discussions could lead to a recognition that rather than being two opposing camps, management and workers were simply two parts of one team.

For such a step to take place, whether at the corporate or the national level, the power of each group must be irrelevant; they must be listened to according to their need, and the reasonableness of their requests or arguments. We must stop assuming that management are entitled to huge levels of pay, merely because of their role in the company. Similarly, we must rid ourselves of the notion that if Westminster wants a motorway, they are entitled to demolish trees, houses, and woodland to build it, regardless of the wishes of local people. For example, the Department of Transport has been pushing the M3 through Twyford Down with an aggression and dishonesty that is totally unacceptable in an organisation that we fondly believe is in some way democratic (*The Guardian*, July 18, 1992).

Also, there must be no pre-conceived notions of what is or is not a valid argument, or what is or is not an appropriate way of delivering the social goods. To borrow a phrase, if minds are not open, they don't work. In an ideal system we would not have our elected servants choosing inflation as a target to control, for the benefit of those with savings, and excluding unemployment from the policy programme. MPs would have to be capable of looking at all issues in terms of the nation's welfare, not in terms of their friends and fellow golf players.

This means there must be no pre-conceived ideology. We should be suspicious of the populist demagogue, or the politician with the easy answer to solve all our economic ills. The danger is that a confident MP is the epitome of the smooth-talking con-man; they have all the answers, and if anything goes wrong, it isn't their fault. The post-1979 Tory governments have been unable to see the disastrous results of their own policies, and have even managed to persuade the populace to accept the New Right view of reality.

After the September 1992 devaluation of the pound, Norman Lamont not only denied that there had been a devaluation, but blamed the whole episode on the Bundesbank. And 55 per cent of the population believed him. This tendency to blame others is a feature of the authoritarian personality, 'the attribution of blame for bad thoughts or deeds to scapegoats — usually minority groups who could not defend themselves' (Stuart Oskamp, *Attitudes and Opinions*, p328).

Not that the Bundesbank is a minority group, but it is less able to defend itself in Britain's media than it would be on its own territory. But it is Lamont's unwillingness to accept responsibility that is the key issue. In all the deluge of memoirs that have flooded out of the Thatcher cabinets, not one has indicated a willingness to accept any blame. Mrs Thatcher sees herself as being almost free of faults; there may be some, but she is unsure as to what they might be. The economic problems are entirely the fault of Nigel Lawson.

All the other memoirs showed the same generosity and forgiveness. Each and every minister was entirely willing to overlook the possibility that he or she might have any human weaknesses whatsoever. We were indeed lucky to have been governed by such flawless gods and goddesses. What a pity it is that within months of their entering office, millions of people lost interest in work, and chose to be jobless.

The most puzzling aspect of this is that after the economic chaos that had been caused by the Tories' policies, the average person still trusted them enough to believe Lamont's excuses. Of course, the government's support from large sections of the press helped, and the total failure of the Labour Party to mount any campaign of criticism ensured that the broad outline of policy was seen as valid.

Also, for discussion to be informed, all those involved in the debate must have a clear idea of the problems and possible solutions. This requires a well-educated electorate, with a good grasp of the policy issues, able to make intelligent judgements about an informed, able, and competent set of politicians. Naturally, a knowledgeable populace is more likely to choose capable leaders. It is interesting that economically and socially successful countries have high levels of spending on education. Indeed, this was how Japan first stepped onto the development ladder, by making education a priority as part of the Meiji Restoration in 1858. Like other wealthy nations, it has continued with that route. Clearly, part of the explanation for this is that government policy aimed at the economy's needs creates success. This is not to say that the Japanese education is a particularly good one; but it is an economically effective one.

Yet there is one further requirement of liberal democracy; that it denies '*that there is any objective science of society or of morals*'. (Italics in the original.) This leads to toleration, 'because if there is no objective science of society or of morals, then clearly no group, not even the government has any moral justification for imposing any creed, philosophy, religion or ideology upon the rest of society'. (S. E. Finer, *Comparative Government*, p65).

Thus, the government may choose a set of policies that can be shown to work, or to have worked in the past. Or it may suggest policies that it believes will work. But there is no automatic validation for the government's approach, either from its office, or its electoral mandate. The acceptability of its stance must be constantly tested via public opinion.

In addition, the government must not rule merely in the interests of any one group, but must be acting on behalf of all (see Finer, p65). This carries the implication that its role is to balance the needs of all to get the best possible outcome. Thus, there is a moral obligation for the state to maximise welfare. Yet as we have seen in Chapter 2, the post-1979 regimes have explicitly chosen to ignore the welfare of the lower and middle income groups, the homeless, and other vulnerable members of society, and have instead directed their generosity towards those who are already rich.

It is obvious that most, if not all, of the specified components of liberal democracy are absent from Britain. Changes are necessary, in order to create a society where the political system is responsive to the needs of the people. Those most in need must have priority, and fortunately the average person has an innate sense of fairness that would support such a priority. Indeed, there are already so many shared attitudes that a new consensus would not be difficult to create. The evidence is so consistent that one could almost play pick'n'mix in order to create a new party platform. What is so intolerable is that this coherent set of attitudes and values has been so thoroughly ignored by both the post-1979 Tory governments, and the Labour Party.

Of course, there have been changes in attitudes during the Thatcherite era, largely as a result of ministers' propaganda. For example, in 1985, 27 per cent of those surveyed did not agree that employees needed strong unions. By 1987 the number disagreeing had risen to 29 per cent. There is no doubt that the New Right emphasis on the individual, and the active contempt for trade unions, has made collective action seem less important. Similarly, the proportion of people seeing unemployment as the most important policy issue fell from 84 per cent in 1986 to 18 per cent in 1990. Over the same period, the proportion seeing inflation as the most important issue rose from 8 per cent to 29 per cent. (MORI, cited in *Financial Times*, June 6, 1990.)

Clearly, ministers' ceaseless propaganda on the party line has had a significant impact on popular opinion, although the effect has varied. Attitudes towards unemployment have changed considerably, perhaps because the government has persuaded people that other matters have to be dealt with before unemployment can be cured. But one could argue that the government has not been quite so successful in persuading people to see inflation as being important. In fact, there are signs that the populace is slowly turning against the Tories. For example, in August 1995 it was discovered that Conservative Central Office had turned down four Party Political Broadcast slots, because had it made such broadcasts, it would have created hostility rather than votes. (*The Guardian*, August 18, 1995.)

In some cases, the changes in public attitudes may be the result of the effectiveness of the Tories' policy. In 1985, 54 per cent of those surveyed thought that unions were too powerful; by 1990 the proportion was down to 40 per cent. A large part of this decline must be explained by the new weakness of unions — the need to ballot their members on strikes, the need to ask members if they want to contribute to the political levy, and the reluctance to strike that has been brought about by the difficulty of defining what is a legal strike.

But what is more interesting is the way in which opinion has moved against the Thatcherite ideology. Crewe states that from 1974 to 1979, there was a swing towards authoritarian attitudes, but that from 1979 onwards, the swing was towards a more liberal approach. (Ivor Crewe, in *Contemporary Record*, February 1990.) The Tories should be aware that it is 'not merely that the tide of public opinion continues on the whole to move against its core welfare policies, but that even its own supporters appear increasingly to have moved with that tide'. (*British Social Attitudes; 1990.*)

There is, the report says, 'a growing consensus among supporters of all parties for a switch to welfarist, rather than individualist, taxation and social spending policies'. (*British Social Attitudes; 1990.*) For example, an increasing proportion of the population believed that the government should raise taxes and increase spending. This rose from 32 per cent in 1983 to 46 per cent in 1986 to 56 per cent in 1989.

The 1994 report found little changed in the public's opinion on the welfare state, compared with 1991. When asked a series of questions on the NHS, housing, etc., Peter Taylor-Gooby found the pattern of answers almost identical to that shown in 1991. People considered most areas of caring to be the responsibility of government, and felt that health and education should should be provided at a standard quality, for all. 'In short, public opinion continues to be set firmly against the thrust of many of the policy changes in the welfare area'. (*British Social Attitudes; 1994*, p34.)

The report said little about changes in public attitudes to the welfare state as a general principle, but it did examine attitudes to health, education and pensions spending. In 1983, 46 per cent had felt that health care should be the same for all, while 53 per cent thought that those who were able to pay for better provision should be able to do so. By 1993, 55 per cent felt that health care should be the same for all, while only 43 per cent said that people should be able to pay for better health treatment.

A Marplan poll for *The Guardian* found that 84 per cent of the population would prefer to forego a one or two pence cut in the basic rate of tax, as long as the money were to be spent on the NHS. This could be broken down into 93 per cent of Labour, and 73 per cent of Conservative voters who would forego the 1p tax cut, while 74 per cent of Labour, and 47 per cent of Conservative voters would forego the 2p tax cut. (*The Guardian*, March 14, 1988.) If we considered the long term change in the proportion wanting a tax cut, this fell steadily from a high of 37 per cent in 1979, to a low in September 1989 of a mere 9 per cent. The percentage of those wanting better services, even if it meant more taxes, rose from 37 per cent in 1979 to 70 per cent in 1989. (Ivor Crewe, in *Contemporary Record*, February 1990.)

From 1983 to 1993 there was a gradual decline in the percentage of people who wanted to maintain taxes and spending at their existing levels. This fell from 54 per cent to 29 per cent. At the same time, the percentage who wanted higher taxes and more spending rose from 43 to 63 per cent. As the report says, 'the call for higher taxes and more social spending is one of the consensual issues of British politics. Only the government and a reducing minority of the electorate appear nowadays to disagree'. (*British Social Attitudes; 1994*, p3.)

The study also said that we could not draw firm conclusions about public opinion because most questions had not been asked regularly over a period of time. 'But we do have one question asked first in 1985, then in 1990 and again in 1993. In 1985, just over one in five said that 'motorways and road-building' were 'the greatest' or 'the next greatest' threat to the British countryside. By 1990 this figure had risen to one-quarter and by 1993 it had grown further to one-third. This represents a substantial rise in people's awareness of links between road travel and damage to the countryside'. (*British Social Attitudes; 1994*, p16.)

Nationalisation is also seen as more attractive than it used to be. In 1973/74 there was a slim margin of support, with 5 per cent more people supporting than opposing nationalisation. By 1981 that margin had swung against, by a margin of 21 per cent, indicating considerable hostility. Yet by 1987 that margin of opposition had fallen to a mere 4 per cent against, a clear sign of reviving public recognition of the advantages to be gained from state-owned industries, and the problems brought by privatisation. And as mentioned above, there has been a growing hostility since then to water privatisation.

The probable cause of this growing antagonism to Tory policy is that as the public have seen the effects of these policies, they become aware that the opposite approach is more attractive, and would probably be more effective. To get inflation down to 5 per cent is a modest achievement; but is not a meaningful or admirable achievement, if made at the expense of 3 million unemployed. To control the loony left councils is fine; but not if it means poll tax, and drastic cuts in council services. Reining in the state-run monopolies may sound appealing; but not if the alternative is poisoned water, train crashes and closed hospital wards.

Although one would expect motorists to support the government's policy on building more motorways, in fact 85 per cent of those surveyed wanted more spending on public transport — and many of these wanted to see the money coming from a freeze on road spending! (*The Guardian*, July 26, 1991.) Thus motorists, who are also ordinary citizens when they get out of their cars, have realised that constant spending on motorways has not made driving any easier. But on the other hand, repeated cuts have made public transport more dangerous, more erratic, and less attractive, prompting more people to use the roads — thus creating even more congestion.

Thus, there is a clear consensus on a variety of issues, which would allow an opposition party to create a coherent, workable and popular platform. Most people would support tax increases, more spending on the NHS and welfare services generally, cuts in road spending, and less emphasis on the market philosophy. And those views form a pattern which fits well with the traditional values and policies that Labour have supported, which should make it even more attractive for Labour to take up such a policy stance.

The rise cited by Ivor Crewe, in the percentage of those wanting better services, from 37 per cent in 1979 to 70 per cent in 1989, is particularly striking, given one of the alleged reasons why Labour lost in 1992. Apart from the fact that Labour pegged the tax increase to affect incomes of £20,000 per year upwards, there is also the fact that their general level of competence was not highly regarded, as will be shown.

It seems likely that Labour could have created a consensus, even with the likelihood of higher taxes. The same seems to be true of the United States. It might be said that Clinton got in by promising to cut taxes for the middle classes, yet polls show a broad willingness to pay more tax. Asked if 'people like you' should make sacrifices to reduce the federal budget deficit, 53 per cent said yes, compared to 39 per cent saying no. And when asked if there should be higher taxes on incomes over $200,000, 79 per cent said yes while 18 per cent replied no. (*Time*, February 22, 1993.)

The response to the first question suggests a broad-based recognition that everyone must help with higher taxes. The more positive response to the second question implies a belief that the more affluent ought to shoulder a greater proportion of the tax burden. The evidence suggests that the British electorate take a similar view.

However, some sections of society have moved sharply towards Mrs Thatcher's ideology. 'That section of the middle class which includes shopkeepers, foremen, and the small self-employed businessmen — the petit bourgeois — has turned strongly to the party since she became leader'. (Dennis Kavanagh, *Thatcherism and British Politics*, p299). Thus, there is a danger of polarisation or conflict between the consensual groups, and the reactionary middle class.

But here is where the nature of consensus comes into play. It involves not merely agreement, but discussion. Where groups have directly opposing views, they should come together, and hammer out a compromise for the good of society in general. This should be particularly easy in this case, given the extent to which the business classes have suffered under the recession. It is clear to many people that the economy has been hit, not by world economic conditions, or by 'exceptional circumstances', but by the amazing incompetence of Lamont and Major. Using the same policies which were condemned by Kaldor in 1979, and which created the 1980-81 recession, unemployment and bankruptcies have reached record levels. A competent opposition party need merely point out that under Keynesian policies, middle class business people would be much better off.

It might be asked, if the Tory policies have become increasingly unattractive, then why did people vote for them in 1992? The answer must be found at least partly in Labour's lack of unity or competence, the lack of trust it inspires, the hostility that its relations with the unions engender, and the unappealing leaders it has had. It has also confused electoral success with policy correctness, and chosen to imitate the disastrous Conservative policies, rather than condemn them. This has put them in the unattractive position of being indistinguishable from the Tories, while at the same time unable to attack government policy convincingly. Thus, voters have not swung to the Tories because the Tories have been seen as the more attractive party. People vote Conservative because they are the less bad, the less frightening, the less untrustworthy of two incompetent, dishonest, dogma-ridden parties.

Whereas the unions helped Labour to lose the 1979 election, it managed to lose the 1983, 1987, and 1992 elections all by itself. It fought, and lost, the 1983 campaign on a manifesto that was primarily the creation of Tony Benn (Peter Jenkins, *Mrs Thatcher's Revolution*, p125). Yet with each lost election, the far left would cry that Labour's programme had not been *sufficiently* far left. This, despite the fact that every opinion poll suggested that extremism lost more votes than either the verbose leaders or the outdated policies.

The squabbling that broke out between left and right wings of the party seems especially silly given the availability of the evidence showing what the public would or would not like to vote for. Apart from the opinion polls, each election campaign was punctuated with detailed analyses of the voters' decisions, with one particularly good series coming from the American Enterprise Institute. Perhaps it was another example of the way in which only outsiders can understand what is going on.

One of the consistent themes in every election since 1979 is the fact that voters are strongly hostile to both left-wing extremism and trade unions. Both can be objected to on a purely democratic basis. For example, in any rational system, there would be checks and balances to preserve democracy; no two institutions could be allowed to overlap. Thus, in the United States the executive, the legislature and the judiciary are kept separate.

In Britain they are not. The most striking example of this is the Lord Chancellor, who holds office in all three branches of government. And this lack of democratic control is what enables the Lord Chancellor to make cuts in the legal aid system. These cuts will save £43 million, small change by the standards of a national government, yet they will affect the welfare of 12 million people who lose entitlement to legal aid. If Britain had the constitutional separation that any civilised country has a right to expect, such cuts would never have got beyond the Cabinet Office. If policy was judged in terms of cost-effectiveness, this particular blunder would never have left the cabinet sub-committee.

The same separation of functions should apply to the Labour Party and the unions. The only justification for the existing links seems to be the fact that the Labour Party is the child of the unions; and for some reason it wishes to be tied to its parent for the rest of its life. Thus, we have people like Tony Benn writing of the party, 'based as it has always been, on politically active trade unionism'. (*The Guardian*, January 7, 1993.) Other than Labour's need for funds, there is no valid reason whatsoever why it should be welded for the rest of time to its unruly parent.

Labour's link with the unions is not as offensive or as economically damaging as the Tories' automatic deference to business and the City. However, that is not the issue. Its electoral impact alone is sufficient reason to reappraise the relationship, while the political and constitutional implications demand instant severance of links. Voters are justified in not trusting a Labour Party which twists its policies to the pleas of unions. It is interesting to compare this to the separation of church and state. In his study of the United States, de Tocqueville says that the reason for the strength of religion in America was its separation from the state. 'The church cannot share the temporal power of the state without being the object of a portion of that animosity which the latter excites'. (Alexis de Tocqueville, *Democracy in America*, pp319-320, 321-322).

Most importantly, many critics on the broad left have often complained about the Tories' more than generous funding from big business. How can Labour ever comment on the impact of that funding on democratic processes, when they themselves are supported by the unions? It could be said that at least Labour's funding is open to public scrutiny. But on the other hand, perhaps such funding should not be allowed in principle.

The matter of trust could not be helped by the thesis which lay behind 'Kinnock's leadership throughout, namely that the Labour Party could be sold to the electorate rewrapped but without fundamental change of content'. (Peter Jenkins, *Mrs Thatcher's Revolution*, p343.) In other words, a public relations exercise that did nothing to remove all the old policies to which many voters were objecting. The 1983 Manifesto had been called 'the longest suicide note in history'. 'Kinnock had seen to it that the 1987 Manifesto was a short list of generalities' (op. cit., p343). It spoke of nationalisation, but without actually using the word, and it was seen as an attempt to pull the wool over voters' eyes. This might have been a dim memory by 1992, but Labour had done nothing in the intervening years — or campaigns — to make themselves more attractive.

Peter Abell, Professor of Sociology at the London School of Economics, says that 'Labour doesn't have much of a clue as to what to do. People can see this and sense this, which in part accounts for their despondency'. (*Time*, March 15, 1993.) The incumbents may be unattractive and untrustworthy, but at least they give the impression of knowing what has to be done.

Blinded by its ideology, and by the electoral success of the Tories, Labour has ignored the consensus, and ignored the voters' unspoken cries for help. There is not even the plea in mitigation that we can blame the party leader, and absolve everyone else, although this is an extremely attractive option to many Labour supporters. Yes, it might be said that Kinnock was more interested in his career than in the welfare of 58 million people. And Tony Blair does not know which way to turn — except right. But how many Labour MPs were fully active in their constituencies? How many MPs or candidates in marginal seats were fully informed on the local impact of national policies? And why was it not until September 1992 that Labour finally started to attack the years of Conservative policies that had brought recession, unemployment and devaluation?

The first two questions can be answered easily — very few. Austin Mitchell suggests that there have been 'several notorious examples among MPs too old, too indolent or too well cushioned by a huge majority to give their constituencies and their party the kind of attention more and more [voters] were coming to expect'. (Austin Mitchell, *Four Years in the Death of the Labour Party*, p38.)

The answer to the third is a combination of left-wing extremism and political short-termism. Because the party is dependent on local activists, it has had to give them a significant role in policy-making. Mitchell describes them as coming from the 'wilder shores of Labour', often from rough hinterlands where Marxism-Leninism is still the creed (p25). Such people accept no ideology but the centralised state, and Clause IV. Voters also find the links between Labour and the unions to be unacceptable. But again, Labour is dependent on the unions for its finance.

One might say that such MPs saw the voters' ideas as being too far to the right. Perhaps they wouldn't want to appeal to any consensus that would have capital punishment or immigration controls as part of its platform, while not including nationalisation. Instead, MPs wanted Tony Benn's ideas, or the Alternative Economic Strategy of Sam Aaronovitch, with its centralisation and state ownership. But this implies the same imposition of policy, out of office, as is being conducted by the Tories, in office. We have a choice between a party that ignores popular opinion, and a party that will listen to it, as long as it is Marxist, pro-nationalisation, and pro-nuclear disarmament. This is neither consensus nor democracy. The only change under Tony Blair was that it became, any policy as long as it is watered-down Toryism. The creation of a consensus should not only imply a compromise between the dominant parties, but also between the electorate and the parties.

With the embarrassing exception of a round-Britain Public Relations tour, party leaders have completely ignored popular opinion. If Britain is to avoid spiralling into total decline, one of the major parties has to start promoting, and applying, sensible, workable policies. By a narrow margin, Labour is the party most likely to be in a position to do that. But if it declines any further, some other party, probably the Liberal Democrats, will happily take the spotlight, the second place, or even the first place, and maybe they will apply consensus politics.

One could argue that the parties create a consensus. For example, the Tories have created a new consensus in which privatisation, free markets and the minimal state are part of a new economic settlement. On the other hand, poll evidence suggests that Conservative policies are actually deeply unpopular, as well as being socially damaging. There has to be a limit to which parties create consensus, simply because they may be wrong in their ideas. The principle of liberal democracy demands that they do not have the right to take persuasion into the realms of imposition.

Labour is paying the price for ignoring the consensus, as any political party is likely to do. Election to high office is an implicit contract in which the party offers a set of policies, and the voters accept. If MPs choose to offer policies that they know — or should know, if they have any sense whatsoever — will be refused, they have only themselves to blame if they lose the election. The Conservatives have skilfully managed to evade this variant of electoral karma, but Labour have not been so fortunate.

Labour politicians — and supporters — have become skilled at finding reasons to ignore opinion polls. These range from asking why they should listen to polls of Tory voters, to the subtle suggestion that voters are irrational, and therefore not worth listening to. The fact that the electorate chose to reject Labour in the obviously 'safe' election of 1992, is cited as perfect proof of irrationality. Yet opinion polls had detected this swing prior to the actual ballot; so it was not totally unexpected. The real question is, why did the swing occur?

The Labour Party and its supporters must accept a large degree of responsibility for the Thatcherite years, for demanding to impose their ideology on the policy-making process, and refusing to listen to popular opinion. By doing so, they made a major contribution towards losing four elections for Labour. They have converted Labour from being a party that cares, to being a party torn between the best career move, and its nineteenth-century origins. Voters are known to be repelled by some of the outmoded ideology; for Labour to add blatant self-interest, and Tory policies, merely increases the electoral disadvantage.

The refusal to listen to opinion polls on what is, or is not, attractive to voters has moved beyond mere determination. By allowing the Tories in time after time, it has become offensive. The failure to act in a way that the voters want must be a reflection on party members' morality. Certainly, many voters see Labour as untrustworthy and dishonest (*The Guardian*, January 5, 1993). A large part of this must be due to the logical contortions that Labour politicians have to engage in to avoid recognising the validity of voters' views. For example, we have Roy Hattersley arguing that the Tories keep winning elections because of their certainty. He then writes that 'ideological certainty requires continued belief in the traditional principles of socialism'. (*The Independent*, January 11, 1989.) Hattersley seeks to impose socialism, even if there is no evidence for its validity or popularity. One has to assume that perhaps he does not care if socialism is valid or popular.

Yet a consensus could be created, based on the values and goals that both voters and Labour share. It is not a matter of Labour persuading the voters that it is correct, but of listening openly to the opinions of others. Simply going by published opinion polls, we can tell that such a consensus would include a moderate but controlled level of nationalisation, a rise in the level of taxation, paralleled by an increase in welfare spending, and greater government involvement in the economy.

If Labour politicians are so dogmatic in their correctness that they insist on creating their policy platform, or they will leave the stage, then they deserve to lose. It is time that the trade unions re-appraised their investment in a party that cannot win an election, and does not deserve to. Perhaps the Liberals or the Green Party would offer a more rewarding investment, one that could win elections, and would do just as much for the average worker as any party that sprang out of the unions. There comes a time when origins are irrelevant; sentimental attachments don't bring job security. Only a party that can win elections can offer the goodies.

It might be argued that the consensus created by collecting different aspects of public opinion would be no more than a rag-bag of ideas, a mish-mash of unrelated policies. Yet a brief consideration of opinion surveys shows that this is not the case. The range of ideas covers a very comprehensive welfare state, with approval for more public spending, better public transport, better health care and improved education, and greater equality. It is very similar to the Labour Party's post-war policy platform, and forms a more coherent programme than anything that Labour has offered since 1979. And its very coherence is a major argument in favour of this procedure.

Some might object to the dilettante way in which the programme was put together, like a shopper going through the pick'n'mix section. But is this really relevant? Is not the real failure the fact that an obvious, common-sense approach has to be laid out like a blueprint before those on the left will accept their moral obligation to carry out a platform that the voters want?

Apart from which, given the coherence, the theme of welfare, unity and community that runs through the opinion polls like a bright thread, there is a natural structure to the platform. It can create a manifesto that any Labour candidate can treat as the basis for a crusade. It is not merely coherent; it is the natural convergence of consensus and practicality.

Only by governing by agreement can Britain avoid the alienation and apathy that leads to fascism, or the policy vacuum that leads to collapse. And only if we govern in the interests of the entire population can we say that the government has legitimacy. A regime that only looks after the welfare of a minority is tyranny.

Galbraith has argued that the middle classes are in alliance against the poor and the underclass. The affluent sections of society do not need access to state provision of health, education and other social services, therefore they have no interest in paying taxes for these things. And they are not concerned about the impact of cuts in state provision on the poorer members of society. Galbraith's argument is that the wealthier groups will remain unconcerned, until the social disruption caused by the poor impacts on the lives of the rich.

However, one would have thought that the United States had reached the point where wealthy taxpayers were aware of the impact that federal budget cuts had on the poor. Many parts of American cities are no-go areas, drivers must keep their car doors locked at all times, and crime levels are at all-time highs. There are suburbs in the US that have graduated from middle-class ghettoes to walled fortresses, patrolled by guards, with security cameras, and entrance only by invitation. Yet the affluent members of society still do not recognise any link between government spending cuts, and the deteriorating life-styles of the poor. This raises the question of which factors encourage — or prevent — the middle classes realising their relationship to the poor.

Many goods and services are provided more cheaply, because unskilled, low paid workers help to provide them. And of course, taxes can be lowered if welfare benefits for the poor can be reduced. But equally, the quality of life in a society which exploits its weaker members can become intolerable, even for the wealthy. The point at which people react against such a system depends on their awareness of the interdependence, which in turn depends on the quality of education, and the analyses given by politicians. Smooth Tory MPs might deny the causal link between tax cuts and crime, but a genuinely caring party could point out the relationship, and establish the need for alternative policies.

The wealthy need to be made aware of the fact that they do not greatly benefit from their tax reductions, because by shifting wealth away from others, they impoverish the entire country. Their income will be a larger proportion of a shrinking cake. And if there is a gain for any given individual, it may be outweighed by the loss of quality of life. In addition, every member of society needs to realise that they have an obligation to put into society, according to the advantage they have gained from membership. Great wealth and luxury cannot be a person's right, without any corresponding responsibility. The citizen has a duty to return to society some payment for the gains they have received. The rich must be made aware of their gain reciprocity; their implicit contract places an obligation on them to contribute financially to society. Surely, they cannot expect to continue drawing enormous quantities of wealth from society, without giving something in return.

This process could be called gain reciprocity. Just as Hobbes saw us entering an implicit contract with the state, in order to gain security, so it can be argued that there is an entitlement for the state to ask for certain returns in exchange for the other rewards of social membership.

Once again, we have a congruence between the morally necessary and the socially efficient, between society and the individual. To leave a large percentage of the population in poverty, with poor housing, second-rate education, and low paid jobs, is morally unjust. It is offensive that a wealthy nation should allow one part of its population to live in great wealth, while others live in squalor.

But also, it is not rational administration that the affluent should try to save pennies on their tax bill, while losing immeasurably in both their quality of life, and in compensatory spending. As well as being too scared to live normal lives, the wealthy middle classes, in both Britain and the United States, have to buy all sorts of defensive devices to protect themselves and their homes. Their fear is a direct result of the society they have helped to create, but they are no better off financially, for all the tax savings they are alleged to have sought. There should be no difficulty in persuading them that in the long-term, higher taxes could improve both the quality of their life, and their material standard of living.

Otherwise, there is a danger that the exploitation of the poor will continue for years. The level of inequality will increase, while the quality of life will deteriorate. The rich would move to isolated ghettoes of affluence, while the poor would be forced to try anything which allowed them to survive. A regime that only looks after the interests of the minority may drag the country down into chaos or civil war. At best, conflicting interest groups will compete so forcefully for society's goods that no one makes any real gains.

This is roughly the situation which has prevailed in Britain for the last fifty years. Management and unions have both felt entitled to take out of the company the maximum rewards possible, while generous payments have continued to be made to shareholders, even when the company's profits did not warrant this. As a result, funding has been squeezed in the one area where there is no constituency fighting for it — investment.

Thus, on the one hand, the competitiveness of industry declines, while on the other, different sectors of society become opposing forces, enemies. It is a war in which there are short-term gains, as there were for the unions in the 1960s and 70s, and for business in the 1980s. But neither side wins the long-term war. The country as a whole loses, therefore all combatants lose. To expect any other outcome is unrealistic.

If we look at countries where consensus has existed, such as Denmark, Sweden or Austria, we can see how it has had a beneficial impact on society. We have to be careful with such an approach, as Partridge has pointed out. There is a danger of taking social stability or success as evidence that consensus exists, and then arguing that consensus was the factor which created that stability. To avoid this, one should look only at countries where the politicians or economists of that country have stated that they have created, or intend to create, a consensual approach to policy. Second, evidence of success must come from economic factors, or aspects of social behaviour which are markedly better than those of Britain.

To begin with, we can consider Germany, which in line with Olson's thesis, was completely re-structured after the second world war. This re-structuring was imposed on Germany by the major powers, and included 'administrative decentralisation, economic decentralisation, and industrial disarmament'. (Carlo M. Cipolla (ed.), *Contemporary Economies*, p208.)

When Germany's own politicians took over running the economy, there was much discussion of the type of economic policy that was appropriate. The planned system imposed by the Nazis was seen as the antithesis of freedom, and a market economy became by far the most attractive proposition. Following the discussion, 'the outcome was a consensus philosophy' called the *soziale Marktwirtschaft*, which has been translated as the social market economy. (Graham Hallett, *The Social Economy of West Germany*, p17.) This phrase was coined by Professor A. Müller-Armack, who argued 'that individuals are not merely isolated consumers in a market system, but are also members of social, economic and political groups whose interests need to be represented and reconciled, with as much devolution of decision-making as possible'. (Hallett, p21.)

Thus, there was the consensus of agreement, where policies would only be applied if everyone accepted them. This eliminates the maverick policy-maker who simply imposes his or her opinions on a nation, as Mrs Thatcher did in Britain, and Kohl did with German unification. In addition, we see consensus as the reconciler of opposing needs, so that where the interests of different groups clash, a compromise can be arranged so that both parties gain.

The benefits of West Germany's *soziale Marktwirtschaft* can be seen in its effects. Throughout the 1950s and 60s, the German economy was hailed as the *Wirtschaftswunder*, the miracle economy. Growth was high, unemployment was low, and standards of living were impressive. Yet this was combined with low inflation and an excellent state welfare system. Indeed, in the immediate post-war period, growth was phenomenal. 'In the four years between mid-1948 and mid-1952, the German GNP rose nominally by over 80%, by 67% in real terms, while the industrial production increased by 110% from the second half of 1948 to the corresponding period in 1952'. (Carlo M. Cipolla (ed.), *Contemporary Economies*, p221.)

It might be argued that Germany had a lot of advantages in the post-war era, apart from the re-structuring. There was Marshall Aid, millions of dollars given or lent by a generous United States, trying to ensure that while democracy thrived, markets grew. Then there was the massive outflow of three million migrants from the former East Germany, most of them highly skilled, young and educated (see Cipolla, p214). And arguably the most important, the high levels of investment, with 'gross investment levels of 20 to 24% of the GNP between 1949 and 1953-4'. (Cipolla. p222.) And it has also been suggested that the average worker puts far more effort into their work than their British counterpart.

However, Marshall Aid went to most of Europe, including Britain, so we can regard that as assisting in Germany's recovery, but not explaining its economic miracle. It has been suggested that one cause of Germany's success is the hard-working workforce. Cipolla accepts that this no doubt helped, but rejects the idea that the German worker was in any way exceptional, or that their behaviour was some sort of explanation of the economic miracle. It has been pointed out by other writers that hard-working employees could explain Germany's advantage, but not its growth; to rely on the 'hard work' factor, one would have to assume that the workers put in more effort every year.

However, there is no doubt that the extremely high levels of investment, coupled with the excellent general education and the high level of training, played a major role in the post-war recovery. Germany has put more money into capital investment, research, design, and quality than Britain has, with the inevitable result that German products are cheaper, better and often more stylish.

One might argue that Germany, like Japan, has paid the price socially for its industrial efficiency. Both countries have created a nation of dedicated workers, who have the loyalty, the work ethic and the materialism needed for a good consumer society. In neither country, least of all in Japan, can one say that people receive a good liberal education. Although we may admire the economic success of these countries, we may not wish to copy all aspects of their society.

Germany also provides an example of how the loss of consensus can wreak terrible havoc on a nation. One aspect of consensus is the existence of agreement between the various groups, requiring for example, that politicians tell voters the truth about policy choices. These can then be discussed — which is the process aspect of consensus — and then a new balance reached. In 1990, with German unification looming, Chancellor Helmut Kohl offered the East Germans a one-for-one Ostmark-Deutschmark exchange rate. This was a deliberately generous incentive, designed to make unification all the more attractive.

The Bundesbank, West Germany's supposedly independent central bank, described the decision as 'purely political', and the head of the Bundesbank subsequently resigned in protest. Chancellor Kohl also promised the West Germans that there would be no tax increases, or spending cuts, to finance unification, while promising the East Germans that they would soon be enjoying Western living standards.

None of this was possible, and no sensible person would have believed these goals could be achieved. East Germany's industry had around fifty years of under-investment to make up for, with inefficient factories, services, transport and communications. The environment had been abused to an extent that was not merely ugly, but unhealthy. In essence, the entire infrastructure of the nation had to be replaced. It had to be dragged from the 1930s into the 1990s. For Kohl to say that this could be done in a short time, and without extra taxes or cuts in spending, was simply unrealistic.

By July 1991, Kohl was ready to admit that he had underestimated the problems of rebuilding the former East Germany's economy. At his party's congress just over a year later, his apology was more open. 'He warned his party executive that he would not go down in history as the leader who had lied twice' (*The Guardian*, October 27, 1992). Yet he was still unable to state explicitly the need for tax increases, talking only of 'revenue enhancement'.

But by this time, the failure of Kohl's unification programme was plain to see. Net public transfers to the east were expected to reach DM 180 billion, or about 6.5 per cent of GNP. This was partly paid for by extra income taxes and consumer taxes; the income component was known as the 'solidarity surcharge'. But it was not enough to cover the massive costs of unification, so the Bonn government was forced to borrow heavily — thus putting up European interest rates. Public debt was expected to reach DM 1.5 trillion by 1995.

Kohl also broke consensus with the GDR, the old East Germany. Many East Germans did not want unification, and if they did, would often have preferred a more organised version of the GDR. East Germany was at least attempting to create an enlightened society, even if some of its leaders lived in excessive luxury. It offered child care for workers, maternity benefits, and universal availability of housing. Brought up in such an environment, many hoped for a discussion of the directions in which Germany as a whole could go. At the very least, they wanted discussion of which developments would be appropriate. What they got was instant unregulated market forces, and total indifference from Bonn.

West German companies were buying up eastern supermarket chains, and then supplying them from western factories. Other one-time state-owned companies were simply closed down, through lack of demand. The result was inevitable. Unemployment in the eastern region, officially 1.3 million, may actually have reached 3.3 million. By 1991 unemployment had soared to 50 per cent, although by 1992, it was down to a more manageable 15.5 per cent. Thus, not only were Kohl's predictions totally unrealistic, but having initiated the unification process, he failed to manage it in a way that would be best for the population of east Germany.

For east and west Germans, unification has not been the glowing vision they were promised, and one obvious result has been to blame Helmut Kohl. Even the German president, speaking at the official celebration of German unity, said that the affluence promised by the mid-1990s was 'too big a promise to be credible' (*The Observer*, October 4, 1992). Quite explicit promises were broken, and the implied duties of leaders to listen and be accountable were totally ignored. Voters were unimpressed, and opinion polls found that they were less likely to trust the federal government or the political parties than they were to trust the media. The breach of the consensus had caused an inevitable distrust of politicians.

But the most disturbing result has been the swing to the right. This has not been as significant in numerical terms as might have been thought. A 1990 survey estimated that 32,300 Germans belonged to far-right organisations. By 1992, this had risen to 40,000. It is quite likely that as federal government crackdowns on illegal parties intensify, fewer right-wingers will be willing to admit to membership. But what is quite clear is that the level of violence has increased. The number of attacks by right-wingers has increased, and a blatantly racist trend has been clearly visible in those attacks. The increase in unemployment may be part of the explanation for the growing violence, but political cynicism must also play a role.

Even more worrying, the political influence of the right has grown out of all proportion to its apparent numbers. The violence carried out by small gangs of skinheads is supported by large numbers of Germany's more soberly dressed burghers. Hostility to Turkish and Arab immigrants is acted out by youngsters in combat jackets, but felt by millions. Because of this, Bonn is more likely to see the immigrants as the problem than the thugs. Indeed, it took Kohl two years to publicly recognise that there was a problem of racial violence. Being vulnerable on his failings with economic policy, Kohl bowed to strong feelings on racial matters.

Senior Bonn politicians do not want to alienate voters by deploying 'excessive' force against the extremists, in case the mainstream parties lose votes in the next election. Kohl's abuse of the consensus has now led Germany to the point where fundamental political attitudes might change very radically indeed. Tampering with a nation's consensus can unleash forces that can destroy the fabric of society. In two years Germany went from being the locomotive economy of Europe to being plunged into an echo of the 1930s, with racism and recession on the rise.

Not that Kohl's abuse of consensus alone created this. It was the particular form of policy incompetence, combined with the way in which it was carried out. However, had Kohl sought a consensual policy-making process, none of this would have happened. The process of discussion and analysis would have brought out the faults of Kohl's suggested plan.

If we view consensus as a method of political decision-making, we can see that it allows everyone the right to express their opinion. In an open debate of that sort, some opinions would be seen to be unfounded, or irrational. The more informed and reasonable views would tend to get a better hearing. This is not to say that democracy and discussion ensure that the correct view always triumphs; past elections have shown that is not the case. But in an informed and educated society, the functioning of consensus will tend to lead to the better choices.

If in addition, the society is a liberal democracy, such a government will, for the good of the people, seek to create an educated and informed populace. It will seek to maximise their well-being, and offer them an open, accountable and participative political system. This in turn will encourage mature and rational decision-making. As long as the electorate maintains their control over the body politic, it will provide the nearest there can be to the ideal society; the liberal democracy.

Yet we have seen that not only is Britain not a liberal democracy; it is not even a genuine democracy. It is neither open, nor accountable, nor participative. The post-1979 Conservative governments have been democratic only in the least important of the three possible definitions: the 'one person, one vote' structure. And far from society being based on consensus, the Thatcherites have actually ignored the consensus. They have deliberately ignored the opinions and wishes of the population.

In the absence of formal democratic processes, one can sometimes say that at least the outcomes are socially beneficial, as for example in Japan or Singapore. Up until recently, the Japanese system has been inherently biased against town dwellers and parties of the left, and towards rural voters. While in Singapore there is something close to dictatorship. In Britain, the process is largely undemocratic, while the outcomes are without any redeeming features whatsoever. We lack the democratic processes, and lack the beneficial outcomes. We have actually regressed since the middle of the century, both socially and economically.

The time is long overdue for all political parties to recognise the need for democracy, in the fullest sense. For politicians to pretend that we are in some way a civilised society, while we are surrounded by all the manifestations of inequity and injustice, is hypocrisy in the extreme.

5

The toolbox of science

For Mrs Thatcher, her carefully fabricated policy framework was so far beyond dispute that she was able to say about it, 'There is no alternative'. In fact, such was her conviction, or her need to appear convinced, that she was able to say it over and over again, until it became one of the political catchphrases of the 1980s. Yet as mentioned in Chapter 2, the 1979 Conservative manifesto had various logical flaws 'masquerading as empirical laws'. (Lord Kaldor, *The Economic Consequences of Mrs Thatcher*, p53.)

Karl Marx also believed that his writings had the stamp of infallibility, and referred to the various laws he had discovered, most of which have been exhaustively analysed, but with no actual proof.

Some types of personality, especially the authoritarian ones, need absolute certainty in their lives. The authoritarian personality is noted for its need for rules, rigidity and totality. The aura of science reassures the ideologue that they genuinely wield truth, and not some weak imitation. Perhaps they are not able to have faith in their beliefs without this fragile reassurance, as they more than anyone are aware of the flaws in their belief system.

The purpose of this chapter is to set out the rules necessary to ensure that the social theory being considered is not merely a morass of words, a hotch-potch of shallow, but emotionally dazzling ideas. If we are to rule people's lives with our policies, we must be able to put forward some evidence that people will benefit.

In seeking to improve society, it is not enough to list its faults; a list by itself gives us nothing. We need to put our facts into some sort of structure, locating the relationships between the facts within some explanatory theory. There must be a methodology, a pattern to one's investigation that puts the ideas into a scientific framework, so that one is dealing with predictable effects for policy.

This is not to say that one's analysis will lead to absolute proof, because in science there is no such thing as absolute proof. According to Nobel-prize winning nuclear physicist Richard Feynman, science is concerned with what is more likely, or less likely.

In the absence of a methodology, one might as well be writing fiction, and many writers have done just that. Thomas More's *Utopia* was fiction, as was an ideal society briefly mentioned by Aldous Huxley in *Brave New World.* But the work of Marx and Engels, supposedly scientific, was in reality no more than description. Marx endlessly calculated the amount of surplus value, as if repetition would prove its existence, despite his use of purely hypothetical examples. And the ideal future society postulated by Marx had insufficient evidence for an objective reader to have more than a vague idea of what he was proposing.

Yet for some reason, Marx felt that he had created the scientific study of society. Presumably he had not read Hobbes' *Leviathan.* This had been published two hundred years earlier, in 1651, and may have been overlooked by Marx. Hobbes admired the scientific laws of motion and inertia that Galileo developed, and sought to apply to society a similar set of laws.

The Marxist slogan, 'The point of philosophy is to change the world', is, as with so much from that ideology, a simplification. The point of any given social science — which is what Marx meant when using the word 'philosophy' — is to understand the world. When we have an understanding, we know what needs to be improved, and how it can be done.

This was one of the more notable failings of Marxism — that Marx did not use a methodology, so that his arguments could not be linked coherently to his philosophy. He claimed that his theory was scientific, but it failed at the most fundamental level to achieve this. Marx established no clear link between nineteenth-century problems and the cure he proposed; therefore, there was no evidence that his solution would cure the ills of that society.

In fact, there was not the slightest logical connection between the failings of capitalism, and the proposals that Marx put forward. Worse, there was no relationship between the type of world he wished to create, and the manner in which he proposed achieving that goal. He talked about exploitation of the working class, and then suggested a totally centralised state. There is nothing more likely to ensure the subservience of the populace than an all-powerful state. Marx's failure to recognise this is a major flaw in his ideology. His failure to link goals with methods, or faults with cure, means that there is no logical support for many of his arguments.

Having failed to establish even a basic connection, clearly Marx did not even get to the next stage, which is how to locate the evidence that is needed. We must collate the facts, putting them into categories, and seek some causal relationship linking them. But to have a cause supposes either evidence of the cause, or a theory suggesting such a link. Yet the prior existence of a theory may imply bias, while the absence of a theory puts the link in question. One may have any quantity of facts; but if one cannot give coherent reasons explaining how the facts are linked, then the facts in isolation are meaningless.

Later writers such as Pareto, Milton Friedman and Mancur Olson also sought to develop a methodology. Friedman and Olson sought to create a scientific basis for their analyses, demonstrating that their approach was credible. However, Pareto, like Marx, sought to emulate the absolute certainty of the physical sciences, which is an inapprpriate goal for any social study. (Peter Winch, *The Idea of Social Science and its Relation to Philosophy.*)

In fact, it is not possible for a social science to achieve the same level of proof as the physical sciences. In studying society, there are few laws, if any. The behaviour of individuals or masses varies from one situation to another, depending on the influence of external factors, many of which are impossible to measure. Therefore, one cannot talk about laws in the same way as an engineer or physicist can; but undeniably, there are rules. However, in some areas of the physical sciences, such as quantum mechanics or particle physics, one talks about probability rather than certainty. It is ironic that some academics in the social sciences have tried to claim absolute proof, just as the so-called hard sciences were surrendering the idea.

Any valid ideology would be able to start its analysis by describing its ultimate goal — the morals it will be based on, or the welfare gains it will bring. Thatcherites cannot do this honestly because their hidden agenda is to benefit the rich, to give to those who already have. They wish to empower the powerful, and impoverish the poor. Along the way, they wish to destroy all the enemies of the state, a classical ingredient of fascism. Usually, the enemy is external, and a war can be conducted to unite the people and defeat the foe. Under Thatcherism, the enemy has included trade unions, the Greater London Council, the miners, the television companies, and most especially, the BBC.

As an ideology, 'destroy the enemies of the state' is not all that heart-warming, especially if the nation is attacking its own citizens. Had the Tories announced this as their plan, they would not have won so many elections. But of course, they would not have made such an announcement. It is in the nature of this campaign for the attacks to be carried out step by step, with elaborate justification for each attack, until the last battle has taken place.

The New Right paint a different picture, claiming a necessity for each act of legislation. It has to be done to cut inflation, remove over-staffing, eliminate out-dated work practices, or to bring workers' pay down to the market level. There is always a carefully argued reason, with the depth of analysis needed for a one minute sound-bite on News At Ten. But underneath the polished phrases, there is no truth, no evidence to show the value of the theories, so that ultimately, they are worthless.

Neither Thatcherites nor Marxists have created a methodology for their ideas, although both share a similar approach, which suggests what their scientific method is. Both ideologies analyse their principles verbally, linking one concept to another with elaborate reasoning. For example, they will argue a relationship between incentives and tax levels, or between ownership and production. The argument will be thorough, even more than thorough, so that the reader feels that every possible stone has not only been turned, but upended and sandblasted.

The reader understandably feels, it must be right, it has covered every possibility. In fact, the purely verbal approach allows the devious to cover up a multitude of illogical sins. Thus, one can analyse the link between tax rates and savings, with the implication that the subject is income tax. Halfway through the argument, one can change tack onto savings taxes, make a point that savings taxes affect investment, and then having established that idea, make it apply to income taxes.

Indeed, purely verbal reasoning allows one to twist facts, twist words, ignore definitions, introduce half-truths, and throw in a powerful emotional argument as a clincher. Indeed, persuasive communication is nowadays a separate field of literary study. One uses such words as 'obviously' or 'naturally', or reasonable phrases like 'we cannot go back to the past', or 'society must progress'. This allows the skilled communicator to present the opposition as old-fashioned, and themselves as modern, up to date — and to hell with the exact rights or wrongs of each alternative!

The fact that many words have multiple or vague meanings allows one to make a variety of arguments, taking advantage of the vagueness. For example, if one was writing about British culture, working class culture, middle class culture and culture in the literary or artistic sense, one could skip over the range of meanings in order to make a general point about 'culture'.

An American writer, describing the difficult position in which large companies find themselves, writes, 'Once the basic requirements of life have been generally met, then the way in which consumers will channel their purchases is quite unpredictable'. (Clare E. Griffin, from Howard D. Marshall (ed.), *Business and Government*, p98-99.)

On a first reading, this sounds perfectly reasonable. But how does one define the word 'basic'? Products like radios, televisions, video recorders and CD players once seemed like technological miracles. Now, no home is complete without them. Does the writer's definition of 'basic' cover such modern consumer goods, or does it stop at food, clothing and shelter? Or perhaps telephones, central heating and a car? Also, what do we mean by 'unpredictable'? In the context in which the word was used, it was intended to convey that the consumers' choices were so uncertain that companies lived in permanent fear of being swamped with unsold goods. In fact, the mild fluctuations in sales are rarely significant.

However, misrepresenting the beliefs of the opposition is where one can make full use of distortion, half-truth, and the many wonderful games one can play with words. It is always possible to present any argument in a negative light, using emotive language, making unfair comparisons, or by some similar means. One can present nationalisation as Stalinist, the poor as scroungers, and progressive taxation as motivated by envy. In ordinary conversation, people often come out with gross abuses of logic. And as the conversation flashes past us, we usually fail to pick up even the wilder excesses, often because we are not sure exactly what was wrong with each statement. Watching politicians on television, we do not even have the chance to challenge them.

Some speakers are particularly adept at creating emotive phrases that sound good in a speech. We understand instinctively what the person is saying, perhaps because the turn of phrase is at just the right angle for our liking. Yet if examined in the cold light of an early-morning policy conference, the words have all the conviction of a used car salesman. For example, Michael Heseltine promised that as Imperial Grand Vizier of the DTI he would intervene before breakfast, before lunch and before tea. This graphically pre-prandial phrase went down well with the Tory listeners. But its factual content was zero.

And as mentioned in Chapter 3, the ideology of the market has given way to selected phrases, such as 'level playing field'. Being vague, it can be used in any context, for or against any policy. It has connotations of fairness, so whatever decision is made can be presented as a fair one. And it takes for granted the actual condition of the playing field, allowing speakers to disregard gross inequities. The policy which ministers criticise is presented as the real threat to fairness.

Also, with most arguments one has the ability to set the agenda, setting out what are the important issues, and which are the key causes. But in a purely verbal analysis this agenda-setting is less obtrusive, and easier to cover up. For example, a politician talking about economic policy might say they don't want to get into ideological debates, and thereby avoid all discussion of poverty, or inequality. Or a judge or school head may say that they cannot talk about individual cases, and thus avoid talking about a case where they were obviously in the wrong.

The legal profession use this ability to set the agenda to impose their own view of society on those appearing in front of the court. For example, High Court Judge Rose Heilbron argues that a woman's sexual experience with various partners is 'indicative neither of untruthfulness nor of a general willingness to consent'. Yet the Court of Appeal takes the view that if a woman has had a varied sex life, she may either be a liar, or may have consented to what she alleges was rape. In this way, the Court of Appeal makes the rape victim's past relationships part of the court's agenda in determining the guilt of the rapist. (Jennifer Temkin in *The Guardian*, December 29, 1992. Temkin is Professor of Law at the University of Sussex.)

A more worrying example is the trend of research in the United States into the causes of crime. Most academics agree that poverty and social factors are a large causal component of crime; therefore, cure the social problems, reduce the crime. The American approach is to identify those youngsters who probably will be criminals, and treat them with drugs. A secondary implication is that all the other youngsters suffering a poor home environment can be ignored. Thus, the rationale of this approach is probably wrong, while the eventual application will be immoral.

Objective research papers tend to look at a wide range of factors, for example, Lord Kaldor's study of the money supply, which also looked at bank lending. Quoting such research could open up the analysis more than a New Right thinker might wish. But by sticking to 'common sense', and what masquerades as logic, a writer can give the impression of covering a subject comprehensively. The New Right also avoid the open-ended method by starting off with a clear idea of what they wish to prove. They then confine themselves to looking only at factors which relate to their chosen theory.

The Tories, and their academic supporters, have created a very credible agenda. It appears to be informed by what has failed in the past, and what we therefore know to be practical. But it is based in a very limited area of economics, one which is almost entirely theoretical, and which ignores social and psychological factors.

Ideally, political parties should have to stand up before the electorate and explain their platform in detail. The Conservatives associated with Mrs Thatcher in 1979 could not have done this, and had to maintain a hidden agenda. They could not have described their real agenda in detail, given the democratic consensus of that time. In a fascist society there would be no difficulty in presenting a fascist programme. But in the Britain of the 1980s and 90s, propaganda and obfuscation are an essential component. Not only is there no scientific justification, no methodology validating New Right policies, but the hidden agenda means that there is no truth either. As we have seen in Chapter 3, the average person is worse off under Thatcherism, and this is not what governments are supposed to do.

For this author, there is no problem. All the components of this study revolve around the wish to improve the well-being of the individual, and to allow the individual greater control over their own lives. To do this requires giving more political power to people, giving them more access to the corridors of power, and giving them more knowledge of how decision-making is carried out. If one is going to talk about increasing choice, it can only add to people's welfare if one is going to improve the quality or number of the options available. To add underfunded options to a previously high-quality range is not improving the choice available.

The one limit that does need to be mentioned is that the individual's freedom of action must be constrained by its impact on others. On an everyday level, some people need to be prevented from hitting or attacking others. Some abuse the right of free expression, and utter verbal abuse or threats. At a mass level, we have to obey the operating laws of society, and make our contribution to its continued operation.

However, when people are able to choose what they want, and control the political system, rather than be controlled by it, then one has a society that is run the way people want. To pretend that Britain in the 1980s and 90s has been run as a democracy is, at best, an irony. Yet democratic control is what is needed. But it is not sufficient. One also needs economic policies that utilise society's resources for the maximum benefit, in a long-term, socially beneficial and environmentally sustainable manner.

Some people might wield dramatic facts, or selected examples in order to prove their case. That is, rather than describing a typical situation, or the overall impact of an event, they carefully choose an example which highlights the argument they are making. Their example might be totally unrepresentative, and an utterly unique case. But its dramatic impact may outweigh its utter irrelevance. When the Thatcher regime was trying to persuade the nation how good the Poll Tax was, it publicised the plight of little old ladies living alone, struggling to pay their rates, when next door was a huge family of all ages, using all the council services, but paying only the same amount in rates.

Or when European Monetary Union was being touted as an economic necessity, the EC apologists concocted the story of a lone traveller, hurtling around all the 12 countries of Europe on £100, and mysteriously not spending any of it. Due to the massive exchange costs, this lonesome traveller would return to their country of origin with only £24 left. The dishonesty of this tale lies in the fact that few people, if any, would carry out such an escapade. Anyone who genuinely was visiting all the 12 countries would need to take more than £100, and they would need to spend at least some of it. And nobody who did not need to spend any money would go to the (modest) expense of changing it.

To paraphrase Shaw, to do this once would be misfortune; to do it twice would be carelessness; to do it twelve times would be insanity. In fact, the cost of exchanging money is quite small; smaller than this carefully distorted example indicates. However, by choosing a small sum, one is able to exaggerate the percentage loss. And for the people who really want to see one European currency — big business — exchange costs are trivial. When a company spends a million pounds on imported goods, the cost of exchanging currency is a minuscule proportion of total costs.

If we are to attempt any analysis of society, then we are operating within the realms of social science. And we cannot claim to be scientific unless we have a coherent methodology. To look at the ideal economy, or society, in any meaningful way, we need to have a method of operation which gives our arguments and our theories some credibility.

Instead of digging newsworthy stories out of the popular press, social scientists should be investigating the typical impact of a policy. What does it do, not to a vulnerable and telegenic section of the populace, or in a hypothetical example, but to the nation as a whole? In short, what is its total effect? Occasionally, some members of society might be disadvantaged as a result of a given policy, because resources are limited, and different groups have different interests. Thus, a road-building scheme may create jobs and stimulate the motor industry, reducing unemployment. But in doing so, it takes funds away from public transport, has unknown environmental impact, and leads to greater use of scarce fuel. But the argument against the scheme is not that it may harm some individuals, but that its overall impact may be harmful.

When looking at the overall effect of a policy, we must also discount personal prejudice and self-interest — not an easy thing for some people, but the mere fact of rational analysis must make a biased view less tenable. A person who owns a large house might find rates cheaper than a poll tax, but on examining the broader social effects of the two, may be forced to accept that rates are more egalitarian.

Much existing economic analysis, especially that of the New Right, supply side economics, monetarism, or even Marxism, has lacked this scientific underpinning. The quality of this vast range of ideas has of course been widely variable, and in much of it, there has been an element of truth, or a basic grounding in reality. For instance, monetarism has an undeniable core of truth, that extreme variations in the money supply affect price levels. But the claim by Friedman that money, and only money, causes inflation takes that core of truth into the realm of fantasy.

This is particularly clear when we consider the many adjustments that Milton Friedman has made to his facts in order to 'prove' his hypothesis that money, and only money, is the cause of inflation. Friedman's claim to academic respect rests on the empirical studies that he and Anna Schwartz have carried out on the money supply in Britain and the United States. However, David Hendry, writing in the

Bank of England journal, argued that Friedman manipulated the data to a degree that was 'simply incredible'.

Friedman arbitrarily reduced the money stock for the years 1921 to 1955, a time-span equal to almost a third of the entire period he studied. This was allegedly to allow for the fact that in times of uncertainty, such as recession, people keep more of their money in cash. He then 'adjusted' the actual price levels after the Second World War to allow for the effects of price controls and rationing. His arguments for these adjustments was that there was a link between money supply and prices, and the artificial events of the time had repressed that relationship. He then used the manipulated data to prove the link between money supply and prices. (*The Guardian*, December 15, 1983.)

This would be unacceptable in an academic paper claiming any degree of validity, unless there were good reasons for the changes. But the years 1921 to 1955 were so diverse, ranging from the boom years of 1921 to 1929 to the depression of 1930 to 1938, that no single adjustment can meaningfully describe that era. It also included the high inflation periods prior to the Second World War, and the Korean War. At those times we had high inflation due to high levels of demand. And with the aid of a less than honest adjustment, Friedman manages to lose the impact of those eras from his data. In scientific terms, this is dubious. However, to carry out mathematical juggling on a theory that is used as the basis of government policy is irresponsible in the extreme.

Another problem with Friedman's monetarism is the absolute certainty with which he presents its powers. He argues that 'inflation is always and everywhere a monetary phenomenon', and that the only way to cure inflation is by controlling the money supply. In fact, the control of the money supply has merely created the likelihood that prices will stabilise. Not only has this mastery of inflation not taken place, but it is not in the nature of social science to display this sort of rigid causality. There are few situations, if any, where one event will automatically lead to a fixed outcome. What one can say is that a given event will probably lead to a specific result. Thus, a rise in price will tend to lead to a fall in sales; but there have been products where a rise in price has led to a rise in sales.

Also, when economists and politicians say that a given result will take place, what they usually mean is that we can disregard any side effects. It is a bit like Dr. Jekyll claiming to make a natty cocktail which doesn't cause any nasty hangover. The implication is that any side effects which do occur are so minimal as to be of no concern. The social costs are outweighed by the benefits. For example, Chancellor Lamont described unemployment as a price worth paying to keep prices stable. This attitude is offensive as it ignores the anguish of literally millions of people. When a theory ignores real-world side effects, then that theory is totally invalidated for all practical purposes.

One problem with monetarism, supply side economics and the New Right in general is that they focus on limited aspects of human activity, and try to generalise from one indicator to the entire socio-economic system. For example, in the case of

Friedman and monetarism, he argues that the entire economy can be controlled using only the money supply. Similarly, supply side economists argue that unemployment and total output can be controlled via the incentive-creating effect of tax and welfare cuts.

This is far too simplistic. Yet that simplicity is a major part of the theory's appeal. Politicians are able to grasp the concepts with ease, and preach them to the electorate with equal ease. But given the multitude of social, economic and psychological factors influencing society, to choose any one indicator as the only variable to be controlled is simple-minded. It is essential that any rational study look at all aspects of society — the economy, the culture, the political system, and so on. The narrow approach of isolating one academic discipline as the basis for all social truth allows us limited understanding of a small area. Our politicians are able to control the economy partially, according to the guidelines set by their limited ideology. But the narrow assumptions in their theories reduce their effectiveness. Thus, Keynesian ideas were fine for lowering unemployment, and were suitable for a time when unemployment was high. But Keynes' view that any form of spending was sufficient to create jobs translates badly into an era when concern has moved on to include social problems, when unemployment may be low, and when money is scarce.

To quote Richard Feynman again, having established a theory, we then test it against reality. 'If it disagrees with the experiment, it's wrong. It doesn't matter how beautiful the theory was; it doesn't matter what the name of its creator was... If it disagrees with the facts, it's wrong'. And this is the most damning indictment of New Right ideas — they do not work. It doesn't matter how many experts, ministers, or civil servants say that we need to get inflation down — *the theory doesn't work.* And that is the end of the discussion — in the scientific sense, at least.

All aspects of society interact in a way that is clearly beyond the comprehension of the New Right. To take one example, the values of society influence our views on work or unemployment; that is, we take on the values of our culture. But the government's opinions and its perceived views are a part of our culture, part of our socialisation process. And under the Thatcherites, there has been a regime which tells people they have to make their own way in life, that there is no help, no compassion, and no allowance for the needs or problems of others. It should not be surprising if young people who perceive themselves as disadvantaged use their strength to take from those whom they see as privileged.

So we have a clear causal link between government policy and the rising crime rate. We could also make links between cuts in education, and the increasing materialism of our society. We could also argue that the statements made by politicians help to form attitudes in society, thus influencing which forms of behaviour are acceptable or not. In fact, there are no borderlines between one aspect of society and another. One cannot say, 'This is purely an economic policy, therefore it will not affect social issues'. The real world does not recognise textbook social laws.

Although methodology may at first sight have seemed like an academic abstraction, there is a detectable link between the Conservatives' lack of a methodology, and the disastrous failure of their policies. The social and economic destruction caused by the Tories is not coincidence or misfortune. It is the inevitable result of the fact that their ideas are simply wrong. The theories, the concepts, the arguments are all based on the half-baked opinions of bigots. In a scientific sense, the policy failures have merely been the symptoms of the incorrectness of the underlying ideas.

What we need is an approach to policy based on proven, workable ideas. It must be possible to demonstrate that the ideas can work, and indeed that they have worked at some time. This is not a problem, because so many different approaches have been tried, in various countries, at various times. Not that by itself the existence of workable examples would constitute proof. Indeed, we need to consider what it means to have 'proof', and what is necessary to achieve it. Therefore, we need a methodology.

For this, we need an approach that is scientific, in the sense of being logical and rational. It must also use the knowledge gained from the relevant sciences. For example, some sociologists argue that humans are socially constructed, with social factors being the only ones. Yet geneticists argue that we are the result of both social and hereditary factors. Clearly, the geneticists are more qualified to comment on the impact of inheritance than the sociologists.

We should also have an integrated or wholistic approach, in which we collate information from all scientific disciplines. Many areas of study cross the academic borders from one discipline to another, and it would be pointless to be constrained in one's analysis by the empty border posts of academic isolationism.

Some of the most fruitful academic research and most useful social policy occurs when people ignore these borders. For example, the inter-disciplinary research of George Katona fuses economics and psychology, while the American writer, James David Barber, applies psychology to politics to investigate the motives of politicians. Leopold Kohr, the man who persuaded Schumacher that small was beautiful, mixes history, politics and sociology to present a fuller picture of the weaknesses of large nations.

In the field of social policy, in British Columbia, Canada, child abuse policy is 'based on a handbook which is a combined production of the ministries of the attorney general, solicitor general, education, health and social services'. (*Social Work Today*, April 11, 1991.) The Canadian method of dealing with child abuse is integrated at source, creating a unified and coherent approach.

These inter-disciplinary methods allow a fuller understanding of events, and offer the best way of dealing with issues. Rather than be tied down to a mono-causal explanation or a single-discipline solution, one can examine all causes and all possible answers. One of the things we have learnt from Thatcherism is that single-cause solutions are very likely to be wrong or incomplete. The multi-disciplinary approach is more likely to generate a range of answers to one's study of an issue.

We would also look for evidence which seems to conflict with our chosen theory, partly because it may just be wrong. It is unhealthy to simply assume that one's theory is correct. But more importantly, one should try to test the theory because it may be right — but only under certain conditions. For instance, some writers have suggested that Britain should offer tax incentives for investment, to encourage British companies to put more money into modern equipment. Cynics reply that this has been tried — and it didn't work. But this does not mean that tax incentives are ineffective. Studies of British industry have suggested that what stops firms putting money into long-term projects is the short-termism of the City and other financial institutions. Businesses are scared to sink funds into long-term investment, in case profits are harmed in the short term, the share price falls, and the company gets taken over. If the threat of take-overs were removed, tax incentives might become more effective.

This methodology must also include a careful use of words. Many so-called social scientists misuse words in such a way as to invalidate much of what they say. They use words without making their meaning clear, they use emotive but generally acceptable terms, and they use one several times with several different meanings. The nature of language being what it is, this is almost unavoidable. Often, however, the use of vague terminology will result in a single phrase or argument being at best unclear, and at worst, meaningless. But when the term is used repeatedly, it can make the thesis as a whole contradictory or deceptive.

For example, we talk about capitalism, but this is a vague term with a variety of unclear meanings. Yet for some people, 'capitalism' is automatically a bad thing. Others have a similar reaction to the word 'socialism', again without really knowing what it means. Those on the far left tend to see capitalism as synonymous with exploitation, yet under the Thatcheroids, inequality has increased significantly, and could have done so without Britain becoming any more 'capitalist' than it was.

We must also consider the structures and policies that we intend to propose. We need to have evidence that they are workable, which ideally should involve the ability to analyse actual examples of those structures and policies. If that is not possible, we should be able to give clear evidence of the likely characteristics of our suggested structures.

For example, suppose we were suggesting an entirely new economic system, say, with companies owned by charitable trusts. We need to look at what evidence we have relating to the structure as a whole, or its likely operations. Thus, it could be said that charities are by their nature caring organisations, and therefore would provide greater welfare than purely commercial bodies.

On the other hand, it could be said that even charities have been known to suffer corruption and incompetence, and so might not be suitable bodies to control other people's finances. Also, knowing little about business, and not being focused on profit-making, they might not be effective managers of commercial organisations. The normal concerns of a charity include the welfare of others, and the beneficial use of donated money. There could be a conflict between making a profit, and improving welfare, and this conflict could immobilise the charity, or reduce its efficiency.

This analysis could be continued further, but the point is clear. It is possible to analyse even a purely hypothetical structure or policy in an attempt to demonstrate its probable operation. That is, even with a purely theoretical construct, we can postulate likely characteristics, probable modes of behaviour, and so on. There are rules of human, social and organisational behaviour that we can apply even to a system that does not exist.

We can imagine the probable impact of the structure on the life of the individual, using psychological insight. We know that people are vulnerable, acquisitive, sociable, aggressive, neurotic, and a host of other characteristics. A proposed society might emphasise the negative features, or it might calm them. It might encourage certain aspects, while discouraging others, so that on balance its impact might seem neutral. For example, the deregulated Thatcherite market economy seems to encourage business aggression and acquisitiveness, but it may also encourage self-reliance, individuality, and independence.

A hypothetical system could be judged in terms of its probable effects, either on people, or because of human nature. Many sociologists deny the existence of human nature, primarily following the Marxist view that the individual does not matter, and is only the product of social forces. But the individual does exist, and can influence their environment. Naturally enough, changes in the environment affect the individual.

There are methodological problems here, because if we carefully study the life of one person, they could unknowingly be an unrepresentative example. Our study might have chosen a person whose characteristics are not typical of the group we were studying. Thus, we might know exactly why they behaved in a certain way, but not have proved a behaviour pattern for people in general. On the other hand, the link between unemployment and other social ills that Dr. Harvey Brenner found, mentioned in Chapter 2, was purely statistical. He had no evidence of a causal relationship between unemployment and suicide, heart disease, alcoholism, crime, or murder. He had studied the figures for a large mass of people, and observed a statistical relationship. Perhaps by chance, when one variable rose, the others rose as well. It doesn't seem likely, and one can imagine a causal link, but that is not scientific evidence. To prove a causal link as well would have required some knowledge of the psychology of those people, of what caused them to take the paths they chose.

So if we are attempting really detailed proof of a hypothesis, there can be severe methodological difficulties. Ideally our sample should be large enough to be representative, and provide evidence of a general tendency. But it should also be small enough for one to study the psychology, the behaviour patterns of the people involved. In a scientific sense, tabloid stories of jobless youngsters killing themselves prove nothing; they are selected examples. However, they may be used as case studies, showing how the impact of unemployment can affect a person.

We also need to consider the impact of events on society and on the social aspects of life. Some sociologists argue that we are all the creation of our own surroundings, that identity is socially generated. If this is true, and it must be at least partly so, then any alterations to the structure of our society must necessarily change our character. In instituting change we might hope for human behaviour to be more pleasant in a better society, but our structures must be able to deal with the less pleasing aspects of human nature. One would not incorporate our faults into the theory by saying, as Marxists do, that such failings will cease to exist when the ideal world comes into being. This is a weak excuse of an argument, and is totally unfounded.

If some ideal system does exist, we can analyse how our chosen variant functions in the real world, looking at its strengths and weaknesses, its good and bad points. For example, if we wish to propose a Keynesian economic system, we can point to the workings of a Keynesian system during post-war Britain and America, or pre-war Germany. We can analyse how it worked, how it failed, and why it failed in particular ways. We could then say (hopefully) what the reasons were for any failings of the system, and modify our proposed structure accordingly.

If we take the human, social and organisational aspects as the basic modes of analysis, with the policy content as the operational content, we could say that Keynesian economics were beneficial in a variety of ways. First, a system that is based on creating employment is focused on the welfare of the individual. This must be obvious, even if there is no prior information on the social or personal effects of unemployment. We know from our own needs that most people would wish to have a job rather than be unemployed. And the function of society as a construct must be to improve the welfare of its members.

Second, reducing unemployment must be beneficial for society. Again, assuming no prior knowledge, a society in which a large number of people are unemployed is likely to be less stable and less fulfilled than one in which most people had jobs. We might reject the very idea of 'employment' as a way of life, seeing it as demeaning or lacking creativity, but most people need the two basic components of a job — work and income. That is, some useful application of our abilities, and the necessary wherewithal to provide all our personal needs in life. In most economies this means money, which some pundits reject as being a creator of materialism. However, they have not been able to create an alternative that can be shown to be workable according to the same criteria as money.

It is not being argued that people should be forced to take employment, by cutting welfare benefits. Nor that they be persuaded by schools that they should become employees, as was done in many British schools in the 1950s and 60s. What is being suggested is that a Keynesian based economy would seek to create jobs for those who wanted them. Those who wanted to start their own companies should also be encouraged to do so. But not everyone has the desire to run their own business. Society must allow all options, including the people who wish to contribute outside of conventional employment.

The third aspect of our analysis, the organisational component, again leads us into Keynesian economic policy. It can be said that businesses may have an advantage if many workers are without jobs; companies can then offer lower wages. But on the other hand, if people lack pay, then companies will lack customers; and that is not good for business, although it is not such a problem in a monopoly economy, in which the big corporations can set either output or prices to maximise profits.

Most policy proposals can be studied in terms of existing knowledge. The problem here is that British social scientists have not always studied the world around them in as much detail as is needed for a full understanding. For example, when the left was in the ascendant in the 1960s and 70s, few studies were done on the faults of nationalised industry, or the benefits of capitalism. The New Right has its own blind spots, being unable to see the complexity of human response. But during both periods, sociologists have failed to study attitudes, and underlying belief systems. As a result, there is not now sufficient information on popular beliefs and aspirations for a really detailed study, although what is available gives a reasonable picture of British society.

The traditional requirements for a methodology include consistency with known facts, verifiability of observations, and the ability to generate predictions. In effect, one needs these things in order to prove the value of a theory. To these, Karl Popper has added falsifiability, arguing that ultimately one cannot prove a theory, as disproof may always lurk unseen around the corner. For a theory to be scientifically valid, it must be open to disproof.

As this work is based very largely on existing knowledge, there is little conflict with existing facts. However, there is the occasional clash with current theories. For example, there is a belief that companies are able to obtain economies of scale as they grow larger — the greater their output, the lower the unit cost of production. There is only limited evidence for this idea, and some impressive academic research refuting it. In addition, it is possible that some cost reductions attributed to economies of scale are really due to monopoly power, or lower quality products. In the absence of objective research, it is not possible to make any definite statements.

There is also the need for verifiability. This is primarily an issue with laboratory experiments. If one scientist discovers a really amazing reaction or technique, it can only be accepted as valid if other scientists can achieve the same results under the same conditions. This was the central concern in the 'cold fusion' controversy, when two researchers from the University of Utah claimed to have created nuclear fusion in a glass jar, at room temperature. The problem was that nobody else was able to re-create the experiment in their own laboratories.

It is even more difficult to achieve verification in the social sciences because there are so many variables in the normal setting that the investigator cannot control. This is a particular problem because the mere fact of observation alters the behaviour of the people being observed. This was first discovered during studies of workers at an electrical assembly plant in the US, and became known as the Hawthorne effect. Researchers were trying to find out to what extent light levels affected the workers' output, so they turned the lights up, turned them down, raised them to dazzling brightness, and lowered them to twilight dimness. They found that whatever they did, production went up. The workers were reacting to being observed.

Even without the Hawthorne effect, there are so many factors operating in society that one cannot carry out anything like a normal laboratory experiment. The other factors may multiply or cancel (to an unknown degree) the variable that one is trying to study. Therefore, severe changes in the social environment may effectively invalidate one's experiment. Thus, monetarism may have failed in Britain during the 1980s because of the rise in oil prices. This raised price levels generally, thus obscuring any value that monetarism may or may not have had.

This allows people to excuse the failure of their pet theories by pointing to all the other variables that distorted their results. They can claim that their policies or methods would have worked perfectly, but external events interfered. Thus, the Major government can say that the 1990-93 recession does not indicate a failing of UK economic policy; there was a world recession, and Britain was suffering because of the general downturn in trade.

A good theory should also allow its users to make predictions about future events. For example, using the Theory of Relativity, Einstein was able to predict that light observed passing close to the sun would be deflected by a certain amount. Observations made during an eclipse in 1917 verified this. In the social sciences, prediction is not so easy, again because of external factors. And once again, this can be used to justify failed predictions. Marx claimed that his study was a science. Indeed, Bryan Magee states: 'The claim that Marx and Engels were concerned to establish before all others for their ideas was that they were "scientific", and this claim is reiterated over and again in their writings; they even refer to their brand of politics as "scientific socialism"'. (*The Guardian*, September 9, 1989.)

Marx believed that because he was using scientific laws, he could make irrefutable predictions. One of these was that the communist revolution was inevitable. Also, it would occur in the most advanced industrial nation — at that time, Britain. History shows it did not, yet latter-day Marxists argue that 'the chain breaks at its weakest link'. In other words, science by cliché. Perhaps the Stalinist purges of the 1930s can be written off as 'the exception that proves the rule'.

Karl Popper argued that verifiability proved nothing in the last analysis. We could endlessly verify a theory, perhaps because we had not yet found the events or places which would prove us wrong. Once we argued that all swans were white, and used this as a logical format. Then we discovered that swans in Australia can be black. This eliminated the 'all swans are white, this is a swan, therefore it is white' sequence. But it also cast doubt on the argument, 'Aristotle is a man, all men are mortal, therefore Aristotle is mortal'. We know from experience that people are mortal, but if a logical structure based on all past observations is no longer valid, it leaves us metaphorically operating with no visible means of support.

Popper eliminated this by arguing that the ultimate basis of science does not rest on repeated verification, but on falsifiability. That is, a theory must be open to being falsified. Verification gives it validity, may be a strong indicator of its worth, and demonstrates that one may continue to use the theory, but it does not indicate the scientific validity of the theory.

Marxism fails this test too, because of its repeated ability to justify its failed predictions. According to H. L. Mencken, 'Communism, like any other revealed religion, is largely made up of prophecies'. The faith of the believers has not given Marxism any protected status. The crisis of capitalism never occurred, there has been no confirmed sighting of the dictatorship of the proletariat, and if there has been a communist revolution, it did not take place where it should have done.

Despite all this, Marxists are still able to argue that the faith has not been disproved. The invasion of Czechoslovakia and Hungary, the collapse of the Soviet Union, the show trials and purges, and the massive rejection of communism by eastern Europe are all written on the wind, minor events, maybe even irrelevant. There is an argument to explain away each of them. But as Popper points out, if the theory can explain everything that occurs, then nothing can prove or disprove it. It is not constructed to be validated by specific sets of events, and does not need the future to conform to its predictions. If this is true, then there is no point in making the predictions; the theory can cope with any event by altering what it claims to be true. The celebration when a forecast turns out correct is hollow if disproof merely brings forth some meaningless cliché.

In effect, Marxism is not open to disproof. In Popper's terms, it is not falsifiable, because it can adapt to any event. And if it is totally unaffected by all events, then clearly it makes no meaningful predictions, because it claims to be correct whatever happens. Thus, the prediction does not really tell us about the future. Nor can the theory be scientific, because it does not add to our knowledge. We cannot be sure of anything the theory tells us, because it is ready to say anything.

These characteristics define what a methodology should be; but they do not show what it will look like. The most perceptive description of a methodology for the social sciences is that given by the sociologist, C. Wright Mills. He argued quite simply that the method had to be appropriate to the problem.

> In these terms, consider unemployment. When, in a city of 100,000, only one man is unemployed, that is his personal trouble, and for its relief we properly look to the character of the man, his skills, and his immediate opportunities. But when in a nation of 50 million employees, 15 million men are unemployed, that is an issue, and we may not hope to find its solution within the range of opportunities open to any one individual. The very structure of opportunities has collapsed. Both the correct statement of the problem and the range of possible solutions require us to consider the economic and political institutions of the society, and not merely the personal situation and character of a scatter of individuals. (*The Sociological Imagination*, p15.)

This leads us to a very clear basic methodology: that we should analyse the problems of society in order to determine their causes, and therefore, the likely solutions. For example, given the problem of unemployment, we can say, to quote Mills, that 'the structure of opportunities has collapsed'. At the time of writing, most commentators in Britain are saying that the cause of this collapse is the lack of demand in the economy. Therefore, the question is, how do we expand demand?

There is a difficulty in that we are making a value judgement when we choose to define certain issues as the key problems. This lays any choice open to the accusation of bias, and by implication, it is not objective. However, for most people the major concerns of British society can easily be agreed. The real issues are the ones that worry us all — after the persuasive Conservative speech has ended, and the authoritative voice has been switched off for the night. The things which actually worry people are the the threat of unemployment, the quality of life, the level of crime, the quality of the health service and of education. These are the main problems focused on in this book, and will be the key subjects for analysis.

Naturally, New Right pundits would claim that the 'real' issues are inflation and the economy. They would say, perhaps sincerely, that unless inflation is conquered, industry and the economy will never be competitive. But this is mere rhetoric, and no economist has yet set out a credible argument as to why industrial success cannot take place until prices are under control. They might say, 'Look at Germany; they are successful, and they have low inflation'. But this would not prove that the success depended on the Germans' ability to control prices. It is far more likely that the stable prices are a result of having a strong economy. Also, to say they have feature A and feature B, does not prove that one is the cause of the other. The Germans all drive on the right, and have low inflation; but that does not mean that driving on the right causes low inflation.

And is a strong economy what we want? This could imply high levels of output of low quality, short life-span goods of modest real worth, with the bulk of the wealth created going to a minority, while society's majority struggle to survive. This describes what others might call a strong economy. Surely what we want is an economy which provides us with useful, enjoyable employment, and a pleasant quality of life.

Moreover, given people's concern about certain issues, the attitudes that politicians have to those issues is irrelevant. It is a matter of fact that voters regard unemployment as a more important problem than law and order. The percentages vary from one poll to another, and from area to area, but in a study of the 1992 General Election, 36 per cent of voters thought that unemployment was the main economic issue, while only 11 per cent felt that inflation was. (Anthony King, *Britain at the Polls.*) Similarly, 61 per cent of a Marplan poll wanted to see the government giving a higher priority to the environment (The Guardian. October 13. 1988). That is, as shown in Chapter 3, there is a broad consensus on most policy issues, and politicians should take note of that fact.

One might say that the government should not always give the people what they ask for; in the case of capital punishment, for example. This would be a retrograde step that served neither justice nor the protection of the individual. Attempting to improve on the local council rates was also a mistake, leading to the poll tax, and putting local authority financing firmly on the agenda as well as stepping up the emotional heat behind the issue. Now, any move towards a sensible system, such as progressive local income taxes, would be lobbied against by the vocal middle classes. Had a pre-1979 government introduced local income taxes, the issue would have raised only moderate complaints.

Ideally, the state should act as a manager or parent figure, carrying out the policies that are the best for the populace as a whole, and dealing with conflicts of interest. In most cases this should involve giving people what they want, if at all possible. But if it is not, then the state should seek a balance of interests to achieve, in a well-known phrase, the greatest good of the greatest possible number. That is, the state's job is to maximise welfare.

Within the available knowledge we can deduce various things about society. But we must also recognise our limits. We cannot see the future, nor does this author have all the information that is available. And for anyone making judgements about policy, their distance from the site of the problem may preclude them from making an informed comment. People on the scene should be able to adapt policy according to their particular circumstances. So the ideas being put forward in this book should not be regarded as being fixed or complete. That would lead to it degenerating into dogma. What is being offered is a partial view of a possible form of economic structure, that is workable and beneficial, and that is suitable for our society at this time.

But given the fluid nature of the social sciences, what would be just as useful as a theory of social structure would be a way of proceeding. Here, too, an empirical and rational approach would be valuable. In the past, the British Labour Party has emphasised state control, welfare spending and nationalisation. The Swedish Social Democratic Party has taken a similar stance, based on a welfare state with high taxes and high levels of spending. Both of them got into a certain pattern of thinking — spend money on the problems, raise taxes to obtain the money, and the state would impose its solutions.

This approach shows no flexibility, no room for local or personal needs and initiative, and does not encourage the creation of new methods. According to Feyerabend, '*the invention of alternatives to the view at the centre of discussion constitutes an essential part of the empirical method*'. (Paul Feyerabend, *Against Method*, p41. Italics in original.)

Feyerabend's argument is that theories must be tested against alternative ideas, and one way to do this is to create those alternatives. For example, this book could be compared to existing New Right ideas, to see if it — or they — are the more accurate. Similarly, politicians could use such an approach. Rather than look for policies within their existing framework, they could look for radical new solutions to each problem, dealing with them as they occur instead of trying to fit all problems into a pre-determined ideology. The Danish government takes this sort of stance, dealing with each issue on an individual basis. Perhaps because of this, Denmark spends a smaller proportion of its GDP on the public sector, but achieves a better quality of life even than that of Sweden.

This book will take the same overall approach of fitting the solution to the problem, and using C. Wright Mills' methodology of choosing a method of analysis appropriate to the problem. Because one is analysing neither society nor the economy as separate units, but an entire entity made up of the two together, academic borderlines will be of no relevance to the study. Information that has relevance to a problem will be used, if it describes general trends rather than one-off occasions. Unique instances will only be used as evidence of a trend if there are no general studies demonstrating a link. Otherwise, such one-offs will be used to illustrate rather than prove a relationship.

Hypothetical examples will not be used to prove anything, but they could be used as an explanatory device. There will be no rigged scientific rules, with hidden alterations, and there will be no spurious certainties. In the real world of social science there are no certainties, only probabilities. Some events or policies are more likely to lead to given outcomes than others, and to pretend that a given outcome is inevitable is simply dishonest.

As academic disciplines are not being allowed to dictate the content of the research, evidence will be taken from any relevant subject. Data on the behaviour of factory workers, for instance, could be taken from sociology, economics, industrial economics or management studies. Theories to explain such behaviour might be taken from sociology, social psychology, or anthropology. No single academic discipline should be seen as having a monopoly on the truth. By widening one's field of view, one can obtain evidence that other writers may have overlooked. For example, the best work on corporate crime, an area that should be of great interest to concerned economists, was written by two sociologists.

Because of this wholistic approach, there will be many links between the different chapters. Economic policy can be seen both as a cause of social change, and a result of the decisions of elected representatives. Where this dual facet occurs, the links will be pointed out. And as we are dealing with the total impact on society, policies will be viewed in those terms, rather than simply their immediate or local impact.

Events will not be seen in terms of single causes, because as will be seen in Chapter 10, with reference to the Enlightenment in the eighteenth century, some events have a variety of causes. This is particularly significant when pundits demolish one cause of an event, and say that given their excellent disproof, the feared results will not occur. If we accept multiple causality, then a single-event disproof is meaningless.

Ideally, the resulting theory will be verifiable, but following Popper, it will also be falsifiable. It will have to be proven, and there will be evidence for most of the causal links. But the theory as a whole is also falsifiable. That is, if a society of the type depicted is created, and does not create the quality of life that is being claimed for it, then the theory as it stands must be wrong. Although, following Feyerabend, if we test this theory against the alternatives, it seems far better than any existing alternative.

Given the data, the next step will be to create a picture of society and the relationships within it, such that the picture allows one to explain how the system functions. To do this, it will be necessary to split up systems temporarily into their component parts, for ease of analysis. These micro-economies or micro-cultures might not allow a full understanding by themselves, but they do allow a complex problem to be dealt with in stages.

To take an example, the micro-culture that one finds inside a company is formed by many factors. One can examine these causal factors, gain an understanding of the local culture, and then move on to an analysis of how corporate culture affects the economy. One could then carry out a separate study of how government policy affected the economy.

The following chapters will use appropriate methodology to ensure that the overall analysis is valid. Clearly, all the ideas described in this book are based on actual studies, and to that extent this is a scientific work. But I will also try to ensure that the logic is valid.

In the social sciences one cannot have the absolute proof of the physical sciences; it is more like a jigsaw, building up a picture of the most likely representation of reality. But using information from a variety of sources, I hope to demonstrate that there is a workable alternative economic system to the unemployment-ridden New Right economy that we have now.

6

The radical economy

MANY PEOPLE ARGUE that New Right economics has failed, while some say that capitalism has failed; either way, we need a new economic system. The question is, which type of economic system?

The social economy was originally seen as being halfway between capitalism and communism. Certainly, this is the view that emerged in Eastern Europe as the barriers collapsed in 1989. That was also the view that I had been working on, up to that time. Two things happened to change this approach — one was the collapse of communism in Eastern Europe which effectively discredited Marxist or state-centralised economies. The other was the shift in the consensus in the western industrial nations, primarily Britain and the United States. The Russian bear had died, but a new monster had arisen, in our own homes.

For many people, communism had been discredited much earlier — in 1921 with the massacre of the Kronstadt sailors, in the 1930s by the purges and show trials, in 1956 by the invasion of Hungary, and in 1968 by the invasion of Czechoslovakia. It seemed that any failure of the system could be absorbed — my ideology right or wrong. As Karl Popper had observed, Marxism was not open to falsification. But when actually existing Marxism ceased to exist, its credibility was destroyed. Its exit from the world political stage may have been of greater impact than the fact that so many subjects of communist countries bore such intense and obvious hostility to the hated ideology.

As an economic system, it did not work; politically, it was undemocratic; socially it was grim and depressing. However, some people said that the Soviet Union was not real communism; it was state capitalism, or it was Stalinism, and its collapse did not affect the validity of Marx's theories.

But this is simply another example of Marxism's refusal to accept any falsification. Firstly, nothing that has happened in world politics has been seen as a disproof of Marx's ideas. The communist revolution took place in a backward nation, even though Marx predicted it would occur in the most advanced industrial country. Reforms took place in the west, even though Marx said improvement in social conditions were impossible. And the working class got better off, even though the iron laws of communism 'proved' they would be increasingly impoverished. All this was brushed aside as the Marxist-Leninist locomotive thundered off into the dark Soviet night.

If any event could be fitted into the Marxist cosmology, including those which were portrayed as impossible, without Marxists seeing their theories as faulty, then the theory was meaningless. If no events could ever act as disproof, then nothing could prove the theory either. It existed independently of facts, evidence or logic; it did not relate to the real world, and was simply a philosophical construct. Its sole function was to pose an alternative to capitalism, not to actually be that alternative.

Yet the failure of 'socialism in one country' was inevitable, given the requirements that Marx had postulated. The state should own the banks, the transport system, all industry and so on. In other words, Marx proposed an all-powerful centralised state that eliminated the need for capitalism by eliminating private ownership. By doing so, it made the controllers of the state apparatus more powerful than anyone else in society. As the theory made no provision for the enormous power that the state apparatchiks held, it implicitly condoned the inevitable abuse of power. Therefore it was quite simply an unworkable theory.

It could be said that Marx intended the centralisation of control to be followed by a 'withering away' of the state. But one has to recognise that the individuals who manage the apparatus of the state are not likely to relinquish their hold on power voluntarily. Having been given near-absolute power over the nation, there is no force that would be able to depose them. And there is no reason to assume sufficient altruism from literal nobodies, the unknowns who will for some reason be the rulers of the state.

Also, Marxism contained a discrepancy between values and policy. Any sensible theory that has a human value content built into it will try to link the moral needs to the objective policy. The Conservatives at least show internal consistency here; their priority is the control of inflation, so their actions revolve around anti-inflationary measures. Marx wanted a system that would improve the lives of the working class; so he proposed a society that centralised all power in the hands of the state. As a result, the working class had no power to control their own lives. It is to Marx's credit that he sought to create a better society. But his was not the ideal way to ensure that one's moral code operates to the full. It is a pity that latter-day Marxists remained so committed to the methods, rather than to the ideals.

Marxism had not merely failed; for many observers, it seemed as if Marxists were more concerned with protecting their dogma than with improving the lives of ordinary people. The millions killed in the Russian purges or oppressed in Eastern Europe were all a historical footnote. The main plot revolved around the triumph of Marxism. This obscenity in the face of suffering must, in the end, lead to discredit.

The same must be said of the Labour Party in Britain. Faced with public hostility to their policies, to their links with the unions, and to the extreme left, many Labour MPs simply puffed at their pipes, to block out the sight of homeless people outside their windows. Their policy reviews were half-hearted efforts; Labour was more wedded to certain methods than to outcomes. As mentioned in Chapter 5, Labour ignored the existence of a consensus, and surrendered electoral victory to the Conservatives four times in a row, like a drowning man rejecting a rope. Because of this, Labour must share responsibility for the social tragedy that has settled on Britain.

Even before the far left started losing ground, the far right was gaining it. In the United States and Britain the ideas of the New Right were taking over from the Keynesian consensus. In a sense, this was not a really new direction for either country; governments in both countries had traditionally been more than sympathetic to the needs of business. (See Galbraith, *The Affluent Society*, and Kolko, *The Age of Conservatism*.) But whereas in the past, government had provided the tax breaks, or the anti-union laws that commerce had asked for, now the New Right had an entire economic ideology justifying a whole range of policies.

In one area, Marxism has finally been proved correct. Whereas in the nineteenth century capitalism did not have a coherent ideology, the New Right has now created one. In criticising capitalism, Marxists depicted the state as an automatic ally of commerce, where business exploited the workers, and the workers were impoverished. Thus, the rich got richer by the exact amount that was taken from the workers' production. This simplistic analysis was made even more unreal by insisting that value was created only in the manufacturing process. Thus, no one was enriched by transport, distribution, communication, retailing or any of the other aspects of a trading nation. It was as if production alone created wealth, and industrialists could become richer simply by paying their workers less.

The New Right demonstrated how shallow this was by incorporating it into their own beliefs. They actually took on the values that had been alleged to be essential parts of capitalism. Keep wages low, and we will have low inflation, greater incentives, lower production costs, and a growing economy. Thus, we will all be better off if the workers have less income. As most of us are workers, it is difficult to see how this feat will be achieved. By earning less, we will be richer. It is Orwellian NewSpeak at its finest.

What this argument ignores is that for an economy to function, all that production must be bought by somebody. It must be purchased by consumers, and it is their money that enriches the capitalists. However, it does mean that consumers must be rich enough to engage in a healthy level of spending, in order to keep the wheels of commerce turning. As most consumers get their income from employment, this means that wage levels must be high enough to allow all this purchasing. If industrialists reduce wages too much, they will be damaging their own economy — which may help explain the UK's 1991-94 recession.

Marxists portrayed capitalism as the sole source of evil, and the ultimate source of power, yet history shows this to be utterly untrue. The state and religious organisations have displayed far greater evil than even the worst flaws of nineteenth-century capitalism, objected to by Marx. Equally, power can be wielded by the state, by religion, by the army, by monarchs, or indeed by almost anyone.

Previously, many people were not even aware of a clear definition of capitalism, and Marxists were able to set the agenda by creating one of their own. Naturally, it was a definition that portrayed its subject as being intrinsically evil and exploitative.

This attitude may have helped stimulate hostility to business in general, as Marxists were unable to distinguish between the Maxwells and Union Carbides of industry, and the Body Shops or the co-operatives.

One could also say that Marxists had contributed to the growth of the New Right by splitting the left, and making the issues emotional rather than logical. The Labour Party had its own inherent contradictions, but the extreme left added to and exacerbated these divisions. Much Marxist dialogue was bigoted, hysterical and closed-minded. Total certainty will always find an audience somewhere, but it doesn't allow rational debate. Policies created in this intellectual vacuum discredited the moderate left, and gave the New Right an apparently more sensible image.

Throughout the 1980s, the Labour Party became increasingly vulnerable when faced with the stonewalling and coherent policy of the Tories. Labour was unable to defeat the Tories in parliamentary battle, and had to move from their own dogmatic certainties to a degree of debate. But their inability to 'win' a verbal battle led to many assuming that the Conservatives had the correct arguments. In fact, it was merely due to the ability of well-informed sophists to be able to find a way out of any argument. Instead, Labour should have concerned itself with presenting the arguments to the voters; offering a coherent set of consensual policies in the public arena, and had it done this, Labour would have won.

In reality, the Conservatives were seen as a winning party. Britain and the US set the tone of the policy debate, and the theme was soon echoed by countries as diverse as Australia, Chile and Singapore. Even more vulnerable to the new ideology were the nations of Eastern Europe, who were actively looking for a new approach to economics. To encourage this trend, the governments, universities and institutions of the west sent as many ambassadors as they could. Anyone who could preach the market philosophy was pointed at the old eastern bloc, and a salvo of libertarian economists was unleashed.

Now, most of us see the ideas of the New Right in a more objective light. In Britain at least, we have seen its failures, its errors and its contradictions. The question is, what system could replace it? But given the methodology agreed in Chapter 5, there is a way to choose that system, i.e. one that works. Reviewing the economic history of the twentieth century, we can see clearly which approaches have worked — they include Keynesian demand management, the welfare state, government intervention in the economy, and a mixed economy.

Some commentators have suggested that Keynes's ideas ceased to work from the 1970s onwards, perhaps due to some change in the structure of the world economy. But clearly they worked under Roosevelt's New Deal, in the United States. They worked in the immediate post-war period in Britain. And they have played a role in most economic recovery and development programmes. Galbraith points out that Germany's recovery after World War II is sometimes credited to the market;

> Ludwig Erhard made the recovery of German industry after 1948 the product of the unaided market. This was a remarkable feat of oratory for it

coincided with the Marshall Plan, a vastly publicized effort in public intervention, and took place in a country where industry is extensively regulated, and where per capita government expenditures are much higher, and those for welfare about twice as high, as in the avowedly socialist state of Norway (as it then was) where the level of individual income is about the same'. (*The Affluent Society*, p13.)

One could say that the entire Marshall Plan, including Germany's post-war miracle, was an excellent demonstration of the validity of Keynesianism. This is not to say that Keynes's ideas represented a perfect system, or that they were only defeated because they lost a propaganda war. There were weaknesses in Keynesian economics. And if nothing else, Thatcherism has taught us the importance of the efficient use of resources. Keynes himself regarded any form of spending as beneficial, and made no attempt to distinguish any particular type of spending. Indeed, he said that it would be perfectly acceptable for the government to pay one set of workers to bury money, while another set were paid to dig it up again. This is comparable to Friedman's attitude that it doesn't matter where any addition to the money supply is introduced.

Both of these statements fail to allow for the variable value of spending power to the economy. Keynes acknowledged this elsewhere in his theory, recognising that as people earned more, they spent a smaller proportion of their total income. The rich would be more likely to save most of any extra money, while the poor would be likely to spend all of it. Thus, an addition to national income would have a different impact, depending on which group of society was to receive the extra money. At the present time, it would be both egalitarian to re-distribute money to the lower income groups, as well as being the most effective way of increasing consumer demand.

Government spending, regardless of whether or not it created a deficit, would create jobs and pay packets. Workers would spend more, and their spending would, in turn, encourage production, therefore creating even more jobs. The process was described by Keynes as being a virtuous circle, in which the spending of money would automatically generate more spending.

As mentioned in Chapter 1, the strength of the Keynesian system was that it was supported by both the efficient administrators, and the morally-concerned social democrats. The weakness was that the pursuit of efficiency was gradually relaxed, as policy was determined by politicians, for an electoral or ideological agenda rather than for the good of society as a whole. Also, the global economic environment changed, while Britain's politicians were still dabbling in nineteenth century ideology, and its mid-twentieth century progeny.

What is needed today is a programme with the same dual support — both the moral and the practical. We need an economy which expresses the sensible pragmatism of Keynesian economics, with the moral fervour of Beveridge. That is, it must be an efficient system, as well as being morally just. But it must also be a system which uses its resources wisely.

Keynes's statement that any form of spending was good enough to boost the economy has made Keynesian demand management an easy target for those who wish to cut expenditure. For example, two American economists argued that there was a positive impact on the economy, but that this was soon outweighed by negative effects. (See K. A. Chrystal, *Controversies in Macroeconomics*, p130.) Spending alone is not, and should not be seen as, enough by itself.

This means not merely using resources cost-effectively, but in a way that is for the good of the population as a whole. All the ideology in the world, all the theories in the groves of academe are irrelevant in the face of the ultimate test — does it improve people's well-being? With that in mind, we have to re-appraise the minimal state, privatisation, deregulation and the conscious lack of any industrial or economic policy.

Thatcherism forced many people to see the error of unlimited spending. It introduced a rigorous study of all forms of government spending. Hospitals are being audited, teachers will be tested on the job, local authorities will be subject to audit as well as to central government control. The concept of cost-effectiveness is now well and truly stamped on the public consciousness. This is not to say that under the Tories it was carried out evenly, objectively or thoroughly; at the time of writing it is very much at the whim of the Cabinet.

But that very recognition of cost-effectiveness means that we are no longer so casual in our thinking about policy. In an era when money and material resources are almost infinitely precious, we cannot waste either on grandiose schemes, or state handouts for every fringe group in the country. It is no longer enough to say that a certain group needs funds, or that they deserve financing. We have to look for other ways to solve the problems.

This is not an argument for cutting spending, nor is it saying that we can ignore the state's duty to minority groups, or those in need. It is simply saying that resources have to be used effectively. Money is the government's most important raw material, and it can be used in a multiplicity of ways; each one having its own peculiar side-effects. So the allocation should minimise both costs, and unwanted side-effects.

Fortunately, Keynesianism is a flexible system, and has a variety of ways in which it can be applied. One may start with the basic tax or spending changes, but given the need to use the state's money effectively, one needs to consider where the extra spending would be applied, or which area might be a target for cuts in spending.

For example, given the differing proportions of income spent by the upper or lower income groups, if demand is mildly over-heating the economy one might raise taxes for the rich, while if the boom is creating excessive demand, one might also sharply increase taxes for the lower and middle income groups. A reverse procedure could be used to deal with recessions.

But tax is a blunt instrument in comparison with spending, as there are so many ways in which state funds can be applied. They may be allocated locally or centrally, used to pay for incomes or for infrastructure, or used in labour-intensive or capital-intensive industries. Thus, their impact on local needs or the national economy will vary, the long-term or short-term benefits will differ, and the impact on unemployment will vary.

There will also be an effect on material standards of living or quality of life. So an increase in funding for NHS running costs would allow for more nurses, thus creating jobs and reducing unemployment. But it would also (presumably) create an improvement in the nation's health, and so would mean a better quality of life. The presumed qualification here is the fact that extra nurses by themselves do not guarantee extra health care. They have to be trained, managed, and placed where they can do the most good. Such a qualification could of course apply to all spending. In the absence of this otherwise obvious warning, politicians would calmly point out that spending by itself is not enough. Such trivial wisdom is an excellent smokescreen for covering up spending cuts.

Similarly, an increase in capital spending on the NHS would create jobs for builders and equipment suppliers. Again, the quality of health care would improve, but because more or larger hospitals allowed a greater number of patients, or because more or better medical equipment enabled hospitals to provide more advanced health care. Thus, the two different approaches to health spending would both improve care, both would create jobs, yet the impact would be different, both quantitatively and qualitatively. The rise in current spending would probably create more jobs, but the rise in capital spending might have the greater long-term impact on the level of health care.

Thus, given a fixed sum of money, there is a menu of options the money can be spent on. The option chosen would be determined partly by the economic situation at the time, but also by the impact of each method. So the menu can be judged in terms of the range of likely outcomes it would create. A government that sought to reduce unemployment would direct its finance towards a labour-intensive sector of the economy. A government which sought to reduce balance of payments problems might aim its funds at import-substituting sectors of industry. Trade deficits are a permanent concern for Britain, so the need to deal with imports is always a consideration for the economy.

Such constraints make economic Keynesian management difficult for the government. There have always been the problems of timing, and the size of the state's intervention, but these have usually been managed correctly in the past. In 1951 the Australian federal government completely mistimed its actions, making a mild recession much worse. But usually, the timing of economic intervention involves few difficulties. On the other hand, most of the constraints suffered by Lamont or by other recent Tory Chancellors were of their own making. The lack of any industrial strategy, combined with the credit boom of the late 1980s, created an inevitable balance of payments deficit. And the constant tax cuts, allied with cuts in government spending, shrank the economy, and thus reduced the tax base that subsequent Chancellors could utilise.

If there were a narrow range of policy targets to be dealt with, and a selection of policy instruments to choose from, then one could more easily assess the effectiveness of the different instruments. For example, if unemployment was the only problem, one could measure how good each method was at creating jobs. This could be done with a mixture of past experience, analysis of the current situation, and computer models. So with a little research, one should be able to say how many jobs per £ one should be able to create.

When there are many targets and instruments to manage, one needs to use Cost-Benefit Analysis (CBA), a tool for quantifying the various impacts of a given plan; although by itself, CBA is not enough. In a simple issue that is not complicated by social factors one could use CBA to calculate the total costs or benefits of a project, to see if it is financially worthwhile. Thus, the government, or one of the ministries, might use CBA to evaluate a proposed new investment. One could add up the cost of new machinery and so on, and then predict a likely level of income to be attained from the project. So an organisation can compare in straight cash terms the costs and the income that can be expected. The government must also distinguish between the initial setting up costs, and the long term cost. For example, a project may have a high setting up cost, but be very cheap in the long term, because of its low annual costs.

However, merely to assess the effectiveness of state spending, CBA studies should be carried out on all projects. In this way one could compare the merits of an extra motorway with a boost to public transport. Building a motorway creates jobs, both in construction and in the car industry, because new roads boost cars sales. Similarly, greater expenditure on public transport creates jobs, but it also reduces traffic jams, unlike road-building. Because extra roads encourage car sales and car use, there is no real benefit to traffic flow to be gained from building roads. As traffic jams cost Britain an estimated £15 billion per year, CBA shows public transport to have a significant advantage. If we add on the advantages in terms of lower pollution, and less impact on the environment, the case for public transport becomes irrefutable.

However, CBA is not carried out on all public spending projects. It is carried out on most proposed road schemes, and on all proposed motorways. The method used by the Department of Transport, a system called CoBA 9, takes account of the time that motorists would save, and the reduction in traffic accidents that any given road scheme would produce. However, according to transport consultant Jonathan Bray, each life saved by the road scheme is valued at £680,000. This introduces an element of bias, as it considerably enhances the social impact of a road plan. This may be one of the few times that the Department of Transport puts any value on a human life

One other difficulty with CBA is that some of the side-effects can be difficult to quantify. This is partly because it converts all effects into monetary terms, to put them on the same basis. This means that one can compare utterly dissimilar effects, such as the closure of shops or a reduction in traffic deaths. This apparent ability to compare chalk and cheese makes complex decisions much more manageable.

For example, on a straight cost basis, a kidney machine is cheaper than a transplant, so a purely cost-effective health service will concentrate on providing kidney machines. However, if we do a CBA, and put a value on the quality of life, we find that the kidney transplant is better, as it allows the recipient the freedom to move about.

Transport policy is one of the areas where we can see the superiority of the other nations that have been referred to, such as Holland or Austria.

Amsterdam was being choked by cars, as nearly half of the city's population owned a car. There were two interesting aspects of the Dutch way of dealing with the problem. First, they put the issue to the population in a referendum. And second, voters took the more radical of the two choices. Option A would have fixed traffic levels until the end of the century. Option B created car-free zones, and cut the number of parking spaces by 60 per cent. 45 per cent of voters chose Option A, but 52 per cent chose Option B. (*The Guardian*, March 26, 1992.) Commuters would be encouraged to travel by bus, tram or underground, but of course, being Holland, many would travel by bike.

In Vienna, the Austrian capital, public transport is co-ordinated with outstanding efficiency. A fast, clean, efficient network of trams, buses and underground takes commuters and tourists from one part of the city to another. And given a wide range of specialised tickets, from the one-journey ticket to the card which covers eight travelling days of your choice, using a car rarely makes sense. The result is that jams are few, and most traffic moves swiftly through the city.

However, with purely economic data, like a shop closure, there are complications in valuing the impact. One can put a cash value to the loss of employment for a given number of people, and their new unemployment is likely to last for a given duration. So one can value their personal loss, and the costs to the state, and then add in the cost to the shop owner. But the closure might have ruined the shopkeeper — do we also value the cost to society of having permanently lost a possible source of employment? And all the fittings and equipment in the shop have been transformed into scrap; it may have been written off for tax purposes, but it now represents another loss to the economy. Putting a range of disparate factors on the same cash basis makes comparison easier — but can be misleading.

In general, how far does one take Cost-Benefit Analysis? Do we follow the ripples into the future, or do we merely look at the immediate impact? Also, how do we value intangibles? For example, how do we value the loss of confidence the shopkeeper and the now-unemployed staff may have suffered? And how do we value the possible cash impact of this loss on their future economic activity? And if we have an agreed cash valuation for a social phenomenon, can we assume that it is an objective assessment of the impact?

Because we live in a market economy, with a great deal of inequality of income, it is not always possible to see all cash units as being of equal value. If a waitress spends one pound on a magazine, that £1 is not — as an expression of consumer welfare — exactly comparable with the same amount spent by a City share dealer.

And if they both became unemployed, how would we value the cost to them and to the economy in terms of pay lost?

However, in terms of personal tragedy, unemployment for a low-paid, low skilled worker is generally a much greater disaster than it is for a highly-paid, skilled person. The unskilled worker is less able to get another job, and is less likely to have savings to tide them over a period of unemployment. So perhaps we could adjust the cash values according to the personal impact; but how much should we adjust them? Whatever figure we chose would be purely arbitrary and, in a sense, misleading. The impact on the economy of one City share dealer becoming unemployed would be much greater than the impact of one waitress, simply because the share dealer would tend to earn more. But if we were valuing personal welfare, an addition to the wage of the waitress would be regarded as having more value than any addition to the income of the share dealer.

But if we were analysing the issue in order to calculate state benefits, we might offer the waitress a larger sum, because of greater personal need. However, if we were looking at a typical situation, unskilled workers tend to lose their jobs in greater numbers than highly skilled, highly qualified workers. So we might want to adjust the assumptions made for job creation policy. The complexity of this issue does not invalidate such adjustments, but it does show they are not the clear-cut sources of instant wisdom that some might like to claim. We cannot apply CBA to personal situations, and assume that the same figures will be valid for all situations.

And if the loss of a job is difficult to evaluate, what about the loss of natural resources, or of personal well-being, or even of life? How do we value the personal cost of tragedies like the King's Cross fire, or any one of British Rail's train crashes? The normal CBA approach would be to value each life in terms of lost income for a given number of years. So a dead waitress earning £60 per week, with a future working life of forty years would be valued at 60 x 52 x 40 = £124,800. It sounds like a lot of money, and would represent an attractive life insurance payout; but does it really represent the value of a person's life? Does it compensate the spouse or a partner for the loss of a loved one? And is it an appropriate fine for the corporate criminal? Not to forget that if the City worker died, they would be 'worth' a likely £1,248,000.

Comparisons are often misleading, but suppose the waitress was a single mother, performing an excellent job of bringing up her children alone. And suppose also that our City dealer has been personally responsible for boosting the balance of payments deficit by importing a series of expensive foreign cars. There might be a variety of social, economic and personal aspects to each one of our hypothetical examples, but ultimately we have to say that at the personal level a cash valuation is meaningless, even though in some circumstances we have to make one.

Given this, a government policy which was based purely on CBA analysis of human welfare would be standing on shaky ground. The carefully constructed example exaggerates the problems, and it must be recognised that CBA is far ahead of anything the Thatcherites have used, but it is not the perfect tool for analysis. If a government chose not to build homes or hospitals, or ignored the physical or psychological welfare of its citizens when judging a policy, it might not be able to justify its actions on the basis of CBA, given the weakness of the underlying methodology.

Of course, some governments, such as the post-1979 Thatcherite one, will justify any action they choose to take. When we have sharp-witted, articulate politicians who have used their power over the media to subdue any criticism, it might seem they can justify their policies. The Thatcherite stance was a simple, 'don't spend what you haven't got', an approach which Keynes demolished in the 1930s.

With CBA however, the problem is that of valuing the invaluable, or putting a price on that which is priceless. And there are instances where price is simply meaningless. One way to deal with this is to apply one's Cost-Benefit Analysis in the usual way, and then make a subjective adjustment, based on human considerations. This allows us to add in the intangibles and value judgements that normal CBA does not permit. Despite this, it is as scientific as any other social analysis. For example, economists using computer models of the economy to make predictions will often make adjustments to the final print-out. This is claimed to allow human intuition to make the prediction more realistic.

Given that the computer model is often based on dubious theories of social and economic relationships, and is simplified to bring the economy to a level the computer can deal with, further human interference makes the whole process seem utterly unscientific. On the other hand, CBA puts a cash value on everything that can be valued, and then allows the use of value judgements for those things which are beyond value. Surely this approach is both the more rational, and the more human of the two.

Thus, in valuing the human impact of unemployment, one would treat all people the same. Their previous income would not be relevant to the need to create jobs, although one might say that it was more important to create jobs for the unskilled and low paid, than for the affluent skilled worker. However, in measuring the economic effects of unemployment, we would have to consider the past wage levels of the jobless workers. One would also give the provision of basic services a higher priority than the non-essentials. Thus, building schools and hospitals would have a higher value than new motorways.

Some on the New Right might say that this is totally unscientific, and that policy must be based on facts. The market is better, they would claim, therefore leave all decisions to the market — that is the efficient procedure. But what does it mean to say 'better', or 'efficient'? These are vague terms which only have meaning when carefully defined; in the normal hurly-burly of politics or in the carefully rehearsed television interview, politicians tend to avoid clear definitions. They go for sound bites, quotable comments, and vagueness that will allow them to later claim that they meant something else entirely.

In fact, for the Thatcherite New Right to criticise anybody on the basis of truth or accuracy would be somewhat like Pol Pot attacking Jonathan Ross for making cruel remarks. Since 1979, a whole succession of Conservatives have demonstrated only a vague understanding of the concept of truth, while adding whole glossaries full of euphemisms to the English language. We have heard of people being economical with the truth. We have seen Norman Lamont try to count phone calls as part of manufacturing production, so that he could say that output was rising. We have heard Mrs Thatcher say the NHS was safe in her hands — failing to mention that she wanted to carry out surgery on it, probably using an axe. Or we have John Major announcing that the NHS saved his life when he was born, this of course indicating the emotional depth of his commitment to that revered institution. What he failed to mention was that the NHS did not exist when he was born — in 1943.

There is a tendency to regard politicians as dubious scoundrels who are slightly lax with their definitions of truth, but under the Tories, this has become a romantic misconception. These are politicians who knowingly, deliberately, lie. It is not that they misunderstand the nature of truth, or fail to clarify the issues. It is simpler than that; they lie.

And the evidence they give in support of their opinions may also be lies. When they claim that their research or their civil servants tell them that a given policy is effective, that too may be a lie. Journalist Melanie Phillips has said that many civil servants in the Home Office were deeply upset at being misrepresented by Michael Howard. It is very likely that other Tory ministers have been equally casual about the 'actualité'.

In fact, we should make a point of seeking the flaws in anything that Conservative politicians say. Much of it has no factual content whatsoever. Rarely were Shakespeare's words more apt. It is a tale told by an idiot, full of sound and fury — signifying nothing.

One of the requirements of a democracy is accountability, that ministers must be seen to be responsible for failures, errors and incompetence on their part in the performance of their duties. Yet for the electorate to exercise this accountability, they must know what is being done by the government, and how successful it is. Thus, a secondary characteristic of democracy is open government. And this requires honesty.

The record of the post-1979 Tory regime in terms of its honesty is less than impressive. It may even be the worst on record this century. It ranges from the coy evasion to the gross exaggeration, from the half-truth to the outright lie, and from group collusion to cases of evasion of individual responsibility.

Some instances may be regarded as errors of judgement, as for example, when Norman Lamont accepted taxpayers' funds in 1991 to help evict a tenant from his London home. At the very least, this was questionable. It is normal for the Treasury to pay ministers' expenses, when incurred as part of their ministerial employment. Where the expense arises from a minister's private life, the Treasury should not offer public money, and the minister should not take it.

The Treasury gave Lamont £4,700 so that lawyer Peter Carter-Ruck, an expensive specialist in libel law, could handle the eviction of Lamont's tenant. Not only that, but the Treasury failed to inform the Auditor General of this dubious use of public money.

As the Treasury is charged with the control of government spending, it should have been unwilling to pay for a minister's private and personal costs. For that very reason, Lamont should have known better than to accept the money.

Michael Portillo may also fall in the error of judgement category, with his claim that foreign students buy their A Levels, and that government contracts abroad are obtained through corruption. These remarks were reported from a speech of his to students at Southampton University, and although he claimed that they were 'a slip of the tongue and that he had inadvertently exaggerated', this seems odd given that he had made the same sort of comments in a speech at Eton a few days earlier. (*The Guardian*, February 17, 1994.) Perhaps it was more than a momentary lapse, and may represent a recurring theme in Portillo's thought processes.

It probably indicates something about Portillo's view of foreigners, although it may also represent the over-enthusiasm of the recent immigrant — Portillo's parents came from Spain, and perhaps he himself does not feel truly, deeply British. But he clearly respects Britain; in his Southampton speech, he also told students that Britain was the most honest country in the world. Although at one point, he did refer to 'the British people, as a whole,' one wonders if he included politicians in his praise. He subsequently apologised for his remarks, although it has been said that merely by making them, he has demonstrated the xenophobia that lies in the heart of the Tory party.

One of the constitutional weaknesses of the British system of politics is the lack of any separation between the judiciary, the executive, and the legislature. The Lord Chancellor sits at the apex of all three, and is placed in a role which must be personally awkward as well as constitutionally unhealthy. As a member of the Cabinet, he advises on the legality of government policy, while as the head of the judiciary, he determines what the law actually is.

The flaw in this role was shown up when the Lord Chancellor, Lord Mackay, tried to persuade a judge to eliminate preliminary hearings, at which it had been decided whether alleged victims of racial or sexual discrimination had indeed got a case. Despite being head of the judiciary, the Lord Chancellor does not have the power to tell judges how to interpret the law. The judge, Mr Justice Wood, refused to end these hearings, saying that they were correct in law, and that Lord Mackay's suggestions would harm the quality of justice, merely so that the process of justice could be cheaper. Mackay's reply was that he was not interested in legal niceties, and demanded that Wood do Mackay's bidding, or 'consider his position'.

Quite clearly, Mackay was asking Wood to resign — something which Mackay did not have the right to do, even as Lord Chancellor. And given that Wood's stance was correct in law, Mackay did not even have a reason to ask for Wood's resignation.

One has to assume that the Lord Chancellor, influenced by arguments and ideology floating around the Cabinet, saw it as his duty to impose spending cuts on the judicial system. Given his ambivalent constitutional role, this was a dubious stance to take. But when Mackay described the chain of events to the House of Lords, he claimed that the request for Wood to 'consider his position' meant that he wanted Wood to explain how he could justify his arguments. But Wood had already given detailed explanations of his views, at a meeting, and in a letter. (*The Observer*, April 3, 1994.)

But the prize example of Tory economy with the truth must be the arms for Iraq affair. The government set up guidelines in 1988, banning the export of arms to Iraq, as it might prolong the Iran-Iraq war. But it was estimated that the loss of arms sales would cost Britain £1bn a year, as well as having serious consequences for public spending. On the other hand, the United States wanted Iraq's cheap oil. So the guidelines were changed, although Alan Clark says they were merely interpreted more flexibly.

This view is difficult to understand, given that the guidelines banned exports, and subsequent events showed that exports actually carried on throughout the war. In 1989, Mrs Thatcher claimed that the guidelines had been followed. And William Waldegrave claims that they could not have been changed, because if they were, Parliament would have had to be informed; it wasn't, therefore there was no change.

Yet if one Conservative leader is honest, it is John Major — presumably. After all, he is known to be a nice man. A very nice man. Yet Major suffers from terminological imprecision to a degree that suggests a loose grasp of reality. In one speech, he made so many dubious assertions that a Conservative MP was forced to write a rebuttal.

In December 1992, Major spoke to the House of Commons on the Maastricht Treaty. He claimed that under the Treaty, Britain was not committed to a single currency. Nicholas Budgen MP replied that we are legally obliged to enter the process of economic convergence, as well as to stage two of monetary union.

Major also claimed that immigration was specifically excluded from the Treaty. Nicholas Budgen replied that immigration is covered in Article K1. The third error made by Britain's then Prime Minister was to suggest that education was also 'explicitly' excluded from the Treaty. Budgen pointed out that under Article 126, the Community 'shall contribute to the development of quality of education...' by encouraging member states to co-operate with one another.

The Prime Minister also announced that defence was not a matter for the European Community. This was even harder to believe. Budgen cited the treaty's preamble, which spoke of 'a common foreign and security policy'. Defence is so much a part of the EU, that Austria nearly did not join, because EU military commitments conflicted with Austria's neutral constitution. Britain's obligations tie us to the Western European Union, a pan-European force with close links to NATO. It is beyond the outer limits of credibility that the Prime Minister of Britain did not know that the Maastricht Treaty involved deep and fundamental defence commitments.

Major's last, and least believable claim was that the citizens of Britain would always be British citizens. In a change even more central to the Maastricht Treaty than defence, a European citizenship is established which, in the opinion of some, supersedes and eliminates old-style national citizenships.

Earlier that year, Major had shown his grasp of statistical data by claiming that 'between 1981 and 1991, the British economy grew faster than the German economy, the French economy, the Italian economy, or the economy of any other country of Europe'.

One has to wonder at the source of John Major's figures, although the usual source for European statistics is the OECD, or the EU itself. Neil Kinnock, the Labour Party leader at that time, produced figures showing that over the period cited by Major, growth had been 25.9 per cent, or 2.3 per cent per year. Far from being the fastest-growing economy in Europe, we were in fact only 12th, below either the OECD average or the European Community average.

A few years later, William Rees-Mogg showed a similar inability to interpret raw statistical data, in an article for *The Times* which announced that Britain was 'the world's success story'. This grand claim was based on OECD figures, and suggested that Thatcherism was the fount of this amazing economic performance. Similarly, the refusal on the part of France to follow Thatcherism led to their poor performance.

However, economist Wynne Godley pointed out that Rees-Mogg had completely misinterpreted the OECD figures. Two days after his original misunderstanding, Rees-Mogg apologised in the pages of *The Times* for 'having misconceived' the OECD statistics. However, as Godley pointed out, Mogg did not withdraw the claims for Britain's economy, or for Thatcherism, made on the basis of the misunderstanding.

The reader was left with the impression that although the figures might be mistaken, the underlying conclusions were still valid. In fact, both the figures and the deductions drawn from them were wrong. Britain's performance over the period in question was actually very poor. The conclusion that should be drawn is that Thatcherism was a total disaster.

It might be argued that statistical data is difficult to understand, and that Rees-Mogg was only a journalist — although many journalists would understandably resent the 'only'. On the other hand, John Major was, at the time, the Prime Minister, which if nothing else means that he had access to a team of researchers and speech-writers, all of whom should have been capable of distinguishing between a high growth rate and a low one.

It might be argued that ministerial dishonesty is nothing new, that governments have always suffered from a degree of corruption and evasion. Yet under the Conservatives, this was such a problem that Major was forced in 1994 to set up guidelines for dealing with the press, which not only require overt honesty, but explain why there is a need for it. He also set up a sleaze test for MPs, which most of them had failed within a week of its inauguration.

A previous approach to dealing with leaks and unwelcome facts emerged from the health service, when William Waldegrave was Health Secretary. Public relations consultants for the NHS Management Executive suggested in 1991 setting up a news management service which would promote success stories, and carry out damage limitation on bad news. Naturally, this device to present the public with a more tasteful view of the facts was to be funded by the taxpayer.

Was the post-1979 government really so different in its moral standards? Was it being more economical with the actualité than previous governments? Or was it, for some inexplicable reason, subjected to more ferocious attacks by a normally friendly media? One answer comes from yet another Conservative. Sir Hal Miller, talking to *The Guardian* about the arms to Iraq affair, said that he had never seen 'so much lying in high places'. (*The Guardian*, January 16, 1992.)

Anything that ministers say about Keynesian demand management — or any other aspect of policy — must be viewed in the light of this integrity. It is not that deficit finance has been proved to be economically disastrous; it is simply that Tories, because of their ideology, dislike it. In order to depict opposing ideologies in a negative way, or portray their own policies as superior, they will say whatever is necessary to give the impression they seek to convey. Factual accuracy is simply not an issue.

It is a duty of government to ensure that the economy proceeds in an orderly manner. We need to avoid sudden and artificial growth, like the Lawson boom of the 1980s, while also avoiding severe recessions. That is, we need a counter-cyclical management of the economy. And regardless of the Conservatives' claims for the minimal state, there is a clear need for government intervention in the economy. The recession which started in 1990 is a good example of what happens when governments ignore the need for economic management.

At the time of writing, Conservatives will no doubt argue that Britain cannot afford to spend its way out of a recession. The tax base is too low, both through unemployment and through low rates of tax, for revenue to cover spending. And the deficits necessary for an effective counter-cyclical policy would be too large for their New Right sensibilities. But they have allowed budget deficits, and to that extent, Tory economic policy is Keynesian.

Indeed, the Tories have painted themselves into a corner. Given their own self-imposed rules as to what government can or cannot do, and the impact they have had on taxes and unemployment, policy alternatives are much more constrained. They have created a £50 billion budget deficit, and must also avoid a too-rapid recovery from the recession which could lead to a balance of payments problem. Or if we imagined another party in office, trying to spend our way out of the recession could run us into a larger budget deficit than the one the Conservatives have already created.

There is an implicit recognition that a large part of the problem is a lack of demand. For example, an article in the *Financial Times* in 1993 called for Japan to boost its economy, to increase demand. And G7 summits, like OECD reports, regularly utter calls for action to encourage demand. Despite this, the recession, low incomes, and the many unemployed, the Tories still argue that there is no lack of demand in Britain. Yet the current (1993) UK budget deficit is primarily the result of the high level of unemployment; if fewer people were unemployed, the amount paid out in benefits would be less, and with more people in jobs, tax revenue would be greater. Far from being a reason not to boost the economy, the budget deficit is actually evidence of the need to act.

According to the Campaign for Local Economic Strategies (CLES), the probable cost of unemployment is around £47 billion (*Economic Sense: Local Jobs Plans*, CLES.). This figure is at 1987 prices, and updated to 1993, the year of the £50 bn deficit, gives a cost of unemployment in excess of the budget shortfall. Thus, there is a very good case for saying that if the number of jobless was reduced to a more reasonable level, there would be no problem.

In addition to the saving on benefits, and the extra tax revenue from the newly employed, there would be the indirect effects. In what is described as the multiplier effect, each newly-employed person spends more money than before, thus creating extra demand and more jobs. Thus, even more income tax is generated.

Much of the problem has been created by the attitude that government must do certain things; it must not intervene in industry, it must cut taxes, it is not responsible for the health of the economy, and so on. One justification for this being, according to Patrick Minford, 'If it's a good thing, then industry will do it' (on *The Money Programme*, May 23, 1993). In fact, industry has failed to act in the economy's interest regarding training, investment, research and development and the creation of infrastructure. And one would not even expect the business sector to deal with counter-cyclical policy.

To announce that certain things are, or are not, the government's job is as illogical as the Labour Party deciding that state ownership is sacrosanct. To argue about what the government should do, or own, is to misunderstand the nature of politics. The key issue is what outcomes the state should be generating.

In a liberal democracy, the government should carry out whatever policies are necessary to generate outcomes such as economic stability, job creation, high standards of living, good quality of life, and low levels of inequality. The main questions are about how to achieve these outcomes, but the fact of them is not in doubt.

If we had an adjusted Cost-Benefit Analysis, it would produce far more sensible, more cost-effective, and more socially unifying policies than those of the Tory government. Typically, the Conservatives have been steadily expanding the British motorway network, arguing this created a better transport system, as well as creating jobs. It has led to such ludicrous spectacles as Mrs Thatcher standing in the middle of the just-completed M25, saying what a wonderful achievement it was for Britain. In the United States it would be just another freeway. Indeed, a few years after the Leaderene's jingoistic photo-opportunity, the government was announcing the need for by-passes round the M25 to take the excess traffic from it!

This should not be too surprising, as everyone knows that the volume of car traffic expands to fill the available roads. Build a motorway, and all the car drivers will come out to use it. The alternative approach, of building roads that will be able to cope will all the likely traffic, is simply impossible. A Canadian study showed that even with their space, it would be impractical to build 'roads which could cope with peak travel demand by car alone. A computer simulation for Montreal in 1980 showed that it would be necessary to have fourteen to twenty-two lanes for every freeway link within six miles of the city centre'. (Harry W. Richardson, *Urban Economics*, p105.)

A rational transport policy would first apply CBA to both public and private systems. Motorways could be costed in terms of the cost of land or housing that had to be bought to lay the road, and then presumably, the cost of extra housing to be built to replace any that had to be demolished. In addition, it should take account of the extra pollution, energy use, acid rain, and noise caused by road vehicles. And finally, it should make allowance for the social value of any land or property destroyed by the motorway. For example, a road that requires the destruction of historic buildings, woodland or wildlife habitat should have extra cost penalties set against it.

The total cost of alternative systems could be compared, with the proviso that in considering an urban system, the cost of congestion also has to be taken into account. In Britain, traffic jams cost £15 billion per year, and any road-building would simply add to the congestion. Then one could look at the benefits of each project. Whether road or rail, the planned scheme would create jobs — the question is, how many? Given the knock-on effects that road-building has on the car industry, the motorway scheme might have the advantage here. On the other hand, a rail link would have a saving in fuel resources, and other factors mentioned above. But in addition, there is a rail manufacturing industry. Cuts in rail funding, like the privatisation of buses, reduces the UK's manufacturing base. So while we allow for a motorway's impact on the car industry, we should also allow for a rail scheme's impact on rail manufacturing.

Then one would look at the longevity of the project. To judge by the M25, some motorways have a very short useful life. But most infrastructure investments have a very long life; schools, hospitals, railway lines, houses, and so on, all have very considerable lifespans. Because of this, investing in infrastructure is one of the most cost-effective uses of state funds. Motorways, uniquely it seems, have to be repaired within months of opening.

All these factors could serve as the basis for a well-informed decision, on the basis of the costs, benefits, and side-effects of each method. Under the Conservatives there has clearly been a subjective evaluation, coming down in favour of motorways, and disregarding all other forms of spending. This is a political decision, taking account of the demands of the road transport lobby, rather than the needs of the country as a whole. Most influential in this decision-making process would be the impact of road-building on the car industry. In other words, economic factors are taken into account, but only in a narrow way.

Ideally, policy should take total welfare into account. This need not mean that everyone will be made better off by every policy, as some policies would tend to work for particular targeted groups. The important feature is that the policy platform as a whole will be to the advantage of all. Also, some people do not need enriching, so their needs would have a lower priority than others. Nor would we focus purely on material well-being. Also, one cannot expect every single policy to benefit even a majority. Some rules may help low-income groups, others would aid people in rented accommodation, and so on. But the broad trend should be to help the majority, focusing primarily on those most in need. Unless the economy is run for the welfare of the people — all people — the managers have no moral legitimacy.

If the state carries out policy purely for the well-being of a selected minority, but ignores those who are most in need, and disregards society as whole, that state must be regarded as little short of criminal. If it compounds what can, at best, be incompetence, with superficial presentation, self-serving propaganda, and outright lies, then it lays itself open to impeachment. Morally, the Tory regime that first took office in 1979 lacks the right to be in office.

However, although we may be concerned with those in need, with the clear implication that there must be a welfare state, that does not necessarily mean spending more on all individuals. In the past, welfare spending has been seen by some as giving money to those in need. This is fine as a short-term palliative, but it does not solve the person's long-term problems. What they want for the future is a job or a career or an education, not a subsistence level dose of parish relief.

But targeting does not equal low levels of expenditure, as it has done under the Conservatives. Targeting should mean effective spending, yet in many cases, the Tories' cuts have simply resulted in low quality services. The trend has been to provide the service at the lowest possible cost, and it is in the arena of welfare, especially health care, that low cost most obviously equals inferior provision. For example, would a person needing heart or brain surgery wish to have the operation performed by the lowest cost surgeon? This might be a trainee vet, with no insurance, working from a converted meat store. Perhaps this example is slightly exaggerated, but clearly, lowest cost is not always the best bargain.

The Thatcherite argument for cutting welfare spending was that generous state benefits encourage people to become (or remain) unemployed. It was said that incentives are needed to persuade people to work, rather than be idle, so taxes and benefits would be kept low. Logically, the reasoning should be that low dole payments should be allied with high wages — the carrot and the stick. However, the New Right follow a line that goes from low taxes, to more take-home pay, to workers being better off. This ignores the fact that the same government that is lowering taxes is also weakening trade unions, and eroding the bargaining position of workers in general. As a result, it is lowering wages even further, and making employment even less attractive. Either ministers are totally unaware of the contradiction, or there is a hidden agenda. The implication is a tacit ratchet effect; lower wages require even lower benefits for incentives to employment to exist.

In an attempt to prove this dubious theory of incentives, the Treasury instigated a research study 'to examine evidence for the Thatcherites' conviction that tax cuts are crucial to improving the supply side of the economy'. (*The Guardian*, December 15, 1986.) This study took from 1979 until 1986 — and found no evidence whatsoever for the thesis.

Expenditure needs to be targeted, to be sufficient for the task, and to be directed at root causes, rather than temporary issues. That is, government policy should deal with the problem, rather than the person's immediate need; it should cure the causes, not the symptoms. People become vulnerable to unemployment because they lack the skills the market needs, or they lack the education to be adaptable in what they do. Or on the macro side of the equation, people are unemployed because there is not enough demand in the economy. If the government was to concentrate on providing all the necessary training and education for the entire workforce, people would be less likely to become unemployed. And if Tories were not so obsessed with reducing government spending, there would be more purchasing power in the economy, and therefore more need for workers.

Once again, the moral and the logical operate together. As mentioned above, by reducing unemployment, one creates a taxpayer, where there was none, and one removes a cost to the Exchequer. Therefore it makes financial sense to reduce unemployment. But there is also the moral imperative. Governments have a duty to look after the well-being of their citizens, and this means creating the social infrastructure that any civilised society should have.

It might be argued that if those individuals who lack the appropriate skills got extra training, perhaps they might keep their jobs, but given the state of the economy, someone would have to be out of work. The answer is two-fold — firstly, given a skilled and educated workforce, the economy is likely to be stronger, and wages would be higher. A higher quality workforce would boost the economy's productivity, and therefore sales would be higher, and unemployment would be lower. Also, skilled workers earn more, so the level of demand would be greater. They can ask for higher wages, but they also spend more.

Secondly, the type of government that recognised the need to spend on education would probably also be the sort that recognised the need for state spending generally. Thus, it would be interventionist, perhaps even Keynesian. Yet even if it was not spending in other areas, the additional spending needed to provide the education and training required, would itself create extra demand. The resultant consumer spending would create sufficient demand to create the jobs needed. Therefore, dealing with the workers' needs would be a far better long-term way of solving the problem of unemployment than by simply paying dole money every week.

It should be pointed out that this is not a Workfare scheme which is being suggested. In America, Workfare has been seen by the New Right as a means of ensuring that those in need do not cost the taxpayer too much, that they support themselves, that they gain skills allowing them to get jobs in the future, and ensuring that assistance is properly targeted. British politicians claim to have seen the 'success' of Workfare, and argue that it should be applied in Britain.

In fact, the scheme is not applied throughout the United States, although there are few states which have not applied one or other of the two main schemes. These are, the Work Incentive Programme (WIN), and the Community Work Experience Programme (CWEP). The underlying principles of Workfare date back to 1962, and the predecessor of CWEP, the Community Work Training Programme (CWTP). This allowed states to set up work programmes, so that some welfare recipients could 'work off' their benefits. This was a clear expression of the anti-welfare attitude that exists in the United States, that people have to work to 'earn' their benefits. It is not based on the principle that members of society are entitled to state support, as a right.

There is also a strong element of compulsion in Workfare. In 1980 the WIN programme was beefed up with sanctions against those who refused to participate in WIN, those who refused to accept employment, and those who reduced the number of hours they worked, or in some other way, reduced their earnings (see Louis Burghes, *Made in the U.S.A.*). But the compulsion, by itself, is not the most offensive aspect of Workfare. After all, we have compulsion in Britain, as to whether we wear seat belts in our cars.

The worrying aspects of Workfare can be divided up into the attitudes, and the operations. The compulsion, and the belief that recipients have to earn their dole money, suggest a stern paternalism reminiscent of the Victorian era. The lower orders are seen as lazy, cunning and shiftless. So the state has to force them to work, to earn their keep. As mentioned, the state is not seen as having a duty to the less fortunate, which is a questionable attitude to exist in a so-called democracy.

There is no doubt that this attitude affects the workings of the system. Given that it is intended as a punishment, or as the stick to force the proles to work, little effort is put into ensuring that the training given is of high quality. The evidence suggests that the American scheme provides poor quality training, and one can be sure that if the Conservatives introduced Workfare to Britain, the training would be on a par with YTS programmes. It would not help the jobless to find work, but would condemn them to a life of semi-permanent welfare dependency. Neither the individual nor the state would be any better off. Peter Mandelson's support for workfare, for single mothers and the unemployed raises questions about the attitudes underlying Labour Party policy.

It is also a perfect corollary of a society in which the state recognises no duty to look after the well-being of the citizen. It sees no obligation to create employment, therefore it resents paying for benefits. The system is driven by vocal pressure groups, rather than by a moral imperative, therefore when the big business and middle class tax evaders seek to reduce their tax liability, the jobless must suffer the effects. But as big business has previously sought to hold wages down to the lowest possible level, lower benefits are necessary to make even the most rudimentary employment seem attractive.

The argument that causes should be targeted rather than symptoms can be used in the case of minimum income schemes. Rather than the state paying a minimum income, or imposing such an obligation on employers, it would be better if the government sought to improve the workers' skills. Not that minimum wage schemes are inherently bad, but all they deliver to the recipient is a living wage, while the economy gets a modest input of purchasing power. This is good, but not good enough; it does not cover all needs. The worker deserves more, while society may need certain skills. One of the many obscenities of Britain's unemployment is that while tens of thousands are homeless, tens of thousands of builders are without jobs. A scheme based on providing the education and training that workers need, with benefits paid as grants rather than dole, would serve the long-term needs of both society and the individual far better than a simple dole money.

The same approach could be applied to people caught in the poverty trap, or the career trap. Some workers on state benefits find that if they earn more money, they are taxed more, so that they gain nothing from their extra effort. They suffer a marginal tax rate of 100 per cent. This is no incentive to work harder, and must work to the disadvantage of both society and the individual. One solution would be to raise the income level beyond which benefit entitlement was withdrawn. In effect, we could allow people a comfortable standard of living, rather than a mere subsistence level.

The career trap works in a similar way, and again, operates for the good of no one. There are many people in full-time work who would like to move up the career ladder, but they are unable to do so, because they cannot take time off work to get the qualifications they need. To give up their job to study would be recklessly dangerous in the current economic climate. But to remain in the job could doom them to an industry or profession that has become, or is becoming, obsolete. They need to do something, but the rules allow them to do nothing.

The solution would be to impose on all companies the obligation to keep jobs for people, if they leave the firm for any valid reason. Thus, for pregnant women, or anyone seeking better qualifications, jobs could be held for an agreed term. For example, legislation could impose a one-year freeze on jobs for women who leave to have a baby, or a three year freeze for anyone who leaves to get a university degree. In Austria, for example, women get two years maternity leave.

The state must carry out proper welfare spending, if only for moral reasons. As human beings, we have a duty to care for the less fortunate. If we have an excess of food, and we watch others starve, or if we have more money than we need, and others are poor, then our moral standards are in need of improvement. But the very existence of the nation can also be put in doubt. The state ceases to be legitimate if it fails to care for the well-being of its citizens. It is failing to do its job — that is, the sole justification for the state's existence is that a group of people get together for mutual advantage. If the elected managers of that group fail to carry out that task, they should be sacked.

It is also necessary for social stability; the consensus is strained if a significant minority do not gain from the social order. Most people have certain beliefs as to how society should be run, and extensive poverty does not fit that view. However, one could say that this is simply a matter of socialisation, and that the Conservatives have managed to move the agenda. As a result, unemployment and poverty are more acceptable than they were in the 1960s. Yet this coexists with an awareness that the Tories have failed in their task. And because the Tories have not even attempted to improve society, they have generated a degree of cynicism which is deeply corrosive of all democratic values.

Also, the underclass may react violently against the social order, as with the riots in Brixton, Toxteth, Bristol, and other parts of the UK. This disorder is expensive in terms of property damage, personal violence, and insurance costs. A society that was merely well-run, and made no moral judgements, would seek to avoid such disturbances. But even disregarding the financial costs, the crimes of the poor may be directed against individuals, thus reducing the quality of life for the materially better off. Thus, if only for selfish reasons, the middle classes should be concerned about the level of unemployment or homelessness. One would want the peasants to live sufficiently comfortably to avoid them frightening the horses. But anyone with any shred of moral decency would want the lower income groups to have, at minimum, a standard of living that allowed for reasonable comfort.

But from the economist's point of view, the key argument is that welfare spending creates purchasing power. Those on low incomes — the most likely recipients of state payments — are likely to spend all of their income. This goes straight back into the economy, creating more employment.

Thus, we have a range of separate reasons, all pointing to the need for welfare spending. Each argument can be defended independently of the others, so they do not stand and fall as one unit. One might even say that there was an element of contradiction. Can we plead both a moral claim, and refer to the self-interest of the middle classes? I would suggest that this is not a conflict, but a reinforcement. Sometimes we act in a way that we should, only because of our selfishness. This does not invalidate the ethical aspect of the act, although perhaps it indicates our failure to be morally correct at all times.

The state is subject to a moral imperative to utilise the most effective methods possible to manage the economy, and this requires that it be based on CBA, but go beyond it. It should apply that method to — at a minimum — welfare, counter-cyclical policy, and infrastructure. In addition, one could add the areas that the New Right see as the state's minimum role — enforcement of contracts, property rights, and protecting the rule of law.

I would argue, however, that we should take this minimum level for granted, and that sensible spending levels go far beyond this New Right ideological base. That is, the state is obliged to impose a variety of regulations; but not merely to provide a minimal functioning of the economy. Its role is to carry out the best possible practice for the welfare of all members of society. Claims regarding the ideological purity of deregulation policies are simply meaningless, empty rhetoric. As we have said, the state's function is not to restrict itself to certain types of action, but to achieve certain outcomes.

Given this, the privatisation programme, carried on the back of claims of greater efficiency and rolling back the frontiers of the state, represents a disregard for the proper job of the state. Privatisation has been accurately described as an experiment; hence, it should not be applied freely to all sectors until there is some evidence of its effectiveness.

The issue of privatisation can be divided into two main areas — the sell-off of state industry, and the opening-up to the market of services such as health. With the first group, there is the simple issue of efficiency, although we also need to consider the effectiveness of social provision. Yet privatisation seems to fail here on both counts. Treasury figures show that nationalised industries outperform the manufacturing average by as much as three times. (*The Guardian*, March 3, 1993.)

Victor Keegan suggests that the real key to success is not ownership, but competition. Those companies which have not felt the impact of real competition have had healthy profits and strong share prices. However, there is still the question of whether this is the result of monopoly profiteering, or outstanding efficiency. Anecdotal evidence suggests the former. Keegan argues that those companies which have not felt the full force of competition are struggling, perhaps burdened by the same structural difficulties that drove them to the safety of state ownership in the first place.

Just as Marxists and Labour Party stalwarts used to be obsessed with the state becoming the owner of large tracts of industry, the Tories now see salvation in the state ceasing to be the owner. In fact, neither answer is correct. What we need to create is an economy where the companies are of the right size for efficiency and for reasonable economies of scale, and where there is healthy competition. Occasionally, companies in older industries may have to be guided, encouraged into lines of business that offer better prospects. But the state does not fulfil its obligation to the citizen merely by selling industry to private shareholders.

Similar arguments to those which justify welfare spending apply to counter-cyclical policy. The moral issue is that economic fluctuations cause unnecessary suffering, and if the government can even out the variations in the economic cycle at no great cost, then it should do so.

However, Hayek has said that the bankruptcies and unemployment that occur in a recession might be beneficial, as they allow resources to be re-allocated. Perhaps those resources are being used inefficiently, and the new use will improve total welfare.

But this ignores the fact that in a recession, both the healthy and the sick company go to the wall. An economic slump is no respecter of manufacturing productivity. Because demand has fallen, even some of the best firms are unable to survive; regardless of efficiency, the sales are no longer there. Even in the best of times, well-run companies are driven out of business by the short-sighted attitudes of the banks. But in a slump, good management is no security. It would seem that Hayek's argument applies only to a minority of company closures. The one time it would be valid would be when there is no recession.

Typically, bankruptcy involves the disintegration of a well-run organisation, dispersing skilled workers and specialised machinery, and halting manufacturing procedures that may have been refined over many years. A group of people who may have been brilliant at creating cars, or books, or clothes or farm produce are suddenly out of a job. Machinery that has been selected specifically for that task is instantly transformed into scrap metal. The skills and processes that were learnt over generations may be lost forever, and at the very best, may be difficult and expensive to re-create.

In addition, entrepreneurial skills, management knowledge and finance may be lost. The people running the company may have been through a long learning curve, finding out the practicalities of business the hard way. They may also have put their life savings and their life's work into the company. To see their wealth and their ambitions destroyed may be a hard blow for many. They have created an enterprise, a source of employment for themselves and others, and may be doing something they value for itself. Then, their life's work is obliterated by some senseless whim of government. They may never be able to re-create the finance to start a new business, or they may never recover from the psychological damage. Either way, the entrepreneurial skills are lost for ever.

The total cost of these losses would be difficult to calculate. One could estimate for the lost production of closed companies. But how would one calculate the extra costs for future company start-ups, caused by the dispersal of skilled workers? How could one determine the reduced number of new businesses, due to loss of entrepreneurial capital, or lack of confidence? As a result of there being fewer companies, there would be less competition, but trying to measure the impact of this would be straining the boundaries of scientific validity. It would be measuring an intangible, caused by an unknown. But the relationship would be there.

Given all these costs, one would say that the government had an economic duty, as well as a moral one, to apply a counter-cyclical policy. Both responses are justified within their own realm. The economic argument is that the cost of action is less than the cost of the damage caused. The moral argument is simply to reduce suffering. The wholistic reasoning is that policy relates to, and is determined by, one's moral stance. And if one cares about people, whether workers, management or entrepreneurs, one has to act in ways that deal with their needs. The state's role as a manager requires that it select an instrument that is known to have a good chance of dealing with the problem, and then apply that method in the most cost-effective way.

With infrastructure, ethical considerations are no longer the primary issue. The state spends on infrastructure because it is necessary for the economy, for society, for the efficient functioning of a modern civilisation. We need hospitals, schools, transport and communication, simply for our society to operate. But the better these services are, the more efficiently the nation will work.

A good point for any cost-conscious government to be aware of is that infrastructure spending is the most cost-effective form of spending there is. In Britain we have schools, hospitals, and railways that date back to the nineteenth century. In those areas which are relatively high technology, such as telephone exchanges, some equipment can date back as far as the 1930s. Money invested in these basics will provide a service for decades to come. However, one aspect that the New Right seem to be unaware of, is that these things do need maintenance. Cutting spending on repairs and upkeep is a very soft target. In the first year, the cuts show no ill-effect; in the second year, there may be no problems. But after a few years of such misguided 'savings', the backlog of maintenance may be enormous. This is the problem with sewers, schools, hospitals, and railways. The savings have gone past the point at which they are cost-effective, or where they can be easily made up.

Yet upkeep costs are minimal compared to the total cost of a project, and seen over its usable lifespan. For this reason, infrastructure spending makes very good sense. To attempt to save money on this is short-sighted and counter-productive. As mentioned, savings on maintenance can only be continued for a short while. To attempt to save on capital spending is even more foolish. Capital projects, such as new telephone exchanges, new schools and so on, may cost a lot of money, but in the long term, they save it. The building of canals in Britain cut transport costs, the construction of railways cut costs even more. Each new item of capital investment allows society to function better.

Schools and colleges create an educated population who will invent the next generation of ideas. We also need skilled workers for our factories and offices. Yet we find that by the age of eighteen, only a quarter of the population is in full-time education, compared with 60 per cent in Japan or France. (The Commission on Social Justice, *The Justice Gap*.) It is generally accepted that one of the reasons Britain is falling behind countries such as Germany or Japan is that our workers are not skilled enough, and that we do not have enough graduates — especially in science and engineering, or with commercially useful qualifications. And, ignoring our right to health care, hospitals do a service for society in ensuring that people are healthy, and fit to do their jobs. Thus, without invoking any moral dimension, there are good practical reasons for maintaining social services that even a moderately sensible Thatcherite should be able to grasp.

By offering decent education and training to all, one would also be changing the social environment. As wages rose and opportunities increased, the underclass in the 1990s sense would cease to exist. Not only would standards of living improve, but people's expectations would rise. Instead of seeing the structure of opportunities as operating against them, working class people would see new career possibilities opening up, if not for themselves, at least for their children. As well as creating a better way of life for the ordinary person, this also reduces the incentive, the need for young people to turn to crime. Therefore, it improves the quality of life for everyone.

But at the same time, the government should do all it could to improve the distribution of income. Obviously, the Conservatives are, by their nature, unlikely to take such a U-turn, as the enrichment of the rich is one of its chief goals. However, one can envisage some future government taking on the tasks that government is supposed to do, and trying to improve the quality of life for everyone. In this case, it will take a modest amount of extra income tax from the rich, and use the money to cut taxes, and increase benefits, for the lower income groups.

This need be little more than reversing the inequitable tax changes that the Tories have introduced, along with a return to the old balance between direct and indirect taxes. Direct taxes can be progressive, re-distributing wealth from the rich to the poor. But with the shift to VAT and other indirect taxes, the Tories take disproportionately from the incomes of the poor. This is both unjust and economically damaging.

It has been argued that increased growth is necessary to get Britain out of its recession, and give everyone a decent standard of living. Perhaps we need growth to end the slump, but it is not needed in order to improve living standards.

An expansion of state spending, especially if financed by additional tax revenue, would allow the government to spend more on education and training, as well as expanding job opportunities in other areas. And with a better education, and a more useful range of skills, the worker who is currently unskilled and low paid becomes a valuable and valued contributor to the workforce. If at the same time, the economy is expanding because of Keynesian stimulus, there would be more jobs available for everyone. So the skilled worker would be more likely to get a well-paid job.

Thus, we have the reverse of the Thatcherite downgrade. Thatcherism has shrunk the economy, shifted the tax burden onto the poor and the middle income groups, cut benefits, de-skilled the workforce, and reduced the total number of jobs. The social market approach would expand the economy, shift the tax burden back to the rich, raise benefits, add to the knowledge and skills of the workforce, and increase the number of jobs.

It is not a difficult thing to do. The surprising feature is that we allowed the Thatcherites to carry out the downgrade in the first place. If we look at the moral aspect, the state has an obligation to its citizens to provide some benefits. The social contract between state and citizen means that membership of society yields some advantage. The more advanced the society, and its technology and facilities, the more that society must be capable of offering its people. If a nation has sufficient wealth to give every person a life of exquisite luxury, it is guilty of negligence or worse if a significant number of those people are living in poverty.

But a return to economic health is not simply a matter of reversing every aspect of Thatcherism. Some of those policies may actually have been beneficial. But other, more important changes are needed; the pre-1979 status quo was not perfect.

The post-1979 Tory regime did not seem to recognise the concept of infrastructure. It was aware of the need for railways, transport and communication, and had policies for each of these. It was concerned that they should be subject to competition, so where necessary, the Tories would, where not already carried out, introduce privatisation. The forces of the market would then ensure that everyone operates at the maximum level of efficiency. So prices will be low, and the consumer will — in theory — be better off. Where there is not sufficient competition to guarantee this, regulation is applied.

Thus, competition is presented as a stimulus to efficiency, which is seen as a good thing in itself. But as mentioned above, we need to define efficiency, and decide how we measure it, before we impose it as the universal solution to all of society's ills. To judge it simply by lower prices and lower costs can be very misleading. It could simply demonstrate poor quality and lower wages. The danger is that the New Right view of the economy sets an agenda in which efficiency may seem to be more important than welfare. The Conservatives seek to make workers poorer, and offer inferior products, allegedly to make everyone better off. It is not a credible argument.

Also, we need to define efficiency, to determine what it implies in practice. What may appear to be a cold, rational, economic distinction is in reality a political matter on which voters have a right to be consulted. If 'efficiency' means lower wages, fewer jobs and inferior products, one cannot meaningfully argue that society is made better by it.

We need to distinguish between long-term and short-term efficiency. Most of the faults of current economic thinking are visible in the contemporary situation. For example, mass production of cheap consumer goods uses up huge amounts of raw materials. But low price manufacturing seems necessary because of universal low wages, and the desire of big business for mass markets. If more nations had affluent, educated markets, consumer goods would be less in demand, and bought with both an eye to their value for money, and to their environmental impact.

Also, can we meaningfully refer to 'efficiency' if all that has happened is that wages have been cut? Or if the number of staff has been reduced? If, for example, the Royal Mail reduced the number of deliveries, in order to cut staff, we could not say that it was operating any better. Efficiency means a greater output from a given input; if one reduces both input and output, one has achieved nothing. One has lower costs, but also the customer gets a poorer service.

As part of its privatisation plans, the government intends that the Royal Mail raises its productivity. In fact, ministers want the Mail to achieve a 15 per cent increase in mail volumes, but with 10,000 less staff. It is hard to believe that the result will be greater efficiency in any meaningful sense, or that the public at large will be better off in any way.

In some cases the cost cuts might have a wider social impact, with the burden of provision simply shifted to the consumer. If the NHS refuses to care for the elderly, then families must look after their own relatives, sick or not. This is no gain for society in terms of the utilisation of resources. Or if the Crown Prosecution Service reduces the number of cases it prosecutes, as has happened, not only is justice not served, there is also the danger that criminals will come to regard the law as little more than an inconvenience.

What we find is that in many cases of so-called increased efficiency, all that has happened is that the allocation of resources has altered. It is not that the resources are being used better. It is not that there is a more effective use; it is simply a change in the identity of the users. Thus, companies or individuals are providing a service instead of a state-owned body. This implies that efficiency is not a simple, mechanical measure, but is merely a political judgement. This would be acceptable, were it not covered up in a shroud of pseudo-scientific pretence.

There may also be a trade-off between efficiency and democracy.

The question of whether or not competition does create greater efficiency is usually taken for granted by the Tories. And both privatisation and merger policy have ignored the need for competition. We have seen such examples as British Airways being allowed to buy up British Caledonian, as well colluding with other companies to destroy Laker Airlines. The Tory government deliberately chose not to guarantee competition when privatising British Airways, and gave only half-hearted attention to it in the public sell-off of British Telecom. Equally lukewarm was its attempt to create competition in the brewing industry.

It is worth noting that in the business world, efficiency is not seen as a central goal. And this is particularly true, according to one American economist, when there is insufficient competition. Leibenstein says that when there is little competition, workers will exchange effort and control for the feeling of not being under pressure, and having better personal relations at work. (H. Leibenstein, 'Allocative efficiency vs. X-efficiency', in *American Economic Review*, June 1966, cited in Devine, Lee, Jones and Tyson, *An Introduction to Industrial Economics.*) That is, the workers will enjoy the job, rather than being controlled by it.

Very often as companies become larger, rather than becoming lean machines, and gaining the economies of scale that are assumed to be the automatic feature of big business, they actually become bureaucratic. Management employ more staff in their own private empires, and white collar workers multiply like flies. Managers' status within the hierarchy is measured by the number of staff under them, or by the make of their company car. But each individual executive is too far from the pressures of competition for anyone to know how efficient their department is.

Shielded by corporate size from the cold winds of the market, office workers are able to play at business. Playing with their new technology toy, the ubiquitous computer, they can have fun with software rather being obsessed with work. An American study showed that while 18 per cent of capital investment went on computing during the 1980s, the productivity of the office worker declined by 1 per cent per year. (*Computerworld*, 1989, cited in *The Guardian*, August 12, 1993.) The only apparent explanation is that employees are playing with Windows, Desk Top Publishing (DTP) and other clever devices, to produce beautiful reports and elegant graphics far beyond the company's actual needs.

Given top management's ambivalent view of workers, this is no cause for concern. Although manual and industrial workers are seen as a blight on the factory, white collar workers are seen as both necessity and status symbol. Company reports may boast about the amount of money spent on research or the sum spent on computers, and no one sees the money as wasted. Yet management grudges spending on capital investment that will make the manufacturing side of the business more efficient.

It would seem that efficiency is no more than a stick with which to beat the small company. It is merely another part of the New Right armoury, fine for shooting down competitors and ideological opponents but of no importance whatsoever in practice.

What is needed is a genuinely competitive economy, with lots of small and medium sized firms — and with those big companies that do still exist being very closely monitored. Large corporations can be aggressively anti-competition — and again, BA is a good example. One possibility is to copy the American triple damages legislation; in the United States, when one company damages another company in some way, the victim is entitled to claim three times its costs from the aggressor. For example, in BA's attack on Virgin, Richard Branson would add up the cost of all the harm done to Virgin, triple it, and that would be BA's bill.

It could be argued that there are a whole range of other corporate activities that need to be eliminated, from the eagerness with which companies now get rid of surplus staff, to the casual abuse of the environment. The first is symptomatic of the market philosophy that Thatcherism has brought to Britain. Companies no longer see either workers or staff as assets, but as resources to be exploited; and in the case of workers, to be acquired or disposed of as cheaply as possible. It is to be hoped that Thatcherism is on its way out, and that with its demise, the harshness of the New Right will also disappear. The tragedy is that Thatcherite policies are already built into EU economic policy.

Environmental issues are increasingly of concern to the socially responsible corporation, but in most cases there need to be external pressures for a company to realise its need to be socially responsible. This requires that the firm be vulnerable to outside forces, and if the firm is so multinational that each country is only a small percentage of its global profits profile, then it is going to be less susceptible to outside pressure.

The issue of competition, and of small business, will be examined in detail in the next chapter. But clearly, this is an area of major concern. Most governments since the war have been so indifferent to the existence of competition that it has been almost eliminated from the UK economy, even while it retained a prominent place in ministers' speeches.

The New Right stance is that the state should not impose its policies on society, but let the individual choose for themselves. Privatisation and deregulation allow the market to function effectively, so that, they say, the individual has more choice. Parents can choose which school to send their children to — although education as a whole has been so underfunded that it is a choice between one undermaintained school and another. It is intended by the Conservatives that in future people with lower qualifications and no teacher training will be able to work in teaching. This will no doubt be presented as allowing schools to use their funds more effectively; the schools will have the choice as to whom they can employ on their shrinking budgets.

Patients will also have more choice. They can go on the register of a local GP of their choosing, rather than be stuck with one they cannot trust or sympathise with. However, their GP will now have limited funds, and will not want patients with expensive diseases on their register. One might think that unlimited funding was a recipe for disaster, but the local GP was one part of the NHS that most people were not dissatisfied with. This may be partly because of the size and the accessibility of the local practice. Local provision, by itself, may be an excellent way of ensuring a high quality service.

However, the government should should not be obsessed with the economy as a mechanism for providing material goods. In the 1980s the Conservatives talked about a shrinkage of the industrial sector, parallel to a rise in the service sector. All the evidence suggests, however, that what they really felt was mere apathy towards industry. What would be more constructive would be a positive switch from industrial production to personal well-being.

Thus, instead of the Tories' passive acceptance of rising unemployment in industry, we need monitoring of the resources used in manufacturing, and more resources put into the services and welfare sectors. Many people get an enormous improvement in their quality of life from education, leisure, and personal development. Some of this is currently provided privately, but education should be available from the state, free at all times to all who want it. Some politicians might complain about those who switch from one degree course to another, but this is a small price — if indeed there is an overall cost — to pay for the benefit of having a skilled and educated workforce.

And as well as the boost to the economy, there is the gain to the individual. Most people find education the most satisfying investment they can make; or seen as a leisure activity, it is the most rewarding one. Yet access to education is controlled as tightly as possible, while the quality is held as low as possible. Many writers have seen this sort of approach as a social control mechanism, and with the Tories, there is no doubt of the truth of this.

The careful use of resources could improve the sustainability of our manufacturing processes, and the quality of the environment. The way we collect raw materials, the throwaway goods we produce, and the glossy consumerism of our society all promote an unthinking abuse of the planet's resources. The major industrial corporations all seem trapped in a short-term profit-seeking mentality, each one apparently caught by the attitudes of all the others. However, there is no doubt that when we are down to the last few forests, mines and oil wells, the corporations will simply use the scarcity to push prices up.

Ultimately, the economy should provide quality of life rather than simply better material standards of living. That means providing well-being, happiness, and personal growth. However, even these things need some material production, and therefore require access to resources for their continuation. Perhaps more to the point, it might not be possible to maintain a liberal quality of life in the harsh corporate economy of the future. Now is the time to change that economy.

To conclude, we need a return to the Keynesian demand management of the past, but with more effective use of all resources, including financial ones. To this end, we cannot afford the wasted skills of the jobless or the poorly educated; the economy needs all the skills it can get.

To create an educated workforce, and employ them in the necessary tasks, requires an active welfare state. And higher taxes are needed to pay for such intervention. Yet this will not involve any greater tax burden on the lower income groups; it only requires a reversal of the inegalitarian tax changes that have occurred under the Conservatives.

One of the most damaging aspects of Tory government has been its links with big business, and its willingness to impose the policies that commerce seeks. There is plenty of evidence that a liberal, welfare economy would be both practical and highly efficient. It is time that we stopped listening to the smug clichés of an ideology that has so obviously failed.

The next chapter will look at the advantages of small businesses.

7

Small is essential

WE HAVE SEEN that the New Right ideology serves the interests of big business and the upper income groups. It might be clumsy or ineffective at this, and even at times counter-productive, but it is usually providing what those sectors think is best for them.

Whether or not those policies are genuinely good for them is another matter, but what concerns us is that they are quite clearly not good for the rest of us, or for the economy in general. However, one of the characteristics of a big business economy is that power and money carry more political clout than social need. The big companies seem to be important to the economy, because of their contribution to production, employment and exports. Their wealth allows them to lobby government, hold conferences, carry out PR campaigns, or influence public opinion directly via advertising. And the fact that the big corporations are so few in number, and therefore are controlled by a small number of people, means that it is easier for them to get agreement on common policy, or gather together to lobby ministers.

Using their influence they have asked for — and got — low taxes, low levels of government spending, lax competition policy, tariffs on cheap imports, and selective spending to help their chosen industries. The result is exactly what we see around us — an economy of low taxes and low spending, except for a hyperactive road-building programme, and more than generous defence spending. Mergers are allowed almost automatically, but little is done to protect small firms from the rigours of recession or the maulings of big business. And in the EU, businesses' lobbying organisations have persuaded the Commission to use GATT rules to impose additional tariffs on cheap Far Eastern imports.

But this is just part of the picture. With low taxes on the corporations and their executives, someone has to cover the shortfall. Even in a minimal state there is a minimum industrial infrastructure that a modern society must have, and so the burden falls on the lower and middle income groups. Some of these carry out insufficient spending to support a thriving industrial economy, which is part of the reason for the recession. The greater financial inequality leads to falling living standards for the lower income groups, and the government's bootstrap ideology means that those who are struggling have to survive on their own resources. Not surprisingly, some of those who feel excluded from the visible affluence of the upper income groups react by turning to crime. And not surprisingly, the feeling of division and isolation in society increases.

In fact, there are a whole range of ways in which economic and social deterioration has occurred as a result of the increased influence of big business in government policy. It ranges from the pervasive culture of fast-food outlets and sanitised shopping malls, to the commercialisation of politics, to the cult of the personality. We live in a society that wants soundbites, instant food, instant analysis of news, and easily digestible entertainment. The rise in crime, especially organised crime, is one of the more worrying aspects of anonymous, centralised business, combined with the 'justice for sale' attitudes of monopoly capitalism.

There is also our growing acceptance of high pay levels for top corporation executives. While the average worker is restricted to a pay rise in line with inflation, the top bosses are getting rises of 58 per cent or more. According to John Banham of the CBI, pay had to relate to performance if we were to avoid large increases in unemployment. And, he said, there was evidence that pay levels were running at half the rate of inflation. (*Financial Times*, January 24, 1991.)

But then we find the chief executive of National Power getting a 58 per cent pay rise. The year before, the boss of Standard Chartered Bank got a 58 per cent rise, while Cadbury's boss got 59 per cent. Tiny Rowland's pay rise took him from £656,000 to over a million pounds. The record so far seems to be the staggering 320 per cent rise awarded to the executive in charge of breaking up British Rail, prior to privatisation. (*The Guardian*, June 23, 1993.)

The usual excuse for such generosity is that the director has done so well for the company that they must be rewarded. One wonders what the executives of Pilkington, Smith New Court brokers, and Unigate have to say, because profits for all of those companies collapsed by between 25 per cent and 50 per cent. (*The Guardian*, July 1, 1991.) Perhaps they would say that the recession accounts for the disastrous drop in profits; but what justifies the stunning pay rise? If they had had any sort of rise in profits, would they too be demanding a 193 per cent pay rise, like the chief executive of the Midlands Electricity Board? (*The Guardian*, July 9, 1991.)

In a sense it is unfair to single out particular companies, because so many of them have played the same game. Surveys have shown that there is rarely any link between pay and profits, so the company director's right to the pay rise is not based on performance. Any arguments that the market rewards ability or hard work can be dismissed immediately. The free market rewards those with the power to take what is available.

In a sense, it is understandable. These people are not in business for the good of society; their motivation is the classic New Right desire for money. And they work for companies that are sufficiently large to have lots of spare cash swilling around. Thus, the existence of large companies encourages inequality. In addition, the nice kind Tories have created a tax regime that allows the top executives to take home a large percentage of their earnings — not including their non-taxable perks, of course. As if the previous regime of tax allowances and deductions was unduly mean to top earners, the Tories cut the rates of tax, so that top directors would no longer have to struggle to buy that second Rolls-Royce or French chateau.

It is not surprising that executives take eager advantage of the tax breaks. The money is there for the taking, the tax regime is generous, and greed is acceptable. There is no clear set of values to say that their pay rise should wait until after the poor have got a reasonable income. Peter Drucker, the management guru, and by no means a radical leftie, says that these highly paid executives 'offend the sense of justice of many, indeed of the majority of management people themselves'. (*The Frontiers of Management*, p140.)

It is interesting to compare the ease with which one can — modify — one's tax liability, to the near-impossibility of claiming benefit fraudulently. Not only is tax avoidance perfectly legal; one gets the impression that tax evasion, although technically illegal, is regarded by many high income earners as a sport, somewhat akin to fox-hunting. But when it comes to claiming state benefits, mere entitlement is simply the first obstacle in a gruelling marathon of paperwork. The implicit message is that the rich are entitled to be economical with their tax bill; the poor, however, should not feel that they are entitled to sponge off the generosity of Her Majesty's Government.

Supported by government, inequality is increasing, but at the same time it is widening the gap between workers and bosses. It adds to the 'them and us' conflict, and makes the difficult job of running a large company even more complex. It is obvious that there are double standards operating; pay must be kept low, but only for the workers; incentives encourage hard work, but only for the executives. This institutionalised hypocrisy is bound to cause resentment within the workforce, and will surely affect the quality of the work.

But it is not just pay levels that big corporations seek to influence. They would wish to have control over all aspects of economic, social and industrial policy. They may want tariff barriers to keep out imports, and thus reduce competition, they may want a lax minimum wage policy or health and safety legislation, so they can deal with their employees in their own way, or they may want artificial spending booms, generated to keep their factories busy.

Olson puts it in terms of the distributional groups which influence outcomes within society, and the factors which determine their ability to do this. One of the factors is that for a group to get benefits, it must be small enough so that all members receive some noticeable advantage from membership. However, the group need have no interest in increasing the size of society's cake; it merely wants more for its members. But, says Olson, as the number of distributional groups increases, the complexity of legislation also increases, '*and changes the direction of social evolution*'. (*The Rise and Decline of Nations*, p73. Italics in original.)

As society becomes more complex, so we need a new breed of bureaucrats to handle all the laws, rules, tariffs, etc. Thus, the existence of complexity creates its own vested interest group which in turn will seek to create even more complexity. One of the side-effects of this is the creation of abstruse economic theories, such as monetarism, and the promotion of grand transnational schemes, such as the European Union. The British government has been particularly successful at presenting economics as an incredibly difficult subject, in which only it has the answers. Nothing can be dealt with directly, nothing operates the way common sense would lead one to expect. Inflation has to be dealt with before unemployment can be reduced, and wages must fall, so that we can all become rich again.

The centralisation of politics becomes a tool which the vested interests can use against the people. The sheer scale of society and its problems become a lever that can be used against any simple answers. And naturally, the larger the nation-state, the more effective a weapon is the complexity of the system.

This is especially useful for big businesses, many of which are multinational. Such companies can claim to be threatened by the global economy, thus introducing a concept which sounds incomprehensible to many people. All they mean is that they face competition from cheap foreign producers, but 'global economy' sounds so much more daunting.

The corporation can then use its new-fangled excuse to shed a few thousand jobs, The workers no longer face their ex-employer as an enemy; the attack has come from unknown economic tides, washing their way around the world. Faced with a docile domestic work-force, the corporation then opens up new factories, in Mexico, China, or Singapore, producing exactly the same goods as before. But as a result the home economy can no longer afford to buy the products so easily.

Little of this would happen in a genuine small business economy, as it would be simple, local, accessible and transparent. It does not involve, or create, the complexity that a multinational business must generate. It must be recognised, however, that the nature of a small business economy cannot be determined by looking at the behaviour of a random sample of British small firms, and multiplying by a few million. It is a different type of economy, with different drives and characteristics.

Because of this, it is important to distinguish between the small business economy being proposed here, and the empty words of concern uttered by Thatcherites in defence of small firms. Even if we accepted their statements as sincere, one has to say that the Tories claim no more than a belief in competition. What is being argued here is that the small business economy is inherently different. It is not simply a scaled-up version of a typical British small company. That would tend to be a typical company operating within monopoly capitalism, and so would be representative of its environment, rather than of its potential.

It is useful to consider the characteristics of small companies operating in Britain, but we cannot prove the nature of the small business economy from them. We have to recognise that it would be a completely different type of system, and then work out what its characteristics would be.

The political influence would be less likely to appear, as small firms lack the clout necessary to dictate to either government or the consumer. They are seen as relatively unimportant — yes, governments pay lip service to small firms, but a single large corporation can claim to achieve billions of pounds worth of sales, or exports, or tax payments to the Exchequer. Thus, it is tremendously valuable to the economy. The individual small firm lacks this high-profile impact, and although as a sector, small firms play a major role, the entire sector does not have the same impact or visibility as the single corporation's billions.

So in a country where small companies are the predominant structure, and in the absence of any other organised power centre, political power reverts, almost by default, to the electorate. The small firms do not create all the features that can be associated with a small business economy, although they do have some direct impact. The key aspect is that when small firms are the largest sector of the economy, and the large firms are few and lack influence, then business as a whole ceases to have a major input to government decision-making. It is not that small firms create democracy, or any other item; it is that they fail to destroy those things.

Small firms are also closer to the perfectly competitive free market economy that the New Right apologists claim to be so besotted with. The evidence is that a genuinely competitive market does benefit the consumer. When companies are actively struggling to attract the consumer's cash, they have to make their product better, more stylish, more reliable, better quality, or cheaper. They may even need to achieve all of these. But as a single voice in a busy market, it may not be enough to build a better mousetrap, as the old adage goes; the small firm may have to offer after-sales service as well.

This competitive market only exists if there are a large number of buyers and sellers, and none of them has the power to influence prices. If any market is dominated by large companies, those companies are able to impose conditions on retailers, or demand bulk discounts from suppliers. They may use their massive sales as a lever to discredit smaller firms — the big seller may say that they are the most popular, and therefore the best. It can be gently implied that less popular products are simply less desirable. And of course, the massive corporate advertising budget allows the company to persuade consumers in a dozen subtle ways, making consumers see the product as the key to a better social life, to new friends, to greater status, or whatever.

All of this means that instead of a competitive market, with companies trying to provide what the consumer wants, we have what Galbraith called the Revised Sequence, in which the corporations persuade the consumers to want what the corporations can most easily produce. One example of this is lager beer; it is easy and cheap to produce, has a longer shelf life, and is more profitable than real beers. Backed by heavy advertising budgets, and some very clever ads, the brewers have made lager the pub success story of the 1970s and 80s.

There has been a modest return to the real ales of the past, mainly as a result of the campaigning efforts of the Campaign for Real Ale (CAMRA). This organisation has publicised the products of the small brewers, the distinctive, nutty or wine-like beers made in small quantities. Yet as the local breweries have become successful, the big companies have taken them over. Regional names like Ruddles and Theakston's have become a small part of a national brewing combine, and have tended to lose their individuality.

In theory, the government has some sort of stance on competition. But the Monopolies Commission is not a strongly pro-competition body, and rarely refuses a suggested takeover in any industry. Arguments that a takeover will create economies of scale are accepted with little or no evidence. Indeed at times, it seems as if the mere existence of industrial logic is enough to justify a takeover. Yet industrial logic simply means a relationship between the two companies' operations. If one brewer seeks to acquire another, one cannot deny the logic; although whether or not that will lead to benefits for the economy or the consumer is quite another matter. However, the main limit to acquisition activity is simply the cost of buying target companies. So it is no surprise that brewing in Britain is dominated by just six companies. Most other industries in Britain display the same degree of concentration.

In short, in a big business economy, we are no longer dealing with competition, we can no longer assume that consumers are getting what they want, and we can no longer assume that consumers' welfare is maximised. The key certainties of economics melt away. Neither economists nor the New Right can claim any value for their patent nostrums, if instead of competition we have Galbraith's Revised Sequence.

It has been said that competition is wasteful and destructive, that with many firms all producing the same type of goods, too much will be produced, and all of those firms will be carrying out competing distribution systems, therefore resources will be wasted. In fact, because they will be more local, transport costs will be minimised; deliveries will only involve short distances. And producing too much simply means that the market will be well supplied, therefore prices will be lower.

The commercial battle between companies is also seen as negative. It implies hostility and conflict, and does actually lead to some firms being destroyed. From that point of view, competition is seen as morally unappealing. However, as real hostility and conflict are rare in the world of everyday commerce, the implication, or more accurately the inference, tells us nothing about real business life. The assumed moral weakness is merely anthropomorphising the metaphorical clash of corporate titans. They are not vicious human beings fighting; they are simply organisations, trying to do a better job than the others. The issue is, what does competition do? And the answer is, it encourages entrepreneurs to try harder, to sell more, and to make things better. What it does is provide a better standard of living.

On the other hand, the commercial battle between big companies is simply that of advertising, and the takeovers mentioned above. In the market place, it is a conflict between two manipulative advertising budgets, both trying to part the consumer from their money. In the takeover, it is a struggle between one set of management and another, with the victim company as the prize. The two embattled giants will advertise furiously in the national press, pointing out the rationale for their purchase. They will each announce that they can do better with the company's assets than the other management can. And they will emphasise the industrial logic, and the economies of scale that will occur.

One wonders about the logic of say, Boots the Chemist acquiring (in 1989) Halfords (car and bicycle parts), Payless DIY, and a wallpaper and decorating chain. Not surprisingly, the deal proved unsuccessful, and severely damaged Boots' profits for 1990. In fact, far from industrial logic, most acquisitions are failures. According to one survey, only a third of takeovers 'can be regarded as successful, in the narrow, financial sense'. (*The Guardian*, September 24, 1991, citing *Acquisitions Monthly*.)

Yet even though the takeovers are not successful in terms of efficiency or profits, they still increase the corporation's market power, and its management's access to funds. Thus, the executives can pay themselves more from a bigger company's cash turnover, and the company has greater power to set prices in the market.

If there were many small companies, it is probable that the pattern of commerce would shift towards the single outlet, owned by someone living in the same area as the business. Some small companies would be multi-outlet, or owned by absentee directors, but local ownership becomes at least more likely than it is now. If the owner is living in the same area as the factory (or shop), then they would have the same concern for local amenities as the workers. They would want the schools and hospitals to be well-run, they would want decent parks and libraries, and they would want a good quality of life. There is more likely to be civic pride, and the old worker-management divisions of industrial society become much less probable. (For a fuller analysis of the advantages of the small business economy, see *Economic Power*, by the same author.)

But are small firms as efficient as their big buddies? Economists differ on this, some arguing that small companies cannot achieve the mass production methods needed to bring prices down. However, as a small firm is defined as a company with up to 200 employees, whether or not they can achieve mass production depends on current technology. For example, there are factories in Japan where there is only one worker, who goes in, presses a green button to start the machinery, and then simply monitors the flow of production. If all goes well, there is no need to press the red button until the end of the day. That is what modern industry regards as efficient.

But there is a cost to pay, for this type of efficiency. There is the imbalance between production and consumption, as such automation is very capital intensive. It is simply not possible to have a global industrial economy based on that sort of manufacturing system. There would be a tiny workforce, millions of unemployed, and few people with the money to buy the goods flooding onto the market. Such a system would be a totally artificial one, but it would also be an ironic misuse of resources. The industrial West has enough capital to virtually eliminate work, while the Third World nations do not have sufficient capital to feed and house their populations. This is just one of the global imbalances that make today's economic order so unacceptable.

In manufacturing, the big corporation tends to focus very strongly on the cost of production, which is why managements are so obsessed with cutting wages. But they also seek to cut production costs in other ways, such as reducing the cost of making the components. They will analyse how each item is made, and try to find a way of making the same sort of thing cheaper. For example, in assembling a car, instead of bolting door handles to the door of the car, they might pop rivet them in place. Roof panels can be simply pressed into place, held with plastic studs.

There are various results. The reduction in component costs means an unavoidable drop in component quality. In some cases this may be harmless, but in others it can be extremely dangerous. Cutting costs on brake or steering parts is not a recipe for safe driving. But cutting costs on the suspension or on the petrol tank can also be a potential hazard, as General Motors learnt with the Corvair, and Ford learnt with its Pinto. The Corvair would flip over with the slightest change from straight line driving, such as pulling out to overtake. And the Pinto occasionally burst into flames when hit from the rear, because the petrol tank was located right behind the back bumper. The whole issue would have been less repellent if the corporations concerned had admitted the faults, and corrected them as soon as management knew about them.

Even when product quality is not overtly lethal, it can add to the consumer's costs by reducing the product's lifespan. The immediate purchase price may be low, but the product's useful life will be shorter; so the cost per year will be higher. Also, when things are made to be cheap, and easy to assemble, they may become expensive to repair. The quick and easy pop rivets and press studs of the assembly line become a nuisance for the repair shop. Or perhaps motors, dynamos and similar items become sealed units, where repair is totally impossible. This would also mean that recycling would become extremely difficult. Whereas most mechanical goods can be disassembled for recycling, it might not be possible to dismantle sealed units.

This style of manufacturing has developed because of the emphasis on low costs through mass production — the one thing that big business is good at. It does not demonstrate a wish to be competitive, but merely implies a desire to grab a larger market share, or boost profits higher. It is also a form of setting the economic agenda — big business is good at low cost production, so the way to keep out the high quality competitors is by devaluing their competitive edge.

As the big corporations steadily promote their own values, through PR, advertising, paid pressure groups and tame politicians, cheapness becomes more and more the touchstone for economic efficiency. The European Community, which is supposed to be for the good of us all, announces through its allegedly scientific research that lower prices will be the main benefit of the single market. In fact, the Community is the perfect ploy for a monopoly capitalist empire — it creates a protected market for the corporations, with the nasty little foreign competitors kept at bay by high tariff barriers. It is the antithesis of free trade, and has never been opened up to informed public debate.

Smaller manufacturers can offer individual, personal products, of high quality, reliable, and with good service. Perhaps not all small companies do this, especially in a big business economy, but it is something that small firms are more likely to be good at. This is partly because they have to find a competitive edge somewhere, and quality is an excellent selling point. But also, small firms are more likely to be run by people who believe in their product, who want to make something of which they can be proud.

The small company also seems to be more vulnerable to recession. It is notable that in the 1989-92 recession, small firms suffered particularly badly. The Conservative government was busily promoting the idea that it was an international recession, and that only the weak and inefficient companies were closing down. It is difficult to believe either of these desperate claims, as British exports were booming right up until 1992. This makes claims of an international downturn very dubious. Also, many companies had borrowed money to fund investment — a perfectly normal business practice. They then found themselves in a changed environment, with interest rates shooting suddenly and unpredictably upwards. Others found themselves plunged from boom into slump, as demand collapsed, also as a result of government policy. The excuses that were blandly paraded for the media had a glib persuasiveness but as much substance as candy floss.

The evidence suggests that small companies are more vulnerable to a recession when operating in a monopoly capitalist economy. In a genuinely competitive economy it would be valid to say that the weak and inefficient go to the wall. But when the financial institutions are either owned by or influenced by the big corporations, and the political system is run by Old Etonians and ex-company directors, the small firm does not get a sympathetic hearing anywhere. For years, these corporate dinosaurs have been making the rules, building up their social and family contacts in the City and Westminster.

Virgin, like Freddie Laker, is more likely to get justice in the United States than in Britain. The legal system in America is more open to consumer interests, and less open to lobbying by the old school tie network. It is not surprising that the politico-financial oligarchy that runs Britain is highly sympathetic to the needs of big business; they are more or less the same social group.

Total con artists, like Robert Maxwell, can go to one of the major banks, and ask for a few million pounds with the same casual nonchalance as the average person asking for a £20 overdraft. Those same High Street banks will happily lend hundreds of millions of pounds to Third World countries, with no more than a perfunctory check on where the money is going. But when a small business wants £20,000 for expansion, then they need a business plan, the owner's house as security, and a government guarantee before the banks will part with their customers' hard-earned cash. Of course, banks find it easier to lend £20 million in one lump, than to tout around a lot of little companies, out in the sticks. Why should they bother themselves with a measly ten thousand here, and fifty thousand there? They have a business to run.

And when a recession rears its ugly head, the banks will call in loans and overdrafts, without any consideration of whether or not the stricken company can survive in the long term. Auditors will wind up a company, rather than get it on its feet again, because they make a percentage on selling the bankrupt firm's assets.

Governments too, despite their smooth PR utterances, are not going to be bothered with bailing out a lot of little firms here and there. In an average recession there will be hundreds, maybe thousands of penny ante operations, each of which would have to be investigated, have its finances checked, someone has to see if there's a market... Oh, it's all too much effort. Just let the, er, let them sink.

In a small business economy, small companies are less likely to go bankrupt, because they will have a more supportive environment. There is a saying that if you owe the bank a thousand pounds, you have a problem; if you owe the bank a thousand million pounds, the bank has a problem. In the United States, banks were limited in the amount of expansion they could do across state lines. Hence, most American banks are limited to one or two states. As a result, if a company is threatened by economic conditions, the bank will do its best to help that firm. If your customers are primarily small businesses, one valued customer is just as important as another. They are all important enough to need saving.

Given all these arguments for small businesses, one could ask, if they are so good, why do they disappear? They get bought up, swamped by competition from big companies, and wiped out in recessions. Does their vulnerability prove they are not very worthwhile? After all, if they were strong and viable, they would survive — wouldn't they?

On the other hand, fragility is no indication of inherent value. Democracy is also a delicate creation, that needs constant attention for its proper survival. In 1992, in Algeria, the people were willing to vote democracy out of existence. In Britain, we effectively surrendered the liberal component of democracy to a Conservative government, regarding it as a price worth paying to gain their certainty on economic policy. Since 1979 we have effectively lost open government, accountability, independent broadcasting, ministerial responsibility, and the rule of law. If these things are so valuable, how can they be lost so easily? Perhaps their vulnerability is not related to their importance.

Small businesses are fragile, but if they are of value to society, then they are worth protecting. Existing laws, financial institutions, and economic policy do little to support small companies, even though politicians are warmly insincere about the contribution of small firms to the economy. They talk glowingly of the seedbeds of future industry; phrases like 'the big businesses of tomorrow' trip lightly out of their speeches. But rarely has any real action emanated from Westminster.

In the United States, it has been found that some big corporations have allowed prices to fall below the profit level in order to drive out small firms. And it is suspected that the same has been done in Britain. Corporate muscle has been exercised on both sides of the Atlantic to buy up small companies; these are either closed down, or incorporated into the big company's pricing strategy. The result — less competition. In the US, the Justice Department would respond by launching an antitrust suit. The small firm that was harmed by an oligopolist's attacks could sue for triple damages — for three times the cost of any damage done to the smaller company. There is nothing like this in British monopoly law.

This is not to say that American legislation is perfect. Far from it. But it is so far ahead of the norm for the Monopolies and Mergers Commission (MMC) as to be embarrassing. In theory, if the combined market share of the two parties to a prospective merger (or takeover) exceeds 25 per cent, the Office of Fair Trading will consider whether the bid should be referred to the Monopolies and Mergers Commission. Allowing up to 25 per cent of a market is more than generous. The UK brewing industry is dominated by six big brewers, only one of which — Bass — has more than 15 per cent. The others are all in the 10 to 12 per cent range. Yet these modest market shares have still been sufficient to allow the big brewers a virtual stranglehold on British beer.

In fact, 5 per cent of each market would probably be a better limit if we want real competition, rather than merely the appearance of it. It is worth noting that in the German beer industry there are 1200 brewers, or 75% of the total number in the EU. It is unlikely that any of these has as much as 25 per cent of the market. On the other hand, it is probable that most of them are known for the quality of their product.

Since 1960 there has been an enormous concentration of British industry. In 1953 the largest companies accounted for 27 per cent of total output. By the early 1970s, they accounted for over 40 per cent. And most of this growth has been the result of takeovers. That is, companies are growing larger, not by expanding their own manufacturing capacity, but through buying up other firms, and reducing the amount of competition.

Sometimes the acquirer is attracted by the management or investment record of the target company, and sees a takeover as an easy way to acquire skills or high productivity. The fact that this is an easy way to expand a business is slightly suspicious; people who take short cuts are the ones who want to avoid the effort and the sweat.

One example of this type of business is Hanson Trust. Led by Lord Hanson, the company is renowned for being constantly on the takeover trail. It owns Consolidated Gold Fields, ARC (a manufacturer of construction aggregates), and a part share in Gold Fields of South Africa. In 1991 Hanson tried to buy the chemicals giant, ICI, and in 1992 it launched a bid for Rank Hovis McDougall. A company with such diverse activity is called a conglomerate, and fortunately, both acquisitions and conglomerates may be going out of fashion.

'The nature of conglomeracy is a product of Britain's over-developed financial system which damages industry because it focuses attention on the wrong criteria and encourages directors to close rather than develop businesses'. (*The Guardian*, October 24, 1992.) Like so many other aspects of the British financial system, it encourages short-termism, while wheeler-dealers see companies as assets to be used, rather than businesses to be built up.

Britain cannot build up a strong industrial sector if all we have is a lot of sharp operators looking for a way to take advantage of someone else's effort. We need an economy where all companies are investing, training, and producing high quality goods.

But this lazy approach to industry is the least offensive aspect. The worst part is the reduction in competition. Research has found that one of the reasons companies engage in takeovers is to reduce competition. Sometimes this is put in terms of acquiring monopoly power, which is the same thing, although the managerial motives may be completely different. Some companies may wish to buy up other firms, simply because competition is too much effort. It involves constantly worrying about what the other company is doing, and whether one's own products are of the same standard and price as theirs, and all the other little details that must make the life of top management so fatiguing. One feels quite sorry for them.

The other way of describing that motive, the desire to increase one's monopoly power, is slightly less reputable. It is not merely laziness, but actively taking advantage of the reduced competition. One has more power over one's customers, the consumer has less choice, and one has the ability to control prices to a greater degree. But unlike the lazy manager, one is seeking more than an easy life; one is trying to exploit the customer. This might involve high prices, or it could allow manufacturers to force entire product lines onto retailers, or it might allow sellers to impose certain types of product on the consumer. In other words, we are coming back to Galbraith's Revised Sequence. A degree of monopoly power allows the corporation to tell the customer what to buy.

There is no clear indication as to what percentage of the market a company needs for such power, but as mentioned earlier, most of the so-called big six brewing firms each have around 10 to 12 per cent of the beer market. There is no doubt that is too great for real competition.

A third motive is that the firm will acquire economies of scale. So if two companies making 100,000 cars a year merge, their post-merger capacity will be 200,000 cars a year, and will no doubt offer them economies of scale. As a result, they will be able to produce much cheaper cars than before. This might sound like the most valid of the main reasons. However, if a company wants to increase output, it can do so by expanding its factory, or introducing new machinery. If mergers and takeovers genuinely do offer economies of scale, any benefit to the economy is moderated by the loss of competition. Although it is understandable that a company might see it as an easy route, the government should take a broader view.

In general, British industry ministers have been lax in their approach to competition policy. When Nestlé put in a £2.1 billion bid for Rowntree, Lord Young chose not to refer the bid to the Monopolies and Mergers Commission. Mrs Thatcher's attitude to the bid demonstrated an 'appalling ignorance of economics', according to Rodney Atkinson, a member of the right-wing Bow Group. Atkinson also said that Lord Young did not understand the regional importance of Rowntree.

Lord Young's other clumsy contribution to competition policy was to back down from a Monopolies and Mergers Commission plan that would have freed 11,000 pubs from the control of the six big brewers. The MMC's report in 1989 found that over a ten year period, beer prices had risen faster than inflation — a typical indicator of the absence of competition. Also, the big brewers, through their ownership of pubs, and loans to pub landlords, dominated the trade, again harming the consumer. New brewing companies were effectively excluded from the industry; and pub tenants were in a weak bargaining position, in respect to the big brewers.

The Monopolies Commission decided that the big brewers would be required to sell or lease a proportion of their pubs — half of the number they held, in excess of 2,000. They also had to allow pubs to sell a 'guest' beer, so that customers were not tied to the company's products. This is not an extreme suggestion, and is less than would be needed to create real competition; nonetheless, the big brewers objected. They instigated a highly emotive publicity campaign, even taking out full-page adverts in the national press. After months of lobbying by the big six, Lord Young decided that the brewers could keep all of their pubs.

The original intention was to separate the pubs from the breweries, so that landlords would be free from brewery control, and able to offer a range of beers. Instead, Lord Young alllowed the big six to keep all their pubs, but asked that half of those pubs above a 2,000 limit would have to be operated independently from the brewery company. In theory, it should have meant 11,000 free houses, owned by the big companies, but managed by the tenant landlord. But clearly, the balance of power between owner and tenant was such that 'independence' could easily become a movable concept.

Some of the big brewers felt forced to leave either pub ownership or brewing, and devised skilful ploys to evade the rules — like the GrandMet/Elders pubs-for-breweries swap. GrandMet, the food and restaurants chain, would sell four of its breweries to Elders, a conglomerate which already owned three Courage breweries. Then, a jointly-owned GrandMet/Elders company was to be set up to manage the two founder companies' pubs. In this particular arrangement, the jointly-owned company would have finished owning 6,950 pubs, more than 6,500 of which would have been tied to Courage beer. The theory was that not being owned by one of the major brewers, the new firm would have been free of the 'no-ties constraint. (*Financial Times*, October 17, 1990.)

However, the Monopolies and Mergers Commission decided that the companies' undertakings, for example, to weaken the ties to Courage, were not sufficient to make the deal beneficial to consumers. Some people saw the 'arms-length' deal as allowing GrandMet/Elders to evade the MMC's regulations, without actually giving up its control of pub prices and profits.

Two years later, a report from the Consumers' Association found that pubs were overcharging, and that prices had gone up by 13 per cent from 1990 to 1991, double the rate of inflation for that period. (*The Guardian*, March 5, 1992.) With pubs charging up to £4.75 for a pint of orange juice, the Consumers' Association argued that the government's attempt to break up the big brewers had not created competition, nor had it benefited the consumer.

In 1992, CAMRA found that since 1989 pub prices had increased 17 per cent faster than the rate of inflation. The big brewers clearly cannot say their price rises have been caused by inflation — rather, those rises are the cause of inflation. This ability to control prices is a natural result of the concentration of ownership. And indeed, CAMRA found that the top three brewers share of the market had risen from 47 per cent in 1989 to 62 per cent by 1992. (Campaign for Real Ale, *Submission to the House of Commons Agriculture Select Committee.*)

Labour's trade spokesman, Bryan Gould, condemned the abandoning of the break-up, and asked whether it might have anything to do with the big brewers' lobbying power, and the fact that they were hefty donors to the Tories' treasure chest. Certainly, it was very little to do with either competition or the welfare of the consumer.

This is not to say that Thatcher and Young were blocking an otherwise effective Monopolies Commission. In fact, the Commission is sometimes less than radical in its efforts to control abuses of monopoly power. For example, when it examined the car market, it found that car prices were too high, and that a 'complex monopoly' existed that 'favoured car suppliers and operated against the public interest'. But it did not suggest breaking up the too-close relationship between suppliers and dealers, nor was any major change sought to deal with the 'complex monopoly'. (*The Guardian*, February 6, 1992.)

Similarly, when the Consumers' Association complained about the price of Compact Discs (CDs), to the Office of Fair Trading, it got a lukewarm reaction. The Association said that CDs are more expensive in the UK than they are in the United States, costing £11.99 in the UK as opposed to the equivalent of £7 in the US. And it is well-known that although the manufacturing cost of CDs is about the same as that of LPs, the retail price is significantly higher. Few companies have the technology to make CDs, and just one company controls the rights to manufacture them. However, the OFT's response was a decision not to refer either makers or retailers to the Monopolies Commission.

There is a consensus in the corridors of power that big business is a good thing generally, and if we have to put up with the occasional price increase, lack of choice, low quality products, or imposition of corporate needs on the market, then that too is a price worth paying. This argument, like so many of the Conservatives' beliefs, is not open to debate.

This is not to say the Labour Party were any better when they were in office, in the 1960s and 70s. There was a near-obsession with corporate bigness that would make a Freudian psychologist wonder what they were compensating for. And there was a belief that economies of scale existed without limit, that any increase in size could be justified by the wondrous boost to manufacturing productivity that would occur as a result. This may be related to the 'giantism' that was applied in the Soviet Union under Stalin. With the Conservatives, it is passed off as the effect of market forces, allowing businesses to carry on as they want. But whatever the underlying belief system, the result is the same; and the openness to debate is just as absent.

It is time that we did have a competition policy that actually meant the control and promotion of competition. But not merely through the control of mergers, although that by itself would be a significant step forward. There should also be an entrepreneurial environment, that allows people to see the advantages of small companies, provides support for them, and encourages the formation of new businesses.

Strict control of mergers must be taken as absolutely essential. It should no longer be allowable for corporate marauders to buy up their competititors with all the casualness of a High Street consumer buying a radio. For a company to interfere with the level of competition is an act of self-interest and an abuse of power. No enlightened government that is making any sort of claim to look after the welfare of its citizens should allow such corporate banditry.

As stated above, there should be a general limit of 5 per cent of a market, and any merger or takeover that would lead to a company exceeding that limit would result in an automatic referral. However, a referral would not mean an automatic block on the takeover; it would be allowed if the two companies could prove that it was necessary, and that it would benefit both the consumer and the economy. For example, if one of the firms was in danger of going out of business, and the acquisition would assure the existence of one healthy company, then it probably would be good for the economy.

If however, there were two thriving companies, both capable of active competition, then a takeover would simply increase the likelihood of a misuse of monopoly power. They might be both actively competing at the time, but that is given the market shares and the competitive environment of the time. If the merger is allowed then the market situation changes. The result of this is that the behaviour of all companies in the market also changes; including our two prospective mergees. And this is if we assume only normal market behaviour; if the companies have a reputation for being less than consumer-oriented, we can virtually guarantee an increase in monopoly misuse.

If we look only at the industrial logic, we see in the first case, where one company is in danger of going bankrupt, there is a justification for allowing the firms to combine. In the second case, involving two thriving businesses, the companies would have to prove that joining together would provide some economic or industrial advantage that could not exist otherwise. That is, there would have to be a gain that the two companies could not achieve by themselves. For example, the greater size could allow economies of scale, or greater manufacturing productivity. However, to achieve this, the companies might have to close a branch, and concentrate all operations in one site. But from past observation, we see that most businesses that are bought up are kept open; in other words, the combined operation does not do what is necessary to obtain the economies of scale that are the alleged purpose of the merger. So if a government was concerned that the merger be allowed to create a more efficient industry, it might say that rationalisation of the business would be a condition of the merger.

However, in some cases there are efficiency gains to be made from the expansion of a company, but they are not gains that can only be made through a merger. It is like the Inland Revenue's definition of allowable expenses — they must be from spending that is 'solely and exclusively in the performance of the job'. Work tools are allowed, because they are used in the performance of the job. But expenses travelling to and from work are not allowable, because they are not part of the job. The efficiency gains might arise after the merger, but they do not occur 'solely and exclusively' because of it. That is, they could arise through some other cause.

For example, expanding the company via takeovers allows the firm to get cheaper supplies, through bulk purchasing. This reduces the cost of its products. However, this is not the only way it could get bulk purchasing discounts; it could also join a buying co-operative, and get lower prices that way. Many UK retailers get low-cost supplies by joining retailing groups like Londis or Wavy Line.

In their own way, both economies of scale and competition offer the consumer lower prices and better products. By implication, the government allows takeovers because the trade-off results in a higher manufacturing productivity that outweighs any loss of competition. If there is no need for companies to combine, to cut manufacturing costs, then there is no justification on industrial grounds.

Having looked at the competitive issues, and the industrial logic of the merger, the next step is to look at the social impact of small firms. This would include such factors as the likely impact on unemployment, job creation, training, investment, or community involvement. If a buyer was likely to close factories, cut jobs, move the head office to London (or Tokyo, Detroit, etc.), cut investment and training, or ignore local needs, then it should not be allowed to take over a thriving local business.

For example, given the regional importance of Rowntree, Lord Young should have blocked the takeover by Nestlé. The change of ownership harmed the local economy, but offered no gain at all, either locally or nationally. The only gainer was Nestlé, which acquired a well-known company, with a wide range of famous brand names that it could sell all over Europe. In theory, this would generate more sales and higher profits for Rowntree. In practice, the sales, and therefore the jobs, could go to Nestlé factories in France or Belgium, while the profits would head off to Vevey, Switzerland.

Similarly, a company like Union Carbide, renowned for spreading methylisocyanate around the region of Bhopal, India, should not be running a chemical plant in a brewery. If they ever applied to buy anything more expensive than a pot of brewers' yeast, they should be asked to kindly leave the stage. Union Carbide gained a lot of PR coverage in the United States over the compensation they paid in India, although there is some doubt as to whether they were generous payers, or merely sharp negotiators.

Exxon (known in Britain as Esso) became famous for owning the Exxon Valdez, an oil tanker which dumped several million gallons of oil over the Alaskan coastline. The clean-up operation was expensive, probably quite thorough, and gained Exxon even more publicity than the spill itself. However, one hopes that they did not organise their celebration in a brewery.

Companies which fail to meet all the legal and moral requirements for a socially responsible organisation should be subject to more than legal sanction. It is not just a matter of setting the Monopolies and Mergers Commission or the Antitrust Department on them. In some cases, government bodies are not able to prove wrong-doing, or fail to prosecute, or levy a minor punishment. If law-breaking has occurred, but cannot be punished, the state may have to use other routes. And if the state fails to do so, then the consumer must find some way.

Other companies are known for their failure to contribute locally, or their failure to invest. GEC has been known for years for its pot of cash, which has been as much as £1.5 billion. On the other hand, it has not been known for its fevered investment activity, nor for its search for new consumer goods to bring to the market. It has plodded along in heavy industry, taking part in international consortia. With a track record like this, it should not be allowed to buy any consumer goods companies, as it has shown a total disinterest in that line of business.

Thus, when an acquisition is suggested, the regulatory authorities should first examine its impact on competition; then the industrial logic of the purchase; and finally the social impact. One might reasonably expect trade-offs to be allowed, so that if a merger reduced competition, but was likely to increase efficiency, and the buyer was known for its social conscience, then such a purchase could be allowed to proceed. In the past, however, governments have tended to ignore social factors, treat competition as a side issue, and take a superficial view of the industrial impact.

What needs to be done is for all factors to be taken into consideration, and for the overall effect to be analysed. One could justifiably argue that in some cases, an acquisition could be allowed, even if it reduced competition, if at the same time it increased efficiency and created social gains. But one has to have the information in order to make the judgement. In a monopoly capitalist economy, evidence against the interests of the big corporations seems strangely difficult to obtain.

There is little research on the benefits of economies of scale, or on the size needed to achieve full economies of scale. What little evidence there is has been carried out by independent economists, and suggests that no great size is necessary for optimum efficiency. Nor is there much research on manufacturing quality and product life. Nor is there much work on the political impact of centralised power groups. Daniel Moynihan, US presidential adviser, noted that there was very little work done on the causes of road accidents; a fact that he linked directly to the power of the US auto industry. Quite simply, the big corporations finance any research which will advance their interests; they will publish articles, lobby governments, and give speeches. But any path leading to uncomfortable truths will be discreetly ignored.

One problem is that giving economies of scale academic respectability allows the big corporations to justify their desire for growth. Perhaps it even encourages them in this irrelevant obsession. But growth is exactly what the major industrial economies do not need now. Since the 1960s all the major nations have had enough wealth to give all their people a decent quality of life; what is needed now is the re-distribution of that wealth, not the creation of more. If the poorer nations demand growth, for themselves, that is understandable. But for the businesses or institutions of the West to claim that greater wealth is necessary in the West, is a dangerous deception.

There is a fear that big business will manage to impose its economic agenda on the world, and continue their expansion. There is already a clear trend in this direction within the European Union: the move towards a single European currency and the use of anti-dumping tariffs are a result of corporate lobbying. Similarly, the Maastricht treaty, with its emphasis on monetary control, inflation and exchange rates, was a straight copy of Britain's New Right policies.

At the global level, the IMF and the World Bank are both keen supporters of New Right ideology. Third World debtor nations are forced to adhere to the IMF's Structural Adjustment Programme (SAP), which limits government spending, opens markets to imports, and encourages cash cropping. In nearly every case, the result of the SAP has been a decline in living standards, and an increase in poverty and unemployment. In Brazil there has even been the re-emergence of slavery. There has also been a recession within the Third World countries, reducing their capacity to buy from the West, and adding to our recession. But for the IMF, the main concern is ensuring that all those peripheral nations pay back what they borrowed from US banks.

To finance further capital-intensive investment for corporate expansion will exacerbate an already unstable global imbalance. And to provide the raw materials for continued growth will require the big corporations to buy or control ever-increasing supplies throughout the world. Having seen how the Japanese zaibatsu have misused the forests of the Far East, one is not optimistic about their future reverence for nature as the search for resources becomes desperate. One can envisage a future, not very far away, in which the big corporations own or control all the world's resources, and no threat to their economic dominance is possible.

This represents the ultimate monopoly power. And it is not even negotiable; the corporations would have the basic resource power, but would not be able to surrender it, as their survival depended on it. Even worse, there is the possibility of the big companies continuing their blind rush for growth, consuming all the forests, the mines, the oil fields, until nothing was left. From that point a catastrophic economic collapse would be inevitable.

For the time being, we have to control the structures that do exist, and what we have now is a competition policy based around a quango like the Monopolies and Mergers Commission. Disregarding the problems of information, the rules that the Commission operates on can be tightened up, and the need for evidence of social gain can be emphasised. But whatever we do, we are still talking about an organisation attempting to impose an economic structure on society. And if there are forces operating within the economy that have a natural bias towards big business, then the quango will have an uphill — and permanent — task. It will be perpetually working against the tide of society, pushing a stone forever uphill.

Quite simply, imposing a compensatory mechanism on society must be regarded as a second best solution. Ideally, the forces of society should reinforce the needs of the economy, and vice versa. So policy should use society's tendencies, rather than ignoring them, or working against them. For example, there will always be people who want to start up their own business, but in a country where interest rates are high, and there is a bias against small businesses, it is a less attractive option than it might be. One way to support the work of the quango would be to create a more small business friendly environment. In fact, wherever these beneficial forces are weak, for one reason or another, the sensible government should look first at strengthening the forces, rather than creating some organisational compensation mechanism.

This autonomous equilibrium — where a multitude of forces create the social balance — would be cheaper, if only in the long term, as it allows ordinary people, in the process of doing what they want, to create a stable system. With luck, it will also be the society that they want.

Many people want to run their own business, seeking independence, greater control over their lives, and a type of business in which they are interested. A recession, or unemployment, are an added incentive. What people need is the finance, the culture, the support, informed advice, and a reasonable level of demand. It would be useful to have in addition a stable economic environment, and a healthy economy. In terms of recent years, the key factors are no recession, and stable interest rates. Some politicians, on both sides of the house, go on about stable exchange rates, but these are less bother to the average business than interest rates have been since 1986. If the Chancellor sets a bank rate of 15 per cent, that can wipe out thousands of businesses, as we have seen. The exchange rate would have to be unbelievably high to have the same effect.

A small business economy would also be more able to adjust to changing demand, and produce goods of the type, quality and price that consumers want. The small firms might be able to lobby government, but could not do so on a power basis; they could not push their ideas through into legislation. This is because they would not have the money, the social contacts, the lobbying power, or the advertising clout needed to sway public opinion.If the small firms did want support, it would have to be on the basis of evidence, and proven gains for the economy.

In the absence of any centralised pressure group, leverage in the political system reverts almost by default to the electorate. We may talk about democracy, and hope to mean liberal democracy, but what most countries have is a system of competing power groups, all struggling to get their chosen wish-list fulfilled, without it becoming too obvious to the voters. In some countries, even this perfunctory nod to the populace is absent. The power group may be the military, organised religion, drug dealers, organised crime, political cliques, class interests, or commercial interests. Military dictatorships, such as the Pinochet regime in Chile, are especially renowned for ignoring the needs of the people. However, there is little to distinguish them from the ideological cliques that rule China, and once ruled the Soviet Union.

It is difficult to say which of these is the worst, although at the present time, some are actively more harmful than others. Certainly, none of them should be responsible for managing a nation. And none of the groups should have a privileged relationship in dealing with the government. At the time of writing, there is much protest by Britain's Muslims, who feel that their religion is discriminated against. While the Church of England has the protection of blasphemy laws, Islam does not. Given the alleged separation of church and state in Britain, the answer is to complete that separation, and abolish the blasphemy laws. No group should have special protection for its beliefs, and in a democracy, no group should have a special relationship with the government.

This is just as true of the working class as it is of the church or business. One of the more dubious characteristics of Marxism was its insistence that the working class shall be the rulers of society. Even when this group numbered 75 per cent of the population, to elevate it to the status of the ruling elite was undemocratic. The Labour Party carried on the same error until recently by allowing trade unions to dictate policy to it. For example, after the 1992 election defeat, it was suggested that John Edmonds of the GMB was pushing for John Smith to be the new party leader. In actively promoting their own interests, unions reduce the credibility of Labour, and may harm its ability to formulate useful policies, or be elected to office.

In the absence of any centralised elite, power will tend to revert to the people. Naturally, there may be cliques and empire builders within the structure of the state, and the voters must monitor the politicians to ensure that they are doing their jobs properly. But the usual threat comes from outside government. In the absence of an external agency, and assuming reasonably honest politicians, one can at least say that the government will be able to focus entirely on the needs of the people. And in all probability, it actually will do so.

Then there are the social factors associated with small businesses. A distrust of bigness has long been a part of the American ideology, dating back to the origins of the United States. Thomas Jefferson, one of the founding fathers of America, has a vision of a society of 'free and equal small communities of upright farmers'. McConnell describes this as a 'vision that might have brought a society in which inequality and tyranny would have found no place'. (Grant McConnell, *Private Power and American Democracy*.)

Although Jefferson saw the United States as a farming nation, it being 95 per cent rural at the time of its first census, the small communities he referred to could equally have been made up of farmers or factory owners. The nature of their employment would have very little impact on the dispersal of power; the key aspect that Jefferson would have had in mind would be the small, self-governing community, with a lot of independent workers. McConnell describes this belief in small units as one of 'the tenets of American orthodoxy'. (*ibid.*, p91). It is a part of the American identity, and can be seen in such diverse sources as Norman Rockwell's paintings for *Saturday Evening Post*, or Bedford Falls, in the film, *It's a Wonderful Life*.

It is worth noting that where McConnell refers to 'small units of social and political organization', this could apply equally to small towns, small businesses, or even small countries. The arguments for smallness, local control, personal knowledge, and a community spirit apply to organisations of almost any type.

Of course, the images created by Rockwell and others are fiction; reality could be different. But some of the characteristics of the small town must be true by definition; even to say it is common sense is to be more analytical than is necessary. For example, local people will know their own area, and its problems. They will know which needs can be met from within the community's informal relationships, and which require an official solution of some sort. In knowing the locality, they will naturally have more effective local government. 'This knowledge will extend to details of terrain and to personalities and character. Moreover, since locally chosen officers will be responsible directly to the people of the locality and to no others, the government will be more responsive to the local people and hence more democratic'. (*Private Power and American Democracy*, p73.)

Also, simply because fewer people are involved in local politics, it is easier for a single individual to get their voice heard. It is often said that in big city or big nation politics, people struggle to get heard, fail to be more than a single voice in an urban din, and give up. After all, it is quite apparent that in Britain at least, neither of the two main parties is actually listening to what people are saying. One opinion among millions has no impact; but with televisual persuasion politics, even the millions can be ignored. The best the individual can do is vote for the party that is nearest to their personal beliefs. Some people might simply abstain from voting — in the 1992 British election this was put forward by some people as a constructive alternative.

In a small community, there would probably be more uniformity of interests, and therefore less conflict between citizens. 'There are fewer families, and these are frequently interrelated; there are fewer economic interests, and often lesser extremes of wealth and poverty; there are fewer religions and races. The same will generally be true of almost any dimension of social difference'. (*Private Power and American Democracy*, p94.) As a result, there would be less reason for animosity, jealously, racial tension or any other traditional source of friction.

One writer, describing American small towns in the early nineteenth century, paints a picture of relative harmony. 'By all evidence debate was lively at a town meeting, but when there was strong dissent to a proposed action by a significant group, the moderator would defer a decision until all could be won over. When conflict got out of hand, it was a sign that the basic cohesion of the town had broken down'. (Richard Lingeman, *Small Town America*, p50.)

One would not expect everyone to be happy with every decision, as that is often not possible. One cannot always be happy with one's own decisions, let alone with someone else's. There will always be conflict between differing goals, as our needs pull us in so many different directions. For example, a person seeking promotion may work late at the office to please the boss. They may also want to buy a house, and want to find extra paid work. They cannot do both. Such conflict will be multiplied many times over in a community, where the goals vary, the interpretation of those goals differ, where willingness to compromise varies, and where people's ability to see the other person's needs vary.

In the small community, one will not necessarily understand the other person's motives, or their needs, but one is at least more likely to do so. One will not necessarily sympathise with them; but one is more likely to do so. And because of the physical proximity, one can discuss the disagreements face to face, explaining one's view personally. In such a situation, compromise is more likely to occur, as people find ways to introduce policy with the minimum amount of upset.

Because of this informal, co-operative way of dealing with conflict, there is less need for formal rules. 'What must be dealt with in a large social unit by rigid rules, procedures, and precedents can in a small community be handled in humane fashion and settled on the basis of the merits of the individual situation, avoiding the procrustean bed of a system of law based on analogies. In this sense the small community is at once more efficient and more just'. (*Private Power and American Democracy*, p98.)

Thus, it is more efficient in the sense that less effort and fewer resources go into ensuring that justice is carried out. There is less need of courts, police officers, lawyers, and all the other paraphernalia of the Western legal system. Few people in Britain or the United States would say that we have an efficient system of justice; it is too slow, too expensive, and too often punishes the innocent while allowing the guilty to go free. Yet it may be the best that is possible in an urban, industrialised, mass society. We have to have a system that is impersonal, that protects all who appear before it, to reduce any chance of miscarriage, and that ensures that all legal technicalities are observed. The more complex the legal process, the more necessary it is that all the rules of justice are observed, and seen to be observed. All of this requires the attention of hundreds of highly qualified legal personnel, from police officers to forensic scientists to barristers. In a society that seeks an impersonal, mass produced justice, a lot of effort is needed to show everyone that justice is done.

As the complexities of social, technological and financial relationships multiply, the difficulty of making simple moral judgments also increases. The wrongness of taking a life is called into question when we can keep people alive for years, even when their mind is dead. The rights of parents are open to doubt in a society which knows of child abuse, and foster parents. But as these additional factors proliferate, and the difficulties of deciding right or wrong increase, so it becomes more important that the legal system go through all the procedures, publicly. Justice must not only be done, it must be seen to be done.

In the small community, justice may be done personally. The victim of theft might know who stole from them, and need nothing more than a chat over the fence. A young tearaway has been stealing apples? Well, have a word with their mum and dad over coffee, and tell them to have a word. Someone has smacked into your car? Well, who has recently acquired body damage on theirs? Have a word with them. And if they don't pay up, spread the word about their miserliness throughout town.

If all else fails, there may be recourse to the local bobby, a rural Dixon of Dock Green who greets everyone, 'Evening all'. The law in such an environment is not an ass, but a friend. It is not an expensive bureaucracy, but an informal settling of disputes.

And of course, there is the community spirit that we associate with small towns. There is 'the common belief that "anybody can visit anybody" and "everybody can join any club he wants to"'. (A. Vidich and J. Bensman, *Small Town in Mass Society*, p23.) This is the small town where everyone is popping in and out of other people's houses, chatting, borrowing sugar, or the lawnmower, and generally socialising. It is a community in the truest sense. It is friendly, supportive, a resource to draw on when needed, and people to turn to when one is down. Relating this spirit to the business environment, there is the team spirit or family atmosphere that one often finds in small companies. For example, a worker at the Morgan car company described it as being one big family.

C. Wright Mills points out that members of a small community know one another as complete persons, rather than in the single role we meet in the big city. We meet others in their roles as waiter, bus driver or shop assistant — as Mills puts it, we 'know one another only as fractions'. (*The Power Elite*, p320.) This makes it more likely that we will stereotype others, that we will make glib and superficial judgements based on little or no personal experience of the other as a human being. Few of us have social circles that extend across class boundaries, which makes our understanding even more limited.

The self-made, upwardly-mobile politician (or 'sumpy') usually rises from the Essex middle classes to the shire classes of Westminster. Such people, and their business-world friends, make sweeping statements about trade unions or council workers on a basis of complete ignorance. In a small community, voters would be less likely to make ill-informed judgements about other sectors of society, as very often they would know members of that sector personally. They would understand the need for workers to join trade unions, the justification for nurses to go on strike, and the unjustness of imposing a greater workload on teachers or factory workers.

Finally, if the small towns (or regions) are legally autonomous, they act as a counterbalance to central government. They have control over their own lives and their own sphere of influence. They can apply different policies from those of central government, and hold to different ideologies — which is why the Thatcher regime was so eager to dispose of the Greater London Council. Who wants independent opinion, when one is so vocally announcing to the world that one has the only vision of society that can exist? The problem is that in Britain, local authorities get their legal powers and existence from central government; it is perfectly within the law to simply abolish an elected body like the GLC.

The mere existence of independent local government is an additional control on the powers and excesses of central government. Even if local authorities were not inherently more democratic themselves, they would be contributing to democracy merely by being there. They act as a limit to the power of central government, they can demonstrate the effectiveness of differing economic policies, and they act as a school for future national politicians. But we need greater constitutional support for local authorities so that future rulers of Whitehall cannot make themselves look better by making the Town Halls vanish.

However, small communities or small businesses are not utterly without fault, and are not by themselves the solution to all of society's existing problems. And one might well object that we have painted a highly idealised view of small-town society. People in small towns can be parochial, and unwelcoming to outsiders. Lingeman refers to 'the conformity, the suspicion of strangers and new ideas, the informal, personal politics... the "neighborliness" accompanied by a proclivity to pry into the private lives of those neighbors...'. (*Small Town America*.) At its worst, the small town could be a stifling, oppressive place, where one's mistakes or indiscretions hung round one's neck like albatrosses for the rest of one's life. The big city does allow people the anonymity and privacy that some seek.

In this idealised view of small town life, we see the green fields and the cottages, and we overlook the smell. At a distance, all things can become more attractive, and we can ignore the blemishes that we cannot see. For many people, life in a small town could be boring, narrow, restricting, lacking in culture or inspiration. The usual range of big city facilities might be lacking, leaving few options for social life or entertainment. There might be no theatre, maybe no cinema, and perhaps only the most basic of eating out. In short, no stimulation.

Some people might say this does not matter, we take our own stimulation with us, and find mystery on a blade of grass. But many would find the small town dull. Perhaps we have got used to the flashing lights, hustle and bustle, and permanent sense of danger. Certainly, some Europeans seem to find London's crime rate an added attraction rather than a put-off. It adds an element of excitement that is lacking back in their home country.

This is one area where one can quite clearly not state that one structure is better than another. One can pose the faults of the urban sprawl, but one cannot say that small town life would be better. This would be too much of a value judgement, given the negative features. But it is worth noting that many Londoners have moved to the north of England, because the quality of life is so much better. Perhaps the medium-sized towns, such as Leeds and Huddersfield, combine the best of city life, with the best of the small town. But the most important feature is that we should have the choice as to where and how we live. At the present time, most of the work is in the big cities, and in effect, those with the power have decided how much work there shall be, and what sort it shall be. This is not the way society should function.

We can contrast the small community with either the large industrial society, or what sociologists call mass society. Definitions of mass society vary, but 'in its most extreme form, the mass society is devoid of individuality and community; separateness and the attendant freedoms are gone. People respond to central agencies run by an elite so that their behavior comes to be "controlled" by that elite'. (Philip Olson, *America As A Mass Society*.)

We could see Britain or the United States as mass societies. Education, food, entertainment, and even social values are all acquired as a mass, according to the views of the mass. Traditional society has broken down or simply evaporated with the rise of the big city, and so traditional beliefs and constraints on behaviour have also vanished. We are highly mobile, Britons moving house on average every seven years, and often we do not even know our neighbours; so the opinions and censure of neighbours is a weak constraint. If we steal, harass or mug someone, we just have to disappear round the corner to become totally anonymous. With neither parents nor schools teaching any sort of moral values, young people grow up with the values of their peer group, the mass media, and what they can get away with.

This is part of our process of socialisation, in which we learn from childhood the values of the society we are brought up in. But whereas in traditional society, this occurred in the family, at school and in the community, these sources have either given up or vanished. What occurs now is socialisation by default; politicians and the mass media promote their opinions for their own various reasons, and in the absence of any strong alternative, children take these half-formed, half-baked ideas on board. Hence the generation known as 'Thatcher's children'. They had grown up while Mrs Thatcher was Prime Minister, and absorbed all the simplistic clichés and vacuous certainties along with everything else on nightly television.

We need a society where people can grow up as human beings, not as ballot box fodder for politicians, bombarded by mass media propaganda. People need to be able to make up their own minds, weigh the evidence, choose their own values and their own way of life. And one of the many changes needed to achieve this is to abolish the centralisation that exists in the economic and political realms.

The small communities described here are simply part of a return to the traditional society. It is hoped that parents, family, friends, teachers, and so on would all contribute to the sense of community and the formation of traditional values. This does not mean the values of the nineteenth century, but the values of unity, friendship, compassion, and personal growth.

To achieve the small business economy we need to encourage the creation and use of small firms, and discourage, dismantle, and where relevant, boycott the larger ones. In the world of the near future, we literally cannot afford their socially and environmentally destructive ways.

8

The dictatorship of the commissariat

SINCE THE END of the nineteenth century, Britain's economy has become increasingly centralised. An economy of medium-sized businesses has become one that is dominated by big business. Yet under the Thatcher Imperium, that centralisation has both accelerated, and broadened, extending into more areas of society. We have seen the rise of the hypermarket and the shopping mall, consortium building projects, the rise of the EU, and centralisation of state power in Whitehall.

The shopping mall usually has the external appeal of a warehouse, combined with the interior design sense of a Rupert Murdoch canteen. It is environmentally harmful, inviting consumers to drive many miles just to fill the weekly shopping basket. It is socially damaging, putting a blight on inner city areas, encouraging further concentration in the retail sector, and contributing to the run-down of shopping centres generally. In an energy-intensive, artificial atmosphere, centrally heated and air-conditioned, consumers are surrounded by just enough cold, austere elegance to persuade them to buy. They are the unwitting targets of a carefully thought out marketing campaign, designed to clinically separate them from their money. And naturally, almost as a side-effect, these shopping centres promote the big retail chains at the expense of the small local shop.

The development projects also centralise resources, because the really big building schemes usually have some component of state funds. The government's aim is to create jobs, preferably in one fell swoop, thus saving effort, and in a high-profile operation, thus ensuring maximum credit for the ministers involved. For example, in a regime committed to the minimal state, there has been generous state aid for the Canary Wharf project, once said to be the largest building site in Europe.

The main problem is that these large projects draw government funds away from a hundred small, local developments that could use the money more effectively, and create more jobs. Healthy profits for the big building companies are matched by job losses in a dozen small construction companies. Just as bad, the finished product does not reflect a local need, and very often is a blight on the community, as well as being a blot on the landscape.

Then there is Westminster's avid accumulation of power. The Gnomes of Downing Street have no social concerns, other than their own careers and the welfare of their social equals. To this end, they feel obliged to weaken the ideological opposition, somewhat in the manner of Pol Pot. Aiming at the same targets, although not with such fatal ammunition, they seek to shoot down the teachers, the media, the intellectuals and local government. The value of these individuals or of the work done by them is of no importance; the demands of Year Zero are that only one ideology shall reign supreme.

Allegedly, the policies used have been aimed at increased consumer choice. Thus, for example, schools can opt out of local council control, doctors can run their own budgets, and hospitals can opt out of the NHS. The theory is that each organisation can run itself, and in the school's case, the parents can take part in the decision-making. The reality is that cost-cutting is imposed, resulting in the decline of the quality of services. Nevertheless ultimate power to decide the level of spending on these services will remain in Whitehall.

More power will move from Britain to Brussels, as the nations of Europe move towards 'ever closer union'. Yet the Maastricht Treaty, the essence of this closer union, pays scant attention to the need for democracy. The foreign ministers who have negotiated it see no need to explain their justification for the union. Nor is there significant concern for social welfare, as the main issues in the treaty are interest rates, exchange rates amd monetary union. Indeed, much of the treaty is Thatcherism formalised. There is neither explanation, justification, nor evidence. It is simply — this is what the European Union will do.

If the market philosophy is allowed to spread throughout Europe as it has done in Britain since 1979, and the Union extends itself as it has done in the past, by the third decade of the twenty-first century the views of business will dominate both North and South America, and a Greater Europe of more than 40 nations. This will not mean a wealthy Europe, simply because of the self-destructive nature of the market ideology. The world's economic centre of gravity will have shifted to Japan and the Asian dragons, like Taiwan and Singapore.

These nations, learning from the success of their interventionist neighbour, Japan, will be highly productive, with high levels of investment, and skilled, educated work-forces. Government intervention will be taken for granted, just as it is in Japan, and no doubt they will target markets, products and niches as successfully as the Japanese themselves. And they will compete with the West with the same disdainful ease as the Lords of the Rising Yen.

The economic failure of the West will be combined with a political centralisation that is noteworthy even now for its refusal to listen to the average person. At the time of writing, the Maastricht treaty has been rejected by the Danes in a national referendum, and EU pundits are loudly citing the 25,000 Danes who opposed Maastricht. Like the number of communists in the State Department, the number varies, so the Portuguese minister was able to talk of the 50,000 Danes who voted. But he put it as if these Danes had opposed the decisions of 12 governments; as if the will of politicians was more important than the will of the people. And with the added implication that it was 'only' 50,000 Danes who did this. To be exact, Maastricht was opposed by 50.3 per cent of those who voted, but quoting the smaller number of 50,000 (the margin by which the 'no' vote exceeded the 'yes' vote) allows those with no interest in the truth to dismiss all those who voted against Maastricht. Such people were so disturbed by the 'no' vote that they demanded a second referendum. Douglas Hurd, Britain's foreign minister at the time, argued that the question should be put to the Danes, until they 'got it right'.

The EU is extremely centralised, with a non-elected commission, and whose last president, Jacques Delors, once looked set to stay in his job for life. This is a trick that is usually played only by the dictators of Third World republics. The nearest federal comparison is the United States, which from 1815 gradually became more centralised, with powers being re-allocated from local or state level to federal government, and new powers being created explicitly as federal powers. Whereas the US became centralised, the EU started that way, yet is becoming more so.

The problem with a centralised political system are various. There is a physical, social and cultural distance between politicians and electorate that makes access and communication near impossible. Firstly, the geographical distance makes the government physically less accessible. Voters would find it difficult to actually get to their leaders, in far off Washington, Brussels or Beijing. This makes a mass lobby of government a daunting task, even when people may be deeply concerned about policy. In a poor country, the mass protest may be financially impossible, while in a richer country, it may be merely an added burden on the organisers, already overloaded by the distance itself.

Conversely, that distance makes it less likely that politicians will have any personal knowledge or experience of local people's problems. We all live relatively isolated lives, and can travel as much as we like, without ever seeing the decaying 1960s estates, the inner city slums, and the cardboard box shanty towns. Even if we assumed normal travel patterns, this would be especially true of politicians. As they travel in chartered jet or chauffeur-driven limousine, from their country house to a speaking engagement in front of a selected audience, they are unlikely to see any members of the underclass. Indeed, they are unlikely to meet anyone who is not on their carefully-planned schedule. Their journey is a military exercise, planned with care, and executed with precision. A meeting with a total stranger is a meeting with a potential critic, and no politician wants that.

They want the whole process of political life, especially the elections, to be tightly controlled, and as free from the unknown and uncontrollable as is humanly possible. The media are subject to government legislation, funding constraints, and an assortment of semi-official pressures. As a result, interviewers will not be as dogged and ruthless in seeking answers as the public deserves. So even a 'probing' television interview will tend to be more of a rehearsed PR job.

But a meeting with a member of the public can be very disconcerting, as Mrs Thatcher has found out. Ordinary people can be sharp, well-informed, and not subject to media controls. So they can say what they like, argue, disagree, and even prove the politician wrong. They can reveal the true image of the emperor; wearing the faded remains of an old potato sack. Or as Dan Quayle, the US Vice President under George Bush, spelled the word in an unscheduled school conversation, 'potatoe'.

In the 1992 election, John Major was heckled during a walkabout in Bolton. He was unable to deal with their criticisms at the time, but he made up for this by talking about 'Rentamob' in subsequent interviews. Like the entire Tory regime, the lack of content was compensated for by skilled presentation.

Many politicians cannot deal with the unscheduled, uncontrolled public, and actively avoid them. This is a loss for democracy, because we need to be able to judge our elected masters. But just as important, they must be able to judge us, and our needs. For government to be effective, politicians must have a clear idea of what has to be done, as well as the best way to carry out that action — assuming that they wish to do what is needed by the people. And if we assume benevolent intent, they need to be in touch with people in some way to carry out their good wishes.

If they live and work a thousand miles away from the mass of the populace, in an insular, protected cocoon, in a different culture from the rest of society, they will have little understanding of the way of life of the average person. It is possible that some outstanding leaders would somehow keep in touch with mass society by reading popular papers, or through academic studies of the conditions of ordinary people. But this does mean a positive effort, and it does not guarantee any real understanding.

The cultural differences simply add to the gap, and even if a politician comes from the same background as their electorate, there is the possibility of eventual incomprehension developing. The government, in the far away capital city, may generate a culture of its own, in the same way that many institutions do. It rules the individual's life, it protects the member against the outsider, and ultimately, it influences the individual's values. This is particularly true of the House of Commons, which is sometimes talked of as being Britain's most exclusive gentlemen's club. It has taken to admitting women in modest numbers, but the insular culture remains.

It is quite certain that the European Parliament in Brussels has also developed an institutional culture. Regular visitors to Brussels and Strasbourg believe that Europe's leaders are more than the formulators of policy; they are also entitled to say what is right. And when the people reject the chosen policies, the alleged servants throw hysterical temper tantrums. They ignore the direction in which obedience is supposed to flow, and they forget to get the technical details right. For example, after the voters of Denmark rejected the Maastricht treaty, the Portuguese minister spoke of the number of Danes who opposed Maastricht, in the comments referred to above.

The institutional culture often develops into this sort of 'them and us' attitude. This has become quite clear in some of the statements uttered by EU bureaucrats, and by some national government leaders who have been dealing with the EUfor a prolonged period. The attitude is that the mandarins of Brussels have chosen, in their infinite wisdom, the correct policy for the 320 million people of Europe. And the people, ignorant fools that they are, reject this wisdom!

This 'them and us' attitude is a result of the cultural isolation, but once the attitude has been given voice and made explicit, it becomes a stronger part of the policy process. Ideas are presented in a way that will appeal to 'them', or are initiated secretly, or they are preceded by increases in the power of the bureaucrats. In that way, the difficulty of influencing the legislation becomes an argument against attempting to change it. In effect, power has become a justification for the policy.

From here it is just a short step to blaming the ordinary person. In Britain we have seen the Conservative government blaming the victims of society, saying that those who are homeless, unemployed, rioting, drug addicts or criminals are to blame for their own problems. Occasionally ministers will blame the church, the decline of the family, the rise of the one-parent family, parents in general, or the lack of fear concerning hellfire and damnation, as John Patten did. But they will not accept that the government might be responsible for unemployment or homelessness, or that social factors might cause riots or drug abuse. The automatic response is to blame the victim. Or in Tory terms, the individual must accept their own responsibility.

For this approach to work, it must be accepted by a large proportion of society. One cannot accuse the homeless of being responsible for their own plight when the mass of the electorate are strongly sympathetic to their plight. In the long term, the government would seek to change people's attitudes, but in a here and now of sympathetic voters, verbal attacks on the homeless could be political disaster.

But by bland reassurances and skilful propaganda, the government can change attitudes, as the Conservatives have done over unemployment. When the Tories came into office in 1979, one and a half million jobless was close to being politically unacceptable. By constantly telling the electorate that inflation had to be got down first, for economic recovery to take place, that the economy had to be cured before jobs could be created, and by saying that one could not spend to create jobs, gradually the public view of unemployment altered. The Conservatives had reconstructed the political agenda. Not by saying that unemployment was unimportant, but by emphasising the other issues that they claimed had to be dealt with first.

This allowed them to ignore the unemployed, even when there were two or three million of them. The same supply side agenda allowed the government to reduce the benefits paid to the unemployed, thus saving the state money, and cutting the level of taxes that needed to be raised. This allowed the higher and basic rates of tax to be cut, which then shifted the income distribution in favour of the upper income groups. The concern of the middle and upper income groups for the unemployed would be dampened by their belief that the victims were to blame, that things were being done, and that they were better off under the Tory government.

This tactic could be seen as divide and rule, an appeal to self-interest, or as mere capitalist exploitation. But in essence it is that a group that is neither of, nor for the people, will use any ploys it can to benefit its own chosen constituency. It has limited sympathy for the victims of society, and limited understanding. In an extreme case, such as the New Right Conservatives, it simply does not care about the underdog. This is an ideology whose creator actually condemned those who 'drool and drivel about caring'.

It is interesting to compare Mrs Thatcher's hostility to compassion with Norman Tebbit's hostility to the 1960s. This was expressed in one of Tebbit's mild-mannered rants against the BBC, an organisation which probably represents everything the Conservatives hate. 'The word "Conservative" is now used by the BBC as a portmanteau word of abuse for anyone whose political views differ from the insufferable, smug, sanctimonious, naive, guilt-ridden, wet, pink orthodoxy of that sunset home of the third rate minds of that third rate decade, the 1960s'. (Norman Tebbit, February 1990, quoted in *The Guardian*, December 31, 1990.)

Reading this, one comes away with a strong suspicion that Tebbit dislikes the 1960s. Apart from the 60s being wet and pink, one wonders what other objections spring to Tebbit's mind. Could it be the fact that in the 1960s, the working classes were not only wealthy, but they were downright enjoying themselves? They had money, working class heroes such as David Bailey or the Beatles were seen as role models, while working class needs were a major issue in politics. Could that be part of what Tebbit objected to?

However, many of the arguments above apply even if we assume that our politicians have the best of intentions. We can imagine them to be kind, benevolent, and wise; and they are doing their best for us. But if they are out of touch, a thousand miles away, and understand neither us as individuals, nor our culture, then they cannot be expected to provide us with the best government we can get. They will be benevolent, but incorrectly informed; kind, but misguided. In other words, if we imagine the perfect human beings we would like our politicians to be, they would still be unable to act as perfect leaders. They would not have the information necessary to do so.

But if we then imagine that as a result of the social gap between rulers and ruled, there develops a lack of sympathy, a difference in cultures, and probably a 'them and us' attitude, we come closer to normal human behaviour. Allowing for the gulf between us, we can expect bureaucracy, empire building, minor compromises on the general population's needs in order to protect the bureaucrat, misunderstanding, and indifference.

This sort of behaviour exists in every organisation, in every historical period. We can see empire building in the actions of MI5, threatened with the loss of operations by the end of the cold war, seeking to move into activities that have traditionally been the role of the police. We see cuts in public transport or NHS spending by the Conservative government, few members of which are obliged to actually use the services the state provides. The larger and the more centralised the organisation, the easier it is for the institution's apparatchiks to justify their actions. Just as the mandarins do not really understand the populace, so distance lends enchantment, and a second-rate education adds mystique to the pen-pushers of Whitehall. This allows the bureaucrats an impressive range of exotic explanations as to why the schools are still crumbling, and railway safety is still appalling. The complex system of government and administration is incomprehensible to most people, so the bureaucrats can continue in their self-protective ways.

Given the likelihood of a chasm of indifference between the rulers and the population in general, the constraints of democracy become ever more crucial. One small control would be to insist that politicians be open to regular interrogation by the public. These could be reported by the media, and if a minister was unable to answer a criticism by a member of the public, it would make entertaining front page news the next day. There could be security objections to this, which only makes it more important that the media be able to question MPs without any hindrance whatsoever. Interference with the press and broadcasters is actually an assault on democracy.

So far we have looked at the politicians' distance from the electorate, and its effect on the politicians. It is also worth looking at the effects of distance on the people. The most significant impact is on elections. We talk about democracy as if holding an election every five years justifies the whole charade, as if that one moment of choice means that the populace is being ruled wisely and properly.

Because of the physical and cultural chasm that so often yawns between politicians and the electorate, there is considerable mutual ignorance of the other side. What few attempts at understanding there are, are purely one way. Nobody really cares what the voters are actually like, but politicians do care how the voters see them. So the Conservatives being the skilled, manipulative masters of the Saatchi arts that they are, seek to understand the voters, so as to present a ballot-friendly image.

As a result, elections are not the expression of democracy that some of us would like to imagine, but a struggle between two opposing forces. In the blue corner, we have Sugar-Coated Pill, backed by most of British industry, and fighting under the Marquis of Grantham rules. This contestant has had acres of publicity from the press, while any lingering disapproval that the camera crews may bear is irrelevant, as they have been gagged. The small, occasional voice of objective comment is more than drowned out by the steady drone of tabloid attack. The editorials, the political columns, the cartoons, and the emotive personal attacks are a near-guarantee of electoral success.

In the red corner we have Claws Four, an old-fashioned socialist, backed by several well-known trade unions. This provides a diminishing amount of money, but a steadily increasing amount of public hostility. Claws does get good value for money from the advertising budget, but this is dissipated by the attempt to present several key themes, and eight core messages. Parallel to the main bout, Hattersley, Benn, and several other contestants are all carrying on their own fights.

The result has been an unequal struggle in which the Tories have often been an odds-on cert to win. Some of these items may not seem very important, but together they reduce the effectiveness of democracy. Democracy is not a standardised product, like wheat, nor is it like a television, that is either off or on, there or not there. It is a complex political concept that can exist anywhere along a spectrum of positions, and any given country can move subtly along that spectrum at any time. Many people are unaware of their society's position relative to other countries. And few of us are aware of the discrete, day to day changes that take place.

The combination of the distance, the lack of personal contact, the Cabinet's indifference to the population's needs or opinions, and the electorate's inability to influence the direction of politics, leads to the alienation described in Chapter 4. Thus, the distance may start as a purely geographical concern, but if the gap is too wide, or it is used by politicians as a barrier, then it becomes an emotional distance as well. But if the electorate is alienated, then regardless of the democratic institutions or the checks and balances, democracy is effectively dead. As we can see now, it is only a short step from ineffective controls, to authoritarianism.

But if voters and leaders do not understand one another, and one another's problems and culture, then communication between the two will be minimal. Voters will have a distorted view of what politicians are doing, and politicians will have a distorted view of what the voters need. As a result, the government is less likely to do what is needed, while the electorate is less likely to realise that they are only getting a loose approximation to the correct policies. In many cases, voters will be moderately happy with the fairly competent policies that are applied. Few voters know exactly what is needed, and they tend to accept the plausible excuses offered by their elected bosses.

The fact that they have voted this particular set of elected representatives into office does not make it a true democracy. There must be more to democracy than simply having a vote. For example, one might imagine a country where everyone had the vote, but voters were deliberately misinformed and misled. This is especially likely when the politicians are both plausible and articulate, able to persuade the electorate that the chosen policies are the best of all possible policies. Or consider the way in which Germany became an elected dictatorship in 1933, or Algeria nearly did in 1992, and in which Britain moved imperceptibly towards one during the 1980s and 90s. None of this is acceptable from a government which claims the moral right to rule. Legitimacy does not come merely from universal suffrage.

Nor is it acceptable to impose policies that harm or ignore the interests of any of the electorate. To disregard the welfare of a majority of the population, as the Thatcherites have done in Britain, is a total negation of the state's responsibilities. It might be argued that the government has a mandate from the people to follow a given course, but it has no moral right to continue that course, regardless of the damage done to society.

What we need, as stated in Chapter 3, is not merely a democracy of one person, one vote. That is little more than an organised formality, which can be eroded by the death of a thousand cuts. Information on policy becomes a little more difficult to obtain, government statistics become a bit more misleading, politicians become fractionally more evasive about the impact of their policies, and so on. Bit by bit, our voting power is devalued by the legal chicanery of our alleged leaders.

For genuine liberal democracy we need to have an informed electorate, elected representatives who wish to do a job rather than find a career, and open political processes. That is, we need an educated citizenry which has free access to public debate and an unbiased, uncensored media. We need politicians who represent us both in policy and as a peer group. And we need a political system that, like justice, is not only done, but can be seen to be done.

What we actually get is smooth-talking MPs, elegantly stonewalling media questions, a biased media, and an electorate that does not understand the choices. We have politicians selected in closed enclaves, and who are largely white, male, middle or upper class, and from business backgrounds. Our legislative process is carried out at least partly in secret, and is influenced anonymously in ways that we may never hear about.

In terms of what we read in the papers or see on TV, informed debate has virtually ceased to exist since the early 1980s. Politicians have become adept at giving bland interviews which reveal nothing except the party line. They answer pointed questions with a fluent and articulate monologue that sounds like the voice of compassionate expertise talking. They cover all the necessary points, and although well-practised, it never sounds rehearsed. These are image control experts who rarely have to resort even to such blunt tactics as refusing to answer a question. Although when South Georgia was recaptured, Mrs Thatcher and John Nott made a brief statement, no questions were permitted, and Mrs Thatcher disappeared into Number 10, saying, 'Rejoice!' (*The Coercive State*, p125.) And at the slightest sign of criticism, Norman Tebbit would attack the BBC vehemently, and of course, attacks by a key member of the government carry at the very minimum the implied threat of the withholding of funding.

Instead of debate, we have presentation. Ministers have expert research staff to ensure that they are at least as well-informed as any interviewer. And there is no doubt that ministers have had the same sort of speech and image training as Mrs Thatcher, ensuring that they present themselves in the right way. They have also learnt to put their argument in long speeches, in which they cover so many points that their analysis must seem exhaustive to the average viewer. And usually there is too much for any opposition speakers to deal with every issue that has been raised in the minister's monologue. In fact, most opposition speakers do not even try to do so, and by default allow a whole string of specious arguments and half-truths to go unchallenged. When their turn to speak finally arrives, they launch into a statement of their own policies, thus giving the impression that they accept the government speaker's dubious opinions, but have opposing opinions themselves. Every interview like this has carried the implicit message that the minister's arguments were irrefutable.

Also, much of the agenda for debate is presented as a foregone conclusion. The government announces what it will do, what it has decided and what actions it will take. For example, our representatives go to Maastricht with a predetermined agenda, or the education minister states that schools will be re-organised in a certain way. There is little or no discussion, even with the people involved. For example, when Kenneth Clarke decided that teacher training should place more emphasis on in-class learning, and less on specialised teacher training institutions, there was consultation — but not on the change itself, only on the implementation of that change. (*NATFHE Journal*, July 1992.)

But when professionals object to the changes being imposed on them, ministers throw petty temper tantrums. To take an example from education again, testing of seven years olds, as well as testing too early, imposes a heavy workload on the teachers, for no extra pay — as has been the case with many so-called reforms. John Patten's response to the teachers' union, NUT, was a letter saying, 'I find your union's troublesome behaviour over this matter grossly irresponsible.'.

The impression given is that once the government has a mandate, all public discussion ceases. It has been given a job by 'the people,' and although it will not be looking after the interests of all the people, the mandate allows it to make what decisions it wants. It does not need to discuss its idea with the workers involved, nor listen to expert opinion. And there is no reason to assume that the public want to know what the underlying reasoning is. The government's manner gives the impression that it is both expert and trustworthy. No doubt, many voters will accept this view, believing that governing is a job that some people have been chosen for, and the public should just let them get on with it. In other words, the government's cavalier attitude may be generating respect among the electorate.

For democracy to work properly, we need educated and perceptive citizens who can take an active part in debate. It should be clear to most people that to cut spending, and then impose more demands on a sector, cannot be done without some strain occurring. Yet this is what the Citizens' Charters do; they impose requirements, without any obligation to provide finance. But with the government constantly cutting education expenditure, loading extra work onto teachers, and deskilling teaching, one can only expect an ill-informed electorate. What we actually get is much worse than that — an apathetic, politically illiterate electorate. Professor Harry McGurk of Surrey University says that Britain's young people have no conception 'of the characteristics of different political systems; and they are hardly aware of the policy issues, let alone the philosophical differences, which distinguish the principal British political parties'. (*The Independent*, December 3, 1987.) Similar research five years later showed the same depressing picture. (*The Guardian*, February 14, 1991.)

Once again, this works in favour of the Conservatives. Young people have traditionally been the most radical sector of society, and have tended to vote Labour rather than Tory. As their political apathy has increased, encouraged by a government that deliberately refuses to listen to anyone, so the Labour vote has fallen.

Although our politicians are elected, one cannot call them representative of the society they rule. MPs are mainly white, middle class, or upper class males. In 1979, when 60 per cent of the population was from a manual working class background, only 5 per cent of Conservative candidates came from such a background. (*Britain at the Polls, 1979*, p15.) And this was a rise compared with earlier elections: in pre-1970 elections the number of working class Tory MPs was between 5 and 7. (Stanworth and Giddens, *Elites and Power in British Society*, p33.) The typical Conservative MP will be ex-public school, from a law or business background, or perhaps a landowner.

Given this, it is not surprising that Tory legislation tends to favour business, especially big business, and the upper income groups. And although Tory antipathy towards closed shops has hit Fleet Street printers, the television industry, the police and trade unions generally, it has been strangely soft on restrictive practices in the legal profession. Solicitors have been savaged by a dead sheep, while barristers have suffered nothing more violent than a thwack from the jester's bladder.

This is not to say that elected representatives can only be of benefit if they come from the same social class as their constituents. It has been said that British rule of Hong Kong has done wonders for the Hong Kong economy, despite the Brits' total lack of understanding of the local people. The combination of British respectability and Chinese energy has proved tremendously successful. Whether this same synergy can apply in non-colonial situations is another matter.

This concern that one's needs are ignored or misunderstood lay behind many of the nationalist movements of the twentieth century. The Basques, the Catalans, the Welsh, the Scots, the Lombards and the Lapps have all felt that their central governments had failed them. Some might include the Tibetans, but this is a different situation. Tibet has been invaded; there is no democracy there to fail. But in the Western examples, politicians from majority cultures have been seen as totally inappropriate for the needs of a minority group.

Finally, we do not have an open political system. Parliamentary debate is veiled by the mystique of its complex rules, yet that is the more open part of the legislative process. It is Cabinet that decides the Parliamentary programme, and what Cabinet agrees will almost certainly pass the Commons. But the Cabinet, usually ten to twenty people, does not itself have full access to the facts, and to the decision-making process. Civil servants deliver long discussion papers to ministers, immediately before cabinet meetings, so that ministers have little opportunity to actually read the documents. As result, 'the Cabinet more often acts as a rubber stamp for decisions taken elsewhere'. (Paddy Hillyard and Janie Percy-Smith, *The Coercive State*, p51.) The real decisions will often have been taken already by a Cabinet committee, probably dominated by the Prime Minister and a few acolytes.

Indeed, one of the tendencies of the post-1979 Tory governments, although less significant under John Major, has been the willingness of the Prime Minister to push through their chosen legislation, regardless of Cabinet, the House of Commons, or the public in general. It has even been said that under Thatcher, Britain approached an American, presidential style of politics. Political power, already over-centralised in the Houses of Parliament, becomes vested in one person.

This extreme centralisation is the effective opposite of genuine democracy, because it lacks transparency, accessibility, and openness to control. What we need is a decentralised society, where decisions are taken in line with John Major's much touted, and little used, rule of subsidiarity. That is, they should be taken at as low a level as possible. In fact, the EU flouts its own policies, as the Maastricht Treaty proposes that 'decisions are taken as closely as possible to the citizen'. As has been noticed, the EU has not asked the member citizens about its integration or expansion, or acquisition of new powers, or indeed any other aspect of its actions.

'De Gaulle, in one of his moments of exasperation with the French, had asked how was a nation which made 1,756 — or whatever it was — different kinds of cheese to be governed?' (Peter Jenkins, *Mrs Thatcher's Revolution*, p360.) Surely, one of the characteristics of a nation is diversity, and the institutions of government should be arranged to recognise that, not to repress it.

We need to decentralise the institutions of our society, both regionally and locally, so that the average person can once again take control over their own lives. The first stage is to decentralise national politics, with power in Britain being moved from Cabinet to Parliament, and from party headquarters to local branches. Cabinet procedure should be arranged to be as open as possible, with briefing papers delivered to ministers at least 24 hours beforehand, and major decisions, where secrecy is not essential, to be taken only in full Cabinet sessions. For example, there can be no conceivable reason why economic policy decisions should be taken in secret, therefore they should be taken by all ministers collectively.

Ministers should be made more answerable to their colleagues in the Commons, perhaps by abolishing the party whips, and by increasing the powers of the All-party committees. These committees should have the power to summon any MP, to demand full and honest answers, and to impeach any MP who either lied to the committee, or concealed important information.

Many of the powers that have accrued to government over the years — especially those years since 1979 — could be put back into the hands of local authorities. For example, education, housing, health, and the decision as to the exact level of expenditure should all be taken locally, or at least influenced by local input. The type of education, and the allocation of housing funds could also be decided locally.

The decentralisation could also be applied to the local authorities themselves. Prior to the 1974 re-organisation there were 1,400 local authorities in England and Wales. According to Jones and Kavanagh, 'dissatisfaction with the earlier system had been widespread'. (*British Politics Today*, p169.) But having seen the results of the government's decision to act over dissatisfaction with the rates, one wonders how intense, and how justified, that unrest was. It has been said that the smaller local councils were inefficient, but the new larger bodies are equally inefficient. There is no gain on that basis, yet there is a loss of access, of transparency in local government, and in responsiveness to public needs.

It would be useful to break up some of the less responsive councils, into local or district councils. Some local authorities are already doing something similar, by setting up local offices for many of their services. This could be extended to all areas, so that the existing borough councils become a co-ordinating agency for those services which need to be provided in a planned or integrated way.

Some local authorities abused their powers, ignored sensible controls on spending, and allowed debts to mount to ludicrous levels. They refused to sue tenants who had not paid rent, on the grounds that these people were already the victims of society. In some cases, this may have been true. But properly targeted benefits would ensure that those who were genuinely in need would get the assistance they deserved. And after all this, some council officers refused to discuss policy failings; that is, they regarded themselves as unaccountable. This is a total negation of democracy.

Decentralising local authorities would not only make them more amenable to control. It would also reduce their propensity towards giant development projects. They would be less able to afford or encourage giant construction programmes, and they would be more aware of small-scale local needs. Rather than a 400 acre shopping mall, they could focus on the renovation of 20 houses, 5 schools and a hospital. Small-scale jobs could be handled by local companies, with no strain on the council's budget, and no subsequent debt repayment to City of London financial institutions.

Having re-structured the local authorities, their existence and funding should then be protected by statute, so that no future government could arbitrarily impose its will on them. There are certain tasks that councils have to carry out, and central government should give them the money for this. If Westminster seeks to impose additional tasks, it should provide, or negotiate, extra funding.

Also, the move towards the concentration of state agencies in one location should be reversed. It has been alleged that it is more efficient to have all paperwork on social security or housing benefit under one roof. This is the same 'economies of scale' argument that has been used so unconvincingly by the proponents of big business. In fact, the evidence suggest that not only are these centralised operations inefficient, but that the government actually uses the bureaucratic process as a way of limiting expenditure.

There is good reason to suppose that unemployment benefit is operated on this principle. Those who seek to apply find that it is necessary to negotiate a maze of offices, and a formidable barrier of application forms, before they can get what is said to be their entitlement. The process is so slow and interminable that many people simply give up. Some of them become homeless because they lack the money to get any sort of home, and cannot fight their way through the benefit barriers.

All of these bureaucracies should be localised, so that not even the head office is further than a few miles away. This is especially important for welfare benefit offices, so that the lines of communication between claimant and administrators are kept short, and any likelihood of misunderstanding or loss of paperwork is minimised. Also, localisation makes the agency more accessible, so that if there was a bureaucratic blunder, the claimant would not find it impossible to sort out.

One suspects that the Tories have used centralisation and bureaucratic procedures as one of the barriers to prevent people from obtaining their benefits. In other words, it is probably a form of attack on working people, rather than an attempt to improve standards of living. It is most unlikely that the present system is efficient, or cost-effective, and therefore decentralising it will release funds for other purposes.

In addition, it might be useful to put some of these agencies into local authority control. Funding could still be provided by Whitehall, and based on need, but administered locally. It could also be managed by a quango, but the main issue is to remove provision from central government control. Thus, public transport, health and education could be operated and co-ordinated on a regional or local basis.

The best approach would be to set up a totally independent constitutional monitoring body, with the right to evaluate state spending. It would agree minimum levels of funding with the government, with the clear proviso that if existing tax rates did not bring in enough to fund services properly, then the rates would have to be increased. Of course, given a genuine democracy, there would be a progressive tax system, with the rich bearing a larger percentage share of the burden than the poor.

Clearly, a wide range of organisations could be decentralised, making them more accountable, and more amenable to popular control. This is part of the definition of democracy, and until all our institutions are fully accountable, we cannot call our nation democratic.

But decentralisation by itself is not enough. Our main concern is that decision-making power be in the hands of the individual, that each person be able to control their own lives. Therefore, any power bloc or pressure group that is powerful enough to channel the political process in their own interests must be dissuaded from doing so. Because as long as they are asking for special treatment, the system is giving disproportionate benefits to the pressure group.

The impact is severe because many of these are not just pressure groups in the normal sense, but are highly influential social strata operating at the core of political operations. They socialise with the Cabinet, have regular meetings with ministers, and swing the odd round of golf with top civil servants. Because their opinions are injected straight into the heart of the political process, into people who, because of their social background already agree with the message, those opinions are extremely influential.

In Britain, the core has typically been comprised of politicians, business, church and unions. The influence of the church has been steadily waning since the nineteenth century, while the unions have lost their role in more recent times. But business is still in the front line in the race for political favours, while the average voter is still trapped behind the starting gate.

To remove this imbalance, the political system should be kept separate from business. This would be extremely difficult, given the close social links between business leaders and top politicians. But at least one can maximise the formal, organised separation between them.

The most important step is to abolish the funding of political parties by outside bodies. State funding of parties is normal practice in the Scandinavian countries, and is probably a contributory factor in the effectiveness of their democratic procedures. In Britain, we should make funding of parties by either business or unions illegal. Instead, parties would be funded by the state, in proportion to the number of votes they had got at the last election. And of course, there has for many years been a tradition of allowing the major political parties to broadcast free, at election time.

In the United States there have been cases of companies persuading their employees to donate funds to the company's favoured party, usually the Republicans. Even if the company subsidises each employee's donation, it is still an abuse of the workers' rights, and an infringement of their voting power. And because it gives electoral advantage to an organisation that has no vote, it is actually a form of political corruption. For this to happen in a country where political donations were illegal would be morally offensive, so the punishment should be appropriately severe. But it should be a punishment aimed at the executives of the company who proposed such donations, rather than a fine or other action against the company, which is merely a legal entity.

In Britain, we have the Advertising Standards Authority and the Press Complaints Commission, neither of which impose any controls over what is said in the realms of politics or religion. Both of these areas of debate should be brought under some formal control, at the very least, so that those on the lunatic fringe cannot get away with outright lies.

But perhaps the worst abuses of free speech have appeared in the press, with editorials, cartoons, and so-called news reporting that often crossed the line from bigoted, entering the territory of outright lies. Clearly, the press watchdog should have sufficient teeth to be able to give any newspaper that did tell lies, the mauling of its life. For this to happen, as and when editors stepped across the line, the regulator would have to be completely independent of the press themselves.

In fact, the ideal would be if all the institutions of society were independent of one another, and all answerable either to the public, or to some external monitor. There are no guarantees, and we have seen the vulnerability of Germany's constitution in the face of right wing extremism, but at the very least such checks and balances increase the likelihood of our institutions doing the job for which they were intended.

Given a decentralisation of political power, a curbing of the size and power of business, and a legal separation of business and politics, it is much more likely that power will revert to the electorate. This can be seen as a default setting, which in computer terms, means that if no other action is taken, it will be the chosen setting.

But democracy should not be ours by default; it is something that we should be willing to grab hold of every day, warning off any predator. It is ours. And we have to protect it.

9

The national culture

As MENTIONED BEFORE, one cannot deal with problems in isolation, and this is as true of social concerns as of economic ones. Although it is easy and convenient for the government to blame the victim, the causes of our social ills usually lie elsewhere. Economic factors are often the primary, but not the only causes. Crime, drugs and delinquency are often linked to poverty, unemployment, homelessness and alienation. Financial factors are not always paramount, but they do often play a role.

Some of these are linked to government policy on inequality, housing, education, industry and the economy, as well as to the attitudes and culture of the society. It might be said that the government does not have an explicit policy on inequality, but it does have a very clear taxation policy. The stance of the post-1979 Tory administrations has been to allow inequality to increase, both in number and in the intensity, the breadth and the degree of unequalness. The level of poverty has risen sharply, the number of homeless people has grown rapidly, young people have been almost forced to leave home by restrictive social security legislation, and education has been devalued; the social impact of all this has been tragic. Yet it has taken place amid a backdrop of economic incompetence. The role of industry has been ignored, while economic policy has been aimed at controlling inflation rather than creating jobs or stabilising production.

All of this has been accepted, or at least tolerated, by the electorate. That is, voters have seen all this, awful as it sounds when described bluntly, as acceptable. This acceptability is determined by culture and attitudes, which in turn are very much influenced by the government of the day. It is also determined partly by our socialisation, which is a composite of school, parents, friends, the media and politicians. As most people's opinions are affected by both politicians and the media, many of the opinions we hear are repeated, arriving by different routes. When the Chancellor says we must control inflation, this is broadcast on the radio and TV as news, and quoted in the newspapers. Friends or acquaintances hear this, and comment on it to us. Thus, we may hear it as news, authoritative comment, or expert opinion.

But we do hear it, and repeatedly so. No other voices get so well aired as those of government ministers. Certainly, no opposition voice gets quite so much air time. As a result, the beliefs of those in power are key factors in influencing society's attitudes. Ministers' theories are explained in detail, and repeated many times; and as any marketing manager will agree, repetition is one of the secrets of getting one's message over. Also, the Cabinet's theories on economic policy are the reality of life. The mere fact that they are being applied gives them some sort of spurious credibility. This combination of repetition and reality means that the government's policies, no matter how disastrous they might seem, are regarded by the electorate as valid.

But it is not just *what* is done, but *how* it is done — or to be more exact, what is said to justify policy. A government which allows a rise in unemployment to control inflation may be seen as harsh. But a regime which allows unemployment to stay high for a number of years, even when inflation is low, clearly does not care about the jobless. It may convince a sufficiently large number of the electorate for it to get re-elected, but it is unlikely to convince everybody. Especially, it will not persuade the unemployed. They, and many others, will be sure that the government is simply ignoring the welfare of the weak.

If ministers attempt to justify what is clearly an uncaring policy, they merely throw doubt on the concepts of morality and justice, of right and wrong. There is no morality in allowing millions to suffer poverty and unemployment, just so the middle classes can have stable prices and predictable savings. But given the central role of government in society, if voters continue to support it, despite its lack of morality, the result will be for many a weakening of faith in society, in consensus and in humanity. It creates alienation, and hostility to those who have the consumer goods, the savings, and the comfortable lives. There is a division between those who have, and those who are merely ignored.

And this is what has been happening; government, the main source of political socialisation, has since 1979 been saying explicitly that the key issue is inflation; unemployment doesn't matter. The implicit messages have included — the individual must fend for themselves, they must find their own jobs, and no one else will look out for them, as the government won't use its power on their behalf. The justification for ignoring the jobless is that inflation has to be dealt with first. And ministers have no doubt been able to persuade people that the economy has to be cured before unemployment can be removed.

In doing so, the state has, to a certain extent, changed what people see as acceptable. The Tories have shifted unemployment down the political agenda, while making price stability seem crucial. A large number of voters now accept the argument that unemployment is a necessary price to pay to control prices. Similarly, in America, the US federal government uses capital punishment (including under-16s and the mentally handicapped) as an alternative to an effective social policy. Thus, if you can't control crime, you can at least kill lots of criminals. The agenda is presented as being feasible, outside the realm of morality. The aim of policy shifts from the ideal to the achievable.

Because of other legislation it would be a simplification to say that the Tories have created a two-class society, of those who have and those who have been dispossessed. But this is one aspect of Thatcherism. The result is a nation characterised by selfishness, insecurity, and tension. A nation where crime is on the rise, because those who have little see no reason why they should not take from those who have more.

But the government is not the only influence; business also plays a role in our culture. The products we buy, the shops we buy in, the mass cafeterias we eat in and the advertising that persuades us, all help to form our view of what is attractive, socially acceptable, right or wrong behaviour. We buy electronic games to play, computers to play them on, and music machines of enormous expense. We buy cars which go faster than we are legally allowed to drive, and we spend more on them than the average Czech earns in a year.

The advertisements play on our hidden fears and weaknesses, assuring us that without the hallowed product, we will smell, be anti-social, unwelcome, uncool, and unattractive. The more sophisticated amongst us regard some of the more obvious claims of adverts with amusement; we are not taken in by them. Yet sometimes we find ourselves buying the touted goods. Is it just to try them? Even if we are not taken in by the individual claims, there is the even more worrying possibility that we are affected by the overall atmosphere of advertising. We are nagged by the subliminal message of materialism.

We shop in glossy temples of consumerism, where the act of purchasing is seen as a personal triumph. Some of these palaces are totally isolated from the community, nothing but shops and a car park, so that only the road-using classes can shop there. But nobody will feel that this is their shopping centre, because of the glassy anonymity, whose function it is to make everyone feel relaxed and ready to spend. All sense of personality or human scale is eliminated, so that mass purchasers can flock in without feeling out of place.

The leisurely mix of eating and conversation that can still be found in other parts of Europe, especially in the Mediterranean countries, is gradually being replaced in the fast-food emporium. Skilfully combining the clinical construction of a hospital with the colours of a child's toy, the fast-food cafeteria reduces the pleasure of eating to an assembly line. Consumers enter, make a purchase, and leave as soon as the staff can decently force them out. All that they have lost is the sociable atmosphere, conviviality, and one of the real pleasures of life.

The production-line café creates the expectation of a major social event, but very efficiently separates the consumer from their money. As well as losing the ambience of a real restaurant, the customer often loses out on nutrition as well. Much of the food is highly processed, in order that it be properly standardised, and some of it has a high fat content, which could lead to health problems. In addition, there is concern about the environmental impact of the many beef herds needed to supply the global burger chains.

It is worth noting that those countries which still have a traditional diet that is high in vegetables, have a lower rate of heart disease and cancers than the meat-eating nations. What is disturbing, however, is that the eating habits and lifestyles of the more commercialised nations are creeping into the lives of Greeks, Spaniards and others who had previously retained a healthier way of life.

Whereas in the 1950s, most people would have gained their ideas of right or wrong from their parents, nowadays we get some of our values from the media. Advertisements show us the good guy, selling the company cars in order to maintain the workers' pay levels. Beautiful people in perfect clothes tell us that we can share their lifestyle, if only we buy the correct perfume, aftershave or deodorant. And if we buy the proper drinks, we can have an exciting social life. The mass production food factories are somehow presented as places of fun, somewhere to go for a night out.

Both the content and the forces of socialisation have changed over recent years. In the 1950s, the family was the primary source of socialisation, along with friends and school. Now, the media play a much larger part in our lives, so their output acts as the next generation's input. News and editorial influence our opinions on the world, while leisure programmes and adverts tell us what is fashionable, what forms of behaviour are socially acceptable.

Of course, people know that adverts are designed to sell things; we all know that their whole function is to persuade us to do something we would not otherwise do. But when the message is repeated many times, in slightly different ways, we take in much of it, despite our cynicism. We may not lust after each product advertised, but we will tend to accept the general principle — consumption equals happiness. The gleaming shopping centres, the friendly staff, the pleasure of spending all enter our attitudes. And the result is a culture of materialism. It is a pity then, that the actual purchase is so unsatisfyingly unlike the world of the adverts, and the product itself fails to yield its promise.

However, to take advantage of our increasing materialism, big business is now moving towards the integrated entertainment package — see the film, read the book, play the computer game, play the music of the film, and buy the merchandised toys, T-shirts, shampoo, mugs, etc. Companies like Columbia and Warner Brothers are now owned by Japanese manufacturing corporations, who seek to offer a complete package to the consumer. Not only will the corporation own the software you buy — the video, CD, or computer game — but they will make the hardware that you use to play the software.

For example, a viewer might watch a film from Universal Studios on a Matsushita video, or listen to a CBS tape on a Sony machine. The advantage to the company is that they will be able to sell the consumer everything that is needed, in every step of the process. And they would still have the licensing rights for anything they don't make. These can be worth big bucks by themselves. In the US, in 1981 manufacturers paid $1 billion for character licences, on products which provided over $20 billion in retail sales. (Philip Kotler, *Marketing Management*, p466.)

This means that increasingly, films are seen as part of a marketing unit. The company will seek to create a film that has a saleable music score, with visible references to selected products, and with good opportunities for spin-offs, sequels, or licensing fees. The film becomes a vehicle to promote the album, while the book promotes the film, and so on. Every product in the sequence loses its integrity and its identity, and becomes part-promotion vehicle in a corporate marketing strategy.

This trend has already become visible, as Hollywood has sought international sales. Films have used their New York or Los Angeles locations more self-consciously, music has become a more integral part of the atmosphere, with of course the soundtrack album available at your local record store. Also, some films have used brand name logos discreetly — the name of the airline can be glimpsed on the plane as it takes off; as the main characters drink their highball, a major brand name can be seen on the canopy above them. And naturally, advertisers will gladly pay to get this sort of exposure. There is a danger that some films will become nothing more than a scripted travelogue/advertisement. Some scenes in the James Bond film, *Goldeneye*, may be little more than an advertisement for BMW.

The film as a story about people, or as an entertainment, may cease to exist. The script will no longer be constructed to show the characters' emotions, or their development, but as a plan for maximising the use of product logos and music. A similar trend may already be taking place in the music industry; 'the video has become so central to commercial success that artists may be signed on the basis of looks and acting ability alone'. (Kath Davies, Julienne Dickey and Teresa Stratford (eds.), *Out of Focus*, p111.)

The post-war generation grew up, acquiring many of its ideas of adulthood from Hollywood. Men were strong, silent, and could fight anyone in the saloon. Women were decorative, sympathetic, and sometimes excellent dancers. Of course, films and music in the 1950s were a commercial product. But there are at least two dangers in the current trends. One is that as entertainment gets taken over by big business, independent companies will find it more and more difficult to enter the market. The other is that our screen role models become more explicitly commercial. This is not just in the sense of Madonna, creating an image to sell to the audience, but also in the sense of the role model being used to sell other products. If the star of the silver screen creates gender identity for a million adolescents, what do we say of a society in which the use of certain products is seen as a part of gender identity?

There is also the fact that for young people, leisure is becoming an increasingly technological activity. Sharing one's time with friends and family is being replaced by electronic games with little social input. These games may be tied into a hit film, thus making them absolute 'musts' for young consumers. But they are also addictive, which is always a good product characteristic for the maker. This also takes the games player away from social activities, and away from family influence.

Game players learn some highly specialised skills, but they may also fail to learn normal social skills. They may even develop an ethos that sees all conflict as being resolved by violence. But they are certainly more likely to see conflict being settled by physical activity — overcoming tasks rather than by rational discussion. In effect, the computer game becomes part of the person's socialisation. And some people may not regard these devices as the best basis of a child's upbringing.

The big corporations have an array of brand names, which are instantly recognised by most consumers, and this adds yet another weapon to the corporate armoury. The rapid recognition of the brand name gives the products a significant edge in the high-pressure sales field of the average supermarket. With the act of shopping turned into a well-organised foraging campaign, the consumer makes purchasing decisions in seconds, or even a fraction of a second. The brand name product can be seen, selected and bought in less time than it takes to merely think about an obscure brand.

Because of the sales value of brand names, corporations are actually valuing the names as part of their assets. And naturally, they protect those names avidly. Those who infringe a copyright name will soon find the lawyers on their doorstep. But it is not merely protection; names also have to be maintained. The company has to advertise regularly to keep the name in the public's eye, and to maintain the proper image for the product. This may cost the company tens of millions of pounds a year, but it reaps rich rewards. And it is yet another way of excluding newcomers to the market; that is, excluding competition.

It is also a rich source of merchandising. Well-known brand names can add to the sale price of totally unrelated products. For example, a cartoon character or a soft drink logo on a T-shirt, a baseball cap, a mug, a radio or various other products all add to the status, the street cred of the item. And of course, many clothes already have their own logos to give the consumer a recognisable identity. We are not merely being told what to value; we are being told that certain types of object are the most highly valued. That is, products bearing a widely recognised brand name, even if the name is unrelated, have cachet. They are the things to value.

But one section of business plays a key role in influencing attitudes, and that is the media. And it is important to remember that most of the media is run as a business, and is not simply a public information service. Often, people talk about reading something in a newspaper as if that is evidence of absolute truth. In reality, of course, news is a commercial product like any other, but one that often has powerful political implications. Given that, it is inevitable that ministers will seek to influence how the media present events.

We cannot judge all aspects of the media on the same basis, as newspapers, film and television are all run by different types of people, within differing organisations, which may be controlled by the state or by commercial enterprises. Also, the audiences vary, and approach the media with varying expectations. To attempt a blanket description of all forms of media with one analytical label would be misleading. Therefore, each arm of the media will have to be analysed separately. Having already looked at the film industry, I will now consider newspapers and television.

Although I shall argue that the media have an impact on people's opinions, it is not being claimed that these companies operate as an omnipotent propaganda machine. It is not a hypodermic syringe model of behaviour, in which biased information is injected into an unwitting public. This is as simplistic as the so-called researchers who allege that children who watch violence on television become violent, or that people who watch pornography carry out sexual attacks. Some of these theories have Marxist undertones, and the media are seen as capitalist, and therefore bad, while people in general are seen as pliable pawns in the hands of commerce. There is insufficient space to analyse this in detail here, but such views are far too simplistic.

Traditionally, the most politically important part of the media has been the newspapers. Ruled since the nineteenth century by the press barons of the Harmsworth and Rothermere families, the world that once was Fleet Street held the king-makers of British politics. When Labour won the 1964 election, Harold Wilson offered Cecil Harmsworth King, editor of the *Daily Mirror*, a peerage and a ministerial post. (Simon Jenkins, *Newspapers*, p38.)

But gradually, the old order crumbled, and new press barons moved in. As a result, the face of British politics also changed. The old families were paternalistic and Victorian, but also showed some semblance of caring for the nation. They had established their fortunes, and did not need to make any more. They paid their workers well, not because of powerful unions, but because they wanted their workers to be well-paid. Later on, this became a barrier, a device to keep out newcomers, as no start-up company could afford the pay levels that Fleet Street printers took for granted.

Roy Thomson bought the *Sunday Times*, the *Herald* suffered circulation problems, and was re-named *The Sun*, and was later bought by the Australian newspaper magnate, Rupert Murdoch. Over the years Murdoch gradually shifted the *Sun* to the right, and after Harold Evans gave up the editor's post at the *Sunday Times*, that to moved rightwards. By 1987 only the *Guardian*, the *Mirror* and the *Observer* were sympathetic to Labour. Perhaps the shift in ideology was related to the increase in absentee press-ownership. The *Telegraph* was acquired by Canadian, Conrad Black. The *Sun/Sunday Times* stable is owned by one-time Australian, Rupert Murdoch, who had since become a US citizen to further his media empire. The *Observer* was briefly owned by the Atlantic-Richfield oil company, the *Mail* tried to move offshore to Holland, while Robert Maxwell became increasingly international as his fortune grew. It seems that proprietors with global media holdings do not feel in any way tied to one country; each place is simply a market to be exploited.

One key issue for proprietors is to ensure a political environment that allows them to continue expanding their holdings, as and when they see fit. This might mean acquiring other newspapers, or it could mean radio or television stations. This means that almost as an inherent part of newspaper ownership, press barons need to support the pro-business party in each country. In Britain of course, that means the Conservatives.

The bias is not obvious, because of the newspaper's ability to select what it wishes to portray as news. Not only can the editor ignore stories and facts that conflict with the paper's political stance, it can also set the agenda on what 'news' means. Thus, talks on whale hunting are not news. But a scandal in the life of a TV soap star is news. It is gossip, the personal, the trivial, celebrities, royalty, and the dramatic. A single plane crash killing 500 people is news; the steady slaughter on the roads of 10,000 people a year is not.

It is an entertaining diet, but not an analytical one. Not that this matters, given the declining standards of education, and lack of parental interest in school performance. For many people, education is seen as unattainable or pointless. Life has become subject to powerful but uncontrollable forces, and our lives are wracked by economic storms of incomprehensible origin. For those who think beyond the struggle to survive, the lives of the successful and the cult of the personality, or some form of substance-induced escapism, are more attractive than the tedious arguments of politicians.

In such a culture, it is easy to reduce politics to the level of personalities; one set of politicians are good and trustworthy, the other lot are sneaky and inexperienced. There is no need to lie about the candidates, although the tabloids are not averse to doing that. All that is necessary is to emphasise the emotional content of the issues, and get the reader's emotions responding to the journalist's critique.

This does not necessarily involve lying. It is just a matter of emphasising the aspects that the reader/viewer will find interesting — the dramatic, the unusual, the personal. One may see this as popularisation or trivialisation, but it affects our way of life profoundly. For example, our perception of social workers is largely the creation of the media. And our attitudes to social workers partly determine their working restrictions.

When a special school head teacher was sentenced to 12 years in jail at Shrewsbury Crown Court, the judge, Mr Justice Fennell, praised the joint team of police and social workers. The profession's magazine asked, 'Will there now be banner headlines? ... [But] we all know that "social workers get it right" is not a very sexy message as far as the larger world is concerned'. (*Social Work Today*, April 18, 1991, p2.)

Whenever social workers are mentioned in the media, it is usually to do with a failure of their procedures, or their failure to do what the public believes they 'should' have done. Much of the work is very high profile, being the sort of thing that will easily attract headlines if problems arise. For example, child abuse is an instant target for attention. As a result of this concern, social workers have to accumulate much more proof before they make allegations of child abuse, because if they fail to prove their charges in court, they will be seen as having smeared an innocent family. It is a good thing that this burden of proof exists, however, there is a danger that many valid cases are not going to court, as it is not possible to get sufficient evidence to satisfy the court.

The obvious implication of the quotation above is that the image projected by the media is a powerful and influential one. Yet it is also apparent that the media have to respond to what the customers are willing to buy. That is, content is determined by the audience, as well as by the media proprietors. A readership survey in 1960 'showed that most readers who were questioned deplored what was described as "the sex, violence, scandal and gossip" in popular papers and wanted more "real news". Yet the papers which might be accused of specializing in the things they complained about were the ones most sought by readers'. (F. W. Hodgson, *Modern Newspaper Practice*, p61.)

Academics Patrick Barwise and Andrew Ehrenberg argue that the simple model of information as something which is 'injected' into a passive audience is a misrepresentation of how real people behave. The agendas are set, and persuasive methods of expression are used, but the comments made have to fit into the audience's existing framework of opinion. That is, the customer has to 'buy' the product, in one sense or another.

Clearly, newspapers also persuade by their presentation. News is what is happening now, which means that newspapers are not usually given to detailed explanations of the background of an event. The degree to which they do so will vary according to the nature of the event, and the paper. Thus, if a Labour government got the country into severe economic difficulties, the analysis, especially in the tabloid press, would be limited, and hostile. If the Tories did the same, the analysis would show that the problem was inevitable. A recession — under the Tories? Well, there's a world recession. High unemployment? Yes, but we have to control inflation first. Thus, the reader or viewer is persuaded of the rationale behind the government's actions.

And to add to the tone of objectivity, experts of various sorts would be wheeled out to add their fund of wisdom. To many people, the views of a stock market analyst or the Governor of the Bank of England would sound like knowledge personified. But in fact, these are people from the same social class and with the same economic agenda as any Conservative minister. Their authority is dubious, and their objectivity is a sham.

However, it exemplifies the power of the government, not merely to set the agenda, but also to define the nature of truth. The post-1979 Tory governments have made full use of their ability to control what has been published. This has extended all the way from news blackouts during the Falklands campaign, to the total destruction of Thames Television. There has been a campaign of harassment waged against the BBC, and the industries' unions have been virtually demolished.

Having gained a significant degree of control over the media, Tory ministers have gone on to ensure that their view of the truth is the one which is most often repeated. Their ability to set the agenda, control the interview, or phrase the analysis in various ways allows ministers to give the impression of complete openness of discussion. They can talk about the ideology, the needs of the economy, or the success of the policies that have actually been carried out. The fact that the various approaches all fit together must seem impressive to the average viewer or reader. And the fact that the politician can express complex or controversial ideas, while the interviewer is apparently unable to find any fault in the logic, adds enormously to the politician's credibility.

Given the much-vaunted professionalism of journalists, especially those on the Fleet Street 'heavies', or in the BBC, one might assume that biased experts would only be used when their knowledge was relevant. That is, given a liberal democratic view of mass communications, one assumes that those working within the industry are seeking to do their best for society. They wish to do their job to the best of their ability, and seek informed, objective opinion from among all the voices that are available.

However, as has been pointed out, journalists are middle class, and would tend to have the same values and attitudes as others of that class. Within the BBC there is a disproportionate number of Oxbridge classics graduates, whose knowledge of Latin and Greek literature may be impeccable; but their understanding of the rest of society is extremely limited. Such people, when looking for 'objective' experts, will tend to sympathise with pundits from a similar social background, and ignore opinions from working class speakers. (See Abercrombie, Warde, et al., *Contemporary British Society*, p410.)

Newspapers are unlikely to be able to change people's minds about the issues. But they can change how people see the issues. They can make John Major's niceness or Neil Kinnock's baldness seem important. They can present the policies in an easy to digest form that dramatises and exaggerates the situation to a point that would be lying, if it were made explicit, but which in a simplified form merely seems like a summary. For example, on the day of the 1979 election, the *Daily Express* carried a cartoon referring to the Liberal-Labour pact. It showed a voter putting a ballot slip into a ballot box with David Steel's face on it. Inside that was another box with Callaghan's face, and inside that was a box held by Tony Benn, and a hammer and sickle painted on the front of the box. The message was that a vote for the Liberals was an indirect vote for Moscow-controlled lefty policies. (*Britain at the Polls, 1979*, American Enterprise Institute, p166.) At the time, the Soviet Union was still seen as both powerful and dangerous, so this was a very powerful political image.

In the 1992 election one newspaper carried the election day headline, 'Will the last person to leave Britain turn the lights out,' with a photo of Neil Kinnock. For people who presumably respect the newspaper they choose to buy, this would be a very powerful emotional message indeed. Its total absence of any rational content would be no disadvantage whatsoever. But a reader who was fed a sustained diet of such bias would, even given political neutrality, eventually feel some negative thoughts concerning Kinnock.

'There is a tendency to assume that workers do hold a clear, consistent and coherent image of society and a tendency to mould data into neat, tidy categories'. (M. Haralambos, *Sociology: Themes and Perspectives*, p64.) In fact, workers, and no doubt everyone else, hold views that could be labelled left or right, and have varying degrees of coherency in their images of society. Indeed, they 'seemed to have no problem with holding apparently contradictory views'. (Ibid., p64.)

Given this, one would expect voters of all sorts to be quite susceptible to persuasion by the skilled wordsmiths of Fleet Street. First, because they had no clear view of society that could be contradicted by the newspaper's stories, and second, because given the contradictory nature of people's existing beliefs, almost any message could be accommodated within the pre-existing framework.

R. M. Blackburn and Michael Mann 'found that both right and left-wing views co-existed in the workers' ideology and concluded that they do not possess "consistent and coherent images of society"'. (Ibid., p65.) So the terms 'right' and 'left' do not help us to understand or label voters' behaviour, or their understanding of society.

Given the average person's unclear ideas of the nature of society, the media find it relatively easy to persuade people to view politics in the way that the media barons wish. And as we have seen, they are assisted in this endeavour by the fact that they share an ideology with the Conservatives, who are adding to the New Right message.

In recent elections, they have also been helped by the electoral incompetence of the major opposition party. 'Voters' two strongest impressions about the Labour Party were that it was dominated by 'extremist' activists, and that its philosophy leaned towards directing people into a drab, uniform culture determined by trade unions and bureaucrats'. (Colin Hughes and Patrick Wintour, *Labour Rebuilt*, p153.)

Some leading members of Labour were so unimpressed with their party's performance in 1987, that they felt Labour did not deserve to win. (See Hughes and Wintour, p28.) Given Labour's ability to lose an election in the middle of a major recession caused by the incumbent government, one hopes that party leaders feel the same humility as some of them did in 1987. However, all the indications are that many Labour MPs are playing the usual game of ignoring public opinion, and saying the party did not go far enough to the left, it was all Neil Kinnock's fault, and so on.

Regardless of Labour's contribution, clearly voters' attitudes are influenced by the media and by the Conservatives. These are the two most important factors in determining what is politically acceptable in Britain today. Other organisations, such as the CBI, the SMMT, the IoD and so on also play a role, but they are more like a backing group for the two lead singers. They are not seen by the public as major players, but are of sufficient importance to add to, or detract from the leading ideology.

The message that is broadcast, untainted by any hint of disagreement from the Labour Party, is that New Right ideas are the best possible course for the economy. Any problems, such as a recession, have either vanished, under a tossed salad of green shoots, or else are caused by world economic conditions. The government cannot intervene, it must not impose its ideology, and it must put the battle against inflation first.

And as the policy stance is integrated with our political culture, we find new explanations for why things should be like that, how it all fits with human nature. The state cannot do anything for the poor, the unemployed or the homeless, because it is those people's fault that they are poor, homeless, etc. It is not our problem, it is theirs.

Gradually we move towards a culture in which the forces of the economy are seen as vast, global movements. They are incomprehensible, yet invincible. We as individuals struggle within the whirlwind, and if we cannot understand the factors affecting the national economy, we can at least try to protect our own welfare. It is not only a sensible course, it is also implicit in Thatcherism. The concepts of 'society,' 'community,' or 'solidarity' are replaced by different forms of self-interest.

Fortunately, we in Britain have only had the New Right in power since 1979; in the United States, they have had the materialist, full-strength version of capitalism for 30 or 40 years. They have had that much longer for the values of individualism and selfishness to entrench themselves in society. As a result, life in America is much more of a struggle between various individuals with different forms and amounts of power, with few of them displaying any concern for the well-being of the others.

There is time for Britain to reverse the socially and economically harmful effects of the New Right. The tragedy is that the main opposition party is busy destroying itself in futile ideological battle. Its MPs are too blind to see what they are doing, or too career-minded to care. But clearly, something must be done.

10

There is an alternative

ONE OF THE many tedious hangovers left behind by Marxism is the belief that there is some mystic secret to social change. It is not something that can be fathomed by ordinary mortals, but needs the word of some old guy with a beard and a German accent? He will then reveal the truth, the one true way to social change. It may be a violent revolution, leading to a dictatorship of the proletariat, or it may be a catastrophic upheaval. But certainly, a revolution is good; it is dramatic, and therefore an emotionally attractive way of changing society.

For some people, there is a clear desire for disaster. Even before the sado-monetarists were elected into office, many bar-room pundits would talk about nuclear catastrophe, the collapse of capitalism, and the difficulty of getting a good cup of tea. They would relish the scale of the upheaval, the number of deaths, or the destruction of existing institutions. Marxism merely justified their wish for the end of civilisation as we know it.

In fact, there is no reason to assume that a complex set of events, which we label 'changing society', can be dealt with by just one policy instrument. What we are talking about is creating a situation in which the quality of life is better, human values are more caring, our behaviour towards one another will be more compassionate, and our material standards will not only be higher, but will be achieved in ways that are less harmful to the environment. This is merely a fraction of what we seek, described very briefly, yet some hangover from the nineteenth century tells us that if we just press the right button, it will all happen.

There is some dispute as to whether, in seeking change, we should change the system, or change the people. Some argue that we first have to change the economic and political structures of society, and that will create a more enlightened populace. Others say that if we all transform our own consciousness, that will lead to changes in society. They argue that no real change can occur until the personal and the social structures have been totally transformed.

Thus, if we are all better people, the world will be a better place. So they chant, meditate, or take up personal growth, with the intention of changing themselves, and the world. It is a very Buddhist approach, putting ourselves at one with the universe. It is also selfish and isolationist, and often does nothing directly for society's problems. While the enlightened middle classes chant, or hold consciousness raising sessions, the poor are starving or freezing.

In fact, it is because of the social problems that many of us cannot become better people, or else will find it extremely difficult. One might think that those with limited income or education will find it hard to alter their patterns of thinking; and this is undoubtedly true. But educated people also get into fixed patterns of thinking that can be very hard to break. To get out of the unhelpful ways of thinking, we have to be very open-minded, and we need to persuade others to open their minds as well.

We need to recognise what, if anything, we as individuals get from this society. The rich may get the largest share of the rewards, but we have all received benefits from our membership of society. We need to point out to others that perhaps they do not gain in proportion to the riches that are available. We may point out that they do not need to be locked into the existing social system, and that its harm to them and others demands that it be replaced with something more caring.

We have to step outside our own lives and needs, and deal with the needs of others, because we have to change the opinions of others. The job of changing society is too big for those few of us who are already converted to be able to deal with it. If we put it in numerical terms, the converted include those who vote Green, and some Labour voters, plus a few who do not fall into the obvious categories. Perhaps this is 5 per cent of the population. At the time of writing, we haven't even got enough people to vote an intelligent government into office. Sweeping change does not normally come from such numbers, if they are operating in a democracy. If we want real radicalism, we need millions of people to lobby, protest, vote or complain.

But as mentioned in earlier chapters, the parties themselves need to change. Labour's faults are legion, but even the Green Party needs some shaking up. For example, the split in the party, repeated in both Britain and Germany, between the realists and the fundamentalists, shows a lack of consensus. Worse, it suggests a lack of genuine internal discussion. Perhaps the Greens also need to be open-minded as regards policy, and ways of achieving office.

Self-improvement of the few is not enough, given the scale of the task. There is a need to do something that is active and visible. It is not enough to think; it is not even enough to care. If we are concerned about the poor or the homeless, we must take some action that will do something for those groups. We must deliver soup, write to politicians, collect money, stir up publicity, support campaigning groups, and so on. But it must be real, and it must be powerful.

If we can all develop our skills and awareness, that will be great. But considering the power of the forces of regression and irrationality, we have to expand our personal power as well. We are opposed by groups who can spend millions to influence government policy, sometimes just to achieve one policy change. They advertise, have PR speakers and spin doctors, and representatives in business and politics, all of whom put over different aspects of the group line. Sometimes one reads articles in the papers by a representative of the CBI or the Society of Motor Manufacturers and Traders (SMMT). As quasi-journalists, they objectively discuss aspects of New Right ideology that cannot be covered by the politicians' soundbites. The apparent unity of these diverse sources implies a jointly-discovered truth. So when MPs, the CBI, the Adam Smith Institute, the SMMT, the *Daily Mail*, and the

Centre for Policy Studies all say that monetarism or the EU is a good thing, naturally voters assume that here is objective truth.

Their direct influence is impressive. For example, when the big brewers' control of the market was threatened by the Monopolies and Mergers Commission, they retaliated with an expensive, and very effective, advertising campaign. The business community's contacts with government are extensive, and most politicians, especially Tory ones, have close social and business links with the City and the big financial institutions, and may even have worked in such places.

On a global scale, these large corporations have helped with the downfall of the Allende government in Chile, pressured the Bangladesh government into continuing to buy expensive Western medicines, and persuaded the Indian government to accept a very modest sum in compensation for the Bhopal tragedy. In a more commercial arena, Japanese lobbyists have even persuaded Washington to treat imported Japanese trucks as cars, for the purpose of import tariffs. Lobbying is an expensive process, but its success does not depend on the result leading to improved well-being for the nation. The legislators have their own agenda, one that speaks in the language of money and power, and does not listen to altruistic pleas, unless they are supported by one of these two.

Occasionally, the corporations are backed up by powerful and sympathetic organisations like the IMF and the World Bank. These ensure that the economic policies of Third World countries are not inimical to Western industry, or specifically, to US corporations. For example, in the Philippines, the World Bank created its own policy clique within the Philippine government. For such people, welfare is not an issue, although the interests of the United States do seem to take precedence over that of any other nation.

Noam Chomsky argues that these global institutions have become a de facto world government, with the power to control nations. One needs massive countervailing power to deal with bodies of this scope and influence. Because of the harm they do, through such policies as the Structural Adjustment Fund, and the growth in their power, it is essential that they be controlled. But for the very same reasons, it will be enormously difficult to control them. Therefore, it is essential that policy for change, whether long-term or short-term, local or global, recognises the influence of these institutions.

The same imbalance of power can be seen in Britain. But at the local level, it is more obvious that the problem is not best defined in terms of business influencing politics, but rather that business people and politicians come from the same social backgrounds. They share the same values, and the same beliefs as to how society should be run.

Thus, although one may talk about commercial interests lobbying government, it is more comparable to two arms of the one social class communicating together. But outsiders lobbying the citadels of power are at a double disadvantage; they are socially distinct, and they lack pre-existing influence. Galbraith argues that groups must have some degree of organisation before they can achieve recognition or assistance from the state. (*American Capitalism*, p152.) That is, one must already have a significant amount of strength, before the state will consider bestowing additional benefits.

There is a danger that people will assume that society has progressed steadily since the nineteenth century or earlier, and will continue to do so. But this is not the case. Whichever point we take as our base line, we find that progress, however we define it, has been erratic, and occasionally marked by reverses. The whole Thatcher era has been one long decline, socially and economically. Further back we see the unemployment between the wars, the Great Depression of 1873-1896, and the appalling conditions of life in the very early part of the nineteenth century.

Improvements only take place when the conditions are all working in the same direction. For example, the Enlightenment of the eighteenth century took place because of 'an interlacing pattern in which the "facts" of history, the creations of the arts, the discoveries of science and the speculations of philosophy reacted upon each other and in turn affected men's attitudes to history, the arts, science, philosophy and religion'. (Norman Hampson, *The Enlightenment*.)

At the present time, the conditions are all working with the forces of reaction. Big business is becoming more and more powerful, both nationally and globally. It is acquiring increasing influence both with national governments and with global institutions, such as the IMF. At the same time, political structures are moving out of the control of the average voter. An organisation like the EU is simply too large for any democratic control to exist. Yet it is sufficiently centralised for big business lobbying to be enormously influential. Meanwhile, in Italy the Mafia has become a multinational crime syndicate, a major force in Italian politics, and with growing power in European and American politics.

The corporate lobbying brigades can defeat any skirmishing forces sent out by a disunited and disorganised populace. For example, Europe's Environment Commissioner, Carlo Ripa Di Meana, banned the Department of Transport's motorway construction through Twyford Down, arguing that under EU law, the department was obliged to publish a non-specialist environmental impact assessment. The planned route went through an area of natural beauty, an archaeological site, and a site of special scientific interest. John Major applied pressure to Jaques Delors, and the latter duly removed Di Meana from office. There is no doubt that one of the key arguments was the importance of the construction contract to the survival of Britain's road-building companies. The public interest, a popular phrase in Whitehall circles, was seen as totally irrelevant.

In addition to their wealth and influence, big business has the finance to create and support allegedly independent research units, such as the Adam Smith Institute. It is also respected as a sector, being the source of both employment, and goods, whether the essentials of life or the luxuries. But neither the companies nor the politicians they support show any noticeable desire to prove their value to society. Their infinite beneficence is taken for granted, and any argument to the contrary are whitewashed over with banalities, evasions or outright lies.

As big business expands, becoming more global, our culture, our work and our political systems are taken over by commercialism. The European Union will be Fortress Europe for big business. Satellite television will bombard adults and children with cheap entertainment and trans-atlantic culture. Much of this 'entertainment' will be packaged advert vehicles for popular heroes of cartoon characters. Labour MP Roy Hattersley has pointed out that much popular fiction of the 'sex-and-shopping' variety uses well-known brand names to pigeon-hole characters. Hattersley objects to the lazy writing this encourages; just as bad is the crude materialism that is invading what once might have been literature.

And as the profit motive takes over, non-commercial, non-profit-making groups will cease to exist. The commercial and money-making will survive, and that which is not grossly profitable will vanish. Neighbourhood theatres and local restaurants will vanish, and choices of all sorts will be reduced.

In the shops, the range of goods is already becoming narrower. In the UK, it is difficult enough to buy British, with the increasing imports of Japanese electronics, Dutch biscuits and German dairy products. But it is virtually impossible to avoid the products of big business. At such a point, competition and choice have almost ceased to exist. When they have vanished altogether, and just a handful of manufacturers dominate each industry, then prices in the shops can really be raised. This has been happening in Japan for many years, because the Japanese domestic market is entirely controlled by a few manufacturers and trading companies. As the Japanese market becomes more open to international competition, European markets become monopolised.

There has also been a gradual spread of processed foods. In the United States it is almost impossible to find fruit, vegetables or sweets that have no chemicals in them. In Britain, it is rare to find beer that is simply that, rather than a heady mix of stabilisers, frothers, and clarifiers. Whether it is fiction or food, the cheaper product will drive out the quality one, as Gresham's Law hits the shops. The company that sells a low quality, pasteurised, sterilised, chemical-packed product will achieve a longer shelf-life than the goods of a high quality or organic manufacturer. Whether it is radios, cheese or chocolate, the inferior product is often the more profitable.

The furious drive of the profit motive, as depicted by both Thatcherism and the Maastricht Treaty, ignores all issues but lower prices, and economies of scale. This will have an impact on our lives in all sorts of ways, from cheap food to packaged entertainment. There may also be the disappearance of all non-commercial activities. Even now, campaigning groups like Friends of the Earth and Greenpeace are cutting both staff and activities as a result of the recession. We need to examine the choices available to us, and the motives and justifications behind them, while those choices still exist.

Economic and social trends are combining to make right-wing governments more attractive to voters, aided in Britain at least, by the total failure of the left. The rise in unemployment and insecurity, as mentioned earlier, leads to a general move rightwards. So right-wing policies become a part of the national tradition, so that even allegedly left-wing parties feel that they have to adopt supply side economics.

Many European countries are moving further and further to the right, with racism and fascism on the rise. The last time this happened, in Germany, it took many years to defeat the fascists. This time, the reactionaries might be in control of a Europe-wide government that cannot be dealt with militarily, not that there is any outside force that would choose to do so. Europe would simply be condemned to re-enter the Dark Ages.

One would not say that voting a sensible set of politicians into office is a prerequisite of any improvement, although it will certainly help. But there is a danger that the election of a vaguely liberal party would allow radicals to assume that the war was over, that one could go back to ignoring politics again. Mills points out that the New Deal made politics seem banal and routine (*The Power Elite*, p334), and there is a danger in Britain too, that a liberal government would be seen by some as an opportunity for extremist policies, and by others as an excuse to sink back into inaction. Even worse, the victorious party would feel that anything it did would be wonderful, therefore a few selected displays of legislative generosity would be sufficient to justify a five year term. Certainly, there are no signs at present of any opposition party suffering from policy dynamism.

The Conservative governments have been able to ignore all protests, even when they have been in the wrong, when their arguments were weak, or when a majority of the population disagreed with them. They stayed in office because sufficiently large numbers of people continued to vote them in. This is just one of the things that have to be changed, perhaps in a sense, the smallest change. Because the real step forward is ensuring that future governments base their policy on the needs of the people, not on some irrational dogma.

Yet change can take place, regardless of the elected government, or the power of big business, given sufficiently large numbers of committed people. Instead of one massive change, it will be a lot of tiny alterations, moving society imperceptibly forward. But this does require that thousands, preferably millions of people organise in some way to ensure the changes they seek do take place. Politics in Italy and Japan have been corrupt for many years, but in Japan, popular anger at the Liberal Democratic Party threw them out after thirty years in office. In Italy, that same rejection of corruption may lead to a complete transformation of Italian politics.

Given Galbraith's thesis of a contented middle class, one might ask who would be in the constituencies that would vote for a reformist regime. The answer is that the middle class themselves would be the most likely supporters. They have been conned into thinking that New Right policies are in their interests, but in most countries where such programmes have been applied, no one has been made better off except the rich.

The lower income groups are even poorer, and most people are more insecure in their jobs. But even for those few sectors or individuals who are richer in terms of their net income, the social deterioration is such that overall quality of life is decidedly worse. By the time one deducts the cost of car alarms, burglar alarms, and a myriad other items of protective technology, even the quite affluent cannot be genuinely better off. If one then allows for the anxiety and fear that many people feel in their normal daily routine, then real quality of life has fallen considerably.

The new electoral constituencies would include all those who were worse off in cash terms, or in lower security, or in reduced pleasure with life. All that is necessary is for the politicians to point out the links between New Right policies, and the resultant social and economic deterioration, and most voters would recognise the source of all their past problems.

Assuming that a more constructive government does come to power, it must remain in power for at least two consecutive terms, simply to reverse the damage that has been done by the Tories. It is not merely the damage to the economy, although that has been bad enough. There has also been the massive impact on attitudes, behaviour and expectations. Rates, progressive taxation, the welfare state and a sense of community have all been brought into question by the Tories. And all these changes have to be reversed.

People sometimes talk about Japanese industry as if there was one key aspect, one key secret to Japanese success. In fact, there are a lot of factors, but one of them is the management's willingness to listen to the suggestions of the workers. Every day, in every factory, some workers put ideas into a suggestion box. Over a year, the factory receives tens of thousands of ideas, some of which may make only a very tiny difference to the company's manufacturing methods, and most of which will just make a modest difference. But together, all those small improvements add up to regular, massive annual increases in productivity.

There is a rather nice story of the Prince Buddha walking in a forest one day. He saw a squirrel, dipping its tail into a lake, bringing its tail over the ground, shaking the tail, and dipping it back into the lake. The Buddha asked the squirrel what he was doing, and the squirrel replied, 'Emptying the lake'. The prince pointed out the size of the lake, and the smallness of the squirrel's tail, but the creature replied, 'If I take just a few drops every time, and I carry on emptying the lake, eventually it will be empty'.

The appeal of the story is the squirrel's dedication to a job that was surely much too great for it. It is part of human nature to look for the quick fix and the easy way out. We baulk at tasks that have to be done in tiny steps, or seem too large to ever be possible. That may be the emotional appeal of a sudden and violent revolution. It is the social reformer's equivalent of the hero's escape in the nineteenth century novel; 'With one bound he was free'. How did Jack (the hero) escape? Well, who cares? He had made his fortune, and returned with enough money to pay off the family's debts. It was a deeply satisfying ending, good triumphed over evil, and the family was re-united.

The final revolution that is so fondly regarded by some Marxists has all the same emotional chords. Good triumphs over evil, no effort is involved because of historic inevitability, and everyone lives happily ever after. And the whole plot was concocted by a nineteenth century scribe with a greater sense of drama than of the practicalities of life.

In the real world, change can work through reform just as well as through any other approach, and probably more effectively than most. It is a method of change that neutral observers can respect — so it won't put them off. And repelling new recruits is one sure way to keep a movement small and ineffective. In addition, the slowness of reform allows one more time to vet the opinions of would-be leaders. It also allows the time necessary to get the fine details of change exactly right. One can examine the state's budget each year, consider which are the most pressing concerns, and study which have been the most successful approaches.

However, it is worth returning to the two basic approaches to change. Does one start with oneself, or does one change society at large? We should not assume that one answer or the other is totally true. All methods of social change have to be used simultaneously. Society has to be dealt with as a social, political, economic and cultural construct. Thus, the battle must be fought on many fronts. But as mentioned above, if we intend to do something for any given group, it must be real and direct.

Of course, we have other things to do in our lives. In an increasingly recessionary Britain, we also have to ensure our own economic survival, and may seek ways to improve the quality of life. Thus, social change may occasionally take second place to earning a living, or we may do things that have no overt impact on society. For example, if we seek to recycle all our newspapers, glass, etc., some might argue that we are not changing the power balance in society, but merely allowing mass production to continue for another few years.

But 'changing society' is a subtle process, imperceptible at every stage of the way. The macro-changes may be visible, such as when several million people decide to vote in a certain way. But if one person makes such a decision, it is just as much a social change, if with no public visibility.

For some, the belief that nothing can be done, or that it has to be done in a certain way, is just as much a barrier to change as the inertia of the establishment. To combat this culture of pessimism, the established ideologies and the many other opposing forces, those who seek change must present a coherent and united front of active campaigning. What particular form that campaign takes for each individual depends on their skills and preferences, but it needs to include an element of changing the opinions of others. Only if the minority voice is raised at least to that of a significant minority can there be any hope of any real change.

This means that someone has to persuade people that the old ways of thinking are no longer valid, and no longer valued. It helps if you are a naturally persuasive person, but perhaps more important, you need to have the facts. This book, and many others like it, some of which are listed in the bibliography, are good sources of evidence that the small business, decentralised society offers a better quality of life than any alternative. Other books, like *Straight and Crooked Thinking*, by Robert Thouless, help to pick out all the dishonest ploys that people use in arguments.

Perhaps the next dinner party you go to will lead to a change in attitude for someone.

But a key feature to changing society is that there is no revolution, no instant utopia, no sudden entry of the planet into a perfect world. It is a steady, step by step spread of knowledge. This is why structural or institutional change which fails to take account of human nature is always doomed to fail. The New Right ignores the abuse of power both by companies and by government. It also ignores the impact of economic conditions on the weaker members of society. It fails to see that the market is not value-free, or socially neutral, but is instead a system of power. As a power structure, it affects some people adversely, and it is understandable if those people react in hostile ways. The free market's supporters are utterly incapable of seeing this human dimension.

Yet the human dimension is the fulcrum of change, as well as being the guideline by which to judge the effectiveness of change. To talk about changing the economy or society implies that one will be creating new structures, or modifying old ones. And to be able to do this requires that people accept the validity of the new structures.

We are all attached to the values and attitudes of our society. Insofar as we share those values, we are part of its culture. We do not change our personal opinions easily, but opinions that we share with our culture are built into us, part of our identity. Different parts of society have their own culture, hence the differences in attitudes between the various social classes. But the strength of those beliefs is indicated by the difficulty of changing them. For example, it has been found that some company mergers fail, not for business reasons, but because the cultures of the two companies clash. If an authoritarian company took over an individualistic one, the clash of ideas and attitudes could make management and communication very difficult.

Yet corporate values are probably less deeply held than those we share with our society. And it is the latter that we seek to change when we talk about 'changing society'. In Britain today, those who have been brought up under Thatcherism are often convinced that there are limits to the role of government, indeed, to what government is capable of doing. They have been subject to a coherent, consistent ideology, whose exponents have been able to explain or justify all apparent failures. As a result, Thatcher's children see New Right policies as the correct ones. The government should not spend to create jobs; those who are unemployed lack jobs through their own fault. The poor are themselves responsible for their poverty.

This may be seen as the result of brainwashing or propaganda, but it has to be dealt with on an individual basis: these are people with mistaken opinions. So it is essential that we have the facts and the arguments. Even people who have not been beneficiaries of Thatcherism have taken on the arguments, and will wield them with sincere conviction against anyone who seeks to persuade them of another point of view.

Of course, it is a massive task. To talk about 'changing society' means to change the culture in which we live. This means that the beliefs of millions of people have to be altered, whether this is by politicians, parents or teachers, or by books, newspaper articles, speeches, or demonstrations. The means may be various, but the task is enormous.

Those who hold to one of the current ideologies will regard their own views as perfectly logical; the truth, in their own eyes. Even some Marxists, who have seen the total collapse of nearly every society which followed that path to revolutionary enlightenment, still regard Marxism as living truth. It may be the light that failed, but for them, it is the light nonetheless.

The New Right will be even more firmly entrenched in their views, as they believe they have had some success to back up their claims. They have seen their party carry out privatisation or deregulation, rolling back the frontiers of the state. And they are able to claim 'the highest rates of growth in Europe', or 'the fastest growth of manufactured exports in Europe', or maybe just a high level of 'seasonally adjusted confidence'. But the truth of their claims is often open to question.

The changes we seek can be long-term or short-term — of course, in practice we need both. We can seek action on the local or the national level, in the political or the personal. We can help the process by starting a business, or a protest group. So long as we do something.

Some people argue that all we need is proportional representation (PR) and a new constitution. Certainly, with PR the Tory governments that have been elected since 1979 would have been reduced to being merely the largest elected party — assuming that voting patterns would have been the same under PR. Instead of having 51 per cent of the seats, which they needed to dominate the Houses of Parliament, they would have had as few as 42 per cent. But we should not regard PR as the whole answer, having seen the experiences of some countries. Also, through much of the Thatcherite era, a Liberal/Conservative alliance seemed a very real possibility. This would have given the New Right a majority, whatever the voting system.

In addition, many people have suggested PR as a constitutional remedy, as if the unfair electoral system was all that stopped Labour winning the election. As we saw in the previous chapter, even some Labour leaders felt that the party did not deserve to win the 1987 election, and many Labour supporters felt they did not really deserve to win any of the other elections. It is unhealthy to promote PR, or any ploy intended to give Labour a victory at the ballot box, when as a group of individuals, they are decidedly unattractive. There is a danger that the call for PR will be used as a cover for Labour's faults, allowing those MPs who are the biggest liability to pass the buck yet again. The cover story will be that there is nothing wrong with Labour as a party; all that is needed is fair elections.

In addition, PR gives disproportionate power to small parties. For example, in a vote on Maastricht in 1993, eight Ulster Unionists played a key role in giving the Tories a majority. This could well have been used to demand concessions on Northern Ireland policy that would not normally be considered. It has also been said that PR contributed to the political instability of Germany in the 1930s, by so accurately reflecting the divisions within German society. In the absence of consensus, PR adds to the conflict.

Also, a written constitution is not by itself an answer, as it would be a reflection of the values and biases of the establishment, and it would need to be enforced to be effective. John Patten has claimed that the 'Citizen's Charters' have started a process that will lead to the creation of a new constitution by the year 2000. Yet all the so-called charters offer is paper promises with no financial support. In reality, there would have to be independent protection of the constitution, and enforcement by a non-partisan permanent authority. This body would have the right to veto or nullify any existing or proposed legislation, and judge governmental actions in terms of their constitutional legality. The continued existence of the authority could be protected partly by guaranteed funding from the Home Office, and partly by a legal right to accept funding from any source, including local government (having guaranteed local government independence, as mentioned in Chapter 6.)

But although it would be nice to have a safe, permanent body to look after our welfare, in reality there are no guarantees. Social changes could take place that allow a reactionary government to cut funding to a constitutional quango, or to fill it with right-wingers, as Nixon and Reagan did with the US Supreme Court. Some thought that West Germany was protected from any re-creation of fascism by the written constitution. In fact, politicians have done almost the same as they always do in the face of extremism — they look the other way. The German government was reluctant to confront the racists head-on, in case it lost them votes. So rather than act, they dithered.

The only real guarantee of civil liberties is the determination of the people not to accept political manipulation of society's institutions. But this means constant action, monitoring of government responses to extremism, and mass action to combat extremism.

It is an easy answer to political problems to create a quango for every need. In the past, British governments have tended to do this, especially Labour ones. They have created the Commission for Racial Equality (CRE), the Equal Opportunities Commission, the National Enterprise Board, the Prices and Incomes Board (PIB), the Arbitration and Conciliation Advisory Service, and so on.

The underlying message has been that if there is conflict, or a failure in the economy or in society, a new organisation will be created to deal with it. If someone is racist or sexist, their behaviour will be punished; if their prices are too high, they will be controlled; if there is a problem, the state will impose a solution. There is no attempt to change attitudes or social structures, it is the simple exercise of power. The state is more powerful than the individual or the company, so it will settle the argument.

The first problem is that this does not change anything. Any number of racist or sexist landlords or employers could be taken to the relevant commission, and punished, and the number of people with dubious attitudes is not altered one iota. As it happens, the levels of racism are actually higher than they were before the creation of the CRE, although of course, this is a Europe-wide problem, and one which has been exacerbated by New Right policies. However, one can say that the CRE was neither intended to, nor able to, reduce the level of racism.

One could say the same of the PIB. It was set up to control prices during a period of high inflation, yet it found that the number of price changes it had to monitor was just too many for it to cope with. So first, its scope was limited to price rises by the big companies. Also, 'it could handle only a relatively few of the many thousands of price and wage changes taking place each year'. (Wilfred Beckerman (ed.), *The Labour Government's Economic Record 1964-70.*) Nor did the Board's recommendations have any statutory standing with companies.

On the other hand, as each price investigation involved detailed analysis of the company's costs, profits, and so on, ministers and public learnt a lot about corporate activity. There is much secrecy in British industry concerning costs and profits, because directors would like it to appear that all costs are unavoidable, and that whatever profits are made are minimal in terms of total sales or the costs of production.

However, there is little evidence that the PIB was very effective in controlling either prices or wages. What little restraint in prices that did occur could be put down to other factors. But one factor that is almost universally agreed to constrain prices is competition. And although the Labour government of 1964-70 recognised that many companies made excessive profits because of their market power, it did little to minimise that power.

The probable explanation for this is that just as the Tories, working within a market-driven ideology, cannot see that markets fail, so Labour could not see the advantages of the market. Labour's world-view was based on socialism and state intervention; it was an ideology in which the state stepped in to cure any and all problems. This approach is by no means absent from modern Labour thinking, nor is it entirely absent from some in the Green Party.

Labour was applying the same symptom-driven remedies in many of its plans for nationalisation. For example, British Leyland was created because the British Motor Corporation was seen to be struggling, while the Leyland truck company was efficient, being run by an outstanding management. The government assumed that by putting the weaker company under the good management, Britain would have a better and larger company. And because it was larger, it would have access to the supposedly beneficial economies of scale. In fact, the resulting merger led to the creation of British Leyland (BL), the state-owned disaster of the 1970s.

A similar tale can be seen in the Upper Clyde Shipbuilders. This was created by government pressure, in an attempt to cure the shipbuilders' 'low productivity, late deliveries, bad design, bad labour relations, inept management, and Victorian marketing. ...£329m of public money later, the same diseases afflict the industry'. (*The Economist*, February 14, 1976, cited in P. Maunder, *Government Intervention in the Developed Economy*, p147.)

In such cases, nationalisation not only failed to cure the disease; it was not even the correct cure. And it is unlikely that Tony Blair's vague assertions about stakeholding would cure the problem today, either. The real fault lay with the incompetent management. The proper solution would have been to analyse the companies' many structural weaknesses, and find ways of curing them.

A second objection to the quango- or symptom-driven system is that one is complicating and expanding the mechanisms of government, without necessarily creating any value for society. It creates a top-heavy state, exactly the sort of monster that Thatcher and Reagan promised to sweep away. They got into office by promising that the bureaucracy of Whitehall or Washington would be replaced by slimline government, the minimal state, and efficient use of the taxpayer's money.

The quango-creating approach is one which says, whenever faced by a problem, 'Let us create a more powerful force that will overwhelm the people or organisations who are causing the difficulty'. In essence it says, here is an enemy — let us attack it! The institutions of the state become a weapon to be wielded against the wrongdoer, to force them to stop doing whatever it is that we object to. And sometimes this is the best approach. But there are many times when this is not the best way. We may formalise the conflict, or moderate it, but we are not actually getting rid of it.

It is not just the matter of imposing quangos; even if they could be shown to be cost-effective, they might still not be the best answer. The problem is that very often one is imposing a solution to the symptoms, rather than dealing with the causes. In the United States, as in Britain, there has for many years been a problem with youngsters stealing cars. So the car manufacturers created sophisticated anti-theft car alarms, coded ignition, stronger door locks, and other security measures. The result — car thieves carry guns, and hijack both the car and its driver. Dealing with the car owner's immediate concern has not really been a successful approach.

In a similar manner, Britain's Conservative government approaches road congestion with its market ideology in its hands, and seeks to impose a market-driven answer. Road-pricing is the solution that springs naturally to Tory minds — charge drivers for the amount of use they make of congested roads. However, apart from the fact that the technology does not yet exist to monitor road use, there is also the fact that the real need is to reduce the amount of use, but without hindering the ability of workers to go to work. Therefore, any sensible government would seek to improve public transport, because it is the most efficient method of moving large numbers of people.

In any rational system, the first step should really be to find out what causes the problem. And maybe, even consider why it is of concern. And we also need to be aware of any additional or external constraints. If we know the cause of a problem, we can deal with it more directly. We may be able to demolish it at source, instead of spending all our efforts constantly curing the symptoms.

The Labour Party's Commission on Social Justice takes as given the concept that society has changed; we no longer have full employment, the nuclear family and a strong state. Therefore, say the Commission, we must completely re-evaluate the welfare state. (*The Justice Gap*, IPPR.) But if we examine the problem, we find that unemployment is high because of the mistaken economic policies of the

Conservatives, not because of any change in society. To know what must be done to deal with such issues, we need to examine the extent to which modern social and economic faults are endemic, or artificial.

There are a variety of issues which politicians of one party or another claimed to be able to deal with, within the rules of their particular ideology. The Prices and Incomes Board was an understandable response to inflation, from a party whose economics were based in Keynesian ideas. And strict monetary control, combined with high interest rates, was a natural choice for any party following New Right ideas. Both parties treated inflation like a nail that had to be simply hammered back into the wood. It is the economics of confrontation. Dealing with the causes of inflation would have been much more effective.

The post-war period, and especially the post-1979 era, have seen a dramatic rise in the levels of crime. The natural response to this is to increase funding for the police, and this is undoubtedly the best immediate reaction. But it ignores the entirely separate issue of the long-term social causes of crime. If one could identify the various social factors which exacerbate the level of crime, the long-term gain for society would be much greater. We would spend our money on better education and housing, improve job opportunities, and ensure that worthwhile activities were available for all.

And extra spending for the police is essentially the same as trying to solve a problem by creating a new quango. It is dealing with social forces using a political institution. The only difference with creating a new organisation is that it would tend to see the issue as a unit, and would be subject to political pressure to 'cure' that single issue. This would lead members of the institution to think about the item as a single unit, and try to deal with it in that way. The 'short, sharp shock' treatment and the heavier prison sentences are an expression of the belief that all we need to do is impose more severe punishments, and criminals will immediately be too frightened to commit crimes.

However, we do need to recognise that even in the best society there will be people with emotional problems, unpleasant attitudes, and perhaps even downright anti-social behaviour. Even in the best of all possible worlds, there will still be crime. On the other hand, putting people in prison is not the best way of curing crime. It simply removes convicted wrongdoers, temporarily, from society, and in most cases makes no attempts whatsoever to cure their problems.

We can regard crime as a single issue when reading a tabloid, or discussing it down at the 'Dog and Ferret', but in real life, 'crime' is unemployed youngsters, skilled workers boozing too much, flash lads on bleak council estates, and a dozen other types. It is individuals suffering from too much time, too little money, no job, no future, or in one way or another, a life that does not fulfil them. Changes have occurred in society which have increased the number of people who feel that way, and although more police on the streets is a logical reaction, it does not cure the underlying issues.

The increase in crime under the post-1979 regimes suggests that the causes relate to government action, and specifically to the deterioration in the social environment as a result of the Thatcherites' policies. We have seen an increase in unemployment, in inequality, and in the number of homeless. At the same time, there has been a decline in the number of people with genuine job security, greater materialism, and a growing acceptance of the belief that government is not obliged to look after the weaker members of society.

It cannot be a coincidence that these increases in anxiety, insecurity, low pay, and unemployment have been accompanied by a massive rise in the crime statistics. In some cases, the links are well-documented and well-established. For example, research has existed for many years, showing that a rise in unemployment is followed by a rise in the rate of crime. Also, the financial stress caused by low pay and job insecurity adds to the emotional burdens of the family, causing marriage breakdown, and sometimes leading to children running away from home.

Alcoholism and suicide have also been liked to unemployment, and given the known link between drink and violence, it would not be unreasonable to suggest a possible connection between unemployment and violence. Given the number who are jobless — not fully recorded by the government's statistics — it is not surprising that many turn to crime as a way of life; hence the rise in organised crime. This is a double threat to society. First, the high levels of crime can reduce the police clear-up rate. Second, the existence of criminal organisations could lead to deliberate attempts to interfere with the wheels of justice.

What needs to be done is to get to the root of the various problems, with all of them being dealt with as separate issues. There must be job creation programmes, better quality training, an expansion of education, and legislation protecting jobs and pay levels. And all of the government's programmes of privatisation and deregulation need to be examined for their effectiveness — have they saved money, improved services, and been justifiable overall? Or have they simply reduced costs and prices, at the expense of safety and workers' pay?

But more spending by itself is not enough. The expansion of education must be accompanied by a change in the quality of education, expanding the content of education, while encouraging parental involvement with schools and colleges. Research has shown that getting parents involved in their children's education considerably improves performance. It is possible that the actual amount of work the parents do is less important than the attitude they impart to their children. The unspoken message of their involvement is that we, as parents, care about you, and we believe that success in education will be good for you. That message would be extremely powerful for most children, and encouraging in every sense.

State education needs to be expanded at all levels, not on the basis of what we can afford from our national purse, but what the country needs. This can be seen in terms of the economy's needs or the desires of many individuals to have a rounded education, a full knowledge of all the things they wish to understand. Perhaps such freedom would result in a lot of people choosing to study literature, psychology, or other liberal arts subjects. If the government objected, it could offer incentives for students to go into engineering or chemistry. But as such services should be provided for people as a right, the government would not have the right to do any more than offer incentives. It should not, for example, be able to cut education in the miserly way that the Tories are doing.

There should also be better training, especially for young people. There is supposed to be a Youth Training Scheme, which is why youngsters under 18 are not entitled to social security benefit. Not only is YTS provision patchy, but where places are available, the training provided is often minimal. If we want British workers to have the skills that a genuine manufacturing industry needs, then they must have both the education and the training.

This would allow young people to go into jobs with career opportunities ahead of them, and with skills that they could be proud of. They would have a life of employment to look forward to, which is a considerable improvement on what they are offered by the New Right. In addition, it would be a life doing an interesting job, a well-paid job, and ideally, something which they enjoyed doing.

Employment is not everyone's choice of lifestyle, but we are now talking about creating a society in which people have choice in their lives; not the 'your choice out of three underfunded options' that the Conservatives regard as choice, but genuine, full range choice. So those who chose a given career would do so because it was their preference. Others might seek higher education, a life in the arts, or some form of voluntary work. It is not our place to pre-empt, or judge, any of these choices.

What is important is that everybody has the opportunity to develop their abilities to the full, and then use those abilities as they wish. If everyone is employed, in the broad sense, and all necessary services are being provided, then comments about saving the taxpayer's money could become mere quibbles. In addition, it is likely that the members of such a society would be much more fulfilled personally, happier, and therefore less likely to commit the crime that so concerns us now.

Policy should also be applied via monitored feedback; that is, the results of policy should be carefully observed. This is so that if the effects are not as expected, one can moderate the policy. For example, suppose that in trying to control a wild boom, one raised taxes; but the rise was too great and caused a dip into recession. Monitoring the events leads to a feedback in policy, so that as the economy turns down, taxes can be lowered again to reduce the deflation.

The post-1979 regimes have not done this, and this failure was the greatest cause of the 1988-93 recession. Interest rates were clearly too high in 1990, and were causing a slump in consumer demand. Yet the Chancellor at the time, Lamont, did nothing whatsoever to alleviate the problem, until the pound was forced out of the ERM. To maintain an economic policy without some sort of feedback mechanism is nothing less than stupidity. Yet this was in effect the Conservative approach to government.

One issue that is equally deep-seated is the conflict between management and unions. The Thatcher government solved this by weakening unions to the point that they ceased to be a threat to management. A previous Labour government had dealt with it by creating the Prices and Incomes Board, while Tony Blair hopes that stakeholder participation will generate a new culture in the workplace.

In fact, British management has for many years held short term views on how to run a company. They have cut back on capital investment, and completely ignored innovation, product quality, design, and other factors. They have used the companies as sources of money for perks, company cars, and other ego-inflating pleasures. The wrath of the shareholders has been bought off by paying them higher dividends than companies could afford. It is only in the post-war period that workers have also tried to get every penny they could out of companies.

There was not a genuine consensus that could break down, but at least one could say that in the 1950s and 60s, there was wary consent, and that the two sides were more or less evenly matched. Mrs Thatcher simply altered the power balance, without changing the fundamental social conflict. As mentioned in Chapter 4, it is possible to have consensus in society, and in the workplace, and anything that can be done to create better industrial relations would have enormous benefits for industry generally.

The culture of the workplace is primarily the creation of management, and they need to be persuaded that there is more to life than glass offices, big cars and dark blue suits. It is a pity that under Thatcherism, management attitudes have actually moved towards the nineteenth century exploitation that Marx so vividly condemned. The latter part of the twentieth century is not a time to be looking for enlightened bosses in any part of Europe.

It is to be hoped that at some point in the future, rational debate between the two sides will be possible, and this should not be based on the amount of power that one side or the other wields. It would be far more sensible to try to create a working environment in which both sides co-operate, in the interests of the business, and of its customers. It should be apparent that neither side can succeed without the other, and that the business cannot survive if one side or another permanently withdraws. And in recognising that both parties have to take part, one would both side-step, and subsume, the argument about who should have the most power; both sides would have exactly the same power.

But this recognition cannot be created, simply by Labour reversing the Tories' anti-union legislation, and returning to the unions the power they previously had. That, by itself, would simply recreate the old enmities with the old balance of power. What is needed is for both sides to recognise the logic of sitting down at the negotiating table, and working together. Co-operation could lead to fewer strikes, a more flexible workforce, and perhaps higher levels of investment and training. Whether or not the stakeholder approach would help remains to be seen.

The culture of exploitation is deeply embedded in the minds of some leading business executives, and has been encouraged by Thatcherism. But a persuasive government that created a competitive environment could also persuade the two sides of industry to sit down and discuss planning and development in a rational way.

Indeed, it seems that most social problems and conflicts could be dealt with by locating the sources of the problem, and dealing with them one by one. With the aid of better communication, better understanding, greater compassion, and greater willingness to listen to the needs and opinions of others, we can create a way of life in which issues are resolved by discussion, rather than by the exercise of power.

Many of us will have to look at our behaviour, and eliminate the myriad ways in which we exercise power. As parents, employers, or customers, we seek to impose on others when we can. As we replace this with communication and understanding, in all areas of life, we will gradually create the sort of society we seek.

We need not create great social institutions and structures to deal with society's problems. In fact, this may be futile. But we do need to monitor the changes in society, so that the pace and degree of change is as we would wish it.

But by changing a multitude of forces and attitudes, we can move towards creating the sort of nation we would wish to live in, or which we would want our children to live in.

11

A menu of options

BY THIS STAGE, it must be agreed that there is a need for change in the world; not just in Britain, not just in the party orientation of the government, but in many aspects of society. The question is, how do we achieve that change? And as mentioned in the previous chapter, it is not a matter of a violent revolution, or pressing the right button. Attitudes, economic policies, even whole ways of life have to be transformed.

The next question is, how do we create that change? The answer is, by using every method or action or policy that leads to some net improvement in our quality of life. That does not mean simply improvement now, or for Britain only, but anything which makes the world a better place.

There are a range of social and institutional structures that have to be transformed in one way or another. These include family relationships, education, work, and politics. It may be useful to take these structures as the basis for our analysis.

To introduce the changes we seek, we have to make politicians quite clearly aware of our demands and opinions. And it is best to do this in ways, and at times, when they are most vulnerable to critical comments: given the lack of interest in the welfare of the average person that has been displayed by politicians, we have to force them to do what we want. Our political leaders do not work out of sheer altruism. One course we could take is to write letters to our MP, or even to other MPs — they do usually reply. But they would be even more sensitive to our opinions if we wrote to the local paper at election time, or campaigned noisily against them. They would be even more attentive if large, vocal and informed groups turned up at election meetings.

This would be particularly effective if applied in marginal constituencies, where a candidate is fighting to get in — or stay in. (This is the key to what little success Militant Tendency had in Labour areas. They targeted marginal seats as suitable sites for entryism.) Others could target vulnerable MPs as suitable candidates for the pressure treatment. Fear of losing their seat would concentrate the mind wonderfully, and remind MPs of an oft overlooked truth — that they are elected to serve people.

It might be best to begin this reminder at the selection process. We need to pay attention to the selection of candidates, before they get started on the career ladder, and before they start seeing voters as ballot fodder. It is not in our interests to have candidates chosen by left-wing extremists or party headquarters. We need to take an active part in constituency politics, so that our own personal or local wishes are considered. And we need to examine the motives and attitudes of prospective local candidates, to ensure that they wish to serve, rather than simply be elected.

This could be applied to any party, indeed, it might be useful if MPs could be encouraged to separate their policy statements and opinions from those of the national party. Their election to office depends on convincing the local people to vote for them, not on obeying the rules of party national office. If party headquarters were too finicky about MPs toeing the policy line, then perhaps the campaign could be taken to some more appropriate spot — e.g., the party chairman's constituency. This could be made the site of an all-out campaign, with publicity statements aimed at both a local and a national level, perhaps with a common theme — does this person have the right to tell elected representatives (in other constituencies) how they should vote in Parliament?

This could lead to political parties becoming more of an umbrella organisation for individuals sharing a spectrum of views, rather than the leaders of an obedient mass of slaves. Centralised parties like the Conservatives have so much power over MPs' voting behaviour that the effect is grossly undemocratic. In the Maastricht confidence vote of November 1992, Tory whips were reportedly frogmarching MPs to the vote, or warning some MPs that their mistresses were known about, with the implication that such details could be leaked to the press. This type of behaviour is an abuse of all the rules of elective democracy, as well as being morally repugnant.

Voters and local constituency members need to take greater control of the choice of MPs, the policy stance of candidates, and of local fundraising. This would be particularly valuable for influencing the Conservative Party, as Central Office is very dependent on local branches for its funds. Locally raised funds could be released to Central Office only to the extent that the party, and the local MP, had obeyed the wishes of the local branch.

It is unlikely that non-Conservatives could influence or affect the fund-raising process, as it is usually conducted entirely by party members. However, an informed campaign pointing out the damage done by Tory government policies might dissuade some Tories from actually giving money to party funds.

Parties must also be made aware of the need for democracy in the fullest sense, both in the creation and the implementation of policy. It is not enough to simply announce what one's policy will be, and then steam ahead with new legislation. That, by itself, would be undemocratic. So the Tories' obsession with privatisation and deregulation, even if it had been proved to be socially beneficial, would still be unacceptable. They had not fully discussed the policy, its merits, and the arguments against it, before proceeding with implementation. They simply acted, as if their opinions were all that needed to be considered.

Parties should present their programmes, and then explain both the intention, the operation, and the advantages of their approach. This should be done not merely because of the need for participation, but also to strengthen the consensus. Without that participation, the party cannot claim to be democratic in any meaningful sense.

We also need to separate politics from business, and although the social links between politicians and business executives cannot be eliminated, the deliberate lobbying does need to be examined. One cannot simply ban lobbying, as there are issues of freedom of speech to be considered. But there should be some controls on the ability of companies to put their point of view directly into the ear of ministers, while the ordinary voter gets completely ignored.

The best compromise might be to ensure that all the details of all lobbying be publicised, and be made fully available to the public. This could be done as part of a Freedom of Information Act, with a public right to know enshrined in law. Any business leaders who objected to this should have it pointed out to them that they operate in a democracy, and that part of the definition of democracy is openness and accountability. Given that, they could be asked, do they object to the requirements of a democracy? Again, the processes of consensus could be very effective in achieving the desired ends.

Pro-business pressure groups would have to publish details of all the arguments they were making to Parliament, or to politicians generally. Any evidence to support their claims would have to be published, and all interested parties, from informed individuals to counter-pressure groups, would have the right to publish opposite opinions.

Ideally, newspapers and television would take part in the debate, with public discussion of the relative merits of the different points of view. Here is where an independent media can work really effectively on behalf of democracy. The supporting arguments from the opposing schools of thought could be subject to public interrogation, and then everyone could decide on their relative merits. Given the quality of many policies sought by business, some of the changes proposed would probably be quietly dropped.

But increasingly, British politicians have become more remote, more career-oriented, less interested in the welfare of the average person. What if, with all the pressure applied to the parties, they still do not react with genuine responsiveness and democracy?

The answer is that decisions must be separated from the political system, and made more local. This could be done by forming local residents' parties, by forming one-subject pressure groups, and by simply demanding that local needs are considered, whether by central or local government.

The decentralist approach could be taken with local authorities, as we saw in Chapter 7. It has been said that the smaller local councils were inefficient, but the new larger bodies are not visibly better. There is no gain, yet there is a loss of access, of transparency, and of responsiveness. One might object that part of the problem was cuts in central government funding, which undoubtedly has had an effect. But there has also been bureaucratic incompetence, and loony left dogmas. More local and accessible authorities might be more amenable to local opinion.

Where local councils are open to pressure or new councillors, people could push for the break-up of the larger authorities. The bureaucracy, incompetence, unresponsiveness and apathy could be used as the basis of an election campaign, as well as the justification for a break-up once in office. In addition, councillors could lobby parliament, the EU, and anyone else for a change in Britain's law, so that local councils had a legal right of existence and funding, independent of central government.

Some local authorities have already decentralised their operations. Tower Hamlets localised its services into 7 mini-councils in 1986, under a Liberal administration. It is based on 7 neighbourhoods, each based on its component wards. The neighbourhoods are semi-autonomous, and have responsibility for housing, social services, leisure, refuse collection, street lighting, economic development, and other services. The result is that elected councillors for each ward sit on all committees, and so can handle any problem. Also, offices are closer to ratepayers, usually 'within walking distance', according to council officer, Ashley Gibbons.

When the idea was first put forward by the Liberals, Labour opposed it. For example, Labour leader Christine Shawcroft said, 'What the Liberals call decentralisation just seems to be chopping everything into seven'. (*Municipal Journal*, February 20, 1987.) She added that the Liberals had failed to make a distinction between council functions, and council services. This could be a major criticism, considering that a failure to deliver services was one reason for the unpopularity of the previous Labour administration.

However, according to councillor Eric Flounders, decentralisation has actually improved efficiency. He says, 'People who say to me that dividing things into seven makes for inefficiency have obviously never dealt with our housing department, one huge department with 50,000 properties and it absolutely cannot cope'. (*Municipal Journal*, February 20, 1987.) For instance, at one time, only 2 per cent of planning applications were dealt with within eight weeks. Under decentralisation, it is as high as 32 per cent in one neighbourhood. To take another example, Tower Hamlets had the second lowest rents and the sixth lowest poll tax of all Greater London boroughs in 1993.

One of the Labour Party's principles on local government, is that when it is in opposition, it does not sit on council committees. Under decentralisation, if it did this, it would have no right to complain about the quality of service provision, as all elected members sit on committees. Any complaints would be met by the Liberal officials saying, 'If you want to run things differently, please take over'. This so weakened Labour's ability to take the high moral ground that they gave up. Now, they take part on committees just like any other council member.

One significant criticism of local provision has been the cost. Jones and Kavanagh describe the pre-1974 arrangement of local government as 'an ancient patchwork system of 1,400 local authorities'. (*British Politics Today*, p168.) The justification for the subsequent re-arrangement was primarily on the basis of cost and efficiency. And certainly, extra staff costs for Tower Hamlets could be in the region of £1 million per year. However, the evidence suggests that the cost-effectiveness of delivering services has improved considerably. The additional costs might be no more than a transitional item. It is too early to pass final judgement on Tower Hamlets' experiment, but the signs so far are that it is a success.

Policy can also be influenced by pressure groups, such as Charter 88, Liberty (NCCL), or the London Cycling Campaign, as is appropriate for one's beliefs and interests. Others — those still in employment, after the industrial sabotage carried out by the Tories — might join a trade union, and seek to influence union policy, or even Labour Party policy. Labour is vulnerable because of its dependence on unions' finance, and perhaps could be persuaded to carry out a rational evaluation of its platform. But given Labour MPs' performance in parliament, it would be nice if they could merely manage to criticise the Tory government occasionally.

Given that Britain is a member of the EU, some pressure groups could seek to ensure that we complied with EU regulations. This could be applied in the realms of wages, safety at work, competition, product quality, water and environment quality, pollution, and a variety of other issues. The EU is said to be influenced by socialists, and Jacques Delors, its most influential president, was said to be a socialist; although one suspects that this refers to old-style, state control socialism. This is an ideology that believes it knows the 'will of the people,' and some exponents think they do not even have to ask the people what they want. They, as Nietzschean leaders, can simply do as they wish.

However, pressure can be applied to British MEPs, or possibly some people could lobby the EU directly. Perhaps with carefully targeted pressure, leading members of the Brussels junta could be persuaded to recognise that constantly yielding to big business lobbying is not in the best interests of the population as a whole. Brussels seems to be full of lobbying organisations, for the consumer electronics industry, for computers, for retailing, and so on. The combination of money, research and proximity to the decision-makers ensures that the word of business is always the loudest sound in the civil servant's ear.

It is time that a counter-lobbying organisation was set up, ensuring that EU politicians paid a little more attention to the needs and demands of the population generally, rather than just those who run very large companies. Given that the EU's justification is so often based in altruism, one hopes that its bureaucrats would be susceptible to some informed persuasion. At the very least, they should be willing to take part in rational and open-minded discussion. However, the past record demonstrates exactly what one expects from a powerful centralised organisation; it imposes its will on the people, whenever and wherever it can, it does not listen, and it is not responsive to popular needs.

The goal of the European Union is a nation-state with a population of 320 million people, and is the epitome of political centralisation. The centre of power will be too distant from the electorate to be either responsive, or aware of the people's needs. It has already attracted the description, 'democratic deficit', but there is a danger of there being a complete lack of democracy. The best course might be to seek the total abolition of the EU as a political unit. As a free trade area, with no federal ambitions, the EU would be totally unobjectionable.

In addition to the sphere of politics, there is plenty of room for action in the realms of work, in the personal sphere, and in ordinary life. That is, we can influence people at work, or in the course of work; we can influence family and friends; and we can talk to those we meet day to day, on the bus, shopping, or whatever.

At work, we can present our opinions of how an employer should treat their employees. Some, such as Rupert Murdoch or British Airways, fall so short of the ideal that they can only impose their New Right ideas under an authoritarian government. Under the cover of moral darkness, aided by the ideology of unrestrained capitalism, employers can revert to the exploitation that Marx accused them of in the nineteenth century.

An active workforce, aided by a vociferous union, could make that employer look like the outdated throwback it is. In the cold light of publicity, with plenty of emphasis on the stress suffered by workers, and the loss of quality in the product that the consumers get, these wicked capitalists might be made to think twice about their short-term abuse of employees.

There is also a lot that unions could do to avoid the destructive style of conflict of the 1970s. The strike-prone mentality was not good for industry, for the company, or for the worker. And because of public opinion's hostility to strikes, ultimately, this tendency to call 'all out' at the drop of a dispute was not even good for the unions. And more importantly, there are other, more rational ways of settling disputes.

Unions need to be run by managers seeking the best interest of their members, rather than by the old-fashioned revolutionary comrades. Most important, unions, like all other actors in the social consensus, need to achieve their results by discussion and negotiation. The first step in any impasse should be to publicise the reasons for the dispute, the union's claim, and its arguments. If management are still stubborn, then the union could publicise the relative pay rises of workers and management.

Consensus is a process which must reach all sections of society, even the most dissensual. And in creating discussion, we also emphasise the essential unity of society.

One can also seek, or create, a job which encourages change. For example, big business depends on the creation of materialism and mass production, but one could reduce the sales of the big corporations by taking sales away from them. Many people have technical skills that could be used in this way, repairing mass produced goods such as cars, video recorders, televisions and so on.

Some people might say that even repairing such goods is encouraging their use, and is therefore bad. But for the time being, these products will be popular, regardless of our actions. So by providing an alternative source of supply, we are not creating a market, but we are reducing the big company's sales. Given that power is one of the key dimensions protecting the structure of the existing system, anything which reduces that power must be seen as a priority. Any marginal encouragement of the use of such products is more than balanced by the big corporation's loss of sales.

Also, given the boycott of some manufacturers (see below), people with appropriate skills could start up businesses making goods in competition with the offending corporation. Perhaps one could co-ordinate such activities with relevant pressure groups, determining which are the offending companies or products. One could then ask environmental groups to identify the products which are the most environmentally harmful in their manufacture. Repairing such goods, in quantity, would not only provide paid employment, it would also be socially beneficial.

One of our key roles is in the family. Many of us play the role of parent, yet in that most important and most difficult role, we often fail to act as a parent. The state has taken on the job of educating children, while television has taken on entertaining them. All we need to do is feed them. Certainly, there is a tendency for some parents to act as if the education of their own children is not their job. There is something unhealthy about the 'not my job' attitude in any society or community, but for people to say it about their own children is even more unattractive.

Yet as parents, not only do we have the legal right to provide a full-time education ourselves, with us acting as teachers, but we can act as a supplement to the state system. We can teach our children all the moral and social values, and the complexities of relationships, that the state system does not see as any part of its job. We can explain the difference between right and wrong, how far one needs to go to keep one's peer group happy, and what to give to, and expect from, a relationship. And this need not involve keeping the children at home, away from the state school, although parents do have the legal right to do this. It could occur in normal conversation, or in relation to school work.

Many parents, even quite assertive ones, talk as if they do not have the right to impose their values on the child. After all, we can be talking about someone as old as 18 years old. What is our moral right to impose our opinions on a near-adult? The answer is, our right stems from our relationship, and from our provision of a family home. That is, if we pay the bills, we impose our values. This might sound authoritarian, but it could involve no more than discussing issues with one's children. (See Michael Argyle, p121.)

Apart from taking a role in the education of one's child, there are also the values and attitudes that can be considered. Many British people seem to believe that what exists in the world, exists, and cannot be changed. They take everything for granted as it is, from the programmes on TV, to the political system, to the quality of food at restaurants.

All of these things should be open to question, to considering why they are like that, what would the most effective or best way be of making or doing this or that. Children need to be made aware that the objects and institutions around us are not designed for maximum benefit for us. They have been put together, perhaps based on a nineteenth century design, often with barely minimal competence. The intention is not always to keep the consumer happy, but may be merely to keep them quiet.

This attitude is irritating in some restaurants, or in badly designed machinery. But when we encounter the same indifference to the end user in our political system, then something is seriously wrong. The people who run the government should be obliged to consider our welfare, under pain of punishment if necessary.

If we can make our children aware of these myriad incompetences, and the casual thoughtlessness, then perhaps they will not have to suffer such appalling social conditions. We need to become aware of every social, institutional, and mechanical clumsiness, so that we can point them out. And we need to be aware of how important each one is, so that we can discuss the amount of effort that could go into remedying each concern. And we need to have some understanding of the origins of each failing, so that we can discuss with the child what sort of cure would need to be applied.

Some parents argue that their effect on children is very limited, that they cannot do much to alter the way the child turns out. Once again, society is blamed for the result. Yet those same people will complain about the way that child athletes, gymnasts and actors are exploited by their parents, pushed into a career they do not want, and lose their childhood because of parental pressure. And this is very true. To hear singer Michael Jackson talk about his childhood is to hear a tale of great sadness. His entire life has been shaped by the forces of his childhood.

However, one cannot and should not take this argument to the extremes used by some ministers. The fact that some parents have caused childhood unhappiness does not mean that one can blame all parents for all social problems, as some ministers would like to do. Single parents are an especially attractive target for this form of scapegoating, as many voters already have some hint of hostility towards them. And of course, the government is delighted for any opportunity to blame someone else for the problems it has caused.

Yet if parents can have an effect for the worse, then they can also have an extremely beneficial effect. They can shape the child's attitude to life, to people, to lifestyles, to work and education. The parent can be the most powerful force for good in a child's life.

Young people do need guidance, and if parents fail to provide it, the young will find it where they can — from the peer group, from television, the mass media, whatever. And some parents encourage that, pushing their kids in front of the box as a way of keeping them quiet. Yet this simply encourages children to absorb the implicit values that are pumped out by the television — might is necessary for right to triumph, material goods are needed for one to have an enjoyable and exciting life, and that technology is an essential part of life.

But all of those sources of culture, together, are analytically a vacuum. The content is little more than soap opera clichés, generalisations, and superficial judgements. If parents abdicate their role, the result will be a childhood like Golding's *Lord of the Flies*. Or it could be like the Los Angeles gangs, where the gang provides the upbringing, the security, and protection on the streets. At best, parents will be breeding an army of unthinking consumers, advert-fodder for the hungry multinationals. In a society in which most parents have given up, the outlook for the next generation is bleak indeed.

Yet all that is needed to prevent this vision, is for parents to create a supportive environment, introduce discipline, and simply talk to their children. The younger the children are when the parents start this process, the better. They can discuss the issues of the day, politics, the problems of work, human relationships, even philosophy.

The important thing is to get children to recognise a series of general principles, including the fact that events and issues are complex, yet understandable; that rationality can solve problems more effectively than the fictional violence of entertainment or the hysteria of some debaters; and that some issues are best solved by communication and discussion. It is also useful for young people to be aware that although good and evil do exist in the world, leaders and pundits do not fall automatically into one category or the other merely because of their job. One politician may do well as Prime Minister, but another takes over and uses the post as a tool for manipulating society.

It is also useful to encourage children to respect education, and preferably be interested in it. Learning is a valuable process that can be fun, as well as maybe leading to paper qualifications in later life. But the two key advantages of education are the understanding one gets of the world, and the ability one acquires for controlling one's life. Some people who lack formal education still possess these powers; but they are easier to acquire if one has a supporting framework to lead one towards them. According to Argyle, the best way to encourage children is with emotional rewards — 'praise and material rewards are no good'. (*Psychology and Social Problems*, p123.) Emotional rewards, on the other hand, create an internalised motivation. Although one suspects that Argyle means that praise *by itself* is inappropriate.

It would be a useful contribution to society to teach one's children a moral code, or a set of values. Some writers believe that this should be taught at school, and although there is nothing wrong with this, it would be best if the parents took on this task, wherever possible. Parents should be the primary source of socialisation, and we should not see the agents of the state performing every task that parents wish to abdicate.

Ideally, this instruction should go beyond a strict behavioural-legal code, and include ethics and values. For example, we could encourage our children to appreciate the new and different, rather than display the more traditional English attitude of hostility towards the different. Instead, we could encourage them to see these things as a source of interest and fascination; there are new ways of life, different foods, new ideas to explore. This would lead to a far more creative lifestyle than the typical English attitude, which for some people is expressed in a total indifference to any new type of food, or in an unreasoning hostility to foreigners, or anyone with a slightly different skin colour.

In addition, the process of education itself has to be re-structured. Since 1979, it has been increasingly the tool of central government, with financial constraints, content, working conditions and wages all decided by Westminster. This has indirect effects as well. Morale is damaged by the increasing insecurity, while teaching quality is reduced by the larger classes — themselves the result of spending cuts. It is time for teachers, parents and local authorities to re-possess their property, and ensure that it is run the way they want it.

Schools and parents could make a powerful coalition to attack Parliament. Many teachers have felt under threat because of the government's new policies, but have responded by going on strike, or other methods more suited to a factory. This tends to put teachers in a confrontational relationship with the local authority, while the parents stand on the sidelines, confused. Thus, no one in this three-sided battle is attacking the government, the group who started the fight.

Parents and teachers need to join together, preferably with the council, to demand that their MP fight for more money for local education. It should be put to the MP in very simple terms — get more money for our schools, or we campaign against you. That is, every parent, every teacher, would be out there campaigning non-stop, explaining the issues, describing the social and economic implications of education cuts. It is a threat that should put the fear of cold steel into any MP, but especially those in marginal seats.

Such a campaign should make a point of ensuring that people see Westminster as the enemy, rather than venting their anger on the local council. There is a tendency for people to assume that cuts in council services are the council's fault; an understandable enough perception. But any protest group should have at the top of their agenda the need to ensure that people point their fury in the proper direction.

There is a tendency for people to see certain activities as 'not my job'. Thus, many teachers feel that funding levels are 'not their job', and that communicating with parents is similarly outside the job description. We cannot afford such demarcation disputes, especially given the chaos that society is rapidly collapsing into.

Where relevant, the 'not my job' syndrome must be dropped. Clearly, one should condemn exploitation by a greedy employer, but apart from that, there are many things that should be part of one's job. Teachers should be concerned about the welfare of their pupils, bosses should care about the well-being of their employees. Also the police should cease to take the attitude that a crime has not been committed, if someone has merely been threatened. The threat itself is a crime, and there are many situations where, even if no specific crime has occurred, it is still the responsibility of the police to look after potential victims. And to take the argument a stage further, would we hold a shop detective responsible for escaping toddlers? In some cases, perhaps we should.

As members of a society, we have to take a stand on the welfare of others. To take the blessings of membership, and then ignore the well-being of all, except those whom one is specifically paid to look after, shows a miserable attitude. Not as callous as the post-79 Tory governments, admittedly; they do not even concern themselves with the welfare of those they are paid to look after — the entire population.

Noam Chomsky argues that the best way to improve society is to do the opposite of what the existing structures are creating. Where big government creates isolation, or destroys communities, he says, we should go out of our way to create a sense of community. Similarly, where the state exudes propaganda and self-righteousness, we should ensure that people are confronted with the facts of Britain's economic situation.

One of the ideological victories of Thatcherism is to de-emphasise the concept of society. Putting social issues in terms of individual responsibility allows politicians to blame society's victims for their own problems. The homeless should earn money and find a home. The unemployed should get on their bike. Blaming the victim is usually very effective, because the downtrodden are usually so unappealing. They look scruffy, they may even be bad mannered. If they are not actually villains, we can safely say they are not looking after themselves. They beg, they drink, and they look untidy; perfect tabloid targets.

Instead of blaming the individual, or the victim, we should make a point of ensuring that we, and everyone else, are aware of the role of society in causing individual behaviour. Very often, the original cause can be traced back to some action taken by government, and if we can show a link between that, and the social problem, then so much the better. Otherwise, we can simply point out the complexity of social relationships, of cause and effect, and show that changes at a national level, whether of purchasing power or attitude, have had their effect on every person in the country.

Perhaps one of the things we need to do, whatever role we play, is to ensure that attacks are always pointed at the correct targets. There has not been enough research in recent years looking at the links between crime and unemployment, poverty, and other causal factors. What evidence there is needs to be placed squarely in front of the public, and repeated until no one is in any doubt as to the state's role in causing many of our social problems.

When making complaints, or targeting campaigns, one should also aim the attack as close to the source of trouble as possible. That is, we should direct our letters, protests or campaigns at the cause of the problem, rather than the most accessible target. Thus, if a government minister proposes spending less on local authorities, we must attack the minister, rather than the local council. If the media presents a biased view of policy, then the organisation or its editor must be the subject of our complaints. And if the government allocates funds somewhat over-generously to some sections of the population, it is Westminster that should be criticised, not the beneficiaries of its misplaced generosity. If too much is spent on the roads, one criticises the SMMT or the AA, but not individual car drivers.

The one exception to this rule is if the beneficiary is one of the sources of political influence. If income is redistributed by selective changes in the progressive tax system, the upper income group has, under the Tories, been the usual recipient of the largest tax gain. This group is usually also the most active supporter of Conservative party funds, of political lobbying, and of right-wing organisations generally. So both sides of this amoral alliance must have their faults pointed out to them.

We may also create change as consumers. One has the sovereign power to buy, or not buy, the goods of one's choosing. And we can vet our purchases in terms of their environmental impact, such as cars or aerosols, or the environmental effects of the manufacturing process. Or, we could take it a stage further, and boycott certain manufacturers according to the social and environmental impact of their global operations.

For example, some Japanese companies are renowned for the huge quantities of wood they consume. This is often used simply for shuttering, when pouring concrete in construction. Wood panels are used half a dozen times, and then disposed of. Whole forests are being decimated in Malaya and Brazil to feed the hungry industries of the West, yet at least a tenth of the trees logged are so heavily damaged by the logging process, as to be completely unusable.

In addition, native people are displaced by the logging, although often it is on land that officially belongs to them. They are paid a fraction of the value of the wood, or in some cases, shot by greedy miners or land-grabbers.

The moral code of some big corporations is so dubious we may wonder how the people managing them can continue in business. There has been Union Carbide, allowing methylisocyanate to escape and kill hundreds in Bhopal, India. The management of the Ford Motor Company in Detroit chose to continue making the Pinto, knowing the petrol tank was located dangerously. And the Nestlé company encourages the use of dried milk for babies in Africa, despite the fact that many countries have inadequate or unsanitary water supplies.

As consumers, we can boycott these firms, and any similar corporate miscreants. Some boycotts are organised, such as the Nestlé one, which is espoused by the Baby Milk Action Campaign. It is worth keeping in touch with groups like this, or Survival International, Greenpeace, Friends of the Earth, or any of the many other groups. There is no doubt that such campaigns are effective. For example, after pressure from Greenpeace and others concerned about logging mahogany on native reserves in Brazil, B&Q announced that it would no longer buy mahogany for retail goods.

Because of their high investment costs, some big companies are extremely vulnerable to falls in sales. Massive sales volumes are needed to recoup their high levels of investment. A highly organised and well publicised boycott could be enormously damaging.

Some lobbying organisations could direct information campaigns at big business, ensuring that top company bosses were more aware of the damage done to the economy and to society by existing policies. For example, there is no point in getting inflation down to 3 per cent, if the cost to the economy is four million unemployed, and a dozen businesses closing down every day. Perhaps corporate executives are too dazzled by Conservative propaganda to see the contradiction, but with skilful argument and persuasion, they might realise that sometimes a pro-business government is not the best thing for business.

It is likely that a well-planned boycott, in collaboration with an information campaign, could be doubly persuasive. Diplomatically explaining the damage that a company was doing, with the unspoken threat that a nation-wide protest was being planned, would at the very least improve one's chances of an attentive hearing.

Some boycotts, such as that of South African goods, have been very effective. Others, such as that of News International, or of Nestlé, have been less so. Better co-ordination, planning and persuasion of other consumers to join the boycott would be a useful strategy. However, one needs to avoid the strident tone of some activists.

It is difficult to avoid all offending products, and it is offensive to seek to impose one's asceticism on others.

In addition to changing society, one needs to consider preparations for the fact that society is changing, regardless of what we want. When Chancellor, Norman Lamont was known to mouth occasional speeches to the effect that the recession was ending, or had ended, but that we wouldn't actually know it until six months into the future. Such verbal garbage can be ignored. Britain is not merely in a recession, but it is more or less a full-blown depression. And we as individuals need to be able to cope with that.

To cope with the economic storms that may be approaching, we need to use all our assets to the full. We need to acquire the appropriate depression mentality, while at the same time still trying to improve society. This means caution with money, preparing for the next unwanted career change, and ensuring that the next generation will be all right. One should do everything possible to ensure that one's children will survive, with the comfort and culture that we struggle to enjoy. When looking after the welfare of future generations, there is no better place to start than with our own children.

For some people, this could mean giving the kids one's family home, saving on death duties, and ensuring that they do have somewhere to live. But most importantly, we must make sure that our children have a proper education. And this does not mean sending them to a private school; we have better things to do with our money. It means teaching them ourselves, discussing all issues with them, rationally, in detail, and with whatever information we have. If we haven't got the full facts on a subject, we must encourage them to go and find out the information for themselves.

But they need to be made aware that one of the long-term goals they have to think about is a choice of careers. They may want to have skills that are of little financial value, they may want a job in a career that is renowned for low pay. But they must at least be aware that money may be very tight in the future.

It is important to remember that we can control our own lives, and this is a valuable lesson that the next generation should also be taught. If we can re-build society in accordance with our beliefs, they at least must be able to choose their own way of life.

Given the many ways in which change can be instigated, it must be possible for everyone to play a part, whatever their skills, whatever their interests, however much or little time they have to spare. To move a nation from its iron railway track, onto a path of our choosing, rather than that of the political and commercial oligarchy, is a huge task. Everyone must play a role, in the way in which they are happiest, and most effective. But no one can be spared, no one can spend their time with fingers crossed, leaving the work to others.

If everyone who can, does what they can, we can look forward to gradual change; imperceptible, but inexorable. It is time that control was taken away from the politicians, and put into the hands of the people.

12

Things we hold dear

Britain was once a pleasant, amenable country, with a high standard of living and a reasonable quality of life. People wrote of its sense of community and of decency, of areas where we left our doors open when popping out, and where neighbours created an infrastructure of social support. Britons typically supported the underdog, and assumed that everything should be fair, people should be given a sporting chance. Now, the images that come to mind are of urban riot, slums and violence on the streets. It is not a society that any of us would wish to live in.

Of course, it is easy to be nostalgic about the past, and some writers have pointed out that the fear of violence recurs every twenty years or so. The tendency to idealise the past tends to recur almost constantly. Yet sometimes, there are valid reasons to say the past was better than the present. For instance, violence is a popular folk devil of the media. Yet it is also a fact; violence has increased. Where once we were horrified by assaults *on* children, now we wince at attacks *by* young children.

Indeed, it is possible to be objective about a whole spectrum of social issues, in each one of which there has been a measurable deterioration. There are more homeless, more people living in poverty, and higher unemployment. And of those with jobs, fewer people have full-time jobs, and for many, wage levels have fallen. Yes, it is easy to be unduly nostalgic, but when one is governed by incompetent, dishonest bigots, there is a temptation to see previous governments as being more attractive.

Not that this is a plea for a return to the policies of the past, although some of those policies do seem in retrospect to have been very effective. One of the themes of this book is that we should re-consider those policies which did seem to work. In this chapter, however, we simply focus on the role of social values in creating our quality of life. Partly, we need to consider the degree to which Thatcherism is responsible for society's deterioration, but also we need to think about the sort of society we want.

It is easy, and very tempting, to blame the Conservative government for everything that is bad, yet perhaps people themselves have played a part, because of their attitudes and behaviour. Our values shape our world, so in a sense, we live in a world that we have created. What we believe is possible or acceptable determines what actually is possible or acceptable. We as individuals play only a small role, but as members of society we support or reject the prevailing culture of our society, and thus contribute to its propagation. The way in which we bring up our children is a reflection of our opinions on the role of parents. Similarly, the way we vote depends on our values and attitudes, our beliefs as to what is right or wrong, what is practical or not, and who should receive the rewards of society.

For example, in the 1992 general election, despite high levels of unemployment, many people voted Conservative. The early support for Labour suggests a recognition that a change of direction was needed, but the last-minute swing away from Labour implies a lack of trust in the Labour Party. In addition, many people felt that the poor and the jobless were themselves partly to blame. This represents a change in attitude from the collectivism of the early post-war years. This, and other value changes that have occurred in Britain since 1979, partly explain why Labour lost an election that all rational analysis suggests they should have won.

The key aspects of our values and attitudes are that they are learned, and that our culture is shared. We are taught from an early age that certain beliefs are correct, and if we were to have doubts, we would find that all our peers held the same views. The urge to conform encourages us to accept those views, and fit in with our fellows. The implicit logic is that one person cannot be more correct than the multitude. And most people respond to these pressures; they adapt their opinions, they moderate their behaviour — they conform. This mechanism acts as a sort of flywheel on society; once the system has built up speed, it can cope with minor changes simply by riding over them. But it is not easy to incorporate new ideas. The speed has been set with the flywheel, and any alterations have to work their way through the whole system.

This is partly because our institutions have been set up to deal with the status quo. They know its procedures, its policies, its strengths, and its needs, and they work within the parameters set by these facts. In a similar way, voters, workers, the media, indeed all members of society, act according to the received wisdom, and reject the unconventional. This is not a universal rule, of course, but depends on the nature of the new heresy.

For example, Einstein's Theory of Relativity sprang to world attention during World War 1. It did not challenge established wisdom, except in the scientific realm. And the great and good of society are not usually concerned with science. But it did offer something above the squalid battles in the mud of France. However, ideas or policies which overtly threaten convention will be at best ignored, and at worst, attacked by the defenders of the social order.

Conversely, existing institutions will be supported by the received wisdom, even when those bodies are of questionable value, or need dramatic reform. The US health system is thought by many to be enormously expensive, inegalitarian, and with doctors who are suspiciously eager to operate for the slightest ailment. According to Ian Kennedy of King's College, these characteristics are maintained by the values of American society — rugged individualism, no government interference, no regulation, the market solves all problems, and an unshakeable faith in technology. These are typically American values, with a clear New Right tinge, yet dating to pre-Reagan days. In fact, they are the values of business, and the big corporations have managed to ensure that the entire United States is committed to commerce.

But the faith in technology is not merely a business ideal; it is also a materialist ideal. A problem in America is solved with money, usually through buying something, and the latest machinery is seen as the best buy of all. Machines, whether watches, steam locomotives or jet planes, exercise their own fascination on the mind. Their predictability, and the ease with which they continue performing their task, makes them very appealing to complex, unpredictable, and fallible human beings. And for some people, modern technology carries the additional potential for expanding the frontiers of knowledge, and triumphing over adversity.

But machinery, especially in the hands of unregulated commercially-oriented hospitals, does not necessarily represent the best way to better health. American medicine is at best, an expensive jumble. At worst, it is taking scarce resources away from other sectors of society, in order to treat those who do not actually need the prescribed treatment, in ways that can harm their health.

Yet despite many complaints about the cost and the inefficiency of the American system, it remains in place, supported by the values of the very people who complain about it. Thus, the subject of complaint is actually a creation of the complainers. Perhaps we in Britain do the same. We are eager to condemn crime, delinquency, dishonest politicians, and the materialistic society, but many people have played a role in supporting those same features. To change the system, we have to change the values.

Similarly, it is said that the success of Japanese industry is due to the work ethic of the Japanese worker. This is a worker who not only accepts the shortest holidays in the industrialised world, but who almost has to be forced to take those holidays that are allowed. It is often presented to the west as a mutually beneficial agreement — the worker gets job security for life, and the corporation gets a co-operative workforce. One would also say that Japan is a society that does not value individuality highly, but values submission to the will of the group. Agreement reached by the majority is accepted as applying to all. A contrary opinion is ignored, even by the person holding it, because the needs of the organisation are more important than the views of one person.

Of course, the success of the Japanese economy also owes a lot to its high levels of spending on education, investment, R & D, and innovation. And unlike Britain, the Japanese government, and its industrial agencies, like the Ministry of International Trade and Industry (MITI), do believe in state intervention; and they intervene very effectively. Yet there is also no doubt that Japan's culture plays a major role in supporting this excellent economic superstructure. The typical Japanese worker does not feel they are exploited by their employer — even though that may actually be the case. But the perceived absence of conflict of interest has allowed Japanese corporations much greater freedom in their industrial policy.

Conversely, economic policy in Britain has been constrained by the general agreement on what is or is not politically acceptable. The post-war consensus ensured that the welfare state and nationalisation were seen as a basic part of British society. For most of that time, levels of unemployment in excess of 1 million were seen as anathema. The 1979 Thatcher government allowed levels of (officially) more than 3 million, claiming that it was necessary, an economic medicine that by its very nature was distasteful to the patient. This government by cliché was extraordinarily effective in changing attitudes, and transformed what was seen as politically acceptable.

Thus, the views of a society can change. What is possible or attractive can change, as can what is perceived as possible or attractive. Times, values, and technology vary over time, as do the messages or ideas presented by the media or the education systems. Leaders can also alter perceptions, as is the case with Mrs Thatcher. She entered office at a time when the old Labour Party, trade unions, and nationalisation consensus was being brought into question; and she offered a range of new ideas which were seen as the answer to Britain's problems. Attitudes have changed since 1979, but a change in attitude was necessary for the Conservatives even to get into power.

This typifies the two basic ways in which values change — through events, or because of people. In most cases, there is an element of both, although one factor may be the more important. For example, the two world wars involved massive suffering, both for military and civilian personnel. After both wars, it was felt that the price paid for peace was far too high, and that those who had suffered most deserved some sort of compensation. Phrases like 'Never again' or 'Homes fit for heroes' were common at the time. The desire for real social improvement was so strong that the term 'war radicalism' was coined, expressing society's wish to create a better world.

More recently, the discovery of a hole in the ozone layer was a significant event for many people, reminding them that the atmosphere is not invulnerable, and can be affected by human actions. As a result, many people became more careful in their use of products, as well as being more aware of environmental problems generally.

It is a good thing that people are able to change their beliefs in this way, as this gives us hope for the future. If the Western world was to continue on its current smugly materialist path, within a few years there would be precious little in the way of resources left to be exploited. And we can safely predict that much of our industrial production will at that time be littering the seas, the air and buried clumsily in the land.

At the present time the dominant culture of what we loosely refer to as the advanced industrial nations is neither healthy nor sustainable. It is gross, superficial and materialistic, and becoming more so with each passing diktat of the EU, and each proselytising mission from the IMF, or foreign takeover in eastern Europe. The previously communist countries of eastern Europe were not renowned for their affluence or their freedom, but at least there were some attempts at egalitarianism. In Czechoslovakia, for example, everyone had a decent home, a modest standard of living, and a job. This is not to say that communism offered a good life, but some variants of it were at least tolerable.

Having freed themselves from the dogma of Marxism, the east is now being subjected to a barrage of free market dogma, from a variety of allegedly unbiased sources. The massed wisdom of the Adam Smith Institute, the World Bank, the Bank of England, and various American universities have been dispatched to the one-time eastern bloc to ensure a complete conversion to the new orthodoxy. There is no doubt that living standards will eventually rise, and that people will be better off — in the sense of having more/bigger material goods. But in most of eastern Europe, a way of life is disappearing.

The EU is longer merely an economic community. It now has political pretensions, aiming at the unity of up to 27 nations, with a single bank, foreign policy, and currency. And with a grotesque emphasis on the needs of business, the Single Market is being presented as opening up a new era for the continent. Many regulations are being made uniform, and some restrictions will be eliminated, so that trade can be carried on more easily between member nations. This is not a bad thing in itself, but the overwhelming concern with the needs of big business ensure that the Single Market will have a major impact on national cultures. The world of the future will not be the global village of McLuhan, or the global thinking of the Greens; it will be the unrestrained commercialism of Santer.

This fits in very neatly with the economist's call for growth. Buying is good, wealth is good, the economy must expand, and then we will all be better off. But in fact, growth is not necessary. Even in slump-torn Britain, growth might not have been the only way to give the lower income groups a decent standard of living. A significant re-distribution of income, via the tax system, would have done the job just as well.

The same insidious belief seems to have taken hold — to varying degrees — in the United States, Germany, Japan, and many other countries. And naturally, the large corporations that seem to own the economies of these countries are not deeply upset about this trend. Each is busily promoting its products as fashionable and desirable. And many corporations are discreetly funding research institutes that seek to 'prove' the importance of business values.

The market philosophy has been applied so universally in Britain, that it may seem to many people that there is no other basis of ruling life. The concept of efficiency is so powerful that even when hospitals have to be closed, the logic seems undeniable. So naturally, there is little or no argument when central or local government chooses to close a community centre, a village hall, or a theatre. The imperative of cost answers all criticisms. Yet in fact, it is not efficiency that has won, but a particular value system.

There is a danger that in years to come there will be no other basis by which to judge policy, other than by the rules of the market. Welfare will be deemed trivial, compared to the need for cheapness and efficiency.

It is clear that somehow the values of society must be changed, in order to allow the creation of a better society. One might also say that many of our current attitudes are wrong in themselves, and must be replaced simply for that reason. But whatever the reason, we cannot allow the continuation of a culture in which the countryside is destroyed for the sake of unnecessary motorways, or for wood to make concrete shuttering. We cannot tolerate an economy which mass produces wasteful goods, wastefully packaged, and then uses many gallons of scarce energy distributing the products from one end of the continent to the other. A society in which the voice of alleged expertise calls for greater manufacturing efficiency, while ignoring essential services, and forcing millions into the emotional desert of unemployment.

As a first step in this process, one could do worse than look at the values of science. But by this I mean the ideal of science as a methodology, rather than the carefully directed procedures of government or corporate scientists. Such people are employed in order to achieve certain results, and represent the triumph of finance rather than the epitome of rational analysis. One must also exclude some of the biased diatribes of the social sciences. Sociology is renowned for its ideologues, whose hostility to capitalism overrides any attempt to understand the world they live in.

Instead, what I am referring to is the science of Einstein or Feynman; not specifically the physical sciences, but the approach, the system of rational analysis. It is a system of thought that seeks to understand the world, to find answers, to explain how things work. It does not start with pre-ordained truths, but with a method, an approach to finding out what is the truth. Nor is it based in certainty; that is a nineteenth-century view of science. Nuclear physics and quantum theory have eliminated the old idea of certainty, and replaced it with probability. We might not know where an atomic particle is, but we know where it is likely to be.

We also have to recognise the limits of knowledge, and given those, probability is a workable tool for understanding the universe. And if we accept that there is no certainty, then we must accept that some of what we 'know' to be true, may not be. Some of what our experts or advisers tell us is the 'truth,' might not be. In effect, everything is up for grabs. If we wish to know the truth, we must research and investigate for ourselves, and find our own answers.

This means approaching the world, and everything in it, with an open mind. Many people cannot do this, or are unwilling to do so. Marxists assume that they have all the answers, based on an unshakable faith in their disproven dogma. The New Right are utterly convinced of the absolute truth of their policies. What they both share is a refusal to listen to anyone's else's point of view, a refusal that often goes beyond the overtly political, into all areas of discussion. Such people are almost incapable of listening to what others say, they are so sure that they know what is correct, and they know what you believe.

The closed mind is an excellent way of ensuring that you 'win' an argument. Apart from the obvious ploys of talking all the time, and interrupting, one can also find fault with anything the other person says. One can find carefully selected examples to prove the other person wrong, or one can find reasons why their evidence is valueless. For example, researchers for the television programme, *Storyline*, argued that British companies were importing goods made by underage workers. So they sent a photo of a young boy, working in a factory, to the British manager of the importing company. 'Obviously', the managing director wrote back, 'a photograph of a person is not proof of their age. Not many years ago, you may well remember, small men who looked like children were employed as bell-boys in hotels'. (*The Guardian*, February 5, 1993.)

All of which is perfectly true. A photograph of a person is not proof of their age. And perhaps some small men could pass, at a brief glance, as children. But the photo was still very convincing evidence, and any rational person should have regarded it as, at the very least, cause to investigate further.

Yet only the person with an open mind will really find out the truth about the world. One has to look for the truth, whether in people, or society, or political matters. One has to listen to what people say, to find out what they mean. One has to study the operations of society or politics to understand how they work. And the whole procedure has to be approached with only one certainty — that we don't know in advance what the answers are.

Our approach to life would be one of finding out the answers, rather than wielding our absolute certainty, like a blunt instrument, to destroy all verbal opposition. The open-minded approach also allows us to see people, the universe, and all forms of study as adventures. Nothing is decided, nothing is cast in concrete or carved in granite, and no expert's opinion is automatically the final word.

We can also learn some useful insights from Einstein's Theory of Relativity. Although it may not seem immediately applicable to ordinary life, we find that many of the principles of Einstein's theory can be quite startling. We can no longer talk about events being simultaneous, or objects moving away from us, without thinking about the caveats that Einstein has introduced to us. The best example is that of the person on a train, who is walking along the coach's corridor. The question is, what speed are they travelling at? The answer is, relative to the train, mere walking speed, but relative to the countryside around them, they may be strolling along at ninety miles per hour.

Given the concept of relativity, we have to accept that everything we see may be perceived in that way because of our position in relation to it. But we can generalise from the physical location, to our position in social, cultural, financial or moral terms. This view is similar to that of the sociologist's conception of reality as a social construct. That is, what we see, what we believe, are the result of our psychological conditioning, our socialisation.

We can use this insight to distance ourselves from what we have been taught, what we assume about the world, to see if our assumptions fit the known facts. For example, many people see politicians as respectable, intelligent, far-sighted individuals, well equipped to deal with complex issues such as managing an economy. Yet when we look at the outcome of politicians' actions in recent years, we see chaos and disaster. We see economies in ruins, masses in poverty, and millions across the world starving. For this deterioration to have occurred so extensively cannot be mere chance. The butter-fingered hand of total incompetence lurks somewhere within the mess.

The recognition that politicians are ordinary human beings, and a host of other insights, can be used to re-evaluate our understanding of the world. But they, and others, victims of social relativity, see the world as they do because of their position in society. They are prisoners of their culture, just as we are locked in the conditioning of our beliefs. Whenever we are dealing with people who are irrational or confused, we need to remember that the person is not necessarily at fault; it is more likely that it is the system.

The most startling example of this is the way that parties of the left see all social action as rooted in collectives, while parties of the right claim the ultimate unit is the individual. There is no apparent reconciliation, yet it is obvious that both views have an element of truth. We live in a society, yet the welfare of the individual must be a key consideration in policy formation. Our laws and our economy recognise this, and our moral system must also accept the duality.

Our legal system expresses this in such areas as car parking; if only one person had a car, the rules of car use would not need to be so extensive. But when millions of people own cars, the law has to take note of the fact that behaviour that would be insignificant if performed by one person, can be a major problem when done by thousands. Unemployment would not be a problem if only one person was affected, especially if it was in some way their choice. But when millions are unemployed, the scale of the problem and the nature of the cure may be very different.

Our moral and judgemental systems should also recognise that we are individuals, living within a society. We are not isolated or autonomous, but are interdependent, social beings. Our origins and upbringing were dependent on, and created by, our interactions with others, as is our current lifestyle. Our education was probably financed by the taxes of others, our first job would probably be in a company created by others, and if we are rich, even through our own efforts, it would be riches drawn from an affluent society.

The material and cultural wealth surrounding us has been created by others, and in some cases, created for people other than ourselves. Thus, on the one hand, we have a huge wealth of knowledge and experience to draw on for our understanding of the world, or for our entertainment. Equally, there are many sources of cultural enrichment for others to choose. This variety only exists because millions of people from varied backgrounds share a nation-state, and roughly similar values. In most Western nations there is sufficient similarity for a consensus to exist on values, whether of moral values or social or entertainment values.

Conflict occurs when the consensus breaks down. For example, in the United States, there are people who are so convinced that abortion is wrong, that it is murder, that they are willing to kill their opponents. Or in Britain, we have puritan souls who seek to impose their views on broadcast television. Both types feel so convinced of the rightness of their views that they feel entitled to impose them on the whole of society. Yet abortion is a matter of personal choice, and personal situation, while television is a service provided for the entirety of a multi-cultural nation. Both are made available for all, with the decision on use, or type of use, in the hands of the individual.

That is part of the nature of society. There is no dichotomy between the individual and the mass. They are simply two aspects of life, and our system needs to be able to deal with all aspects of life. Equally important, we as citizens need to be aware of our role in society. We share a complex socio-structure with others, and we need to recognise the contribution that others have made to our lives, and the resultant adjustment that we need to make to our behaviour, given society's gifts to us.

In re-appraising our life's assumptions, there are a wealth of sources to which we can turn. For business morality, America, so often the home of the worst of corporate misbehaviour, has, perhaps inevitably, also been the home of the most active opponents of big business. Displaying Galbraith's Countervailing Power in action, it has created determined enemies of corporate malice, such as Ralph Nader, and valuable concepts, such as social responsibility. This idea has been active in the United States since the 1960s, and places no limits on the responsibility of business to the community. Quite simply, business must be on its best behaviour at all times.

Some on the New Right, such as Milton Friedman, reject the view that 'corporate officials and labor leaders have a "social responsibility" that goes beyond serving the interest of the stockholders or their members. This view shows a fundamental misconception of the character and nature of a free economy. In such an economy, there is one and only one social responsibility of business — to use its resources and engage in activities designed to increase its profits so long as it stays within the rules of the game, which is to say, engages in open and free competition, without deception or fraud'. Indeed, Friedman goes on to argue that, 'Few trends could so thoroughly undermine the very foundations of our free society as the acceptance by corporate officials of a social responsibility other than to make as much money for their stockholders as possible'. (*Capitalism and Freedom*, p133.)

One can only say that Friedman's argument shows 'a fundamental misconception' of the nature of social organisations. Because they operate within society, their role and function must be determined by society. This is implicit in Friedman's statement that the company can 'increase its profits so long as it stays within the rules of the game'. In other words, Friedman rejects total laissez faire, recognising that some external controls must exist. And although the government enacts the legislation, in a democracy, everyone plays a part in deciding what the rules should be.

Some of us may be directly affected by the corporation's activities, either as employees, as customers, or because we live in the vicinity of the company's factory. Others may not be affected at all, yet may demand the right to comment. And it is essential that they have this right, because occasionally, those directly affected may not feel able to complain about the company. For example, workers may be affected by poor health and safety procedures in the factory, yet feel that if they complain, they will lose their jobs. The outsider who is not affected, may see this as wrong, and they may complain to the government.

Finally, there is Friedman's suggestion that nothing must come in the way of the corporation making as much money as possible for the shareholders. This is actually a very destructive way to run a company. According to *The Economic Report of the President*, capital investment in the United States has declined since 1973. The reason for this is that since 1973, most US companies have paid as much as possible to their shareholders, and have reduced what they put into capital investment. So it was inevitable that manufacturing productivity would also decline.

For Friedman to suggest that corporations maximise their payments to their shareholders is both careless in its regard for other members of society, and short-sighted in its attitude to business. This latter should be of no surprise for students of Friedman's work. He once referred to the 'real' economy, in quotes, as if referring to some hypothetical entity. Friedman's knowledge of the workings of the real world and the real economy is so limited that he simply is not aware of the implications of his statement. His suggestion is not even sensible, much less responsible.

However, once we recognise the concept of social responsibility, we see the corporation, not as an enemy, the dreaded foe of capitalism, but as an integral member of our society. It is responsible to us, in the same way as every other organisation is responsible to society as a whole. It is an inevitable part of our interdependence and consensus.

But this should not imply the intense scrutiny that some on the far left would like. They regard business in all its forms as inherently and automatically evil, and therefore to be subject to the maximum possible level of regulation. This would not be acceptable; however, the level of regulation that currently exists in Britain is equally wrong. At the present time we have weak controls on most areas of commerce, with the odd exception of broadcasting. It is obvious that voluntary self-regulation has not worked, and needs to be replaced by state regulation.

Even more important, we need an environment in which there is open and rational debate about the role of business in society, and in which citizens can put forward their ideas on business responsibility. Equally important, company executives must recognise the moral dimension of their role. Their job is not just to make a profit, or enrich the shareholder. It is also to make a product, to provide employment, and to enrich the community.

This is not merely the nature of business, but is also the nature of the human being. Firstly, if we fail to take account of the needs of our fellows, we may reap the repercussions. Those who live by corruption, by short-changing, by the con-trick, may suffer as a result of their own actions. Secondly, those who do not recognise any moral imperative whatsoever, and who act on purely selfish motives, do not deserve respect from anyone. Perhaps we cannot offer a convincing argument for a moral code, other than the fact that we all share the same society, but the person who totally lacks morality is a repulsive creature indeed.

However, we can assume that corporate executives can be persuaded to accept their social responsibility, because in the past, many have done so. For example, in the 1920s, Gerald Swope of General Electric 'held that management, in effect, was in a position to "define its own responsibilitie"; and when he did so in a 1926 speech, he astonished his audience by putting the public and the employees ahead of the stockholders in the list of those to whom managerial obligations were due'. (From James W. McKie, *Social Responsibility and the Business Predicament*, p30.)

And most of the things we would ask of commerce are undeniably reasonable. One would ask that companies operate efficiently, and that they minimise their use of energy and raw materials. Also, they should keep their waste disposal to the absolute minimum. Very often, the most toxic waste products are also the most valuable — heavy metals such as mercury, cadmium or titanium. It makes both environmental and financial sense to filter out such metals before the wastes are discharged.

Companies should also pay decent wages, offer adequate pensions, and have proper health and safety precautions. Their products should be safe, reliable, durable, and capable of doing the job for which they are sold. Prices should reflect the existence of healthy competition, and no company should do anything which would reduce the level or effectiveness of competition.

Popular attitudes move in cycles, just like the economy, and at the present time, Britain is in a downturn in both cycles. The rise of hard-line attitudes within politics has been accompanied by a more aggressive approach to business management. Some companies have stepped right outside of the legal limits, plundering pensions, or engaging in corporate espionage. Others have stayed within the law, but strayed beyond the borders of what is morally acceptable — raising prices a little too sharply, cutting wages and working conditions a bit too eagerly.

But fashions change in business as in anything else, and without the New Right to protect them, big business will be just a little more vulnerable to public complaints. It may also be more susceptible to the forces of competition, and therefore more willing to bow to consumer pressure, whether on environmental matters or political ones.

But one can extend the concept of social responsibility beyond the business organisation, to cover all groups; that is, by the concept of concomitant responsibility. This simply means that every job, every role, every official position, every activity has obligations accompanying it.

In a way, this is both an extension of social responsibility, and an answer to all those who blame 'society' for all their problems. No one is society, and so everyone can pass the buck. There is always someone else whom one can blame for crime, delinquency, and the fall in literacy. For example, parents do not always accept responsibility for the behaviour of their own children, preferring to blame teachers, society or the children themselves. In some cases, and to a certain extent, this may be true; but when it is used by many parents, it is time to start allocating duties.

Milton Friedman, working from what he refers to as a 'liberal' perspective, sees 'freedom as the ultimate goal and the individual as the ultimate entity in the society'. (*Capitalism and Freedom*, p5: see also p129.) Friedman paints a picture of the individual as being entitled to unlimited freedom, as a right. Paying taxes is seen as an infringement of the citizen's sacred liberties, which implies a failure to recognise the origins of society. Yet as Hobbes pointed out, society is created for the good of the individual, and we must yield some rights to the state for the security it provides.

Friedman sees only the rights and the privileges. It is as if one can belong to a society, gain wealth and security from that membership, yet have no obligations either to the state, or to other citizens. Friedman's view is of rewards without responsibility; indeed, the latter word hardly even appears in his work, except where it is rejected, as with corporate responsibility.

If we take the arguments used by Hobbes, described in Chapter 4, the citizen's responsibility to society must be seen as a natural part of their membership of it. Because they gain from membership, they must surely have an obligation to assist society in its functions and operations. Therefore, they have an obligation to pay taxes; but also to perform any other task that is needed by society for its operations, for any other members. The New Right stance that we only have to pay for what we personally gain is shallow in the extreme, because it ignores social gains, and only considers market purchases.

The corporate executive must be accountable to the shareholders, employees, and customers, at a very minimum. And in the same way, the newspaper editor, the police officer, the local authority councillor, the parent and the car driver all have duties attached to their role. In the case of a job, the duties may be spelled out quite clearly, and will probably be in writing, so that people know exactly where their duties lie. But in the case of roles in society, such as parent, the task has no official standing, so there is no recognised function. Yet there are obligations. However, while the stakeholder economy implies a form of control over the company, what is being argued here is that membership of society carres certain duties with it.

It is necessary that everyone in society recognise their two-way role. They have received benefits from the state, from the community, from the local council, and from other people; and because of this, they have duties to others. These depend on the roles they have, and normally these tasks are learnt as part of our socialisation process. For example, parents have a duty to seek the welfare of their children. But as the institutions of society change under the malign influence of the New Right, so the content of socialisation has weakened. If our roles were formalised via the concept of concomitant responsibility, it could make our lives easier in many ways.

Local authorities could play a part by defining the nature of the responsibilities allocated to each role, and each job. This could then be built-in to local bye-laws, or into training classes, and made available to the public. This would allow anyone who was not sure of their obligations to check with the council, so that they would know what was, and what wasn't, part of their job. Social workers, small claims courts and arbitration panels could also use the stated concomitant responsibility as a guideline in judging disputes, complaints or allegations about people.

In some cases, central government could play a role. With some jobs or activities, the state could impose certain requirements. For example, car drivers could be legally obliged to drive safely, in ways that went beyond those specified in the Highway Code. Or company managers could be made legally responsible for health and safety, regardless of their level in the company hierarchy. That is, all management would be responsible for a given factory, from the works manager up to the board of directors.

However, local and central government themselves have concomitant responsibility attached to their roles. Usually we take these duties for granted, but with the corruption of some Labour councils, and the blind incompetence of the Tory government, it is time that the full obligations of the state were formalised in greater detail.

If people are aware that there are concomitant responsibilities attached to their job or role, they can learn how to handle the task before they take it on. For example, school children can be taught the duties (not just the mechanics of it) of parenthood at school, perhaps from the age of fourteen onwards. House buyers could be given a course on the responsibilities of property ownership when buying their first home. And workers of all sorts would be given a detailed course in the obligations and duties of their role, when they first take up a given post.

This is not a new idea, and many of us already act as if we are aware of it. Most parents, most workers, and at least two of Britain's MPs act as if they recognise the impact of their job. All that needs to be done is to formalise that recognition, so that the irresponsible few can understand the rules better. It is necessary to give advice to the sort of parents who go to Acupulco, leaving their children alone. Or the company manager who pushes the staff a little too hard, regardless of the impact on their health. Or the neighbour who ignores the delinquency of their child. All that we need is for our agreed rules to be written down somewhere, and made available to all those who need to know them.

Perhaps the element of compulsion could be kept to a minimum, because all we really require is that people treat one another decently. All we are looking for is a place in which caring and compassion are more important than manufacturing costs, in which we treat one another as human beings, where rapes and assaults are a rarity.

In an ideal society there would be no compulsion. However, there would have to be information and socialisation. People need to be taught the rules, and they need to have rules explained to them, so that compliance is not merely formal. One is seeking active support for the community's morals, not merely a passive absence of attack.

13

The last word

OCCASIONALLY, SOCIOLOGISTS, PUNDITS and media talking heads tell us about the world of the future. It will be dominated by multinational corporations, allowing us to buy the same products, in the same shops, anywhere in the world. It will be a global village, in which instant news makes downtown Tokyo or Calcutta as accessible as the people next door. It will be a world of giant trading blocs, in each of which travel will be free and unhindered by such nineteenth century trivia as currency exchange.

But who decides these futuristic scenarios? Do we want a global culture, in which every major town in the world is a replica of Toledo, Ohio? There is a trend for the centres of decision-making to move further and further away from the citizen, with a parallel trend for those decisions to take less and less account of what the citizen needs. Is that the sort of society we want?

All the evidence suggests that under the Tories in Britain, the Republicans in the US, and other parties elsewhere, we have put up with a set of policies that do not work, imposed by a government that does not care. It is not that ministers are struggling to do their best for us, in the midst of an unfortunate recession. The problem is that they have created disaster through their deliberately inegalitarian policies. Privatisation, deregulation, and government spending have all affected both staffing levels and service quality.

It has been said that privatisation and deregulation have increased the levels of efficiency in British industry. But even if the once state-owned companies are more efficient, the cost to the nation has been greater unemployment, greater job insecurity, lower wages, and in some cases, poorer working conditions. It is not a case of there being a simple improvement, with no other factors to consider. There has been a disputed improvement, with many negative factors to set against it.

Economic policy also offers us this same ambivalent trade-off. High interest rates reduce consumer spending and corporate investment, thus cutting employment and efficiency. And high exchange rates harm exports and the balance of payments. Worst of all, nine separate acts of industrial legislation have allowed or encouraged wage cuts, making people worse off, and reducing demand. In other words, although the most obvious effect has been to increase unemployment, the overall impact on the economy has been disastrous in every way.

Each item that has reduced staffing, or allowed wages to be held down, has contributed to lower levels of purchasing power in the economy. Workers who are poorer or more insecure or simply unemployed, spend less than they did. This is so obvious that it is on the borders of belief that the exponents of Thatcherism cannot see it.

In addition, every aspect of the quality of life has deteriorated. Working hours are longer, and those in work are more likely to be on shifts, part-time, on short-term contracts, or in some way more vulnerable to job loss. Working conditions have also worsened for many people, with greater paperwork for some, and fewer safety provisions for others. Cuts in public transport spending means that our journey to work is both less safe, and more likely to be delayed. And whether we are at home, or out and about, we are less safe; the level of crime has turned some parts of Britain into near war-zones.

It has been said that the effect of the changes on job security has been liberating. People can change jobs, change careers, go into professions that once seemed barred to them. This is nice; but did we need Thatcherism, the blatant attacks on trade unions, and the massive insecurity and low pay that went with the changes?

Nor is it a government that could be called democratic in any sense, other than the fact that it had been elected. It certainly is not a liberal democracy, as it is not working in the interests of the entire population. It is neither accountable, nor open to inspection. Part of the definition of democracy requires that government be responsive to public opinion, and one cannot say that this has been the case. Instead of enacting legislation which expressed public opinion, the Tories have sought to impose their dubious ideology on the country. It is difficult to see how the Tory government could be called a democracy, except in the most limited sense, the least important of the three possible definitions.

There was massive opposition to the Poll Tax, and only after there were riots in the streets did ministers finally back down. But there was no real retreat on the closure of 31 pits, and on the closure and privatisation of hospitals. Nor did massive public protest halt construction of the M3 through Twyford Down. In fact, state imposition of the road project extended to violent assaults on protesters. This is not merely a failure to qualify as a democracy; it is a step on the path to fascism. Perhaps one should not say that Britain has ceased to be a democracy, but one can say that it is not a democracy in the full sense of the word.

Through all its massive blunders, from the devaluation of sterling, after repeated claims it would be economic disaster, to the continued recession, despite regular choruses of the green shoots are here, no chancellor, no Prime Minister, has taken responsibility. The recovery has quite definitely not been there, and the economy is clearly in a state of collapse. Instead of confessing failure, or incompetence, or at least admitting to mistakes, ministers have simply ploughed on regardless. There has been a total lack of accountability, as job protection (for the Tories) has taken priority over any obligation to do the job properly.

Instead of accountability, we have blaming the victim. The homeless, the unemployed, single parents, the poor are all in some way the cause of their own problems. None of it is the government's fault; it is all due to laziness, lack of respect for authority; it is the Labour Party's fault for their education policies, or it is due to the lack of fear of hellfire and damnation. But there is no sign whatsoever of the government accepting any responsibility.

The government's willingness to blame the victim is assisted by the fact that many people blame the messenger. When funding for local authorities is reduced, and services have to be cut, people blame the council instead of the government. When trains are late, passengers vent their anger at BR, the bus driver or the ticket collector, rather than the transport minister. The actions of the spending ministries are less immediate than the failings of those who actually deal with the public.

The government has also ignored both consensus, and public opinion. It has taken the view that it alone could decide policy, even to the extent of disregarding Parliament. Nor could it claim that its actions did represent public opinion; surveys by all the major polling organisations and academic studies of popular attitudes all showed that voters were growing increasingly hostile to Conservative policies. They wanted more welfare state, and more state spending, even if they had to pay higher taxes to get better services. Yet the voters' opinions were continually ignored.

But without democracy, consensus, or accountability the government has no political integrity, or validity. It is a façade democracy, legally constituted, but with no moral standing. Its victory at the ballot box is a mere technicality, like a horse winning the Derby because all the other runners were disqualified.

Nor is the state interested in the welfare of its citizens. It has removed wage protection, cut state benefits, shifted the burden of tax downwards, and removed job security. The social impact of these changes includes increased homelessness, greater poverty, and enormously increased levels of crime. The social deterioration has been appalling. It is always tempting to be nostalgic about the 'good old days,' but here is a case when the statistics prove that millions are worse off. For example, there is the fact, cited in Chapter 2, that from 1979 to 1986, the number of people earning less than the Supplementary Benefit level rose from 6.1 million to 11.9 million.

Some members of the government have claimed that the lowest ten per cent of the population have actually become better off under the Tories, but this claim is, to quote Chris Pond, director of the Low Pay Unit, 'being statistical with the truth. (*The Guardian*, May 21, 1988.) Displaying his usual grasp of economic data, Norman Lamont claimed on television that the gap between rich and poor had not widened under the Conservatives. Research by the Low Pay Unit found that those earning more than £50,000 per year were £421 a week better off since 1979, while those earning less than £5,000 per year were only £2.50 a week better off. (See *Poor Britain*, Low Pay Unit. See also *The Guardian*, April 22, 1992.)

The increasing inequality has wreaked such havoc with the fabric of society, via the poverty, crime, homelessness and lack of opportunity that now exists, that the political stability of society is also under threat. This is a demon that lurks unseen most of the time, but when it does arise, it is tragically powerful. When it last arose in Germany, it returned that country to the middle ages, and from there to near-total devastation. It is not a force that we would wish to see in our future.

Yet there is not even any evidence that the New Right programme ever could work. It has no scientific validity as there is no proof, no logic, no sign of the policies working anywhere. The economy under the Tories has been one long, sorry tale of continuous unemployment, low or declining pay levels, falling standards of living, near-constant recession, and the devaluation of sterling. It is a tragedy of errors, written by a fool, and signifying incompetence unbound.

Without effective policies, there can be no respect for individual politicians. The Chancellors whose names spring most readily to mind, Lawson and Lamont, are notable both for the damage they did to the economy, and their refusal to listen to the electorate. Given such performances in the recent past, John Patten's request for the deference due to authority is a sure invitation for two-word requests to leave the stage.

And as individuals, it is a government that is not merely clumsy, but untrustworthy. They no longer project the malice that was the trademark of Mrs Thatcher, but the underlying indifference to the opinions of others is just as strong. Its characters run the full range, from comic opera to corruption in high places. It starts with a Minister for Industry who insists on being called President — Herr President? Our Glorious Leader? Then there is a Minister for Agriculture who gets landscape gardening paid for by a private company, and a Chancellor who gets £4,700 from the Treasury to evict a tenant from his flat. And finally we have the attempts to push through exports of bomb-making equipment and supergun parts to Iraq, despite a ban on military exports to that country.

Given the exhaustive range of disaster, from train crash to corporate collapse, from riots in the streets to joyriders on the roads, any sensible person might think that perhaps the policies would need re-evaluating. But with the blind certainty that only comes from bigotry or insanity, the demagogues of Thatcherism insist that the country is on a winning path. We wonder how long they would continue the destruction, in order to save the economy? When the last manufacturing plant shut down, with unemployment at 10 million and inflation at zero, would they then say that the experiment had succeeded? Or is it the My Lai syndrome, where one has to destroy, in order to save?

Because certainly, few are better off under the Conservatives. The average income has risen, but ignoring the statistical lies in the 'average', are we any better off, given all the many ways in which we are worse off? We are less able to get health care, our work is less pleasant, our leisure is dominated by technology, and enjoyed in a home environment with a background of fear. How can anyone claim we are better off?

It might be argued that the list of the Tories' failings is incomplete. They have committed so many errors that needed to be mentioned, which this book has skipped lightly over, or ignored altogether. And this is the problem. There have been so many failings that it was not possible to examine them all. Merely listing the categories of error would be exhausting — their dishonesty, the abuse of the constitution, the ineffectiveness of their policies, and so on.

This short list gives only an idea of the scale of the failure. Other books must examine the Conservative record in detail. But it may take time to get all the necessary information, simply because of the constraints imposed on some workers, for example, the secrecy imposed on NHS nurses. Because of this obstruction of democracy, it may be years before we realise the full impact of the New Right ideology.

But the failings can be summed up quite easily. The unrestrained market makes many people worse off, and hence reduces purchasing power. Thus, it damages the economy. The market also creates inequality, thus creating social problems. And by making people worse off, the government is acting both in an immoral way, and in conflict with the requirements of liberal democracy.

One thing is clear. No matter how detailed, or how glibly explained, the theories of the New Right do not work. And no theory, however consistent or impressive it may be on paper, can take precedence over the welfare of the population generally. Whether it is the elected dictatorship of the Conservatives, or the revolutionary despotism of communism, the theory must be subservient to the needs of the people.

Yet the evidence shows that other policy programmes are possible. This does not mean a return to the Labour Party-trades union duopoly that dominated much of the post-war era, although there should be a return to the days of consensus. Most important, we should return to the style of governing that aims to look after the interests of the electorate. Whatever else one can say about the incompetence and dogmatism of Labour, they did at least do their best, within the constraints of their ideology, for the population as a whole.

But if Labour are not capable of a policy programme that reflects the needs of the nation as a whole, then other parties are waiting in the wings. They might not have Westminster cred, but if they are willing to consider policies that work, and and evaluate their platform only on that basis, then they deserve to win.

The problem is that the closed minds that are keeping Labour out of office would be the same ones making it unpopular if it was in office. There is still a belief in many sections of the Labour Party that Clause IV should be reinstated, and that it can only mean nationalisation. And the relationship with the unions is such that the party is almost obliged to follow union opinion.

Despite ministerial mutterings about such constraints as inflation — or in the United States, the federal budget deficit — a useful policy platform is quite easy to create. All one has to do is look at the countries that are genuinely successful. And in this case, one has to say that the US has not been successful — it has been economically powerful, it has exported its culture on a global scale, but the levels of poverty have been both tragic and socially destructive, while the levels of crime have made life almost unbearable in many cities.

If we are to look for examples, we should look at places like Norway, Denmark, Holland or Austria. These are countries in which consensus has been either an implicit or explicit component of policy, and in which equality has been a conscious goal. The state's responsibility to maintain full employment has also been taken for granted.

In such countries, government, business and unions work together rather than in conflict. Policy is based on welfare, rather than on some predetermined set of methods. And perhaps most importantly, political debate is both informed and rational. Voters consider the validity of the arguments, rather than whether those arguments fit into a given ideology.

Some of Europe's success stories have lost their way in recent years, and the quality of the social environment has declined. In Sweden and Germany, unemployment has risen, while racism and other social tensions have increased. A part of the problem in both countries has been a failure to consider the needs or demands of the electorate. Germany has displayed a particularly blatant example of this, with Chancellor Kohl pushing for unification, regardless of the costs, social or economic.

Yet that analysis suggests that it is possible to achieve success in all the key social indicators. It is an approach that is both morally and administratively valid, as was said of Keynesian economics in Chapter 1. It also seems that the various components of the programme would work together, reinforcing one another, and strengthening their impact. And whereas New Right economics can be described as a failure, at best, the decentralised, small business economy that is being proposed can be seen to have worked extremely well.

Despite some very weak arguments against it, it is obvious that Keynesian demand management does work, although the targeting of government spending needs to be improved. The higher levels of employment that would result from state intervention in the economy mean less would have to be paid out in welfare benefits, yet more workers would be contributing to the Exchequer, while the greater purchasing power leads to more spending, and more jobs created by the spending of those in work.

There is a tendency for Labour and Tories to be obsessed, especially at election times, with exact amounts of government spending, and the precise level of job creation that would be generated by a given expenditure. And some commentators seem to have the attitude that spending needs to be maintained indefinitely at high levels in order to subsidise jobs.

The simple fact is, spending creates jobs; we might not be able to calculate the exact number of jobs, but those newly employed don't need welfare, they do pay taxes, and they do create further jobs.

Because the policies being suggested work with human nature, human needs, and human goals, there is less of a requirement for a powerful state apparatus, quangos and all the paraphernalia of a compensatory mechanism. The changes, the socialisation, the control are all imposed by individuals seeking the optimum quality of life. The imposition of behavioural controls is minimal, with no need for a powerful centralised state. It allows people to choose for themselves what they will do.

This makes such an approach extremely vulnerable. If people choose to do nothing, if they ignore the options, then nothing will change. Or if they assume that they can achieve their goals easily, they may get disillusioned and give up. But in battling powerful forces, one has to wield power in response. However, at times it may be like fighting a Chinese festival dragon; it is large, and of frightening appearance, but there is just one person guiding it. And human beings can, sometimes, be persuaded to see reason.

Change is necessary, change is possible. And everyone can play a part, no matter what they can do, or choose to do. It may be by buying recycled paper, by encouraging parental involvement in the local school, or by boycotting irresponsible companies. It may be through political action or through influencing trade union policy, or by community level action. But the future is in everyone's hands. It is your decision.

Bibliography

Nicholas Abercrombie, Alan Warde et al. *Contemporary British Society*. Polity Press.

Michael Argyle. *Psychology and Social Problems*. Methuen. 1964.

H. W. Arndt. *The Lessons of the the Nineteen-Thirties*. Cass. 1963

James David Barber. *The Presidential Character*. Prentice Hall. 1992.

Bruce Bartlett and Timothy P. Roth (eds.) *The Supply Side Solution*. Macmillan. 1984.

Patrick Barwise and Andrew Ehrenberg. *Television and its Audience*. Sage Publications. 1988.

W. Beckerman. ed. *The Labour Government's Economic Record*. 1972.

Richard Berthoud and Elaine Kempson. *Credit and Debt: The PSI Report*. PSI. 1992.

British Social Attitudes; the 1990 report. Gower. 1990.

Louis Burghes. *Made in the U.S.A.* Unemployment Unit. 1987.

David P. Calleo. *The Bankrupting of America*. Avon Books 1992.

Geoffrey Cannon. *The Politics of Food*. Century Hutchinson. 1987.

Carlo M. Cipolla (ed.). *Contemporary Economies*. Harvester Press. 1977.

Philip Cohen, from Bates, Clarke et al. *Schooling for the Dole?* Macmillan. 1984.

Commission on Social Justice, The. *The Justice Gap*. IPPR. 1993.

W. Connolly. *Legitimacy in the Modern State*. Basil Blackwell. 1984.

Ivor Crewe. 'The Policy Agenda', in *Contemporary Record*. February 1990.

Kath Davies, Julienne Dickey and Teresa Stratford (eds.) *Out Of Focus*. The Women's Press.

Dossier of Despair. Low Pay Unit. 1993.

Peter Drucker. *The Frontiers of Management*. Heinemann. 1987.

R. Eccleshall, V. Geoghegan, R. Jay and R. Wilford. *Political Ideologies*. Hutchinson. 1984.

Economic Sense: Local Jobs Plans. CLES. 1987.

S. E. Finer. *Comparative Government*. Pelican. 1970.

Milton Friedman. *Capitalism and Freedom*. University of Chicago Press. 1972.

J. K. Galbraith. *The Affluent Society*. Penguin. 1958.

J. K. Galbraith. *American Capitalism*. Penguin. 1980.

J. K. Galbraith. *The Culture of Contentment*. Penguin. 1992.

Ian Gilmour. *Dancing With Dogma*. Simon and Schuster. 1992.

Robert J. Gordon. ed. *Milton Friedman's Monetary Framework*. University of Chicago Press. 1974.

Alexander J. Groth. *Major Ideologies*. John Wiley and Sons. 1971.

Graham Hallett. *The Social Economy of West Germany*. Macmillan. 1973.

Mick Hamer. *Wheels within Wheels*. Routledge and Kegan Paul. 1987.

Norman Hampson. *The Enlightenment*. Pelican. 1982.

M. Haralambos. *Sociology: Themes and Perspectives*. University Tutorial Press. 1980.

David Held (ed.) *Political Theory Today*. Polity Press. 1991.
Paddy Hillyard and Janie Percy-Smith. *The Coercive State*. Fontana. 1988.
Thomas Hobbes. *Leviathan*. Pelican. 1968.
Colin Hughes and Patrick Wintour. *Labour Rebuilt*. Fourth Estate. 1990.
Industrial Relations Review and Report. November 1992. IRS.
Peter Jenkins. *Mrs Thatcher's Revolution*. Jonathan Cape. 1987.
Simon Jenkins. *Newspapers*. Faber and Faber. 1979.
Bill Jones and Dennis Kavanagh. *British Politics Today*. Manchester University Press. 1987.
Lord Kaldor. *The Economic Consequences of Mrs Thatcher*. Duckworth. 1983.
Dennis Kavanagh. *Thatcherism and British Politics*. Oxford University Press. 1987.
Dennis Kavanagh and Peter Morris. *Consensus Politics*. Basil Blackwell/Institute of Contemporary British History. 1989.
Philip Kotler. *Marketing Management*. Prentice-Hall. 1988.
Richard Lingeman. *Small Town America*. Houghton Mifflin. 1980.
LRD Guide to the Tory Employment Bill. Labour Research Department. 1980.
Howard D. Marshall (ed.) *Business and Government: The Problem of Power*. D. C. Heath and Co. 1970.
P. Maunder. *Government Intervention in the Developed Economy*. Croom Helm. 1979.
Grant McConnell. *Private Power and American Democracy*. Vintage Books. 1970.
James W. McKie. (ed.) *Social Responsibility and the Business Predicament*. The Brookings Institution. 1974.
Jonathan Michie (ed.) *The Economic Legacy 1979-1992*. Academic Press/Harcourt Brace Jovanovich. 1992.
C. Wright Mills. *The Power Elite*. Oxford University Press. 1973.
C. Wright Mills. *The Sociological Imagination*. Fontana. 1959.
Austin Mitchell. *Four Years in The Death of the Labour Party*. Methuen. 1983.
Kenneth O. Morgan. *Consensus and Disunity*. Clarendon Press. 1979.
Ralph Nader. *Unsafe at Any Speed*. Bantam Books 1973.
Mancur Olson. *The Rise and Decline of Nations*. Yale University Press. 1982.
Philip Olson. (ed.) *America As A Mass Society*. Free Press of Glencoe/Collier-Macmillan. 1963.
Firmin Oules. *Economic Planning and Democracy*. Pelican. 1966.
P. H. Partridge. *Consent and Consensus*. Macmillan. 1971.
Part-Time Workers — a negotiators' guide. Labour Research Department. 1992.
Howard R. Penniman (ed.). *Britain at the Polls, 1979*. American Enterprise Institute. 1980.
Poor Britain. Low Pay Unit.
The Poor Decade. Low Pay Unit. 1988.
John Rawls. *A Theory of Justice*. Oxford University Press. 1973.
John Rentoul. *The Rich Get Richer*. Unwin. 1987.
Harry W. Richardson. *Urban Economics*. Penguin. 1971.
Massimo Salvadori. *Liberal Democracy*. Pall Mall Press. 1958.

Roger Scruton. *A Short History of Modern Philosophy*. Routledge. 1984.

Roger Scruton. *Thinkers of the New Left*. Longman. 1985.

Small Businesses and their Banks. Forum of Private Business, Ruskin Chambers, Drury Lane, Knutsford, Cheshire. 1993.

Paul Stoneham, Derek Bosworth, and Anne Gibbons. *Investment, Productivity and Competitiveness in UK Manufacturing Industry*. Warwick University.

Dennis Swann. *The Retreat of the State.* Harvester Wheatsheaf. 1988.

Norman Tebbit. *Unfinished Business.* Weidenfeld and Nicolson.

Rosa Linda P. Tidalgo and Emmanuel F. Esquerra. *Philippine Employment in the Seventies.* The Philippine Institute for Development Studies. 1984.

Alexis de Tocqueville. *Democracy in America*. Vintage Books. 1954.

The Union De-recognition Bandwagon. LRD. 1992.

Arthur J. Vidich and Joseph Bensman. *Small Town in Mass Society.* Doubleday Anchor. 1960.

H. Visser. *The Quantity of Money.* Martin Robertson. 1974.

Mark Warren. 'Liberal Constitutionalism As Ideology', in *Political Theory*. November 1989.

Martin J. Wiener. *English Culture And The Decline of The Industrial Spirit 1850 — 1980.* Penguin Books. 1985.

Theodore H. White. *The Making of the President 1968.* Jonathan Cape. 1969.

Peter Winch. *The Idea of Social Science and its Relation to Philosophy*. Routledge. 1988.

Index

ALSO PUBLISHED BY JON CARPENTER

BEYOND OPTIMISM

A Buddhist political ecology

Ken Jones

"This deep, wise, broad-gauged book combines astute social analysis with invigorating spiritual insight; it clears our hearts and heads for action. Stunningly relevant and rich in both political and contemplative experience, this superb book shatters dichotomies between 'inner' amd 'outer' work — and shows us the wholeness to be found as we take action together to evolve a sustainable civilization."

So writes Joanna Macy about this unique study of the human predicament, underpinned as it is by the persuasive Buddhist combination of radical vision and earthy prgmatism. Ken Jones addresses the spiritual, social, economic and political imperatives as we try and construct a society for the future.

ISBN 1 897766 06 8 224pp £9.99

ANOTHER WAY

Positive response to contemporary violence

Adam Curle

One of Britian's leading authorities on the theory and practice of violence and conflict resolution, and an experienced international mediator, Adam Curle has for 25 years out of the last 40 been involved in peace-making efforts in eight wars. In this book he shows that although there has always been violence, the post-Cold War trend has been different in both scale and universality. The same is true of gang warfare and violent crime in our great cities. Curle identifies the main cause as alienation brought about by two world wars and their aftermath, coupled with 'decolonisation' in the USSR and Africa, as well as the bewildering social impact of advanced technology. Plus, of course, the legacy of unhappy history.

"A fundamentally positive search for creative and effective ways to peace. Combines a lifetime of experience, study and reflection in seeking a response to contemporary violence." — Paul Rogers, Professor of Peace Studies, University of Bradford

ISBN 1 897766 22 X 160pp £11.99